What the reviewers say about:

TIME AMONG THE MAYA

"Mr. Wright's narrative blends anthropology,
archaeology, history, and politics with his own
entertaining excursions and encounters, and, without
any visible didactic effort, he teaches us a lot about the
ways that a culture endures."
The New Yorker

"One of Wright's many achievements
is to arouse in his readers a sense of political rage
without inducing cynicism and despair. He manages
this delicate feat by juxtaposing recent events with
stories from Mexican and Guatemalan history, and
from the pre-Conquest period of Mayan life — as well
as by means of some wry, deprecating anecdotes
about his own travels. To read this book is to swim
through several different times."
The Gazette (Montreal)

"Outstanding... Wright draws on his experience
to make the old Maya as real as the new Guatemalans
and it is all delivered with great style."
The Sunday Times (London)

"Wright's book is much like making a trip to
Central America: challenging, lyrical, tragic,
uplifting, and, ultimately, magic."
The Hartford Courant

"Any account of the modern-day Maya must be
a tapestry, weaving together past glories and
present destitution. Ronald Wright has managed
admirably... a skillful marriage of history,
archaeology and reportage."
The Baltimore Sun

PENGUIN CANADA

TIME AMONG THE MAYA

RONALD WRIGHT is the internationally acclaimed, bestselling author of several non-fiction books, including *A Short History of Progress, Stolen Continents* (which won the Gordon Montador Award), and *Cut Stones and Crossroads*. He is also the author of the novels *Henderson's Spear* and *A Scientific Romance*, the latter of which won Britain's David Higham Prize for Fiction. He was born in England, educated at Cambridge, and now lives in British Columbia.

For Janice

PENGUIN CANADA

Published by the Penguin Group

Penguin Group (Canada), 90 Eglinton Avenue East, Suite 700, Toronto, Ontario, Canada M4P 2Y3
(a division of Pearson Penguin Canada Inc.)

Penguin Group (USA) Inc., 375 Hudson Street, New York, New York 10014, U.S.A.
Penguin Books Ltd, 80 Strand, London WC2R 0RL, England
Penguin Ireland, 25 St Stephen's Green, Dublin 2, Ireland (a division of Penguin Books Ltd)
Penguin Group (Australia), 250 Camberwell Road, Camberwell, Victoria 3124, Australia
(a division of Pearson Australia Group Pty Ltd)
Penguin Books India Pvt Ltd, 11 Community Centre, Panchsheel Park, New Delhi – 110 017, India
Penguin Group (NZ), cnr Airborne and Rosedale Roads, Albany, Auckland 1310, New Zealand
(a division of Pearson New Zealand Ltd)
Penguin Books (South Africa) (Pty) Ltd, 24 Sturdee Avenue, Rosebank, Johannesburg 2196,
South Africa

Penguin Books Ltd, Registered Offices: 80 Strand, London WC2R 0RL, England

First published in a Viking Canada hardcover by Penguin Group (Canada),
a division of Pearson Penguin Canada Inc., 1989
Published in Penguin Canada paperback by Penguin Group (Canada),
a division of Pearson Penguin Canada Inc., 1990
Published in this edition, 2005

1 2 3 4 5 6 7 8 9 10 (TRS)

Copyright © Ronald Wright, 1989

Excerpt from "Burnt Norton" in *Four Quartets*, copyright 1943 by T.S. Elliot,
renewed 1971 by Esme Valerie Eliot, reprinted by permission of
Harcourt Brace Jovanovich, Inc. and by the courtesy of Faber and Faber limited.

Excerpts from *Popol Vuh* translated by Dennis Tedlock, copyright © 1985
by Dennis Tedlock, are reprinted by permission of Simon & Schuster Inc.

Manufactured in Canada.

Maps by David Bosse
Illustrations by Persis B. Clarkson

ISBN 0-14-305437-6

Library and Archives Canada Cataloguing in Publication data available upon request

Visit the Penguin Group (Canada) website at **www.penguin.ca**

TIME AMONG THE MAYA

Travels in Belize, Guatemala, and Mexico

Ronald Wright

PENGUIN
CANADA

Also by Ronald Wright

NON-FICTION

On Fiji Islands

Cut Stones and Crossroads: A Journey in the Two Worlds of Peru

Stolen Continents: The "New World" Through Indian Eyes

Home and Away

A Short History of Progress

FICTION

A Scientific Romance

Henderson's Spear

Contents

Acknowledgments ix

A Note from the Author xi

Prologue 5

Part I
East: Belize 17

Chapter 1 19

Chapter 2 39

Part II
Center: The Petén 59

Chapter 3 61

Chapter 4 84

Part III
South: Highland Guatemala 101

Chapter 5 103

Chapter 6 124

Chapter 7 145

Chapter 8 162

Chapter 9   181

Chapter 10   195

Chapter 11   213

Chapter 12   233

Chapter 13   251

Part IV

West: Chiapas   261

Chapter 14   263

Chapter 15   290

Chapter 16   303

Part V

North: Yucatán Peninsula   327

Chapter 17   329

Chapter 18   356

Chapter 19   370

Epilogue   399

Glossary   401

Notes   409

Bibliography   419

Index   439

Acknowledgments

Many people helped me during the research and writing of this book, some with information freely given in an interview, a letter, or a telephone call, others with hospitality and kindness on the road. A list of names is never complete, but because of the nature of this journey, an important group cannot be named at all. These are the Guatemalans and others connected with Guatemala who, for their own safety, must be left anonymous. (The names and details of those mentioned in the text have been changed for the same reason.) My warm thanks to everyone, but especially to those I could not include with the following:

Alison Acker; Jacinto Aké; Anthony Aveni; Juan Bastarrechea; Victoria Bricker; Gordon Brotherston; Gord Brown; Robert Bruce; Chan K'in "Presidente"; Chan K'in "Viejo"; Grace Cipparone; Persis Clarkson; Clemency Coggins; Raymond Comiskey; Jan De Vos; Domingo Dzul; Munro Edmonson; Rómulo Esquivel; Ignacio Ek; Isidro Ek; Susanna Ekholm; Mick and Lucy Fleming; David Gollob; Elizabeth Graham; Ian Graham; Coryn Greatorex-Bell; Jim Handy; Grant Jones; Wallace Kaufman; David Kelley; Robert Laughlin; Maryan Lopis; George Lovell; Peter Mathews; Logan McNatt; Alfredo Melo; Elfego Pantí; Merideth Paxton; David Pendergast; Victor Perera; Simón Poot; Samuel Ruiz; Jan Rus; Paul Sullivan; Barbara Tedlock; Maria Tippett; Harriot Topsey; Candelario Uck; Raúl Valencia; Julián Xix; Ermilo Yah.

Thanks are due also to David Kendall, Bella Pomer, and my wife, Janice Boddy. All read the manuscript and made many helpful suggestions; none is responsible for any faults that may remain. I am similarly grateful to the book's editor, William Strachan, and copyeditor, Ed Sedarbaum. Finally, I wish to acknowledge the generosity of the Canada Council during the first year of traveling and writing.

R.W.

A NOTE FROM THE AUTHOR

Since this book was first published, Maya speakers in Central America have grown in number from about five million to eight, and several events stand out in a fragile cultural and political renaissance.

In 1992, Rigoberta Menchú, the Quiché activist and author, won the Nobel Peace Prize and became prominent in talks to end the Guatemalan civil war. The mid-nineties were a time of cautious optimism in that country: fighting and killings declined, and there was some strengthening of indigenous and democratic rights, including a major investigation by the Catholic Church into tens of thousands of deaths and "disappearances." Congressional hearings in Washington uncovered the extent of CIA involvement in the war and in specific murders of both Guatemalans and Americans. Despite an army massacre of returned refugees in 1995, the former insurgents and the government signed a peace accord in December 1996. A United Nations Truth Commission was then set up. In its 1999 report, *Guatemala: Memory of Silence*, the Commission found that 93% of the civilian killings between 1962 and 1996—more than 200,000 all told—were the work of Guatemalan state forces. More than four fifths of the victims were Maya.

Unfortunately, these courageous steps to confront the recent past have yet to bring lasting change to Guatemala. In April 1998, Bishop Juan Gerardi, head of the Church's human rights investigation, was bludgeoned to death at his house two days after releasing his report, *Guatemala: Nunca Más*. A constitutional referendum, intended to enshrine key elements of the peace accord, achieved neither a majority nor a healthy turnout at the polls. The fundamental problem of land tenure has not been addressed, and the authors of the terror, mainly high-ranking army officers, remain immune from prosecution. Even the ballot box seems to be failing: Alfonso Portillo, the new president who took office in January 2000, enjoys the backing of former dictator Rios Montt, whose terror campaigns during 1982–83 are described by the UN Truth Commission as both strategically planned and genocidal.

While a shaky peace was being reached in Guatemala, ethnic war broke out in neighboring Chiapas on January 1, 1994, the day the North American Free Trade Agreement took effect in Mexico. Alarmed by a return to land policies reminiscent of prerevolutionary Mexico, and exasperated by mounting corruption, racism, and violent intimidation, many Chiapas Maya have taken up arms under the Zapatista banner. So far, broad public support and media attention have restrained the government's response and led to inconclusive negotiations.

Turning to ancient times, the breakthroughs in deciphering Maya hieroglyphs continue, returning the Classic Maya to the realm of history and adding a thousand years of written records to the human past. To give just one example, an inscription found at Caracol, Belize, claims that Caracol conquered Tikal in 562 and dominated it for more than a century. Texts such as this have helped explain the Middle Classic "hiatus," when Tikal's monuments fall silent, revealing a time of shifting alliances much like the Hundred Years' War in Europe.

New digging at Copan and elsewhere confirms that overpopulation and ecological damage were widespread towards the end of the Classic Period. Ruins at Dos Pilas, Guatemala, provide a rare glimpse of the resulting political crisis: the city became an armed camp, the people tearing stone from temples to throw up barricades across the plaza in the last days before abandonment.

Uniting ancient and modern times, today's Maya are becoming increasingly involved in decipherment, interpretation, and use of their ancient texts. Daykeepers have restored the Long Count calendar to daily use for the first time in a thousand years, and some of them are optimistically predicting that a Maya will be elected president of Guatemala in 2012, the epoch of Baktun 13.

Ronald Wright
Ontario, January 2000

TIME AMONG THE MAYA

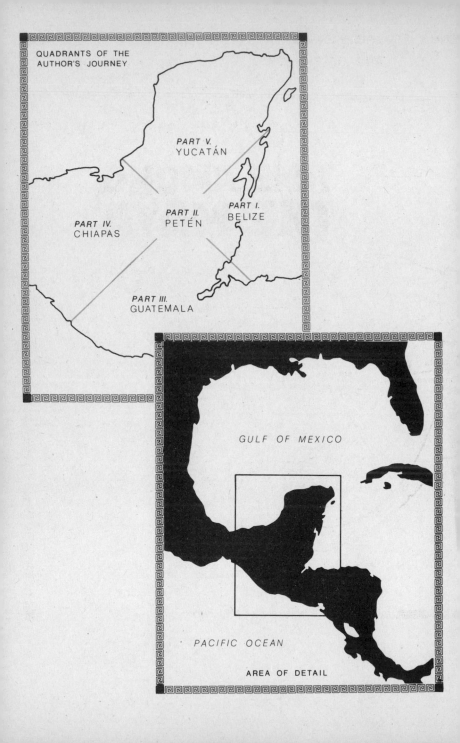

QUADRANTS OF THE
AUTHOR'S JOURNEY

PART V.
YUCATÁN

PART II.
PETÉN

PART I.
BELIZE

PART IV.
CHIAPAS

PART III.
GUATEMALA

GULF OF MEXICO

PACIFIC OCEAN

AREA OF DETAIL

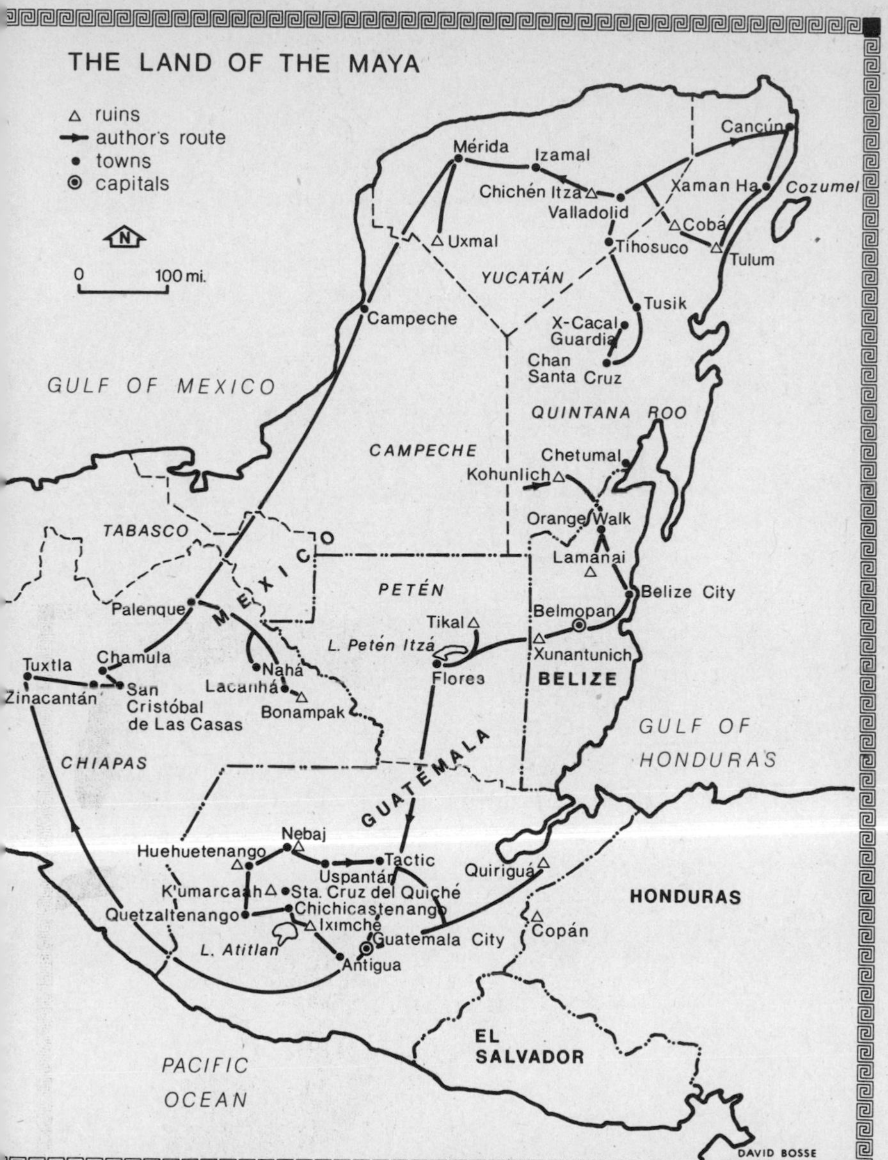

THE LAND OF THE MAYA
ruins
author's route
towns
capitals
N
0
100 mi.
GULF OF MEXICO
Mérida
Izamal
Cancún
Chichén Itzá
Valladolid
Xaman Ha
Cozumel
Uxmal
Cobá
Tihosuco
Tulum
YUCATÁN
Campeche
Tusik
X-Cacal Guardia
Chan Santa Cruz
QUINTANA ROO
CAMPECHE
Chetumal
Kohunlich
Orange Walk
TABASCO
MEXICO
Lamanai
PETÉN
Belize City
Palenque
Belmopan
Tikal
L. Petén Itzá
Xunantunich
Chamula
Tuxtla
Zinacantán
San Cristóbal de Las Casas
Nahá
Lacanhá
Bonampak
Flores
BELIZE
GULF OF HONDURAS
CHIAPAS
GUATEMALA
Nebaj
Huehuetenango
Tactic
Uspantán
Quiriguá
K'umarcaah
Sta. Cruz del Quiché
HONDURAS
Quetzaltenango
Chichicastenango
Iximché
Copán
L. Atitlan
Guatemala City
Antigua
EL SALVADOR
PACIFIC OCEAN
DAVID BOSSE

Prologue

KOHUNLICH, QUINTANA ROO, MEXICO

His name was Ignacio Ek. He was a Maya, born in 1910, the year the Mexican Revolution broke out, and he remembered that his people and mine had once been enemies. We were standing on the steps of a pyramid he had discovered one day when hunting in the forest. His dogs had chased a *tepezcuintle* down a burrow in a mound covered with cohune palms; he enlarged the hole with a stick and saw the giant face of an ancient god, hidden by the jungle for more than a thousand years. Archaeologists later found others, modeled in stucco, flanking the staircase on each of the pyramid's tiers. The faces had the haughty brow and handlebar moustache of Kinich Ahau, Sun-Eyed Lord. In the god's huge eyes was written the hieroglyph for *kin* (sun, day, or time), Logos of the Maya, foundation of their calendar and universe. The archaeologists restored the ruins and left Ignacio Ek to guard them. He picked weeds from the stones and sold tickets to infrequent visitors.

"Icaiché is my hometown," he said when I asked where he was from. "But it's abandoned now. We left when I was a baby, in the time of the Revolution. We scattered in the forest. There was nothing to eat. My mother gave me the sap of trees to drink because she had no milk.

"And you? From where are you?"

"*Inglaterra.*"

"*¡Inglaterra!*" he shouted. "My father used to tell me that Icaiché fought England!" His laugh was like the cry of a raucous bird. He threw back his head, and the dark leather of his face tightened and rippled on his skull. He was only about five foot three, no taller than the ancient masks, but for a moment he looked as if he himself might have posed for the portraits of Kinich Ahau. Despite the baroque iconography, the hieroglyphic eyes, the curling moustaches and flamelike tongue, you could see that the Sun-Eyed Lord and Ignacio Ek were distant kin.

"Nowadays Icaiché is a cattle ranch—inhabited by Mexicans. My people have all left. Some are living down in the Colony, which begins twelve leagues from here." He nodded south, toward British Honduras. "But the Maya exist. I mean the old ones with long hair and bows and arrows. They can come back. From a tree, from a stone." He looked dreamily at the ancient faces. "They are living, but we can't see them. They were magicians." All this he said in Spanish; then added in broken Caribbean English: "Dis a story, Maya story!" And he laughed.

"People come here from Mexico and the United States, very *learned*," he continued, "and they tell me Columbus discovered America. And I tell *them*, look at this!" He waved his hand toward the god. "When Columbus discovered America where were we?" He laughed again—a laugh of extraordinary vigor for such a small old man—and answered his own question by reciting the lands where the Maya lived and live: the Yucatán Peninsula, Guatemala, Chiapas, and British Honduras, or Belize. Then he told me about the events of the last century, the time remembered by his parents.

In 1847 the Maya of Yucatán had rebelled against the Ladinos (whites of Spanish descent and Hispanicized mestizos) in what became known as the great Caste War. The Indians nearly reconquered the whole peninsula from their oppressors, but were then pushed back into this wild eastern region now called Quintana Roo. There, several Maya groups established small independent states that survived until the 1900s. The largest group had rallied around a miraculous Speaking Cross and allied itself with the British of Belize.

"Those people—the Santa Cruz [Holy Cross]—the British used to sell them bullets, gunpowder, rifles, everything to fight the Mexicans!" Ek said. He lowered his voice: "I've been to Santa Cruz. They were still keeping an English flag when I was there. They say they are not only Maya but British too!"

Ek's people fell out with the Santa Cruz over religious differences, and with the British because Belizean loggers and planters were encroaching on their land. In 1867 the Icaiché sacked a sugar estate at Indian Church and chased the British to the swampy environs of Belize City. (The governor ordered ships to stand by for evacuation.) In 1870 they briefly occupied Corozal Town, and in 1872 they besieged Orange Walk. But there they were beaten off by some Confederate Americans who had come to Belize with dreams of founding a second Dixie. The Icaiché leader, General Marcus Canul, was mortally wounded in the action; his successor made peace with Queen Victoria.[1]

Old Ek's eyes were misty by the time he finished recalling what his parents had told him.

"There were many generals in those days," he added. "In those days, when Icaiché fought England!" His laughter echoed among the trees and ancient walls, and before it died on the wind it was answered by the metallic outburst of a *chachalaca* deep in the woods.

It was May 5, 1970, a public holiday in Mexico, commemorating the victory of Juárez over Emperor Maximilian. It was also the sixty-ninth anniversary of the Mexican army's cruel defeat of the Santa Cruz Maya; but I didn't know that then. I had studied the ancient Maya briefly at Cambridge and Calgary, but Ignacio Ek was the first living Maya I'd met. What he told me was new and strange. I had no idea that independent Maya states had existed so recently, let alone that they had been allies and foes of the British. This recent history seemed far removed from the Maya of the Classic period, when great cities were built in the Central American jungle; when writing, art, mathematics, and astronomy reached astonishing levels of refinement during Europe's Dark Ages.

The journey had begun as a summer vacation trip, vaguely intended to sort out my career plans. I wanted to visit Mesoamerica (the parts of Mexico and Central America in which civilizations arose) and Peru. I hoped to find a "thesis topic"— an area of New World archaeology that would fire my interest enough to carry me through several years of study and the writing of a dissertation. I set out from Calgary in an old Austin I'd bought for seventy-five dollars. I remember the car well—it was gray and maroon with funny little tail fins and patches of rust under the doors. I sprayed the roof silver to reflect tropical heat, and a cat left a trail of paw prints on the paint.

In Belize my traveler's checks were stolen, and in Guatemala I had a series of flat tires and breakdowns, but I got as far as Panama, where I parked the car for two months and flew to South America. When I returned and started home the engine bearings failed; I sold my blood in Mexico City to pay for new ones. The Austin and I got back to Calgary, but after another year at the university I dropped out of the doctoral program. A professor had revealed to me the complexity of the Maya intellectual world and the daunting sophistication of the work already done to understand it. I knew I hadn't the mind or personality required—cryptanalytical, photographic, exhaustive, patient. I sold the car and went back to England.

In later years I returned and settled in Canada. I visited Peru and Mesoamerica several times, but as a traveler not a scholar. Thoughts of finishing university faded as time passed. I knew myself now for a dilettante. A scholar dedicates a lifetime to one field; a writer can flit about and sample many.

It was as a journalist that I again visited a corner of the Maya world in 1985. The Royal Ontario Museum was excavating in Belize at a site called Lamanai, and a Canadian magazine hired me to report on the dig. I soon found out that Lamanai was the old Maya name for Indian Church, the place wrecked by the Icaiché in 1867. Three hundred years before that the Spaniards had built a mission church there (whence its English name), and a thousand years before *that* a Maya city of at least twenty thousand people had thrived in that remote region of northwestern Belize.

I got there by bush plane and small boat. The ruins stood beside a long freshwater lagoon, where the New River dilates for a few miles before winding like an intestine through the swamps below Orange Walk and Corozal to the Caribbean Sea. The archaeologists' camp resembled a genteel hunting lodge: small thatched huts in the round-cornered Maya style among clumps of hibiscus, flamboyant, and imposing trees. A grassy slope ran down to the lake. The sun had fallen behind the jungle-covered pyramids; it was already dark beneath the trees, but on the far shore, pools of vegetation were still steaming in the evening sun. Small frogs mewed like kittens in the reeds.

The dig director, David Pendergast, had chosen Lamanai because he hoped it might shed light on one of the great mysteries in New World history: the apparently spontaneous collapse of Classic Maya civilization during the ninth and tenth centuries A.D., when the Maya abandoned most of their cities in the lowlands of Guatemala, Belize, and southern Yucatán. It was clear from the size of Lamanai that much of the city dated from the Classic period, but the presence of a sixteenth-century mission church suggested that not everyone had left:

"Obviously there must have been Mayas still living here," Pendergast told me. "No religious order, no matter how dedicated or fanatic, builds its church where there are no parishioners."

Pendergast found evidence of more than three thousand years of continuous occupation. Early Maya corn farmers had settled at Lamanai around 1500 B.C., and the first stone buildings appeared between 800 and 600 B.C. During what is known as the late Preclassic period (approximately 450 B.C.–A.D. 300) the city became one of the largest in the Maya area. Other centers outgrew Lamanai during the Classic age (A.D. 300–900), but it continued to expand, reaching its apogee in the seventh century. Then Lamanai began a slow decline. There was no clear break at the end of the Classic period. The inhabitants even built a small ballcourt (a stadium for the ritual ball game) when great cities such as Tikal, Copán, and Palenque were already ruins, and until about A.D. 1200 they carried on repairing the fronts of some pyramids while the forest claimed the backs and sides. Then the life of Lamanai gradually shifted a mile to the south, and the architecture became less ambitious. When the Spaniards arrived, the inhabitants were living in the sort of houses the Maya still build: oval thatched dwellings with stone or pole walls, raised on small platforms.

In the late 1630s the Belize Maya threw off Spanish rule, burned the Lamanai church, and, in the words of an outraged friar, "returned to the vomit of the idolatries and abominations of their ancestors."[2] It is difficult to say what happened after that. Old World diseases—especially smallpox, malaria, and yellow fever—struck hard at Indian populations throughout the Americas, and probably reduced Lamanai to a few hundred or even a few dozen people. During the eighteenth century, English buccaneers came to cut logwood, valued for dyes, which grew beside rivers and swamps. And in the last century, British mahogany and sugar interests skirmished with Maya such as the Icaiché, who did not enjoy working for white men and disliked the idea that their ancestral lands belonged to the Crown.

I spent a week at Lamanai and had the run of the place, sometimes with the archaeologists, more often alone. I was drawn to the northern part of the site, where tall pyramids of the Classic period stood cloaked with rain forest, uncut in a thousand years. Pendergast's workers had made trails and cleared the fronts of some buildings, but most of the jungle was undisturbed. Huge tree trunks rose from buttress roots gripping the old stones like octopi. The forest floor was as open as English woodland, paved with rotting leaves; only ferns and philodendrons throve in the perpetual dusk. Here and there a few lean sunbeams, filled with dancing insects, threaded the gloom. The air smelled like a laundry basket—a blend of sweat, earth, and flowers. Fifty feet above the ground the canopy began—a vegetal wrangle in which branches and vines, palms and parasitic bromeliads silently occupied and defended their territories with unimaginable deliberation; each leaf taking the sunlight it could get, until all was absorbed or filtered, and only a submarine pallor reached the earth. Beneath the humus, roots grappled in the same relentless campaigns, sapping one another, seeking the smallest pocket of untapped nutrients, loosening their rivals' grasp. Most of these battles had reached stalemate, and this hostile equilibrium seemed to a busy, short-lived mammal like myself the very fabric of tranquillity.

The main pyramid rose 112 feet, lifting you above the jungle canopy. From its summit you looked out over lagoon, swamps, unbroken forest stretching toward Guatemala. The crowns of tall *guanacastes*, mahogany, and cedar trees swelled like broccoli among feather-duster palms. From below came liquid birdcalls, the croaking of frogs, a woodpecker's tattoo that sounded like a nail being pulled from a board. Occasionally you saw a flash of iridescent plumage or heard the sudden crack as a termite-eaten limb gave way. The whole of Lamanai could be seen from there, and in the morning, when shadows were long, many ancient buildings bulked beneath the trees.

The remote ancestors of the Maya, like those of all American Indians, most probably discovered the New World by crossing a Bering land bridge from Asia between twelve and thirty thousand years ago. At that time they were nomadic hunters and gatherers. About nine thousand years ago, Mesoamericans invented agriculture, gradually developing food staples from wild corn, beans, and squash. With farming came settled villages, population growth, and societies of greater and greater complexity.

Maya civilization seems to have been stimulated initially by the Olmecs, an enigmatic people who built large monuments in the swamps of the Mexican Gulf during the second millennium B.C. After the Olmecs declined, many cultures emerged in Mesoamerica, influencing and interacting with each other as did the Egyptians, Greeks, and Romans of the Mediterranean. An enduring tension—the equivalent of Europe's endless conflict with the Middle East—arose between the Nahua civilizations of highland Mexico (the Aztecs, Toltecs, and their forerunners) and the Maya, separated from each other by Mesoamerica's narrow waist at the Isthmus of Tehuantepec.

The Maya have aptly been called the Greeks of the New World. They lived in squabbling city-states that differed widely

in detail while sharing a rich cultural tradition. Their main
achievements were intellectual, not political. They never built
an empire, yet neighboring Mexican empires owed much to
Maya inspiration and continuity. When those empires fell, the
Maya were shaken but never destroyed. They abandoned some
areas, lingered in others, migrated, merged, and adapted. They
were and are eclectic: the Maya have always absorbed the
culture of their conquerors and remade it as their own. They
survived the Classic fall; and, better than any other Mesoamericans, they survived the Spanish invasion. One pagan
kingdom remained unconquered in the middle of the Guatemalan jungle until 1697, more than a hundred and fifty years
after the Aztecs, Incas, and other Maya had been subjugated. "It
seems almost beyond belief," Michael Coe has written, "that
while students at Harvard College had been scratching their
heads over Cotton Mather's theology, Maya priests 2,000 miles
away were still chanting rituals from hieroglyphic books."[3]
Today, five million people speak Maya languages, and many of
them still preserve calendrical and religious knowledge as old
as their civilization.

D. H. Lawrence saw the New World civilizations as a forest
of great trees felled by the white invader, but he believed the
roots were still alive, sending up shoots through the foreign
soil deposited above them. It was a metaphor the Maya would
recognize. They saw, and see, themselves as part of a great
ceiba, a silk-cotton tree that stands at the center of the earth,
supports the heavens, and symbolizes life itself. On the walls of
Classic temples at Palenque, built eight centuries before Columbus, the world-tree was represented as a leafy cross. After
the conquest, the Maya took easily to the Christian cross,
grafting it onto those ancient roots, converting it from a dead
god's scaffold to a living archetype. In the vertical plane the
tree's roots, bole, and foliage represent underworld, world, and
heaven; seen horizontally, the cross is "the eye of God," axis of
the world's four directions. Each direction has its color. The
East is red; the South yellow; the West black; and the North
white. The center-zenith is verdant and called *Yaxche*, Green
Tree.

No two Maya cities were alike. Lamanai had bald pyramids with smoking altars open to the sky; Copán, in what is
now Honduras, was low and spacious, a city of broad staircases
and wide plazas full of statuary. Palenque was delicate and
ornate. Tikal, the greatest of all, was a vertical place, its tem-
ple-crowned pyramids soaring with arrogant steepness to more
than two hundred feet—the Manhattan of the Maya.

The ancient Maya, like their modern descendants, spoke
some twenty related languages, but in Classic times the upper
classes—scribes, priests, astronomers, and rulers—shared a
hieroglyphic writing system, and possibly a mandarin speech.
On stone monuments, painted walls, and illuminated books
they recorded their history and their knowledge.

The ruins exhale a powerful sense of loss. Of all the jewels of
intellect and art produced in these jungles, only three hieroglyphic books survive. The inscribed stones are threatened by the
slow amnesia of erosion and the rapid obliteration of looting and
development. Inscriptions cut from monuments are irretrievably
scrambled; painted tombs are sacked and vandalized; polychrome vases smashed in carelessness or fear.

The south end of Lamanai, where the inhabitants gradually
moved after the Classic fall and where the British once grew
sugar, is today an area of low mounds and thick bush. In the
last six or seven years, refugees from civil wars in El Salvador
and Guatemala have begun squatting there, planting their corn
in the ancient streets and squares, even using the foundations
of Maya houses for their own. I went there one morning, soon
after dawn, when the lagoon was platinum and still beneath a
sheet of mist that had lifted from the water and begun to lap at
the trees along the shore. It was breakfast time. The aroma of
wood fires and tortillas fought with dung and rotten rubbish.
Smoke was seeping from cracks in roofs and walls. Statuesque
girls were bringing water from the lake. A five-gallon pail
perched on the head does much the same for the female figure
as a pair of high heels and a garden-party hat. The chin is lifted
and the eyes give a measured, haughty stare. The chest is out;

the breasts pert; the whole body taut and poised. The girls' frocks, clean and gay, floated above ground littered with corn-cobs, batteries, pig droppings, and trampled beer cans.

Houses were cobbled together from sheets of tin, cracked planks, palmetto trunks, and tarred cardboard. One shack, boarded up and besieged by weeds, had a truck top for a roof. It belonged, I was told, to a trigger-happy Salvadorean who made himself village policeman and used to stop soccer games, when he felt like it, by shooting the ball with his revolver. Eventually he lost control and sank his own boat in a volley of gunfire while fishing. Such tales have the *opéra bouffe* quality that Anglo-Saxons imagine typical of Latin America.

The village was squalid but not entirely without hope: some people had planted coleus and croton hedges around their huts; and children were gathering beneath a large tree for morning lessons. Despite the drug trade, the gunfights, the nightmare memories, these people were simply trying to build a new life in the backwater of Belize. Belize and El Salvador are the same geographical size, but while Belize has only 150,000 people, the Republic of the Savior has five million. No wonder the refugees were pouring in, and no wonder—after massacres, rapes, murders, and mutilations—some were broken, violent people.

Most of the squatters at Lamanai were Salvadoreans, but a few were Guatemalan Maya, forced to abandon their Indian dress and language to avoid detection. In Guatemala—the border was just thirty miles away—the army recently had admitted destroying 440 Indian villages. The country's bishops had estimated that a million people had been driven from their homes—one Guatemalan in eight, most of them highland Maya. They were wandering in the hills and forests, swarming into Guatemala City's slums. Many were living in crowded camps in Mexico. Some had fled to Honduras and Belize.

Here was another sense of loss. The Maya who had raised the New World's most brilliant civilization, who had entranced me as a boy, and overwhelmed me as a student, were at this moment in crisis. How could I write a glib article about ancient remains, when only a few miles away modern Maya villages

were falling in ruins before helicopter gunships and napalm
bombs?

I wrote it, of course, but decided to come back and travel
more slowly through the Maya lands. A plan for a book
emerged; not a comprehensive book—the subject was far too
big for that—but a look at the Maya as a people who had
endured four thousand years, and who were now threatened by
the worst assault on their lives and way of living since the
Spanish conquest.

A circular itinerary seemed to fit the map. I would start
here in Belize, the east, move into the Petén jungle, the heartland of the ancient Maya, then head south to the Guatemalan
highlands. I would cross westward into Chiapas, and finally go
north to the Yucatán Peninsula. The plan had an appealing
resonance with Maya concepts of space: the journey, like the
Maya world, would have five parts—four quadrants and a center. It would end in Quintana Roo, where descendants of the
Caste War Maya still dream of independence, and not far from
where, fifteen years before, I had met Ignacio Ek.

Part I

East: Belize

Chapter 1

MEXICO–BELIZE BORDER. OCTOBER 21, 1985

"Beliz, Beliz!" a tall black man is shouting. He sees me:
  "You goin' to Beliz, maan?"
  "Are you Venus?"
  "No. Batty. Venus don' com heah no more."
A lie, I later discover, but better to take Batty brothers' old school bus now than wait for the quicker but possibly nonexistent Venus.

We head south across the Hondo River, into Belize. Music pours from a large cassette player in the lap of a young Mexican sitting with his girlfriend at the back. Mexicans consider Belizeans to be light-fingered and it seems he has chosen his *ranchero* songs with mischief in mind:

¡Algún pinche ratero	Some rotten thief
Se llevó mi cartera	Made off with my wallet
Con todito mi dinero!	And every penny I own!

The songs vibrate through Corozal Town, where the road meets the sea and a fishy breeze pushes back the viscous air of the sugar lands; they rebound from the clapboard walls of Bumper's Restorán Chino and Johnny's Place. Gradually the small brown Mexicans and local "Spanish" become outnumbered by colossal black matrons in floral bonnets, little girls with frizzy hair teased into ribboned spikes, lithe young men wearing fringed shorts and T-shirts advertising reggae bands. A

19

jam session of Creole gossip fills the bus; I catch intelligible
fragments declaimed like verse:

"Dat Cooper boy done mek she *fat*."

"Tell me ears now!"

At Orange Walk Town the bus stops at a bar with batwing
doors.

"Lonch time!" calls the driver, who has driven with such
consideration for his vehicle that I think he must be one of the
Batty brothers himself.

"Ow long, maan?" a passenger sings. "Ow long you gi' we
heah?" Before Mr. Batty can reply, a tall, smartly uniformed
policeman gets on behind a small mestizo with a toothbrush
moustache.

"Dat one!" the mestizo shouts. The policeman lopes down
the aisle and grabs a young Creole by the back of his T-shirt.

"Let's go, maan."

"Wha' fo'? Wha' de hell fo'?"

"Let's go. You got someting fo' say, you say it at de police
station. What you got dere in you han'?"

"Jos one bag o' gots, I jos pick up dis one bag o' gots!" The
accused holds up a plastic bag containing pig entrails.

"Let's go, maan," the officer repeats, lifting the accused
from his seat and frog-marching him out of the bus with one
easy movement, T-shirt tightly balled in the small of his back.
As soon as they leave, the Creole jam session resumes, at first
andante, soon allegro.

"Policemaan don' waste no time."

"What's de charge?"

"I didn' heah no charge."

"If dere's de police involve, dere's someting *wrong!*"

Necks crane out the bus windows; down the street the
accused is driven off in a police car. Five minutes later he's
back, freed with a gruff warning.

"Dey jos take him for one car ride!" says my neighbor, who
has a Kenyatta beard and a shirt displaying a monster, half devil,
half machine, called Motorhead.

The young man climbs back on the bus, grinning.

"Wha' happen, maan?"

"I de wrong maan. Spaanish miss twenty dollah, tink I de

tief. I tell de fockin' policemaan, I jos pick op dis one bag of gots."

I get off and walk down to the main square. The clock tower is stuck at ten past four, as it was when I visited Lamanai. Venus Bus Lines' puzzling timetable is still painted on a nearby wall—two columns headed APPROXIMATE TIME SCHEDULE and ACCURATE TIME SCHEDULE. When first I came this way, in 1970, you could have made a frontier movie in Orange Walk without changing a thing, but now several air-conditioned concrete buildings stand out like new teeth between the clapboard storefronts and rusty iron roofs of the high street. Mennonite farmers are loitering outside Haddad's Hardware—lean blue-eyed men in dungarees, motionless and cold as herons, guarding their plain womenfolk. From time to time the younger men sneak glances at shapely Creole girls.

I go into the Vietnam Bar and buy a wine called Night Train Express. Belizeans have a talent for names, but sometimes it leads them astray. During the Falklands War, an enterprising citizen of Orange Walk renamed his disco club the Exocet; one Friday night soon afterward it was torn apart by outraged British soldiers (two thousand British troops are stationed in Belize to prevent Guatemala from exercising an old territorial claim).

Mr. Batty returns from his lunch and starts the engine. Immediately the ranchero songs begin to peal from the back seat. Motorhead calls to the driver:

"Shot op de cassette. Put down de fockin' Spaanish cassette. Put on de wireless."

A reggae song—gloriously loud—thuds the Mexicans into submission: *I man, African race, African song . . .*

We have crossed the ethnic divide. From Orange Walk south to Belize City, Creoles, descended mainly from black slaves brought by the British to cut logwood and mahogany, outnumber the "Spanish" who poured into northern Belize during the Yucatán Caste War. Those refugees were a diverse lot: Ladinos, fearful for their lives, but willing to turn a profit by selling British guns to the Maya; war prisoners, escaped from the labor gangs building the Mayas' holy city of Santa Cruz; Maya deserters, worn out by years of fighting and the imperious demands of the Speaking Cross that inspired and directed the Indian campaign. All are "Spanish" to other Belizeans. On the outskirts of the towns and along the main road one still sees Maya-style houses—walls of plastered palmetto trunks, neat thatched roofs—but the women no longer wear the embroidered shift of their cousins in Mexico, and their children have learned English and forgotten Maya.

Orange Walk prospers these days but not from oranges; nor, for that matter, from sugar. Men here pack six-guns and drive lurid pickup trucks with doughnut tires. The real money comes from a crop known in the United States as "Belize Breeze." The locals, Motorhead tells me, call it "bush."

"See dat fancy house an' trock dere, maan?" He points out an extravagant villa painted red and blue, with an iridescent jeep parked in the drive.

"Five year ago dat little Salvador man was jos a mechanic fixin' cars on de corner. Now look at he. *Bush* buy dat house, maan."

The sugar plantations give way to wild country with Caribbean pine growing on sandy ridges, and tangles of scrub and palmettoes in shallow, swampy basins. Smells of stagnant water; the acrid signature of a skunk. Mr. Batty's wireless is playing calypso, an old standard called "Big Bamboo":

> Chinee man called Dick Hung Lo
> See one gial, say, "Com heah quick,"
> But dis one gial, now she say no,
> She wan' bamboo and not chopstick.
> Oh de big big bamboo, bamboo . . .

Years ago, when I drove to Belize City in my Austin, the road was slow and tedious, a narrow lane of patched and potholed tarmac winding through the woods to little settlements with names like Doubloon Bank, Honey Camp, and Lucky Strike. Now we're on the new Northern Highway, the finest in the country, so straight and broad that drug smugglers use it as a landing strip. (The government put steel poles along the shoulder to clip the wings of midnight fliers, but many of the poles have already disappeared.) It is rumored that the police can be induced to close the road and their eyes for a price.

Mr. Batty stops to fill his radiator from a ditch. Three Bedford trucks roar past; their names: *The Green Hornet, Starman,* and *Mr. Bad.*

The new highway rejoins the old at Sand Hill, a small village with two wooden churches and a schoolhouse on piles with a bell in front. It is midafternoon and very hot. Lessons are being held outside—rows of woolly heads looking up at a blackboard beneath a spreading tree. The teacher's T-shirt says, THE MIND IS A TERRIBLE THING TO WASTE.

Habitation ceases at the edge of the mangrove swamp that stretches the remaining few miles to the city. The Belize River appears on the right, only six inches below the level of the road. The sky turns black and rain falls so hard that we seem to be driving underwater. When we emerge, the bridge across the river's mouth gives a glimpse of the sea, a sheet of weathered lead, trapped and lifeless behind the barrier reef. Mangroves resume, then the sea reappears on the far side of a sandbank being turned into a posh suburb. I notice a particularly ostentatious villa. Was this also built by "bush"?

"No," says Motorhead. "Dat belong to Mr. Aziz. Com in heah thirty year ago from Lebanon with jos a suitcase on he head. Bot he a two-eye maan in a one-eye people town."

BELIZE CITY

You pass a factory or two, then the narrow streets close in—canyons of planking and corrugated iron, gray and rusty or gaudy as a carnival. The houses look like old garages propped on stilts, but some have gingerbread gables and fretted balconies. Only the poorest and most optimistic citizens use the bottom story for anything but storage: the tideless sea can rise without warning in foul weather. Batty's bus fumigates pedestrians and wobbly cyclists with a stream of black exhaust; reggae throbs from a bar. A man looks up and curses. He's got green curlers in his hair.

The name *Belize* is said to be a corruption of Wallace (Walis—Valiz—Baliz), a "notorious buccaneer" active here in the seventeenth century. If the etymology is correct, this is the only country in the world named after a pirate. However, there's a more plausible derivation from the Maya word *beliz*, meaning "muddy water."

Muddy water is everywhere, steaming in puddles, flowing like hot gravy in the river, brimming in the drains, canals, and open sewers that make Belize City a cloacal, clapboard Venice. The first Baymen, as the British settlers along the Bay of Honduras called themselves, were desperate individuals who cut logwood in peacetime and Spanish throats in time of war. The mouth of the Belize, hidden behind a maze of reefs and cays, was a good hideout for galleon chasers. Spain rarely had the nerve to tackle the Baymen in their boggy lair, but natural enemies were less timid: hurricanes, yellow fever, malaria, and cholera kept the settlement free of all but the reckless. Even after 1862, when Belize formally joined the empire, nothing was done to move the town. British Honduras was a "Cinderella colony," the sort of place from which wealth was extracted with little thought for the inhabitants. Belize City grew on its pile of rum bottles and mahogany chips, ragged and transient as a robbers' camp.

I jump from the bus and hop across puddles to a taxi, deafened by the roar of rain on tin, splashed by torrents running from the overflow spouts of wooden tanks. Until very recently cisterns were the only source of drinking water; now a Canadian aid agency is laying pipes and trying to replace the open sewers with proper drains.

Over the Swing Bridge and into the teeming market and commercial district known as Mom's Triangle. This part of Belize City is passed off most convincingly as the capital of a flyblown African republic in the film *The Dogs of War*. (More recently *The Mosquito Coast* was also shot here.) The old bar-restaurant where I was robbed fifteen years ago is gone, replaced by the Royal Bank of Canada. In the Royal's vault lies the national treasure: a jade head of the Maya sun god found at a ruined city called Altun Ha.

*   *   *

Tuesday. The Mopan Hotel, at the "good" end of Regent Street, is a wooden structure with a trellis-screened veranda. The owners are a Creole woman and her Scottish husband, who confines himself to the tiny bar in the lounge, a popular watering hole for local and expatriate whites. "What kind of beer would you like?" he asks newcomers, indicating a row of taps labeled Guinness, Double Diamond, and Worthington. The joke is that they're all connected to a barrel of Belikin, Belize's only beer.

Last night I ate with two other guests in the half of the lounge that serves as a dining room. Fried chicken with boiled cabbage and mashed potato. Rain drummed on the roof, and a parrot kept calling, "What's up, Johnny?" from the kitchen. At the table were a young bearded Canadian working on the sewer project, and Eamonn, an air-traffic controller from Cork.

"The problem is altitude," the Canadian was explaining, "or rather, the lack of it. Anything below street level is also below sea level: sewage can't flow, and must be pumped." He pushed his cabbage and mash around with his fork, as if to illustrate the point.

Eamonn was in his fifties, wanting a change, so he'd taken a two-year contract with the Belize government. His dreams of the Caribbean had not been fulfilled.

"I expected it to have a strand—what we call a beach—but there's nothin' but mangrove swamps. What brings you here, then?"

I said I was doing research for a book.

"That fellow what wrote *The Dogs of War*," Eamonn continued. "He must put a lot of research into his books. I preferred the fillum, actually. The army camp, where all the shooting took place, that's the old lunatic asylum, you know—around there by New Town Barracks."

"Was it empty?" the Canadian asked.

"I should think so." Eamonn laughed. "They're all out on the bloody street! You take your life in your hands every time you go over that Swing Bridge, you do. I've bin accosted several times. 'Give me a cigarette. Give me money. Give me a job'— it's always something. They're very cunning. Cunning even though they're illiterate. A fellow held me op two nights ago—

op there by the corner with the Jehovah's Witness place—I
think he most've been watching *Starsky and Hotch*. Comes
around the corner swingin' his arms, lots of hair, very casual
like. Like he was going somewhere. Out comes this big
revolver—scared the bloody pants off me—'Stick 'em up,
Jesus!' he said. I've never bin called that before. Put his hand in
me pocket and pulled out me money—only had two dollars.
Took me watch. Put his hand in me other pocket and took me
loighter. Beautiful loighter it was, too—all gold. And then he
took me cigarettes as well!"

It rained all night, and was still raining at breakfast. At about
ten o'clock the sun broke through and steam rose from the
streets. I walked one block down to the sea, and discovered that
water was flowing from the harbor *into* the gutters.

Even Government House, not far from the Mopan, is made
of clapboard and roofed with corrugated iron, though it has an
elegant columned porch. A new coat of paint makes it stand
out like a man in a clean white suit at a soup kitchen. Two
guards in a kiosk at the gate are whistling and listening to the
radio. Could I nip in for a quick photo?

"Go awee, maan, nobody comin' inside heah."

I have better luck at St. John's Cathedral across the street.
It's one of the few masonry structures in the city, built in 1812
of a somber factory brick that came from England as ship's
ballast. It would pass without comment in the mother country
as a working-class church or the chapel of a minor public
school, but in the context of Belize it is imposing, a rare example of age and permanence in a town thrown up without
thought for the future or connection with the past. Inside it is
cool and airy, smelling of polished wood and damp prayer-
books. Tall windows arched with fanlights reach almost from
floor to eaves. Plaques on the walls commemorate prominent
victims of the tropics: IN LOVING MEMORY . . . DIED OF YELLOW
FEVER AT GOVERNMENT HOUSE, BELIZE, 28TH MAY, 1905. The
cathedral is empty except for a snowy-haired black verger posting the order of hymns, a sheaf of number cards in his mouth.
The Anglican Church never had many adherents in the colony:

it was always the faith of the elite, wedded to the ideological needs of empire. Here the British crowned the Indian kings of the Mosquito Coast. Mosquitia—now eastern Honduras and Nicaragua—had had links with Britain since before the War of Jenkins' Ear (1739). In the nineteenth century the small Indian state became a protectorate, and Britain did not relinquish all claims in the region until 1907. More recently, the Indians' traditional fear of "Spanish" made them ready pawns in the CIA's war against the Sandinistas.

Wednesday. Trapped by a cloudburst in the Bliss Institute. At first I took this to be another example of the Belizean talent for nomenclature, but in fact it honors a national hero. Baron Bliss was an Englishman with a Portuguese title who enjoyed the deep-sea fishing off British Honduras so much that he bequeathed his fortune to the colony—despite the fact that he never set foot on shore until his sudden death in 1926. His munificence is celebrated annually on Baron Bliss Day (March 9), which, logically enough, is the day he died.

The institute he endowed is the national cultural center and public library. A dance group is rehearsing in the auditorium to drumming and dramatic utterances in a language I've never heard before.

"We practicin' for Garifuna Settlement Day," a black woman in orange leotards explains—November 19, when the arrival of the Garifuna, or Black Caribs, is celebrated. Despite this display of national solidarity, I've been told that these descendants of Carib Indians and escaped African slaves are not well regarded. They are industrious farmers—an occupation most Creoles despise—and have a reputation for witchcraft. The diversity of this tiny nation is extraordinary. In a population of 150,000 there are about 70,000 Creoles (of African and white descent in varying proportions), 25,000 Maya, 25,000 mestizos, 15,000 Black Caribs, 15,000 whites (many of whom are Mennonite farmers), and small numbers of East Indians, Chinese, and Lebanese. The exact number of Central American refugees is unknown.

The Carib dancer goes back to her group; I'm left to wander around the building by myself, drums throbbing in my ears. In the hallway are some Maya stelae—upright stone slabs covered in reliefs—and other sculptures from the Classic site of Caracol. They look rather neglected. There's an old car battery behind Stela 1, and somebody has left a half-eaten sandwich on the stela's altar. A sign nearby says, EATING AND DRINKING ARE NOT ALLOW IN HERE [sic].

Stela 1 shows a standing figure in full regalia with a fat little dwarf squatting at his feet. A caption gives the date as A.D. 593. The altar, shaped like a wheel of cheese, is engraved with a single huge glyph of the day Ahau (Lord) and the number five. Maya numerals are easy to read: dots for units one to four, bars for fives, and a glyph resembling a shell or fist for zero. Seventeen, for example, is written like this: ⸫III The system was presumably based on human anatomy: dots for individual digits; a bar for a full hand or foot; an empty clenched fist for nought.

The day 5 Ahau, like any name-and-number combination in the Maya ritual calendar, recurs every 260 days. It's unusual for a single day to be given an altar to itself, so something momentous must have occurred on this particular 5 Ahau. I have with me the new edition of Sylvanus G. Morley's classic textbook, *The Ancient Maya*. A table of dates at the back shows that a *katun*, or Maya "decade" of twenty years (the Maya counted in twenties, not tens as we do), ended on the day 5 Ahau in our year 593. These twenty-year periods took their names from their final day, and were of enormous significance to the Maya. Every unit of time was a numinous being, influenced by many divinities, and a divinity in itself. The beliefs involved were not unlike the Catholic system of saints' days, but infinitely more complex. To follow the analogy, the Maya would have had saints' weeks, months, years, decades, centuries, and millennia; plus the combination of influences of all these upon any given day.

Inquiry into the mystery of time has been called the soul of Maya culture.[1] Their very name is cognate with *may*, a word for "cycle"—so the Maya can truly be called the people of time. The calendar they devised was both an astrological system of great complexity and a precise astronomical tool; it remains their most famous achievement. Its inventors hit on two brilliant ideas. First, they chose simply to count elapsed days from a datum point in the past—exactly the same principle as the Julian Day Count used by modern astronomers. This eliminated at a stroke all the inaccuracies that accumulate when time is counted in solar years or lunar months. The length of the day is effectively a constant, the fundamental building block of earthly time; but the periods of sun and moon are, by comparison, variable and hard to measure.

To count days for thousands of years you must have an arithmetic capable of handling very large numbers. The other great discovery of the Maya (or perhaps the Olmecs) was the use of zero and place-system notation, in which the same signs can stand for different values depending on position. This elegantly simple idea now seems obvious; but the zero and its implications were discovered only twice, or possibly thrice, in human history. Greece and Rome didn't think of it, despite their advances in geometry. Europe struggled with primitive and clumsy Roman numerals until the Arabs, borrowing from the Hindus, brought ten-base notation in the twelfth century A.D. The Hindus had either invented the idea themselves or derived it from the imperfect six- and sixty-base system of the Babylonians (from which we get our minutes, seconds, and 360-degree circle). The Maya and other Mesoamerican peoples had perfected their vigesimal system long before the birth of Christ. Had it not been for the Arabs, all of modern arithmetic might have had to wait for the discovery of zero in the New World.

Maya dates during the Classic period were expressed in what is known as the Long Count. Put very simply, it resembles a car's odometer, counting days in geared cycles of ascending size. Each cycle increases by a factor of twenty, with one exception: like the Babylonians and ourselves, the Maya were attracted by the number 360 as a rough approximation of the year—so they multiplied the 20-day "months" by eighteen instead of twenty to arrive at a round-figure year of 360 days. This was called a *tun*. A katun is simply twenty tuns. Twenty katuns (roughly 400 years) form a *baktun*. The Long Count date of Caracol Stela 1 reads: 9. 8. 0. 0. 0. This means that nine baktuns (9 × 400 years) and exactly eight katuns (8 × 20 years) have elapsed since the starting point of the calendar.

The numbers on the "odometer" are sufficient to fix any day in Maya history. But Maya timekeepers also had other concerns addressed by other cycles: a 260-day ritual almanac called the *tzolkin* ("count of days") and a 365-day solar year. These were mainly concerned with horoscopes and the farming cycle, respectively; they were probably far older than the Maya's intellectual masterpiece, and they outlived it. Today, more than a thousand years after the last Long Count date was carved on a monument, the tzolkin and solar cycles are still being kept by Maya shaman-priests in highland Guatemala. At least, they were until the recent civil war.

I have lunch at the Golden Dragon—a rubbery conch curry— then down to the Paslow Building to mail letters and buy some maps. What names! Cowhead Creek; Rum Point; Double Head Cabbage; More Tomorrow. Back over the Swing Bridge (so called because it pivots open twice a day to let shipping pass on Haulover Creek). Hand firmly on wallet here. A man in dread-locks shouts, "I sell you some good herbs." Another calls, "Hey, Scarecrow! Give I one dollah!" I give him a quarter, which has the pointed motto TO REAP, PLANT on the reverse. In exchange I ask for an opinion on the new government, the first electoral change in twenty years.

"Elekshaan!" He snorts. "I still livin' like a sparrow, maan."

Sheets of water are falling from an oyster sky, splashing through the trellis onto the porch where I sit. I had hoped that the rains would be easing by now, but Mr. Shaw, at the bar, says they came unusually late this year. I switch from beer to rum.

"Local or imported?" asks Mr. Shaw.

"I'll try the local."

"Yer a brave man."

The consensus is that we're in for at least a fortnight's

soaking; I decide it's time to start heading west through central Belize to the Guatemalan Petén, the center of the Maya world.

WESTERN HIGHWAY

Thursday. Novelo's Bus, also known as the Belizean Queen, is much like Batty's. The road writhes through the swamp, a gravel water snake. Occasionally you see open pools dotted with strange tuffets of vegetation, but mostly the knobbly-kneed, glossy-leafed mangroves reduce the view through the windscreen to nothing but a tunnel between green walls, edged with stagnant puddles and patches of red clay. Once I glimpse the open sea and the hulk of a tramp steamer thrown up on shore by a tropical storm.

The girl in front of me is wearing a red T-shirt and yellow curlers. Her suitcases were brought to the bus by an old man with a tricycle cart on which was neatly printed NAK YU OWN TING: Do your own thing. Two speakers above the driver begin pumping out reggae. The roar of the engine makes the words unclear, but they sound like

> Com awee, com awee,
> I not tryin' to devour you.
> Com awee, com awee,
> I jos tryin' to deflower you . . .

The windows are soon covered by a film of mud. After half an hour the road finds solid ground and acquires some asphalt paving. The rain washes my window; at last I can see out. Flat country reappears—an odd juxtaposition of sandy pine ridges and waterlogged troughs bristling with palmettoes. There are little farmsteads along the roadside: a clearing, a wooden shack, a rain barrel, and grazing cows attended by white egrets. Hills pop up like bubbles on the southern horizon, just visible through the rain. Before long they're joined by others, and then the space between them is gradually infilled until a range of dark mountains nibbles at the sky.

BELMOPAN

I seem to be the only guest at Circle A Lodgings. The rain has stopped, but the sky threatens more.

The bus left the paved road and followed a gravel track to a parking area beside a tree in the middle of a field. There was a row of kiosks selling cigarettes and ice cream, one concrete bench, an oil drum for litter, and a taxi stand with two cabs in it. In the distance I could see a small restaurant, and a brand-new bus station with Novelo's name and orange colors; they seemed unfinished.

"You lookin' at it," the bus driver said when I asked where the town center might be. So this was Belmopan, the new capital, the Brasilia of Belize. How could I get to Circle A Lodgings?

"You'll need a taxi, maan."

It took the taxi ten minutes to reach the hotel and I was still baffled. We drove round a ring road that circled nothing. The only building I saw was a radio station. Opposite the hotel there's a football field with a row of bleachers; next door is another hotel, called the Bullfrog. That's all.

A solicitous young man showed me to a delightfully clean and airy room. He brought iced drinking water with the towels, turned on the ceiling fan, and politely refused my tip. "This is a family business," he said. He had the slightly American accent of the upper-class Creoles, many of whom have been educated in Canada or the United States. I explained I had come to see the archaeological commission and asked where the town was. He pointed out an overgrown footpath behind the hotel.

"Just follow that track all the way and it'll take you right there." He glanced at his watch. "But you've missed them for the day. Offices open at nine o'clock."

It's too early for a drink and supper so I explore. The hotel backs onto a quiet cul-de-sac lined with concrete bungalows well spaced from one another. The buildings are modest and all exactly the same. Each has a rather bare yard—maybe a few crotons and hibiscus—fenced with barbed wire. It looks like an army camp.

The path indicated to me leaves the housing behind and heads across an empty cow pasture. The country is rolling and lush—an outpost of the Maya mountains of southern Belize. Deciduous woods cover the hills. Cicadas and frogs keep up a constant skiffle. Charcoal clouds billow overhead; a few drops still fall. At last, after walking almost a mile, I reach some buildings and realize where I am. There, on the far side, is the bus stop and a row of stalls. These simple concrete structures are Belize's parliament, government ministries, and the central post office—the hub of the nation. It looks like a minor college campus that ran out of money.

Belmopan was planned in the early sixties, after Hurricane Hattie devastated Belize City. It was intended to grow as the old capital withered, but the dream far outstripped the resources needed to realize it. The abundance of space, the long walk-ways and circuitous roads—all emphasize the failure of the new capital to attract any population except the three thousand civil servants obliged to stay here during the week. Belize City stubbornly remains the economic and social heartland of the country, continuing to prosper while weeds crack the paving of Belmopan. It will take another hurricane to change that.

Drizzle falls as I walk back to the Circle A, but a white sun glows briefly through mist rising from the hills. I sit outside in a wicker garden chair on the veranda, drinking the last of my duty-free scotch and reading *The Ancient Maya*.

According to the book's calendrical tables, the present baktun began in 1618 and will end on December 21, 2012. That will also mark the completion of thirteen baktuns since the Long Count began. Some chiliastic "New Age" mystics have popularized the idea that the Maya calendar foretells the end of the world on that day. But sober study of the Long Count will not support such titillating conclusions. It had no beginning or end. Above the baktuns lay other cycles, each increasing by a factor of twenty. The Long Count was a reconciliation of cyclical and linear time. The Maya themselves made accurate calculations millions of years into the past and future, running their great machine forward and backward over temporal spans so immense that they amount to explorations of eternity.

Quite apart from that, it's by no means certain that we

know the right date to "start" the Maya calendar in ours. If the
Long Count had still been kept at the time of the Spanish
conquest, conversion of Maya dates to European ones would be
a simple matter. Unfortunately, the baktuns were no longer
recorded after the Classic collapse; and though the smaller
cycles continued to revolve, they did so without reference to
their starting point. The most widely accepted correlation was
first proposed in 1905 by Thomas Goodman, the Nevada news-
paperman who gave Mark Twain a start in journalism.[2] Goodman's calculations were later refined by others, including the
great British Mayanist, Sir Eric Thompson. According to
Thompson, the starting date fell on August 11, 3114 B.C. Alternative correlations move Classic Maya chronology up and
down in relation to ours, but it is of course internally consistent.

For my purposes, Thompson's correlation is good enough.[3]
Today—Thursday, October 24, 1985—comes out in the Maya
system as 12. 18. 12. 8. 0 3 Ahau 18 Yax. In other words,
exactly twelve baktuns, eighteen katuns, twelve tuns, eight
uinals (20-day "months"), and no single days have elapsed since
August 11, 3114 B.C.—a total of 1,862,080 spins of our planet
on its axis. Today is also the 18th day of the month Yax, meaning "Green," which falls in the middle of the Maya solar year.
And, most importantly for anyone planning something—a
marriage, a business transaction, a religious offering, or a journey—today, in the ritual almanac, is ruled by the lords of the
number three and the dayname Ahau. The Maya would have
written it like this:

The days of the almanac, or tzolkin, are much like our
days of the week, except that there are twenty instead of seven.
Like ours they are named after gods. We have forgotten Sun and
Moon, Woden and Thor, but the Maya were very much aware of
the divinities who presided in endless succession over their
twenty days. The Maya system adds a twist: running alongside
the twenty days are the numbers one to thirteen, also repeating
endlessly. The combined mechanism is like two cogs, one with

twenty teeth, the other with thirteen. It takes exactly 260 days
(13 × 20) for any combination to return.

Not only is each day deeply influenced by the god for
which it is named, but the numbers also have a life of their
own; they, too, are ruled by gods, some dire and irascible, others
helpful and good. In complete contrast to our own superstitions, thirteen was a very good number for the Maya, which is
probably why they chose it as the highest power in the tzolkin
cycle. Besides the bar-and-dot notation, numerals below
twenty could also be written by hieroglyphs—stylized human
faces that give an idea of each number's disposition. Ten, a
number feared by the Maya, has the fleshless jaw of Death.

As far as I can tell, the Maya auspices for my trip aren't bad
at all. Ahau, Lord, is a good day, last in the sequence of names
and senior member of the twenty. His hieroglyph is a full face,
the countenance of the radiant sun god, Kinich Ahau.[4] Three is
also good, a youthful number represented hieroglyphically by a
young man's face in profile. If he is shown with the wind
symbol on his cheek he is a deity of rain and storms. That
influence can certainly be felt today.

Voices in the kitchen are discussing a religious matter of a
different kind:

"An' I tell him no man can take another man wit' him to
heaven—you got to recognize Jesus Christ as you personal
Savior, an' live you life for Him. No one do it for you!"

It all adds up. The spotlessness, the modest integrity, the
lack of ashtrays and bottles: this is a very devout hotel. I go
next door to the Bullfrog for a beer and a steak supper. Afterward I stroll down the unlit road, followed by the sound of a
jukebox and boozy laughter. The drizzle has ceased and the
clouds are torn by patches of black infinity alive with stars.
Frogs and cicadas are playing reggae rhythms in the ditches; a
smell of cow dung drifts from the fields. Fireflies prick the
night around me, answering the shooting stars, which the
Maya believed were cigar butts thrown down by the gods.

4 Imix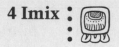

Imix: Crocodile; reptilian body of the planet Earth, first of the twenty days, follows Ahau and begins the sequence again. Today is also Friday.

The government buildings at Belmopan are said to have been "inspired" by ancient Maya architecture. To me the long, low concrete offices look like any others of the 1960s. Parliament is a blend of Maya and Bauhaus in which the latter is unhappily the winner. A curious box on top of the structure—presumably "inspired" by the roof combs that added height to Maya temples—looks as though it might contain a water tank or the air-conditioning plant. The designers have missed the essence of Mesoamerican architecture: effective deployment of geometric mass and space. Admittedly the new capital was built on a shoestring, but given the abundance of empty land at Belmopan there's no excuse for such timid use of elevation and perspective. A few terraces and the choice of a four-sided plaza, instead of a triangle (hardly a Maya shape), could have made all the difference.

The archaeology department is in the basement of one of the office blocks. The passage walls are papered with photographs and maps. A poster warns against trafficking in antiquities.

Harriot Topsey, the archaeological commissioner, whom I met once before when he was studying in Canada, and his assistant, Logan McNatt, have just returned from a field trip to some sites threatened by looting.

"This year is the worst ever," Logan says. "With the government cracking down on the marijuana trade, more and more refugees are being forced into pillaging sites just to survive. We get a few things back when the police catch someone. Trouble is, there's no place to keep the stuff." He takes me down to a small windowless vault guarded by a steel door.

"Before we had this door installed they even broke in here and stole some of our best pieces."

Logan introduces me to Raúl Valencia, the vault's curator—a man in his mid-twenties with a hank of jet black hair
that juts over his forehead like a peaked cap.

"Raúl's a Maya himself, from Succotz."

"That's right, maan, I'm a modern Maya." He laughs nervously. It's a bit of a shock to meet a Maya who sounds like Bob
Marley. I wonder if he's making the point that I shouldn't take
him for a backward Indian—a pejorative stereotype devised by
the Spaniards and perpetuated by British and Creoles. There is
always this ambiguity toward Indians in Latin America. The
ancient Indians—the Incas, Aztecs, and Mayas—are extolled
and raised to the status of national icons. But the modern
Indian—the barefoot, uneducated, potentially rebellious peasant—is deemed an obstacle to progress, a source of embarrassment, even (if he is numerous enough) an object of racist
loathing. For it isn't Indians who rule these republics: no country in America has really been decolonized. Indians may form
half the population of Peru, three-quarters of Bolivia, and sixty
percent of Guatemala; but the rulers are Ladinos—whites and
mestizos—whose blood, or at least whose culture, came with
the conquistadors. Only dead Indians are heroes.

In Belize, Indians are seldom feared or hated—they're too
small and inoffensive a group for that—but they are not generally admired. Discrimination is subtle: Creole politicians have
been known to make speeches about "bringing the Amerindian
into Western civilization." Planning regulations forbid traditional Maya houses in urban areas. The reason for this is said to
be the fire hazard, but it's hard to see why Maya thatch should
be any more combustible than a clapboard shack.

The vault—about fifteen feet square—is packed from
floor to ceiling with artifacts. Shelves line every wall, and there
are more in the middle, leaving only a narrow passage on either
side. Raúl picks up a painted vase of Classic date.

"Look dis one here—it was confiscated from a Salvadorean
by the police. We don' know where it come from, mebbe Tikal.
These two Maya fellows look to be havin' a very intense conversation, or mebbe they're playin' a game."

The vase shows two figures bending toward each other
from a cross-legged position. The scene was painted with a very

free hand, giving movement to the bodies and facial expressions, as in the best Japanese brushwork.

The quality of the finds is impressive, even though several of the best pieces are on loan to a touring exhibition. I'm shown jade masks for the faces of the dead and Maya skulls with jade inlay in the front teeth—an ancient precedent for the gold fillings of today. There are enormous ceremonial flint bars— one is thirty inches long—which were carried by rulers as insignia and often buried as offerings when temples were enlarged. Even stranger are the so-called eccentric flints— elaborate silhouette figures of plants, animals, deities, and what seem to be purely abstract shapes. In pottery, there are tiny naturalistic figurines of men and women, and large, grotesque incense burners in the shape of fanged and snouted gods. It's obvious that Raúl is immensely proud of these ancient things, but when I ask him to translate the Maya name of a site he has mentioned, again comes that nervous laugh.

"Don' know, maan. Like I say, I'm a modern Maya." He changes the subject. "You want to see a stela from Caracol? It over there beside that building." We go outside to the grassy triangle between the two office blocks. It's raining again and the lawn is awash. Raúl goes over to a piece of plastic weighted down with some lengths of scaffolding. Underneath is a Maya ruler in ceremonial pose, similar to the one at the Bliss Institute.

"How long has this been here?"

"Oh, 'bout eight year, I tink. Got no place to put it. Commissioner brought it out by army helicopter to save it from de looters."

For the rest of the day Harriot Topsey lets me use a corner of his office, which is also the department library. I copy down references and we chat a bit about people we both know in Canada. I mention there are a few things I'd like to photocopy.

"How many Xerox machines you think we got in Belmopan?" he asks rhetorically. "One. Belongs to the guy who owns the restaurant behind the bus station. Better get over there quick—he doesn't like making copies during lunch hour."

Chapter 2

5 Ik | ⬛ *Ik: Wind; breath, life.*

SAN IGNACIO, CAYO DISTRICT, WESTERN BELIZE

Pink and blue concrete benches, each bearing the name of its civic donor, surround a dry fountain resembling a three-tier cakestand. Beneath a large cypress there's a plywood bin inscribed: HAVE CITIZEN PRIDE AND PLEASE THROW DIRT IN DIRT BOX. Occasional taxis—big American cars of the mid-seventies—circle this small park, the driver dangling an arm from the window and calling, "Melchor! Melchor!" (They ply regularly between here and Melchor de Mencos, the Guatemalan border town ten miles to the west.)

Some black and gray turkeys are strutting and fanning in front of the police station cum post office, a colonial building with a red roof. From here much of the town drops away; one has a view of iron roofs neatly divided into rectangles of zinc and rust, as the different sheets have weathered. Poster-paint houses shelter among palms, flowering shrubs, and flocks of mist on the wooded hills.

"It's pretty, isn't it? I just love it here." I met her on the bus from Belmopan this morning, a spinsterish woman who said she was a teacher with the Peace Corps. Belize has by far the highest ratio of Peace Corps volunteers to population in the world: almost one for every five hundred nationals. I've got an hour to kill and suggest a beer.

"I'd better not. Wouldn't do to let my students see me drinking with a strange man in a bar. No offense, of course." She touches my arm. "Will you be here long?" I explain I'm waiting for Mick Fleming, owner of Chaa Creek Cottages.

"Well, everyone around here is just so nice. Enjoy yourself and remember not to worry about a thing, because nobody else does."

CHAA CREEK

Evening. Mick and Lucy Fleming have lived in Belize for about ten years. They bought Chaa Creek Ranch in an overgrown state and, like many other back-to-the-landers of the 1970s, tried to make a living with livestock. They had to go into tourism to make the place pay. Now they have several white-washed, thatched cottages in the Maya style and a central dining room whose round plan and conical roof betray Mick's years in East Africa. He's an outgoing Englishman, mid-thirties, with a moustache and a public school accent that has survived Africa, Belize, and marriage to an American. This could have been me, I suppose—a farm like this, the so-called simple life in the tropics. I had played with the idea of buying land in Belize, until I was robbed at Mom's Triangle.

For the first time in almost a week the weather has acted in my favor: the rains made the track to Chaa Creek impassable, and Mick had to use the Macal River, which runs down from the Maya Mountains, past Chaa Creek, and unites with the Mopan (or Belize) a few miles below San Ignacio—a delightful trip. We came up in his dory, a dugout canoe some twenty-five feet long and three feet in beam, carved from a guanacaste trunk.

The dining room is fitted with a bar where guests help themselves on the "honor system." Drips are falling from the thatch onto giant heart-shaped leaves of elephant taro that grow around the building. (The Maya call this plant *macal*—the name given to the river.) It's dark now; oil lamps cast a warm light that polishes the mahogany furniture and loses itself in the great cone of thatch. There are so few insects in

Cayo District that the windows have no glass or screens. I can hear cows chewing nearby, a sound of old men trying out new false teeth. Mick loves cows (something to do with his fascination for the Maasai) and they wander around the place like aged relatives.

Mick and Lucy seem to enjoy the company of guests. They even eat dinner with them. Not that there are many—just myself and George, a commercial fisherman from Alaska.

"How can a fisherman afford to travel all winter?" Mick asks.

"Crabs. Good money in crabs. Cost me forty thousand for my king crab license, but you make that back easy in a good year."

The conversation turns to Guatemala, that magnetic yet sinister republic only a few miles from here. Lucy sometimes runs trips across the border to the ruins of Tikal.

"I must say I preferred my encounter with the guerrillas to the ones I've had with the army. The army are all fifteen- and sixteen-year-old kids. They're nervous, they won't look you in the eye. But these guerrillas were in their twenties and thirties, more my own age. I had two tourists in the back that time and we had had a *hard* day. I was driving the old Ford truck. The power steering hose had snapped, we'd had two flat tires, and the jack had broken. Then up ahead we saw these military-looking types and about half a dozen vehicles pulled over at the side of the road." Lucy stops to light a cigarette, and blows a dramatic puff of smoke at the roof.

"It was the guerrillas! They were very polite—apologized for stopping me, explained that they had a revolution to run and they needed our car batteries for their radios. I said, 'Oh, señor, please don't take my battery because I've had a very bad day.' And he was so nice: 'Of course we won't take your battery, señora.' But they took all the others."

On the wall is a large scale topographical map of Cayo District, and I see that the farm called Negroman—believed to be the site of ancient Tipú—is only a few miles upriver. It's easy to talk George into a boat trip tomorrow.

6 Akbal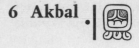

Akbal: Night-House; darkness, underworld, realm of the nocturnal jaguar-sun. The lord of the numeral six is related to Chac-Xib-Chac, red god of the east, chief of the four storm deities who rule the directions of the world. Probably not an ideal day for canoeing.

Mick lends us a twenty-foot cedar dugout built by a local man and exhibited at the New Orleans world's fair as an example of Belizean craftsmanship. For motive power we have two kayak paddles, incongruous with the heavy craft but they work well enough once we learn to keep our weight toward the stern. George is a quiet companion, but it's the silence of contemplation and I try not to disturb him.

The sky is clear and the river still, a pathway of green and black glass between high walls of tangled jungle. A "Jesus Christ" lizard (so named for its miraculous ability to scamper across the water's surface) leaves a score on the glass that slowly softens and is absorbed, as if by the passage of an age. There's a scent of hidden flowers, and the sad essence of decay. Blue herons and kingfishers perch on snags, studying the ale-colored shallows. For a while we don't notice the heavy shapes basking high in the overhanging trees; then one moves, hissing and shaking leathery jowls: an iguana, six or seven feet in length, with a spiky ridge along its back and a ringed black and yellow tail.

After an hour we reach a spot called Big Eddy, where the river turns sharply to the right. Limestone cliffs dotted with bromeliads and hung with frayed pelmets of roots and lianas rise a hundred feet above a dark pool turning slowly like a galaxy. On the inside of the bend there's a bank of yellow sand steaming in the sun. An old black man in a dugout is setting out nets below the cliff. Only his white hair stands out from the olive shade and somber water.

"Mawnin'," he calls out, "I Mr. Thomas. I build dat boat you in. Where you fellas goin'?"

"Up to the Maya ruins at Tipú."

"I got some Maya blood in me. An' I tell you fellas, watch out de Xtabay doan get you. You see any pretty gial in de forest, you tarn de other way."

"The *Xtabay*?"

"Yes, sir, de Xtabay. She wait by de taall trees for you at midnight. Sometimes daytime, too. A man comin' hoom see she, follow she through de bush, follow an' follow, an' den soddenly he realize where he be—lost in de middle of nowhere, maan! She 'chant you, see." He chuckled mysteriously.

"I know of one time, back jos after Horricane Hattie. Friends of mine workin' wit' de timber company, cottin' de fallen mahogany. Well, it was evenin' an' de boys was comin' hoom on de big timber trock with iron wheels. An' dis one fella he say, 'Stop de trock!' An' he go into de bush. An' de other fellas waitin', an' waitin', an' waitin', an' he no com back. Dey tink he gone for one piss, you see. Well, it dark now an' dey go hoom. Tree days dey sarch for he, sarchin' everywhere. Den one week after he disappear dey fine dat man on a little island in de middle of a lagoon in de forest, ten mile from where he walk away! An' he doan remember noting at aall! Well, some say dat was de Xtabay, or maybe *el Dueño del Monte*—de Lord of de Forest!"

Mr. Thomas bends to his net. "I seventy-eight years old. You fellas doan let an ol' maan fright you!"

Noon. After half a dozen rapids we come to the ford at Negroman. Cumulus clouds have been thickening all morning, gradually silting up the overhead river of the sky; now they begin to empty themselves. We run the canoe under some overhanging willows, but it's no use: in five minutes we're as wet as if we had fallen in the water. Soon the rain stops; the sun reappears, and in the stillness that follows the downpour there comes a chorus of joyful birds and the heavy smack of drips on leaves.

We've arrived at Tipú by the same route as the Franciscan friars who came here in 1618 after visiting their mission at Lamanai:

From Lucú one goes up the river twelve leagues against the current in order to reach Tipú. The violence of the water is so great that paddles are not enough . . . and many times the Indians threw themselves into the water to pull [the canoes] by hand. . . .

In three days God was served and they overcame the difficulties of the ascent and [the friars] arrived . . . to stay for whatever time might be necessary to renew the conversion of the infidels.[1]

We scramble up a clay track to a broad meadow, maybe thirty acres in extent, peopled by the placid figures of zebu cattle with enormous humps, dewlaps, and floppy ears. They turn from cud chewing to give us a vacant yet knowing stare, as if in a state of bovine enlightenment.

On a small mound (most likely an ancient house or shrine platform) at the far side of the meadow there's a shack with a man and a woman sitting outside.

The man gets up and comes to meet us. He wears rubber boots, jeans, and his white shirt open to the waist exposes a hairless copper chest and curving belly—the figure of a portly Maya lord. His name is Candelario Uck. He's suspicious at first but brightens when I mention Elizabeth Graham, one of the archaeologists who dug here recently. He shows us the diggings, now covered in scrub. At the edge of the cow pasture are foundations of a rectangular building with beveled corners.

"They say this was a church," Uck says rather doubtfully in Spanish. Only a few stones protrude from heavy sod. Not far from it we come to an earlier and more massive building, overgrown with wild sunflower and morning glory. It seems to be a platform about fifteen feet high and thirty or forty feet square. Excavation revealed that this was a late Postclassic (probably fifteenth-century) temple, one of several buildings arranged around a small plaza. Most interesting was the discovery of Maya incense burners in association with shards of Spanish pottery. These and similar finds suggest that "infidel" Maya were still worshiping here within earshot of Christian rituals in the church.

Tipú, the most powerful town in seventeenth-century Bel-

ize, was a buffer state between the Spaniards in Yucatán to the
north and the heathen Itzá Maya of the central Petén, who were
not conquered until 1697. For years the Tipuans vacillated
between autonomy and Spanish domination, Christianity and
the ancient Mesoamerican gods. A brutal wave of Spanish
conquest had swept through Chetumal and Belize in 1544
under the notorious Pacheco family, whose excesses prompted
one friar to write to the Crown:

> This captain [Alonso Pacheco], with his own hands . . .
> killed many [Indians] with the garrote . . . and, after he
> had killed them, he said, "Oh how well I finished them
> off." . . . He cut the breasts off many women, and
> hands, noses, and ears off the men, and he tied
> squashes to the feet of women and threw them in the
> lakes to drown merely to amuse himself.[2]

Despite, or perhaps because of this, the Tipú and New
River area became so unruly that in 1567 the Spanish had to
mount a second invasion. They destroyed "idols," burned hieroglyphic books, and seized large numbers of Indians whom they
forced to live near the garrison of Bacalar, not far from modern
Chetumal. It was probably at this time that the Tipú and
Lamanai churches were built.[3] Spanish control again slowly
faded until 1608, when a *reducción* of Indians was undertaken
at Tipú. These "reductions" were the sixteenth-century forerunners of the Boer War concentration camps, the strategic
hamlets of Vietnam and Rhodesia, and the "model villages" in
Guatemala today. Indians were rounded up from their scattered
farmsteads and forced to concentrate in a town where they
could be closely supervised by Spanish civil, religious, and
military authorities.

But in the late 1630s the lords of Tipú organized the great
revolt that drove Spanish rule from Belize until the end of the
seventeenth century, when the Tipuans were forcibly resettled
with defeated Itzá in the central Petén.

2:00 P.M. Back on the river. Just as I was thanking Candelario
Uck for his trouble, I noticed a tall tree framed between two

limestone hills to the south. It had a gray trunk, free from any limbs and swelling with the subtle entasis of a Greek column. This graceful shaft supported a perfectly hemispherical crown of foliage. It was a silk-cotton, sacred world-tree of the Maya.

"What do you call that?" I asked.

"Ceiba," said Candelario Uck.

"In Maya it's *yaxche*, isn't it?"

His reply was instantaneous, as if I had asked him a word in Japanese instead of a language widely spoken by his parents' generation.

"*No sé, señor. Yo no sé maya.*" ("I don't know. I don't know Maya.")

Drifting down a river is the most silent form of travel, the stillness broken only by birdcalls and the crescendo of approaching rapids. Usually we hear rough water before seeing it, and its urgent rippling is the signal to sit up and ready the paddles for a few brisk strokes. Then the silence returns, and we drift past iguanas and water birds without alarming them.

Sun and rain compete all afternoon, but it is never cold. At Big Eddy we beach the canoe on the sandbank and stretch out in the sun. Mr. Thomas and his nets are gone. A shower has just ended: sky, rocks, and trees paint themselves on the river as it calms—a pointillist vision slowly hardening into realism, until two perfect worlds are hinged where the water meets the cliff.

7 Kan

Kan: Ripeness; sign of the young maize lord who brings abundance.

In my case, a day to take it easy and nurse sore limbs. Paddling, like skiing, makes one aware of muscles whose existence one had never suspected.

The road has dried out enough for Lucy to drive to town; I

catch a lift and phone my wife from the San Ignacio hotel. A nice clear line to Toronto. She's anxious about my going on to Guatemala the day after tomorrow. I tell her not to worry: neither Left nor Right wants to kill gringos because it's bad publicity. But privately I wonder if I shouldn't follow the Creole proverb: "Coward man keep sound bone."

8 Chicchan

Chicchan: Snake; day of the celestial serpent.

This morning I walked the three miles from Chaa Creek to the main road. From there you can see the pyramid at the ruins of Xunantunich, which lie just inside Belize opposite the modern Maya village of Succotz. I was prepared to walk the whole way but when one of the collective taxis that ply between San Ignacio and the border appeared, I flagged it down. The front was fully occupied by the mestizo driver and two Guatemalans. I got in the back beside a Creole wearing a dark suit with an open-necked red shirt flaring over his lapels.

"You goin' to Guatemala?" he asked.

"Just to Xunantunich today. Guatemala tomorrow. How about you?"

"I go over dere two, tree times a week—on business."

"What sort of business?"

"Oh. I do a little imparting and exparting, you know."

"What in?"

"Tings, you know."

"What kind of things?"

"*Tings*, maan."

He changed the subject: "You know de bes' solution to dis part of de world? Partition!"

I thought he must be talking about Guatemala's claim to Belize, but he had a larger view:

"Like Germany. Let de Russian flag fly over Nicaragua, an' de American flag over de res'. Den all de trobble soon die down." He met my eye and jerked his head toward the three in front.

"Prob'ly in a few years de Russians an Americans push out de other people. Get rid of all de fockin' Spaanish!"

He slapped his knee and roared.

SUCCOTZ

The most striking feature of Succotz today is the central green, perhaps a quarter mile square, around which are arranged modest houses of wood and concrete block, and a few of traditional thatch, half hidden among breadfruit and mango trees, cohune palms, and stands of corn. Tin roofs are glinting in the heat, and the only inhabitants seem to be two sheep grazing on the football field.

I stop for a drink at a tiny store near the road. The storekeeper, an old man, stripped to the waist, is resting in a hammock. He's thickset, with bloodshot eyes. He gets up and, in Spanish heavily accented with Maya, asks what I want. I buy a Coke. The storekeeper pulls a small bench out from the wall and pats it for me to sit down. I glance around at the usual inventory of any small Central American shop: soft drinks and sweets, cigarettes, batteries, files for sharpening machetes, soap, and dye. A large TV set is showing *Dallas*, dubbed in Spanish—from Miami, I presume.

On one shelf, almost hidden among the bright clutter of tinned goods and cigarette advertisements, there's a curious shrine. Flowers are spread before a plain wooden cross, and the cross is wearing a Yucatecan Maya woman's *huipil*, a cotton dress embroidered at the neck and hem. Crosses dressed in women's clothes are found in many traditional parts of Guatemala and Yucatán, but this style was particularly associated with the cult of the Speaking Cross that inspired the Caste War Maya.

"You goin' to de ruins?" the man asks in almost unintelligible English. Then he adds, "Dey say dem Mayas had a whistlin' stoon. How else dey raise up dem big stoons?"

I've heard mention of this whistling stone before. It sounds rather like the Peruvian idea that the Incas built their walls by levitating boulders.

"The people here in Succotz—do they say this? They're Mayas, aren't they?"

"I hear dat. We com from Guatemala, Mexico. Live here. Den dem British com and make dem one Belize."

Belize has always been a land of frontiersmen and fugitives: runaway Indians and slaves; wanted criminals; unwanted politicians. In the last century, while the white governments of Guatemala, British Honduras, Mexico, and Yucatán jockeyed for advantage, various Maya groups carried on equally Machiavellian campaigns among themselves. To these Maya the *dzul* (foreigners) who pretended to rule the region were merely distant players to be manipulated, and the frontiers they had drawn across Maya territory were treated with contempt or connivance as occasion warranted. The politics of the Maya lowlands might be very different today if the nineteenth-century Maya had united against the British, Mexicans, and Guatemalan Ladinos. But unity has always eluded the Maya. Never—not even at the height of Classic civilization—did they form a political structure larger than the city-state.

In the last century, the Maya of Succotz seem to have been generally pro-British, an attitude they shared with the Santa Cruz. But this cost them the hatred of the Icaiché and allied groups, who burned Succotz and the border town of Benque Vicjo in 1867—the same year the plantation of Indian Church was sacked.[4] The British repaid the "rebel" Indians with rocket attacks on their villages, driving many into the Petén. However, other Maya continued to enter British Honduras from Guatemala, preferring Queen Victoria to the anti-Indian "liberal" regimes that arose there after 1871.

To Xunantunich. (The *X* in Maya, following sixteenth-century Spanish spelling, stands for a sound like the English "sh." The name is therefore nothing more formidable than Shu-nan-tu-*nich*, with the stress falling on the last syllable, as in all Maya words.) When the site was first "excavated"—ransacked would be a better word—by an irrepressible amateur named

Thomas Gann, it was generally known as Benque Viejo or Mount Maloney. Gann was told the Maya name and its origin by a citizen of Succotz, one Urbano Patt, "the most renowned shaman, bush-medico, and snake-doctor in all the district."

> [Xunantunich] means in Maya, literally, "stone maiden," and its origin, as told by Urbano, is somewhat peculiar. Some years ago, when the Maya first settled in Benque Viejo and discovered the ruins, one of their number started out hunting one morning. . . . Crossing the mound just below the base of the temple, he was suddenly brought up "all standing" by the sight of a beautiful statuesque Maya maiden, of heroic size. . . . She appeared of a dazzling and supernatural whiteness, as she stood full in the rays of the rising sun, and looked with fixed and stony gaze, as it appeared to him, across the intervening bush to the valley, where later the Indians built the village of Succots.[5]

Was the maiden a Xtabay? Or simply a young man's first view of an ancient stela lit by a sunbeam in the forest? Gann, an Indiana Jones if there ever was one, is hardly a reliable source, but the story is intriguing because it implies that the vision might have had something to do with the choice of Succotz for a village site when the Maya separated themselves from the mestizos at the neighboring town of Benque Viejo.

A small ferry takes visitors across the Mopan (or Belize) River to the ruins. It is just about to leave when I arrive. The old but wiry ferryman begins turning a hand crank attached to a cable. On board are a few locals and an English couple named Roger and Bobbie. Roger is a young officer just finishing a duty tour with the British forces. He has a fine Spanish shotgun; Bobbie is struggling with a butterfly net.

"Oh bother, it's jammed, and I think I forgot my killing jar."

"Darling, you really are quite hopeless."

The butterfly net puzzles the Maya, but they gaze longingly at Roger's gun, which looks extraordinarily shiny and well made beside their own ancient and rusty weapons. One fellow has a percussion musket that might have served in the Caste War.

Roger produces a jam jar containing cyanide from his rucksack.

"You are marvelous. I have a feeling I'm going to get lots of beauties today."

"Nebba caall de crocodile Big Mout' till you done cross de ribba!" Roger says, quoting a Creole saw that doesn't seem exactly apt, but he's a good mimic.

"Thought we'd see a bit of the place before we go back to Blighty," he tells me. "Get a spot of shooting and a few lepidoptera to pin on the wall."

I ask if he's seen any shooting in the course of duty.

"Heavens no! The funny thing is everyone's really quite happy to have us here. The Belizeans like us because we keep the Guats out, and the Guats—they'd never say so of course—but they like us because we keep the border shut. No gunrunning to the Commies and that sort of thing."

The ferry docks at the far side. The Mayas disappear down forest paths to their cornfields, and only the three of us are left on the jeep trail to the ruins. Roger and Bobbie begin smearing themselves with insect repellent.

"Want some?" says Roger. "Quite brilliant stuff actually. British army issue. The only kind that really works."

"Isn't that counterproductive when you're trying to catch butterflies?"

"You don't want ticks. Bloody ticks'll go right up your leg."

"Oh, Rog, how beastly! How far up do they go?"

"*All* the way up," says Roger.

"Oh, do look, Roger, there's a lovely one!" She's off, running from side to side, lunging at the bushes with her net.

"I think I'd better get along to the ruins," I say.

"Carry on."

XUNANTUNICH

The walk—about a mile—is delightful; the trail broad and well kept. Huge palm leaves arch over me—green herringbones filtering the sun. Birds call from the woods: doves, parrots, and once the metallic screech of a *chachalaca*, a demented jungle fowl. Perhaps because of Bobbie I notice more butterflies than usual. Yellow is a common color, and twice I see the spectacular morpho, whose cerulean wings must have inspired the "Maya blue" used by ancient artists in wall paintings, pottery, and illuminated books.

The trail opens in the corner of a clearing surrounded by long mounds. Low walls are visible on top of these in places, but the sides are covered in scrub. To the south rises the great pyramid with mysterious dark doorways and crenellations formed by the base of the fallen roof comb. At 130 feet, this is still the tallest building in Belize—a fact that Belizeans are engagingly fond of pointing out. Here the modern is not necessarily the biggest and best. Even today the country's total population is perhaps one-tenth of what it was in the Classic period. Belize is one of those rare places where one can feel the recession of mankind and nature's subsequent recovery.

Xunantunich stands on the summit of an artificially leveled hill about three hundred feet above the river. The archaeological commission has built a thatched shelter for visitors, and a smaller roof covering three carved stelae found in the ruins.

The warden charges one Belize dollar (half a U.S. dollar) and gives me the visitors' book to sign. He's a middle-aged Maya with a confident gold-trimmed smile and thick hair turning iron gray. He wears a bush hat and safari uniform; his English is very good. Following Mick at Chaa Creek, I mispronounce his name as Ponti.

"It's Pantí, actually," he says. "Sir Eric Thompson thought it was probably a name native to this area." He gives other examples; from the way he rattles off the difficult glottal stops and explosive consonants it's clear that he has not forgotten Maya.

He shows me three stelae, now lying on their backs. One bears the significant date 10. 0. 0. 0. 0—the completion of Baktun 9 on March 13, 830. All are eroded, but where the carving is well preserved one can see that it was deep and rich.

A stela found by Gann shows a ruler or warrior holding in his outstretched right hand a ceremonial bar. On the unspoiled parts of the headdress the treatment of the feathers is particularly fine. The figure stands on a captive or slave crouching on hands and knees, a motif that became common in the late Classic period (c. 600–900) with increasing warfare between Maya cities.

"There was an altar, too," Pantí says. "Part of it is in the British Museum, but Gann cut the glyphs off and lost them."

The date on this one seems to read 10. 1. 0. 0. 0, or November 28, 849: exactly one katun—one twenty-year period—after the other. (The year counted here is the 360-day tun, so a katun is actually about 19.7 solar years.)

When these monuments were being carved, the writing was already on the wall for Classic civilization (the Maya, who loved wordplay, might have enjoyed the pun). Palenque had fallen silent after 9. 17. 13. 0. 7; Copán at 9. 18. 10. 0. 0, or A.D. 800, the year that Charlemagne was crowned Holy Roman Emperor. Tikal survived Xunantunich to celebrate the end of the second katun in Baktun 10; and Tikal's neighbor, Uaxactun, recorded the completion of the next katun in our year 889. But in all the lands of the Maya only one stela marked the close of the fourth katun on January 18, 909; and that date is generally taken by Mayanists as the end of the Classic period.

Despite all the work that has been done, and is being done at sites such as Lamanai, the Maya collapse has yet to be fully explained. We have only the abrupt silence of the inscriptions and a growing body of circumstantial evidence. Theories of plague, invasion, soil exhaustion, and peasant revolt have been advanced; but the collapse of a civilization is likely to be a complex affair. If our own world suddenly ended in something so clear-cut as a nuclear holocaust, what would be the underlying cause? Militarism? Invasion? Or social and political problems that gave rise to those things? And what shall we say gave rise to the social and political problems? The lists are endless and the arguments inevitably circular. Every society creates problems for itself as it develops and expands. The difference between success and failure is the tilt of the balance between the rate that problems are created and the rate at which natural and human resources can be mobilized to deal with them. All such processes rob the future to pay the present; the length of the game must depend on how far the players can enlarge the board and change the rules.

New clues on Maya food production suggest that ecological factors were important. Rain-forest civilizations are extremely rare (the Maya and the Khmer are the only two of any size). The apparent fertility of a jungle is largely an illusion—nutrients are stored in the vegetation itself; the soil is soon leached and eroded if exposed. Shifting slash-and-burn agriculture is possible, but requires very extensive land use and low population density.

Until about a dozen years ago archaeologists were baffled by the apparent lack of an economic base for Maya cities. The breakthrough came when satellite and airborne radar pictures revealed networks of ancient ditches and canals crisscrossing enormous swampy basins—the Classic Maya had converted these wetlands into something like the famous "floating gardens" of Aztec Mexico. The canals were designed to hold water from the wet season through the dry. The fields between them were raised above the water level and kept fertile with muck dredged from the canals, vegetable mulch, and by "self-manuring" with human and household waste. These methods allowed large increases in food production but may have made the Maya vulnerable to climatic disturbance, plant disease, parasites, and social unrest.

Skeletons apparently decreased in size through the Classic period, suggesting that nutrition declined as the population grew. There were telling differences between the upper and lower classes. Nobles and priests were robust, often fat, while the peasantry became stunted with passing generations. It seems that the Maya elite shared the currently fashionable view that the rich work only if allowed to get richer, while the poor need the incentive of hunger to keep them from idleness. If such an attitude led to revolution, then one can only reflect how little things have changed in Central America.

* * *

I ask Mr. Pantí about the rapid culture change that seems to be taking place among the Succotz Maya and about their attitude toward the ruins.

"Well, a certain percentage are really proud, they regard this as our heritage. But there are others, especially the youngsters, who feel alienated. Even though they have Maya blood!" He becomes quite exercised, taking out a handkerchief and wiping sweat from his forehead. "They identify as Caribbean people, or even Americans! It's a different way of thinking. Even people of my generation are not enlightened about our history. I've been trying for twenty years to get cultural activities going in the village. But it's very frustrating. The language itself—all the old stories and things—they're dying out. I've asked the government about getting a tape recorder, and they say yes but they don't do nothing. We need an anthropologist to come in and do a project in the village. Because the younger generation, they're losing it." He stops and stares for a moment across the plaza. We are in a square of space bounded by the tall mounds and the frowning pyramid. Dark clouds have gathered and heavy drops begin to chatter on the grass. His English grammar suffers slightly as he gets excited. His accent is mildly Caribbean, but there seems to be Maya influence in the way he stresses the last syllable of some words; it makes him sound rather like a Welshman.

"One time I heard a little girl in school in sixth standard say the teacher told her Succotz is a mestizo village. Ridiculous! How can from no*where* the village change? The people's names haven't changed, their color hasn't changed. It's ridiculous. And that teacher was an Indian himself, even in name! But it's useless arguing with them. I think it's because some people feel that to be of Indian descent is . . . well, they feel it's an inferior race."

"If they feel that way perhaps they should come up here and see their ancestors' achievements."

"Exactly, exactly. That's what I tell my kids. But we need some education over this, in the curriculum. Otherwise we're not going anywhere, not thinking realistically about our heritage. We're just living day to day like the birds. That's the problem."

Four British soldiers arrive: small men in big boots and camouflage fatigues. They have shaven heads, and generations of working-class malnourishment written in their pinched faces.

"We was told we could get in for nuffink if we was in uniform."

"I'm afraid not. Everybody got to pay," says Mr. Pantí.

"Ow much is it?"

"One dollar Belize."

"Screw it ven."

They shamble off, kicking at the turf in the plaza with their boots.

As you climb the main pyramid, the site falls below you until the geometric outlines of the temple and palace platforms stand out around the rim of the hill like ramparts. Beyond this the forest stretches away to the horizon, broken by bright green dabs of cornfield and pasture. Two miles to the south a cluster of white and red buildings and tufted palms indicates Benque Viejo; to the west lies Guatemala, dark under charcoal thunderheads.

There are six pairs of vaulted rooms in the temple on the summit, three facing north and three south. They owe their preservation to a later enlargement during which they were filled with masonry (removed, eventually, by archaeologists). On the east wall survives part of a stucco frieze that once encircled the whole building: jaguar masks, the face of the night sun, linked by bands of frets and glyphic motifs.

The rain returns, forcing me to shelter in one of the rooms. The end wall has fallen away, giving a view to the west unintended by the builders. The chamber is not remarkable—just a typical Maya room, about fifteen feet long and eight feet wide, capped by a steep corbel vault—but it's exhilarating to stand for the first time on this journey under an ancient roof.

* * *

At three the rain stops, and I climb down to see the rest of the site.

It is cooler now; mist has begun to form at the top of the pyramid, fogging the temple until only its doorways are darkly visible, like sockets in a skull. One could believe, as local legend says, that the ghosts of ancient worshipers are burning incense to their gods.

Part II

Center: The Petén

Chapter 3

9 Cimi

The day 9 Death, a fitting day to enter Guatemala. When the Maya tried to integrate Christianity with their own religion, they decided Death was the day of the crucifixion. "On what day did he die?" asks one of the books of Chilam Balam rhetorically, answering: "On 1 Cimi he died."[1] Death's hieroglyph is a human skull. The number nine has the face of a young man with jaguar attributes: spots and whiskers about the mouth. There are nine gods of the underworld, one for each of its levels; these are the Nine Lords of the Night.

Guatemala does not recognize the border with Belize. I was therefore surprised, when I crossed it in my Austin fifteen years ago, to find a large sign that arched across the road with the words BIENVENIDOS A GUATEMALA. It must have occurred to someone since then that the sign was not quite in step with the diplomatic position of the nation: it has been replaced by a painted map with the *"Departamento de Belice"* conspicuously included in the republic. Belize now has its own sign, staring back across the no-man's-land peopled with money changers: WELCOME TO BELIZE: A SOVEREIGN INDEPENDENT NEW NATION OF CENTRAL AMERICA.

61

The dispute is too old and too silly to be of much intrinsic interest. Very briefly it is this: after Spain withdrew in the early 1820s, six republics emerged from Iturbide's ephemeral Mexican Empire and the stillborn Central American federation. Guatemala and Mexico both claimed to have inherited Spain's sovereignty in what is now Belize. The status of the territory was open to question. Spain had never decisively conquered many of the Maya inhabitants; Britain had never raised the settlement to the status of a colony. Britain nevertheless sought to keep control over Belize, which became a successful trading and banking entrepôt serving its unstable neighbors. After years of desultory negotiations, Guatemala accepted the present borders of Belize in 1859. In 1862 the territory became the Colony of British Honduras. But the 1859 treaty contained a controversial article obliging the British to build a road from Guatemala City to the Caribbean coast "near the settlement of Belize." Britain never built the road; and Guatemala therefore considers her "surrender" of territory to be invalid. One would think that the problem could be solved by a simple payment of cash, but the two sides have never been able to agree on how much. Britain has seldom taken Guatemala very seriously, and too many Guatemalan regimes— especially military ones—have found this foreign quarrel too useful for busying giddy minds at home.

9:00 A.M. No one at customs is the slightest bit interested in my luggage. The immigration officer demands five quetzals for a tourist card which states explicitly in English, "The cost of this document is one quetzal." Everyone is charged five quetzals, whether he needs a visa, has a visa, or does not need a visa. The difference is a compulsory tip; if you refuse to pay it the answer is, "Go back to Belize."

Transport to Flores or Tikal? There will be a *camioneta* at ten, eleven, or eleven-thirty, depending on whom I want to believe. I walk across the long concrete bridge from the border post to the town of Melchor de Mencos, named after the latter-day conquistador who took King Can Ek of the Itzá in chains to Guatemala City. Like all frontier towns, it's a dismal place: a few hardware stores, brothels, and bars; a filling station, a flyblown market, an army base down the road. Tiny Guatemalan soldiers, little Indian boys in their teens, are lounging against walls and fidgeting under the weight of their Galil rifles. Someone is playing Christmas reggae from Radio Belize:

> We wish you a natty Christmas,
> Natty Christmas, natty Christmas,
> Natty dreadlock Christmas. . . .

11:00 A.M. Guatemalan Spanish is very different from Mexican: the *camioneta* is not a light truck or van, as I expected, but a bus. Until now bus travel has been painless but this is a return to the cramped, foul-smelling, and mechanically suspect contraptions of the Andes. There's a huge pile of luggage on the roof; a hundred people got off when it arrived; another hundred are getting on. I am swept aboard with the rest and have little time to choose a seat that (*a*) has padding, (*b*) is not on top of a wheel (no legroom), and (*c*) is not smeared by the droppings of animals and babies, vomit, or the remains of a meal.

We have to wait an hour while the driver has his lunch, meets his girlfriend, disappears with her for a leisurely dalliance, and then returns to fill the fuel tank, a leaking radiator, and a couple of slowly leaking tires. During this time the temperature inside the bus becomes unbearable, but no one dares get out for fear of losing his seat. I look on the bright side: if so many people are traveling they presumably estimate the risk of attack from army or insurgents to be low.

Before leaving home I read several books on the recent history of Guatemala. The statistics had a numbing and intimidating effect: 440 villages destroyed; a million displaced persons; 200,000 refugees in other countries; 100,000 political murders since the CIA ended ten years of democracy in 1954. Guatemala has acquired the mythic status of a nightmare country, a Lebanon or Uganda. Sitting in your back garden with a book and a beer, you ask yourself: How can anyone live there? How do countries like that go on? And the answer seems to be that chaos has become normality: violence feeds on itself; one corpse nourishes another. Human beings have an endless capacity for optimism, a boundless faith that the worst is over, that terrible things happen only to strangers, that the villages destroyed are always tiny and far away.

Guatemala is a country where things are easily hidden, especially the truth. It is cloaked with forest, concealed by clouds, mists, and the smoke of volcanoes; culturally and geographically as convoluted as a brain. The land is repeatedly flooded, buried, burned, and racked by earthquakes. Perhaps such an environment exerts a baleful influence on culture. Perhaps the cycle of violence set in motion by the conquistador Pedro de Alvarado, is periodically given a tweak by the shudders of the Maya earth-monster. One reads that Guatemala is a social pressure cooker with the lid weighted down by repression: the stability of such a vessel is not improved by shaking the stove. There's a symmetry to history and geology. The recent guerrilla conflict gained momentum after the 1976 earthquake exposed and exacerbated government corruption and the misery of the poor.[2]

1:00 P.M. About five miles out of Melchor, the bus slaloms through a large puddle and stops in front of a pole barrier across the road. An armed corporal sticks his head in the door: everyone has to get out to *"documentarse"*—present documents. "Men on the right, women on the left."

Fresh air. When I see fellow passengers waiting nervously to present their papers, I regret my misanthropic thoughts as I sweated in the bus. There's a young woman in a neat gray skirt and white sweater who appears to be a nurse. Three Indian women are traveling with two tiny babies; their beautiful clothes—the multicolored handwoven *traje*, or traditional dress, of some highland Maya group—are faded and in patches, the threadbare plumage of captive birds. They seem frightened, especially of the soldiers. Displaced persons most likely, and I shrink from imagining what might have forced them from a mist-shrouded mountain village to this raw frontier where the badge of their identity is not only a discomfort in the heat but an invitation for further persecution.

"¡Hombres al otro lado!" the corporal shouts; I have to join the other men already lining up with their backs pressed to the side of the bus. Thick peasant fingers produce scraps of yellowed paper bearing stamps, seals, and poorly developed photographs. The soldiers look closely at the photographs and then at the fingers' owners. Occasionally they squint at the writing, and once I see, as Lucy said I might, a document without a photograph being read upside down. Meanwhile other soldiers are going over the bus, looking under seats, prodding bags in the overhead racks, handing down bundles from the roof.

The corporal shouts something. One by one we are taken to the front of the line and made to face the bus, legs apart, hands spread high on the windows. A soldier puts his foot between my feet to trip me if I make a move; another points a rifle at my back. The intrusive intimacy of hands patting under the arms, down the inside leg, around the ankles for concealed knives: a subtle violation that Guatemalans must expect every time they go out. The soldier opens my small bag and takes things out one at a time. Forewarned, I'm carrying no camping or hiking equipment, and no khaki or dark green clothing, nothing that might be useful to guerrillas. I'm worried about my books and papers, but these attract no interest. The soldier lingers over a telephoto lens. Ah! Here's something suspicious—a sachet of white crystals, mysteriously sealed like a tea bag. Gringo drugs? Some newfangled explosive?

"Special crystals," I say quietly. "To keep the lens dry in damp weather." He glances at his corporal; the corporal nods. I'm in the clear.

With few exceptions the seating or standing arrangements on the bus remain as before. I begin to notice the old-fashioned good manners that I remember as characteristic of almost all Guatemalans. Where are the killers, the torturers, the experts in mutilation? They seem to belong to another country, one that existed in the recent past but is now miraculously purged, like Germany after the last world war. I am here at an exceptional time, the interval between the first and second stages of elections for the presidency in a much-touted but not altogether convincing "return to democracy." The country is swarming with foreign journalists. Hard-line generals and death squads are keeping out of sight.

The pole across the road is lifted, and we are waved through, between a wooden watchtower and a sandbagged machine-gun nest. Not far beyond the tower there's a billboard with a naïve painting of a Guatemalan soldier in camouflage fatigues. The soldier is shouting: "If I advance, follow me; if I delay, hurry me; if I retreat, kill me!" An inscription below him boasts: *¡AQUI SE FORJAN LOS MEJORES COMBATIENTES DE AMERICA!*—HERE ARE FORGED THE BEST FIGHTERS IN AMERICA! I have just begun to wonder whether this is intended for Belizean visitors or rebellious citizens when I see the back of the sign, which directs its message to those coming from the Guatemalan interior. It shows a gorilla head in the *King Kong* tradition, or maybe *Planet of the Apes*. Maniacal eyes burn ferociously; the gaping mouth is dripping with blood and armed with sharp fangs; and lest anyone fail to get the pun (not quite as homophonous as it is in English) the creature wears a Che Guevara cap. Above it is the single word *¡ATREVETE!*— roughly, MAKE MY DAY!

Nearby there's yet another sign: a huge death's-head with a knife between its teeth, and two words: *INFIERNO KAIBIL*—KAIBIL HELL. This is a camp of the *Kaibiles*, or "Tigers"—crack counterinsurgency troops modeled on the Green Berets. A witness of Kaibil training reported the following responsorial chant:

¿Qué come un Kaibil?	What does a Kaibil eat?
¡CARNE!	FLESH!
¿Qué clase de carne?	What kind of flesh?
¡HUMANA!	HUMAN!
¿Qué clase de carne humana?	What kind of human flesh?
¡COMUNISTA!	COMMUNIST!
¿Qué bebe un Kaibil?	What does a Kaibil drink?

¡SANGRE!	BLOOD!
¿Qué clase de sangre?	What kind of blood?
¡HUMANA!	HUMAN!
¿Qué clase de sangre humana?	What kind of human blood?
¡COMUNISTA!	COMMUNIST![3]

Just a gruesome training song, or something more? There are several reports, mainly from 1982 and before, when the war was at its bloodiest, that the Kaibiles actually practiced cannibalism. Deserters from Huehuetenango army base in the western highlands reported that they were made to drink the blood of torture victims as an initiation rite. A survivor of the July 1982 massacre at the village of San Francisco said he saw a soldier cut out the heart of a warm corpse and put it to his mouth. (He could not bring himself to watch what happened next.) At Todos Santos, a community of Mam Maya, a peasant claimed that an officer ate a human liver raw in front of the assembled soldiers and townsfolk.[4]

There are more checkpoints, but the sense of menace recedes and the procedure becomes merely a bore, a tedious identification parade. Twice the bus gets stuck while letting off passengers, and on the second occasion we passengers aren't able to push it out. The others resign themselves to wait for a tow, but I stick out my thumb at an approaching van. It stops, and a sharp, blue-eyed face peers out at the end of a leathery neck. A similar face in the passenger seat regards me from under a baseball cap that announces "Jesus Loves You!"

"Where're y'all from, brother?"

"Canada."

"Where?"

"Toronto, Canada."

"Well, we're from Flar'da."

"Are you working down here?"

"Praichin'!"

They are fundamentalists of some sort—Guatemala has proportionally more of them than any other country in Latin America. I've noticed several of their churches along the roadside, at each straggle of huts and clearings. There are Advent-

ists, Baptists, Jehovah's Witnesses, even Presbyterians, whatever that means here; their chapels have names like Bethel
Temple, New Jerusalem, and Prince of Peace. Some are ugly
concrete boxes with hints of Texas Gothic in the shape of a
door or window; most are thatched huts, slightly grander than
the dwellings.

There's been a holy alliance between these American-
based churches and the Guatemalan Right since 1954. Protestant missionaries have been encouraged; Catholic priests
active in community development and civil rights have been
purged. "We make no distinction between the Catholic Church
and the communist subversives," the military commander of
El Quiché once declared.[5] Since the late 1970s more than a
dozen priests have been murdered in Guatemala. The world's
press and the Vatican found this far less newsworthy than the
killing of one priest in Poland.

It should be said that a few Protestant churchmen have
denounced army atrocities in Guatemala and paid for their
courage with their lives, but taken as a group the *evangélicos*
foment anticommunist hysteria and thrive in the apocalyptic
climate of civil war. In March 1982, General Efraín Ríos Montt,
a Guatemalan member of Gospel Outreach of California,
seized power in a coup d'état. Under his bizarre regime fundamentalism became equated with loyalty, and many professed
the new certainties to avoid suspicion. Eventually Ríos
Montt's pious harangues and exhortations began to irritate the
other generals. "Guatemala doesn't need more prayers, it needs
more executions,"[6] said the defense minister, Mejía Victores,
who overthrew Ríos the following year.

In 1839–40, halfway in time between the conquest of the Itzá
and the present, two men from Belize made a little-known
journey through this part of the Petén to the ruins of Palenque
in Mexico. Patrick Walker was a British Honduras career civil
servant who later became an adviser to the Mosquito king.
John Caddy was a Canadian-born army officer with a gift for
drawing and watercolor.[7]

Walker had met the American explorer John Stephens and

his artist Frederick Catherwood when they stopped in Belize City at the start of the Central American explorations that would shortly make them famous. On learning that Stephens and Catherwood were planning to travel through Honduras and Guatemala before heading north to Palenque, Walker decided that a British expedition could and should beat them to that prize by striking due westward through the rain forest. At that time Palenque had become known to antiquarians through several misleading and destructive investigations since the city's rediscovery in the late eighteenth century.[8] Few other Central American ruins had been reported, and none had been ascribed to the ancestors of the native Maya. Palenque was therefore thought to be unique, an outpost of some Old World civilization mysteriously cast up in the New.

Walker and Caddy struggled through the Petén at the height of the rainy season, passing within a mile of Xunantunich and twenty miles of Tikal without ever suspecting these cities' existence. They were an odd pair: Caddy the flamboyant artist and compulsive shot, blazing away at anything that moved; Walker reticent, methodical, and driven. From Caddy's diary:

> Our two rowers were the laziest fellows I ever met with, and did not seem to be at all in a hurry—so we set to work to count the alligators on each side as we passed along. There was not a sandy bank on the margin of the water that had not its occupants, in some places two or three together. Horrid looking monsters some 15 feet in length; they have the most malicious eye of any animal I know, and it was with the utmost pleasure I put a bullet into many of them.[9]

When the two finally get to Palenque they have little to say. Walker gives the ruins five pages, concluding that they were perhaps "of Egypto-Indian origin."[10] Caddy's description runs to ten pages, intended to be published with the fine paintings he produced later from sketches.

The Englishmen were first to the ruins but Stephens was first to press; the huge success of his *Incidents of Travel in*

Central America, Chiapas, and Yucatan completely over-shadowed Walker and Caddy's work, which didn't find a publisher until 1967.

In my view, the importance of Walker and Caddy's accounts has less to do with Palenque than with their descriptions of the Petén. They, too, were traveling in the aftermath of a civil war. Between 1837 and 1840, sporadic peasant revolts had broadened into a general uprising led by Rafael Carrera. Nicaragua, Honduras, and Costa Rica seceded from the Central American federation in 1838; the Liberals, whose fatuous dreams of liberty and progress had brought little but exploitation to the peasants and chaos to the polity, were in retreat.

Carrera has been much maligned. Stephens described him as "with honest impulses, perhaps, but ignorant, fanatic, sanguinary, and the slave of violent passions, wielding absolutely the physical force of the country, and that force entertaining a natural hatred to the whites."[11] Aldous Huxley, in *Beyond the Mexique Bay*, called him an "Indian chieftain" with an "army of savage Indians under his command."[12] Carrera was in fact a Ladino of mixed blood and culture, born in a Guatemala City slum.[13] Like the half-breed anywhere he was caught in an identity crisis. The spiritual and ethnic integrity of the Indians could never be his; and the new society being built by the Liberals, those specious preachers of equality, had little more room for lowly Ladinos than for Indians. Through his marriage to an Indian woman and friendship with the local priest, Carrera came to understand the havoc that Liberal reforms had wrought on the Maya communities of the highlands. Ancient communal property title, long recognized by the Spanish Crown, had been abolished in the interests of "progress" and followed by a massive assault on Indian lands and autonomy. Indians who could not prove ownership of "empty lands"—hard to do in corrupt courts that were as likely to "lose" title deeds as recognize them—had their crops and houses burned by white landowners and ambitious Ladinos.[14] In these and other respects Guatemala in the 1830s foreshadowed the Guatemala of today. Carrera himself was provoked into rebellion after federal troops set fire to his village and raped his wife.

By 1838 revolt had become revolution, and Carrera entered

the capital at the head of a rustic army. At first the tool of various factions, he soon formed an alliance with old Conservative families against the Liberals. In 1844 he took the presidency and held it, with one brief hiatus, until his death in 1865. Carrera eventually became wealthy, corrupt, and oppressive, but throughout most of his regime Indians had more control over their lives and lands than they have ever since.

The Petén was a frontier region, then as now. Walker, as usual, echoed the conventional view: "Under the baneful influence of a weak and contemptible government every relic of civilisation and strength is so fast disappearing, that it would seem as if in this district of the Guatimalean [sic] Republic the Indians were doomed again to become independent."[15] This "doom" would no doubt have been sweet to the Maya. Their backing of Carrera was just one of numerous efforts to free themselves from white domination during the last century.

"This's as far as we go, brother," saith the preacher. It is late afternoon and we've reached the cluster of shacks at El Cruce, the junction with the paved road between Flores and Tikal. I tell him I'm glad to see a decent surface at last.

"This ain't nothin! We jes drove down from Gwoddemolla Ciddy last week. Brother, that road meks this'un we jes done look lahk pavement."

I thank them and walk a few yards past the checkpoint to wait for a ride. I'll go to Tikal or Flores, whichever transport comes first—it's about twenty miles either way.

FLORES

5:00 P.M. The armed forces take charge of the landscape as you approach the capital of Petén Department. A concrete wall, featureless except for barbed-wire trimmings and the occasional turreted machine-gun nest, runs beside the road for two or three miles. Flores airport, essential to Guatemala's tourist trade, occupies one corner of the immense compound. Behind

the wall you catch glimpses of bungalows, barracks, ware-
houses, and rows of armored vehicles, all fresh and neat like the
playing pieces of a war game set out on the floor of an empty
room. According to official statistics, a quarter of Guatemala's
budget is spent on the military; the real figure must be far
higher, especially when one counts American contributions
slipped to Guatemala by proxies such as Israel. Almost all
development is by and for the army; the army has its own
airline and its own bank; high-ranking officers have seized
huge swaths of territory as their private fiefs, sometimes using
terror to remove the Indian occupants. In Guatemala they say,
Hay descontento general, pero no hay generales descontentos:
There's general discontent, but there are no discontent generals.

Lake Petén Itzá is about twenty miles long and five wide, a
blue lozenge in the middle of the rain forest. The old town of
Flores occupies a small island about a mile from the shore; I
decide to walk across the causeway and look for somewhere to
stay. The sun has managed to break through below the clouds
before it sets, gilding the floating town—a tropical Mont-Saint-
Michel of shabby buildings with russet iron roofs swelling
from the water's edge to the small white church that crowns
the whole like a cake ornament.

I find a hotel by the water's edge. The lake has left a
tidemark halfway up the registration desk. Luckily for the
owner, a plump Ladino with the quick eyes of a Spaniard and
the stocky build of the Maya, it didn't stay there. He managed
to reclaim his lower story by filling and raising the floors a
couple of feet—you can tell by the low ceiling and the way the
bottoms of the doors have been sawn off.

"Look at those poor fools!" he says, pointing to some rival
establishments, lower than his, now abandoned. "People come
here and they don't listen to the older folk. We Peteneros"—he
slaps his barrel chest—"we know the lake has a cycle every
fifty years or so. *Lógico:* there is no outlet, although some say
there are underground streams."

The lobby has a coffee table and some wicker chairs beside
a large window. The sill, at floor level, is only six inches higher

than the water; the ceiling ripples with waterlights. I sit and drink a beer. A man fishing from a canoe is a black shadow puppet against the tiger-striped sunset on the lake.

My first strong memory of Guatemala is of Flores's plaza at dusk fifteen years ago. I drove across the causeway to the island and circled the town by its one, narrow road. Nobody was about. I wondered where the cafés and restaurants were. I found a rutted street ascending to the top of the island, and drove up to the church. The square looked superficially like a Mexican *zócalo*. There were the usual concrete benches and an ugly fountain. But where were the people, the chairs and tables on the sidewalk, the music and beery voices spilling from a cantina door?

I left the car and walked across the square. At first I heard only the grackles roosting in a mango tree, but gradually there came another sound, dry, stealthy, like the rustle of large insects. There was only one streetlamp and the neon had not quite caught. The incandescence faltered against the darkening sky; it was hard to make out what was moving in a corner of the square. A pool of shadow halfway up a wall seemed to have a seething, undulating motion, barely visible, like the waving of tendrils in a tide. I went closer but my eyes were dazzled by a naked bulb in a doorway. Two uniformed men were sitting on a bench just inside, and I guessed that this must be the police station. One of them rose and swung himself against the corner to urinate, and as he did so the bulb was hidden and I saw the dark shape farther down the wall. It was a window, with a forest of hands thrusting through iron bars. The occupants dared not speak, but I could hear the susurration of their clothes and a faint, unvoiced moan from deep inside their bodies, an exhalation of terror and despair.

The standing policeman saw me. He did not speak but gestured with his free hand for me to be gone. He was clearly drunk and a pistol was slung at his belt. I could have done nothing for those men, even if I had had the courage to try, which I did not. But their silent appeal prompted me to read and question. They made me aware of Colonel Arana Osorio, otherwise known as the "Butcher of Zacapa."

Colonel Arana had recently crushed a guerrilla movement led by progressive young officers who defected from the Guatemalan army after the CIA coup. His campaign against a few hundred insurgents in Izabal and Petén had cost the lives of eight thousand peasants. "If it is necessary to turn the country into a cemetery in order to pacify it, I will not hesitate to do so," Arana had said;[16] and with the help of American advisers fresh from Vietnam, he created the prototype of modern Guatemalan state terror.[17] Villages were bombed with napalm; death squads prowled the cities at night; people disappeared.[18]

The army was mopping up the stragglers at the time I was last here. In March 1970 there had been general elections, which in Guatemala usually means elections for generals. Arana the Butcher had been "chosen" president.

10 Manik ‖ *Manik: Deer; lord of the hunt; his hieroglyph is a hand. Ten is an old, grim number with a fleshless jawbone; inauspicious for the Maya.*

There's hardly an eating place or hotel in Flores that doesn't have its share of badly stuffed endangered species: moth-eaten jaguar pelts; pathetically small deer heads with painted mouths and plastic eyeballs; snakes that look as if they've been inflated by bicycle pump. Far from a jungle ambience, they give you the impression of a ghoulish junk shop. Outside walls are painted with tawdry Maya gods and meaningless glyphs. The only genuine Indian things I've seen are heavy dugout canoes pulled up in narrow slipways between the houses around the shore.

After breakfasting beneath the grim stare of a flattened ocelot, I walk up to the square. The church is freshly painted, the streets cobbled, and if there are political prisoners in the police station they're well out of sight.

There are two helpful men inside the Archaeology and History Institute but otherwise the place is empty—no exhibits, no maps, no guidebooks for sale. When I ask about ancient Tayasal, one of the men unlocks a drawer and pulls out a blueprinted map. He points out the site of recent excavations on the mainland peninsula opposite the island. There, they both insist, is the site of the last Maya town.

I find this hard to accept; it conflicts with all the written sources. Caddy, relying on a Guatemalan history published in 1808, wrote:

> The Spaniards entered the great town of the island called Tayasal, which they found deserted.... This success was gained on the 13th March 1697; on the following day ... the Pagan place of worship was dedicated as a Christian Church.... So great was the number of Idols found in 21 places of worship ... that the general, officers, and soldiers were unremittingly employed from 9 o'clock in the morning until 5 in the afternoon in destroying them.[19]

In the last twenty years there have been several archaeological projects in the Flores area, but the Itzá state—that living fossil of the old Mesoamerica—has eluded the spade. The peninsula opposite the island does indeed have ruins of a town, confusingly named Tayasal by its excavators, but most of the finds there date from late Classic to middle Postclassic times (say A.D. 700–1300). Unfortunately, the potsherds collected from the island of Flores itself are mostly of the same age.

The history of the Itzá is complicated by its deep integration with the cyclical prophecy-history preserved in the books of Chilám Balam of Yucatán. These books were written in the Maya language, using the Roman alphabet, during the colonial period; they are named after a "Jaguar Prophet" (or prophets) believed to have foreseen the Spanish conquest. Much of their content came from hieroglyphic codices banned and burned by the Spaniards. They are filled with dates in the Maya "Short Count" and associated events, both real and foretold. A recent translation of one of them has the apt title *The Ancient Future of the Itzá*.[20]

Unlike the Long Count of the Classic period, the Short Count is not anchored to a base point: it repeats itself over and over, just as our calendar would if we wrote '66 without specifying whether we meant 1066 or 1966. It is as if the great clock of the Maya Long Count had lost its hour hand. In the Short Count (not to be confused with the tzolkin and solar year counts still kept today) the 400-year baktun was forgotten, but the 20-year katuns continued to cycle on their own. Having lost their gearing to the larger baktun wheel, they were counted and named according to the tzolkin day on which they ended (were completed, in Maya thinking). Because of the mathematical relationship between the 7,200 days of a katun and the 260 days of a tzolkin cycle, a katun always ends on a day Ahau, but the associated number declines each time by two. Thus Katun 8 Ahau is followed by Katun 6 Ahau, and so on; when the progression of even numbers is exhausted, Katun 2 Ahau is followed by 13 Ahau, 11 Ahau, etc. The cycle of thirteen katuns takes slightly more than 256 of our years to run its course.

Because the tzolkin, like the Old World zodiac, influenced destiny, the Maya thought that katuns bearing the same name—and therefore containing an identical almanac sequence—were fated to hold similar events. Past and future became structured in a symmetrical relationship; history became prophecy; and prophecies became self-fulfilling because actions were apparently undertaken to coincide with the appropriate date. Having lost the statelier rhythms of the Long Count, the Maya were trapped in whirlpools of calendric destiny. For them, as for T. S. Eliot,

> Time present and time past
> Are both perhaps present in time future,
> And time future contained in time past.[21]

In the books of Chilam Balam it is written that the Itzá always experienced upheavals in a Katun 8 Ahau: "This was

always the katun when the Itzá went beneath the trees,
beneath the bushes, beneath the vines, to their misfortune."[22]
In a Katun 8 Ahau they had supposedly "discovered" Chichén
Itzá in Yucatán and settled there. In the following Katun 8
Ahau they left Chichén and moved to the Gulf coast of Cam-
peche. They lived there a full thirteen katuns. In the next
Katun 8 Ahau they abandoned their home on the coast and
wandered for forty years, perhaps passing through Lake Petén
Itzá before moving up the coast of Quintana Roo to the island
of Cozumel. From there they resettled Chichén Itzá, but
became engaged in a power struggle with the rival city of
Mayapán, near modern Mérida. In the next Katun 8 Ahau the
Itzá of Chichén were driven out by an alliance of Mayapán and
Izamal. They began their wandering again, finally settling at
Lake Petén Itzá. Some Itzá remaining in Mayapán were in turn
expelled when a shaky coalition between them and their rivals
dissolved into anarchy in—when else?—the following Katun 8
Ahau.

What can we make of all this? Is it really likely that the
Itzá settled twice at Chichén Itzá and twice visited the same
lake in the Petén? Was this not perhaps concocted by a Maya
chronicler-prophet seeking mythic symmetry in history; or
has it been misread by modern ethnohistorians seeking history in myth? It is still not clear whether the second Itzá
expulsion from Chichén (probably the only one based on fact)
took place in the Katun 8 Ahau that ended in A.D. 1204 or the
one that ran from 1441 to 1461. On later events the books are
more specific; there seems to be a clear reference to some Itzá
retiring to the forests at the time of the Spanish invasion of
Yucatán in the first half of the sixteenth century. This passage
also gives an idea of the Maya fascination with numbers, and
their majestically repetitious style of oration:

> Then the great Itzá went away. Thirteen four-hun-
> dreds were the four-hundreds of their thousands, and
> fifteen four-hundreds, the four-hundreds of their hun-
> dreds. . . .
> They did not wish to join with the foreigners;
> they did not desire Christianity. They did not wish to

pay tribute, did those whose emblems were the bird, the precious stone, the flat precious stone and the jaguar, those with the three magic emblems. Four four-hundreds of years and fifteen score years was the end of their lives . . . they knew the measure of their days. Complete was the month; complete, the year; complete, the day; complete, the night; complete, the breath of life as it passed also; complete, the blood, when they arrived at their beds, their mats, their thrones.[23]

To judge from what is said about them in the books of Chilam Balam, the Itzá were not popular with the Yucatec Maya. They were called *dzul*, "foreigners"—a word later applied to Spaniards and gringos, "the lewd ones" (a reference to their alleged penchant for sodomy), and "those without fathers or mothers"—in other words, upstarts. Their original home was probably not Chichén Itzá but the Gulf, for they were heavily Mexicanized. They spoke the Yucatec language brokenly and practiced human sacrifice on the grand scale of Postclassic Mexico. These Itzá seemed unlikely candidates to become leaders of Maya resistance and the culture heroes remembered in legends today. But like all who conquered Yucatán, they absorbed the ways of their subjects, and by the time they settled finally in Petén their language and material culture were essentially Yucatec.

In 1525 the Itzá of Petén briefly reappear in history as the hosts of Hernán Cortés, who had conquered the Aztecs just three years before. Cortés was making one of those long marches with which the Spanish conquistadors confounded the Indians and still amaze historians. He was on his way to discipline a rival Spaniard in Honduras and at the same time reconnoiter the eastern rim of Mesoamerica. With him at the start was Cuauhtémoc, successor of Moctezuma and last ruler of the Aztecs. From time to time Cortés and his men tortured Cuauhtémoc by pouring oil on his feet and setting them alight. They hoped he would reveal the whereabouts of treasure they had been forced to abandon when the Aztecs drove them from Mexico City on the *Noche Triste*. Shortly before entering Itzá territory Cortés discovered Cuauhtémoc urging the king of the Chontal Maya to kill the Spaniards:

> Having heard this, [Cortés] took Cuauhtémoc and threw him in prison, and the third day that he was a prisoner they took him out and baptized him . . . and having finished baptizing him, they cut off his head and it was nailed to a ceiba tree in front of the house of the gods in the village of Yaxzam. . . .[24]

King Can Ek of the Itzá no doubt heard of this, and decided to follow the Chontals' policy of friendship to the Spaniards. The king was received by Cortés at the Spanish camp on the mainland opposite Tayasal Island. An elaborate mass was sung; Can Ek, like any Maya, was entranced by the ritual, which he "closely observed," and the music, which "he praised highly."[25] After mass, the priests and friars lectured him about conversion to Christianity, and Cortés added that he should submit to the Holy Roman Emperor as the Aztecs had done. Can Ek was most obliging: he said he would henceforth consider himself a vassal of Spain, and invited Cortés to his island city "to see his house and watch the burning of his idols."

According to Cortés's secretary the conquistador witnessed the idol burning and left a lame horse in Can Ek's care before continuing to Honduras. It would be fascinating to read the Itzá version of these extraordinary events, but no native account has survived. The fate of the horse, however, gives a clue as to how the religious instruction (no doubt through dubious interpreters) was taken. The Itzá had never seen such an animal before, and it perhaps appeared to them that they were being given the supernatural creature as a replacement for their idols (if these were indeed burnt: other sources question this). They offered it flowers and turkey stew in the hope of curing it, and when the horse eventually died, either from the wound or the rich diet, a statue was erected in its honor. Over the years the cult of the dead horse grew in importance; by the time the friars Fuensalida and Orbita visited Tayasal in 1618, it was being worshiped as a manifestation of Chac, the god of rain and storms.

Fuensalida and Orbita reached the island at ten o'clock one night, and were taken through torchlit streets to meet the ruler, who, as always, was named Can Ek (Serpent Star). Their description of the town fits well with the Flores location, and it seems to have been as crowded then as now:

> It has about two hundred houses, which are around the lake shore, not far from one another. . . . In the high center of the island are the *cues* [pyramids] and *adoratorios* [shrines] where they keep their idols. . . . There were twelve or more temples, of a size and capacity like the largest churches in the Indian towns of Yucatán.[26]

The king welcomed the friars and gave them permission to visit the houses and temples. The two began their work, haranguing the Indians on "the blindness they were in, worshiping the devil in the idols, and with the vanity of so many gods, when really there was only one, living and true, one in being and three in persons."[27] The Maya listened to all this politely but replied that the time had not yet arrived for them to become Christians. Then, in the middle of one of the temples, the friars found the statue of Cortés's horse. The sight of this "Christian" animal converted into one of the devil's falsehoods was too much for poor Padre Orbita:

> The spirit of the Lord descended into him, and carried away by a fervent zeal for the honor of God, clutching a stone in his hand, he climbed onto the statue of the horse and broke it into pieces. . . .[28]

The outraged Maya began to shout and threaten death. But Orbita was by now so enthused that he preached to the angry crowd with a beatific smile on his face, doubtless expecting martyrdom at any minute. The Indians were so taken aback by his behavior that the friars were able to escape and return to their lodgings, where they calmly had a rest before telling Can Ek what they had done.

The king now gave the friars a sermon of his own, pointing

out that although it was true that one day the Itzá would
become Christians as prophesied by the ancient priests, the
time had not yet come. From what happened later, it is clear
that the Itzá were waiting for the fateful Katun 8 Ahau, which
would begin in 1697.

Despite this, the friars came back to Tayasal the following
year. This time a faction lead by Maya priests and Can Ek's wife
threw them off the island. In 1623 another Spanish priest was
foolhardy enough to visit Tayasal with a small troop of Spanish
soldiers and eighty Indians from Tipú. By this time the
patience of the Itzá was exhausted. The group was received
with a show of friendship; then overwhelmed. The Spaniards
were sacrificed to the ancient gods in the time-honored way:
"They opened Padre Diego's chest and took out his heart, offering it to the idols in atonement and revenge for the outrage
which they said had been done them by the other religious."[29]
Soon afterward the Itzá defeated a Spanish military expedition
sent against them. One "idol" at Tayasal was given an impressive set of teeth taken from slain Spaniards.[30] For the next
seventy years the Itzá were left alone by the outside world, and
they even extended the independent Maya realm by encourag-
ing the Belize uprising that began in 1636.

One wonders how long the Itzá could have remained independent had not the approach of Katun 8 Ahau begun to weigh
on their minds. In 1695 the final confrontation of Itzá and
Spaniard was initiated by both sides. The governor of Yucatán
began building a road southward through what is now Campeche toward Lake Petén Itzá, and the Itzá (or one faction, at
least) sent an embassy to Mérida. This was led by Can Ek's
nephew, who is said to have made the following speech to the
Spanish governor:

> Sir: As the representative of my uncle, the great Can
> Ek, king and lord of the Itzá, in his name and on his
> behalf I came to prostrate myself at your feet, and to
> offer to them his royal crown, so that in the name of
> your great king, of whom you are the representative,
> you will receive and admit us in his royal service,
> with his aid and protection, and you will send us

father priests who will baptize us, who will govern us
and teach the law of the true God. That is why I have
come. . . .[31]

At about the same time, a Spanish expedition led by a
scholarly Franciscan, Andrés de Avendaño, was heading south
through the forest between the head of the new road and the
lake of the Itzá. Avendaño was one of those intellectual giants
that the church occasionally produced. He spoke Maya flu-
ently, had studied the katun prophecies, and—most extraordinary of all—had learned to read Maya hieroglyphics.[32] He can
have acquired this knowledge only in northern Yucatán during
the last decades of the seventeenth century, so there must still
have been Maya intellectuals literate in the ancient script.
Avendaño wrote a treatise on his studies, but the only known
copy has disappeared. Maya scholars are haunted by the
thought that little more than a century divides the death of the
old knowledge and the awakening of modern research.

The events of 1695–97 are involved, and their interpretation complicated by the fact that different calculations place
the start of Katun 8 Ahau in any of those three years. Avendaño
himself thought that August 1696 was the time. He reached
the lake in January, and it seems that he managed to persuade
some of the Itzá to accept his reading. They promised to capitulate if he would come back in a few months' time; but there
were others who did not agree. Avendaño soon had to flee and a
Spanish military force was repulsed.

Early in 1697 the Spaniards returned, and this time they
copied, on a small scale, the tactics used by Cortés for attack-
ing the island capital of the Aztecs. A war galley was built in a
fortified camp on the lakeshore, then sailed out against Tayasal. Canoes full of Itzá archers kept the strange craft under a
barrage, but the Europeans were well armored against obsidian. The Spaniards swarmed onto the island with heavy musket fire; before long the Indian survivors were in the water,
swimming for their lives. Not one Spaniard was killed.

On that day the Petén Itzá were broken forever. Can Ek
himself was later taken in chains to Guatemala City; what
became of him there is unknown. A Spanish hierarchy

replaced his lineage at Tayasal; his subjects became peons on the cattle haciendas that took over the grasslands. The prophecy of Chilam Balam had been fulfilled:

> Receive your bearded guests from the east,
> Bearers of the standard of God.
> Receive the word of God which
> Comes to us on the day of resurrection
> Which is feared by all in the world. . . .
> That is the one you shall worship, Itzás. . . .[33]

The Itzá had had plenty of time to get firearms and learn how to use them (as the Incas tried), but they clung to weapons hallowed by tradition. This conservatism continued even after their defeat. When Walker and Caddy entered Petén from Belize in 1840 they were met by a Guatemalan border patrol "which consisted of a Sergeant armed with a tolerable fowling piece and twenty Indians with their bows and arrows."[34] The arrowheads were made of obsidian. Three hundred years of contact with an iron-using people had made no impression at all.

This is a measure of how different Maya civilization was from ours. To us technological progress *is* civilization, a belief most of us still cherish. We keep our faith in technology even though it now promises us nuclear suicide and environmental devastation. The well-known image of the doomsday clock standing at one minute to midnight does not seem very different from the approach of Katun 8 Ahau.

Chapter 4

11 Lamat

Lamat, sometimes represented by the Rabbit, is the sign of the planet Venus.

I had breakfast with the ocelot again. The other occupant was a Californian biker who had driven all night over the Petén roads from Zacapa. He was fortyish, bearded, with the heavy-lidded eyes of a veteran marijuana smoker and an ignorance of his surroundings that was so profound it amounted to a kind of purity. Nothing ever happens to people like him, I thought; how else could he have traveled by night over some of the remotest and most dangerous roads in Central America? Not even the buses run at night anymore.

"Any trouble with the guerrillas?"

"Gorillas? Hey, you're putting me on, man. Didn't see a living thing in the jungle. I had lots of hassle from the *cops* along that paved highway outta Guatemala City, though. They keep telling me my papers say I can't go no farther than Guatemala City. How am I to know? I can't understand a word of their Spanish, and the papers don't make any sense to me either. It's just forty bucks here, twenty-five there, into someone's pocket. I guess that's just the way things are in this part of the world." He scratched under his armpit and rolled his eyes in what-can-you-expect resignation.

"They don't really mind you traveling here, but they don't like you to *have* anything. Man, every night they let down my front tire, and my back tire somehow they put air in! The bike's

84

too big. No one else has one like it. That Honda's a *big* cycle for down here."

"Why didn't you bring something smaller?"

"I tried that once, when I was in Egypt. Bought this little Czechoslovakian bike. Never could get that thing to run right. In Cairo it was just like here. They were always *doin'* somethin'—you know, ripping off the lights, scratching the paint. Man, I'm having a *bad* trip."

I walked along the causeway. Patches of mist hovered above the water and broke in motionless surf against the low green hills around the lake. Ducks were squabbling over their catches but apart from that it was quiet and still. The smell of cooking fires—woodsmoke, rich and exotic like a strange tobacco, and the limy aroma of tortillas—greeted me as I approached the mainland. Twenty minutes later I was on a bus for Tikal.

From Flores to Tikal is about twenty-five miles as the *zopilote* flies and forty by paved road. The airstrip at the ruins themselves is closed now, ostensibly for conservation reasons; aircraft vibration was said to be threatening the temples. That may well be true, but the real reason for the airstrip's closure is that guerrilla bands have been operating in Tikal National Park. Once or twice they've taken over the ruins and lectured bemused tourists on the people's struggle. These occupations are brief; no one has been hurt. The effect is purely symbolic.

The bus stops for passengers at El Cruce, where the evangélicos dropped me two days ago, and heads north across a strip of dry land between the east end of Lake Petén Itzá and a saline lagoon. The small villages of thatched huts surrounded by poinsettias and purple morning glories become fewer; there's one army checkpoint.

The 225-square-mile park, with the ruins of Tikal in its middle, is also one of the few ecological refuges of the dwindling Central American jungle. Jaguar, tapir, deer, monkeys, reptiles, and hundreds of bird species survive precariously here while a similar area of rain forest is destroyed in this country every year.[1] Guatemala probably has the most unequal system of landownership in Latin America; in the highlands, four

million Maya live on tiny plots of poor soil. As a substitute for
land reform (anathema since the coup of 1954) peasants have
been encouraged to carve small homesteads from the jungle.
But this has not been a solution. The unsuccessful colonists
contract debts they can't pay, and end up selling or forfeiting
their land after a few seasons; successful ones are often forcibly
dispossessed after they've done the hard work of clearing the
trees.

What happens next is known as the hamburger connection. Cattle graze the new clearings until the soil becomes
exhausted and eroded—a process that usually takes three to
five years.[2] The stringy beef is sold cheaply to North America
for making beef patties. It's the very worst kind of "development"—profit for a few cattle barons at the expense of the
environment and the poor. A U.S. State Department report
called it "a quick and dirty business."[3] Although Central
American beef production has soared since 1961, the people of
Central America eat far less beef now than they did then; less
per capita than a North American cat.[4]

In the Classic Maya heyday, say A.D. 700, there can't have
been very much pristine jungle in these parts: the cities were
simply too big and too close together. Although some forest
presumably remained as hunting preserves and buffer zones
between rival states, much of the Petén must have been a
domesticated landscape of open cornfields, plantations of food
trees, terraced slopes, artificial reservoirs, and swamps neatly
crosshatched with canals and raised fields. Whether deforesta-
tion on this scale was enough to affect rainfall patterns and
provoke the Maya collapse is something that should be starting
to worry the region's modern inhabitants.

The central zone of Tikal covers about six square miles
and contains some three thousand buildings. Five colossal pyramids and three great "acropolises" occupy about a square mile
at the core. When outlying temple groups and residential suburbs are added, Tikal extends to twenty-three square miles. On
the edge of the city are two large swamps that in Classic times
were probably shallow lakes. These were connected by moats
and earthworks to create a defensible boundary enclosing a
total of fifty square miles. Up to 100,000 people lived within

these limits—as many, or possibly more, than in any city of
Renaissance Europe.

TIKAL

A museum, souvenir stands, and bungalows of the Jungle
Lodge and Jaguar Inn. Both hotels are empty—the combination
of rains, guerrillas, and army patrols has made for a lean tourist
season. In former times a room would have cost a lot; now I
have a chalet to myself for eight dollars. I don't mind the
broken water heater, the blocked shower drain, the damp mattress, the wasps in the ceiling, the decay.

To the outside world and to many Guatemalans, Tikal *is*
Guatemala, a national symbol as powerful as the Tower of
London. The modern highland Indians are regarded in much
the same way, but provoke a condescension and uneasiness that
do not attend architectural relics from the past. Tikal reminds
Guatemalans that this land was once great, and it misleads
them into thinking there is limitless potential in the Petén
forests. Ugly facts can be forgotten when looking at ruins. The
mestizo can for a moment feel pride instead of shame at the
Indian blood in his veins; the Spaniard in him can forget what
his ancestors did to Postclassic Maya civilization. The vision-
ary may entertain the familiar Latin American delusion that a
true *mestizaje* will arise from the Indian and Hispanic pasts, a
hybrid culture more vigorous than either parent. Dreams like
these thrive in the thin jungle soil. But the Indians who once
lived here are long dead: there are no faces rigid with fear, no
hunger-stunted bodies wrapped in splendid weavings to
remind the Guatemalan of the true relationship between
invader and native in his country; no hint that the death-fight
begun by Alvarado still consumes Guatemala with a terrible
malignancy.

The ruins were discovered in 1848, and in that very act the
Indian was deprived of his rightful place. Most books credit
Colonel Modesto Méndez, the Ladino *corregidor* of Petén, with
the honor; but the man who brought Tikal to Méndez's attention was a Maya named Ambrosio Tut. He visited and exam-

ined the ruins a week before the colonel set foot in the place. Méndez was immortalized by having part of the site named after him, but Tut has been buried in the shallow grave of historical footnote.[5]

I spent the afternoon with a beer or two and Sir Eric Thompson's classic, *The Rise and Fall of Maya Civilization*. The rain eased at four—time for a brief foray into the ruins.

I begin walking down a gravel path that I think will take me to Temple IV; it runs through the village where Tikal's workers live. Woodsmoke is drifting through the trees; the sound of women patting tortillas comes from thatched huts; a man sits in a doorway, playing a guitar, accompanied by the splatter of drips in puddles of red clay.

Beyond, the jungle is alive with birds singing out their territories. I count more than a dozen toucans—black and orange garden shears sailing from tree to tree.

After twenty minutes or so I begin to doubt the route; a workman with a wheelbarrow puts me right and sends me down a narrow jungle path. I'm rewarded by the sight of spider monkeys brachiating through the canopy with the aplomb of gibbons. The variety of trees is extraordinary; I recognize only a few species among hundreds: the vicious barbed trunks of "give-n-take" palms (as they're called in Belize); the dark fluted bark and laureate leaves of mahogany; the gnarled *bejuco de agua* vine, famous for giving a drink of pure water if you cut it. The air steams with wild allspice and onion grass, crushed underfoot.

At last I emerge in a clearing below the immense bulk of Temple IV, 230 feet high, the tallest ancient building in the Americas. A dozen ocellated turkeys are strolling about like peacocks at Versailles. Here in the park these birds are almost as tame as their domestic cousin, the *guajolote*. The stairs and sides of the pyramid are forested cliffs. You climb at the north-east corner, scrambling up blocks of stone and roots polished by tourist hands and bottoms.

From the top the forest stretches to the horizon on all sides, diaphanous waves of mist washing across it like an ocean swell. The dark canopy, showing through in lacy troughs, hints at bottomless green depths, and from these rise the steep islands of the five great pyramids. An aerial spray breaks in slow motion against their walls and spires, which seem to recede and approach and recede as they are hidden and revealed.

A vertical iron ladder allows me to climb another thirty feet to the roof. The rungs are wet and slippery, but when a cloud washes over the building all sense of height is lost; there's only an immediate sphere of perception—stone wall, iron ladder, and the outline of a treetop like a Chinese watercolor. This bubble of solipsism falls away with the next ebb in the swell, but the feeling of centrality remains. Here on their tallest building, in their greatest metropolis, I'm at the center of the Maya world.

Until the 1940s many Mayanists thought that there had been an Old Empire, ruled from Tikal, and a New Empire founded in the Yucatán Peninsula after the collapse of the first. As Maya studies progressed it became clear that a city-state model was more appropriate. In 1958, Heinrich Berlin discovered that the major Maya cities had "emblem glyphs" that seem to have been city names. More recently, Joyce Marcus suggested that the political structure of the Classic Maya might be revealed by plotting the frequency with which different centers mention each other's names in their inscriptions. Marcus found that other cities mention Tikal far more than it mentions them. She proposed that the political structure of the Classic Maya lowlands was a hierarchy, with Tikal at the top, four regional capitals below Tikal (one for each cardinal direction), other smaller centers orbiting around the regional capitals, and so on. The structure fits very neatly with the four-part division of space, presided over by a center or zenith, found in most American Indian cultures. The problem, of course, is knowing how much to infer from this evidence. How far can one equate prestige with political control? And to what extent did ideal cosmological patterns influence actual relationships? It seems to me that modern politics can provide a good analogy.

Marcus's method, applied to today's newspapers instead of Maya stelae, would, I suspect, yield very similar results. I'm willing to bet that Canada mentions the U.S. more than the U.S. does Canada; and that Belgium more often speaks of France than vice versa.

Once or twice the sun almost breaks through, drenching the buildings in a warm, buttery glow. The mist drains down through the trees and the true layout of the buildings becomes clear. Temple IV, where I sit, is at the west end of the main axis, with Temple I at the east, and III and II between. They are not quite in line, so all are visible. Temple V, second in height, is off to the south, partly hidden by what appears to be a large hill cloaked in jungle—the unexcavated South Acropolis, five acres in area and almost a hundred feet high.

The pyramid-temples were also observatories. Here, at dawn and dusk and through long starry nights, Maya astronomers plotted the rising and setting points of heavenly bodies against horizon landmarks and other buildings. Their approach was the opposite of ours. We have instruments that enable us to make good observations very quickly. They repeated and refined naked-eye observations over long periods of time. For this they had all the equipment they needed: the superb timekeeping device of the calendar, and a writing system to record their findings. Civilizations, like individuals, have a way of making do with what they have.

All the visible planets were followed by Maya astronomers but none more closely than Venus, whose day it is today. The Maya calculated the planet's average synodical revolution at 584 days, a figure that pleased them because five Venus "years" amounted to eight years of the 365-day calendar, and sixty-five Venus years equaled 146 cycles of the tzolkin.

Five hundred eighty-four days differs from the actual figure of 583.92 by less than two hours per Venus year; but the Maya did much better than that. In the Dresden Codex—one of three preconquest Maya books to survive—they used an elaborate correction table to refine the error to twenty-three *seconds* per Venus year.[6] Such computations show that Maya intellectuals had few inhibitions about testing knowledge handed down from the past, and that they knew their 365-day solar year (which had no leap-year correction) was merely an approximation to the nearest whole day.

If Greek civilization explored the universe with geometry, the Maya did so with arithmetic and time. Their calculations gave them a conception of its temporal scale unmatched by any other premodern people. They didn't contemplate eternity with mere metaphors ("a thousand years in thy sight are but as yesterday"), they actually ran the calendrical mechanism back and forth over immense spans of the past and future, apparently to stress symmetries between human and godly time. Stela 10 at Tikal records a date more than five million years in the past; two inscriptions at Quiriguá refer to precisely pinpointed days—one ninety million, the other four hundred million years ago.

For this work the Maya used cycles of staggering size. Until recently it was thought that the *alautun*, equivalent to 160,000 baktuns, or about 63 million years, was the largest. Some dates have now been found at Cobá, in northern Quintana Roo, showing fifteen cycles above the alautun, each increasing by a factor of twenty.[7] One only has to go two cycles above the alautun to reach a time period greater than the age of the universe according to modern astrophysics. Such exercises, however bizarre, speak of intellectual daring. And they were conceived, as Thompson dryly remarked, "nearly a thousand years before Archbishop Usher had placed the creation of the world at 4004 B.C."[8]

1·2 Muluc

Muluc: Water; symbolized by jade; an aspect of the rain deities.

When I woke at six a thin mist had invaded the hotel grounds and rain was dripping loudly from the trees. I felt damp before I left my room. At the Jaguar Inn I had a stolid pancake washed down with lukewarm Nescafé, a meal redeemed by the girl who served it. A spectacular beauty, and she knows it.

7:30. The tall buildings are invisible until one is almost upon them; the trail opens in a plaza and suddenly what seemed a remote and impenetrable stretch of virgin jungle is revealed as a skin of vegetation over an ancient city occupied so long and so densely that the original ground surface is buried under yards of masonry. As the ceremonial buildings expanded, earlier structures were covered by enormous terraced platforms to provide the bases for newer and grander conceptions. The scale is vast; it takes as long to visit the main building groups as it does to go sightseeing in many modern cities.

The most heavily excavated sector of Tikal is the Great Plaza. Temple I, familiar from every Guatemalan travel poster, rears 160 feet into the sky: nine tapering tiers of limestone ascended by a single flight of stairs. As you climb, other eminences of the city rise into view. Almost a quarter mile to the south, Temple V shoves its 190-foot crown above the forest. It has scarcely been touched by archaeologists, and the roof comb sports a tangle of trees, ferns, and epiphytes above the austere stone face of the temple, like an Easter bonnet. The view to the west—the reverse of what I saw yesterday evening—is the finest prospect in the ruins. Directly opposite, about 150 yards away, stands Temple II, somewhat shorter than I, with its pyramid divided into three massive tiers. Beyond are two more: Temple IV, about half a mile away, and Temple III in between. The roof comb of III, slender and soaring, resembles the summit of an art deco skyscraper with its abrupt offsets and indented corners. Temple IV, broad and massive, dominates the horizon by sheer bulk as much as by height. One sees, above the rippled surface of the forest, a broad smooth wall of dressed stone pierced in the middle by a dark doorway, and the cusp of the roof comb, almost a pyramid in itself, resembling a macrocephalic limestone head.

These buildings, like much of the architecture of the New World and Asia, have a sculptural quality quite distinct from the functional tradition of Europe. They're the product of a warm climate and hierarchical society—intended to be seen from the outside and from great distances. Interior space is insignificant; a dozen people would be cramped in the narrow rooms that stand on top of these colossal masses. It's doubtful that even one ancient Maya in a hundred ever climbed the stairways, and if we accept the evidence for human sacrifice, fewer climbed down. The temple doors at the tops of the stairs have the appearance of pursed mouths, and one wonders if the Maya thought of them that way—as the mouths of hungry gods.

The roof combs, now ragged, were once adorned with faces and human figures, colored cream, red, green, and blue—as surprising and unwelcome to modern taste as the discovery that the Parthenon marbles were originally painted and bedizened with costume trappings. In good light it is just possible to make out the cross-legged giant who sits above Temple I, gazing serenely westward over the city, like a Buddha.

Temple I has nine tiers. These probably corresponded to the nine levels of the underworld, the realm of the *Bolontiku*, the gods often called the Nine Lords of the Night. Heaven, or the upper world, was governed by another favorite number of the Maya: thirteen. It seems likely that temple roof combs represented thirteen levels and a corresponding set of gods.

The Nine Lords and the Thirteen Lords were also regarded as multiple aspects of single gods—one for the lower world or night, and one for the upper or day; and these two—indeed all Maya gods—were but manifestations of the supreme creator, known as Itzamná or Hunab Ku, in whom all opposites were reconciled. Nine was the number of woman, and thirteen the number of man. The Nine Lords of darkness ruled over the moons of pregnancy, and it's possible that the 260-day tzolkin itself arose from the period of human gestation.[9] The Nine were also patrons of the calendar, succeeding one another endlessly like our days of the week.

People sometimes get seduced by the word *pyramid* into thinking that there must be a connection between Mesoamerican civilization and ancient Egypt. Apart from the fact that the dates do not come anywhere close to correspondence on the

two sides of the Atlantic, it was always possible to point out
that Mesoamerican pyramids were temple platforms, and
those of Egypt tombs. But as more and more Maya structures
are excavated it now looks as though the Classic Maya (but
probably not the highland Mexican peoples) did indeed use
their pyramids partly as royal tombs. In 1952 Alberto Ruz
discovered the famous funerary crypt beneath the Temple of
Inscriptions at Palenque, and ten years later a vaulted tomb was
found in the bedrock beneath Tikal's Temple I.[10] Since then
many others have come to light. Some were clearly planned
before the pyramids were built; others were cut into existing
buildings. These discoveries do not invalidate the statement
that Maya pyramids (unlike Egyptian ones) were temple platforms, but they suggest that many of those temples were mortuary shrines in which the dead ruler was either worshiped as a
god or invoked as an intermediary between human and godly
worlds.

At the time that the tomb beneath Temple I was found,
another revolution in Maya studies had begun. The calendrical
content of the hieroglyphs had been brilliantly revealed by
pioneer scholars at the end of the last century; but further
decipherment proved slow and uncertain. Some experts took
the view that the writing system was insufficiently advanced
to be decipherable; others thought its content too esoteric for
interpretation. Because many inscriptions referred to the completion of time periods, Mayanists generally believed that the
personages on the stelae were not human individuals but personified epochs in the worship of time itself. In 1950 Sir Eric
Thompson wrote:

> I conceive the endless progress of time as the supreme
> mystery of Maya religion, a subject which pervaded
> Maya thought to an extent without parallel in the
> history of mankind. In such a setting there was no
> place for personal records. . . .[11]

It seemed that Maya rulers did not share the Ozymandian
ambitions of others, and the relative scarcity of warlike themes
in Maya sculpture suggested a peaceful society governed by

self-effacing priest-kings who spent their days attuning the human realm to the harmony of the spheres. It was therefore a shock when Tatiana Proskouriakoff first suggested in 1960 that the monuments at Piedras Negras (about one hundred miles west of Tikal) commemorated not aeons and eras but the carefully edited lives of kings and queens. Her work was reinforced two years later by David Kelley's decipherment of a dynastic sequence at Quiriguá. The old, idealized image of the Maya was exposed as a seductive myth. For many, it was a terrible disillusionment. How much nicer to believe in a utopian Maya world where ambition was subservient to intellect, where intoxication with astronomy and mathematics had ousted the common obsessions of wealth and power.

Thompson recognized the value of the new work and soon revised his views. But he was never completely wrong: the Maya *were* obsessed with time and the accurate observation of the heavens. It is our understanding of their motivation that has changed. Now we know that they did these things largely to sanction and legitimize the use of earthly power. Their gods, like all others, were made in the image of man.

When I was last here, little was known about the individual found beneath Temple I. Dated monuments gave the outline of the city's chronology but the accompanying inscriptions were largely obscure. Since then advances in the study of Maya writing have transformed the Classic past from prehistory into history. Decipherment is still incomplete, but the fortunes of individual rulers can be traced: we have a good idea of when they were born, took power, got married, and died. We know about their enemies and allies, vassals and overlords, their conquests and defeats; and, after a fashion, we know their names. Temple I has been revealed as the resting place of Ah Cacau, "Lord Chocolate," king of Tikal from 682 until the mid-720s. His reign was a time of renaissance, during which the city recovered power and prestige it had enjoyed in earlier centuries. All the five great pyramids, which now seem so typical of the city, were built in the hundred years after Ah Cacau's reign: a final, glorious florescence before the great collapse.

The city first rose to prominence in the second half of Baktun 8. The earliest stela yet found here bears the date 8. 12.

14. 8. 15, or A.D. 292. This, also the earliest Long Count date in
the Maya lowlands, is often taken as the start of the Classic
period. Soon afterward, Tikal's first great king emerged, known
from the appearance of his glyphic name as Jaguar Paw.

In 8. 17. 12. 16. 7 (A.D. 378) a Curl Nose succeeded to the
throne. With him came an art style heavily influenced by Teotihuacán, the imperial Mexican city a thousand miles to the
west, which dominated Mesoamerican trade and politics until
it declined mysteriously in the middle of the Classic period.
Curl Nose may have been an outsider from the Guatemalan
highlands, which already had strong links with Mexico. At any
rate he married a lady of the Jaguar Paw lineage and produced a
son, Stormy Sky, who presided over Tikal's first golden age.

After the collapse of Teotihuacán, political and economic
patterns were realigned, and Tikal, which had relied most
heavily on the Mexican power axis, lost wealth and influence
until the accession of Ah Cacau late in the seventh century.
Clemency Coggins, who worked out much of Tikal's dynastic
history, has proposed that Ah Cacau timed his inauguration to
occur exactly thirteen katuns—a complete Short Count
cycle—after the accession of Stormy Sky. Stormy Sky's reign
had begun a century of power and prestige for Tikal: Ah Cacau
was announcing that a similar era would begin again with him.
And he was right. In the following 130 years Tikal attained its
greatest magnificence ever. Temples I, II, and V were built early
in the eighth century, soon after Ah Cacau's death; Temple IV,
the tallest of all, went up during or immediately after the reign
of his son, Yax Kin, who may be buried under it; and Temple III,
Tikal's architectural swan song and perhaps the most graceful
of her skyscrapers, was completed in 810. It probably covers the
tomb of Chitam, who succeeded Yax Kin in 768.[12]

If Coggins is right about the timing of Ah Cacau's revival,
this is yet another instance of the Maya using their calendar
not only to record events but to cue them; and it implies that
the destinies of the Short Count were almost as hypnotic in the
Classic period as they were a thousand years later for the
writers of the books of Chilam Balam. Oddly enough, both
Stormy Sky and Ah Cacau came to power in Katun 8 Ahau,
auspicious for them but deadly to the Itzá.[13]

* * *

The stairs up Temple I are so steep and worn that a chain is provided as a handhold. Even so, two people have fallen to their deaths in recent years, one a tourist, the other a guard. Whether human beings were killed here intentionally in ancient times is not known. In Mesoamerican religion, human blood is the essence of life, the substance that informs the living realm and distinguishes it from fleshless underworld and ethereal sky. Life owes a debt to the past and a bribe to the future. The Toltecs and Aztecs believed that the sun had to be nourished by wholesale human sacrifice in order to keep the cosmos alive; but it seems that the Maya (at least until late in the Classic period) generally confined themselves to offering small quantities of royal blood. Maya kings drew droplets from their penises with stingray spines; queens bled their tongues with agave thorns. The droplets fell onto ritually prepared paper that was then burned in the temple doorways at the tops of the red-painted pyramids.

Mesoamerican civilization seems to have been perpetually aware of its own fragility, and haunted by guilt for the demands that culture puts on nature. This ecological penitence—rather admirable when compared with Western man's belief in his right to treat creation any way he wants—was shared by most Amerindian societies. Perhaps it was a memory of the time when people had taken possession of this empty hemisphere. They were not expelled from Eden; they had intruded there, and still felt the obligations of the guest.

13 Oc   *Last number in the sequence, the propitious thirteen. Oc is the Dog, who guides the night sun through the underworld.*

Back to the Great Plaza. The north side is lined with two dozen stelae, many with round altars in front of them. Behind these a monumental stairway rises to the North Acropolis, where there are about fifteen "small" pyramids dating from the first period of Tikal's greatness in the early Classic. This was the ceremonial center of the Jaguar Paw dynasty, a human reef built on older constructions reaching back centuries before Christ.

It is hard nowadays to imagine the nobility of Tikal living in the palaces of the Central Acropolis. The corbel-vaulted rooms are dark and close, running with moisture, reeking of bat guano. But they weren't damp and smelly when in good repair, and presumably much of life was lived outdoors in the court-yards, beneath palm and feather canopies.

The Five-Story Palace is still quite habitable. Part of it has fallen, but on the fourth level there's a fine gallery with its plaster white and dry, and original carved tie beams spanning the vault. The preservation of lintels and beams at Tikal is astonishing—logwood and *zapote* have lasted more than a thousand years, despite rot and insects. There's a colony of bees here now, strange stingless little creatures that drop suddenly when they leave their holes and tumble around on the floor before flying off. The Belize Creoles call them "drunken Bay-men."

1 Chuen .

Chuen: Monkey; the great craftsman, patron of arts and knowledge: a good day.

Near the hotels are rows of stalls selling Guatemalan weav-ings: beautiful, authentic trajes of the highland Maya; gaudy tablecloths, bags, and place mats for the more practical tourist. I stop to look while waiting for the weather to clear. Some Americans have arrived in a taxi; they begin bargaining with the saleswoman, a Quiché Maya in her traditional huipil and wraparound ankle-length skirt. She has long braids tied together with an orange ribbon at the ends, and a gentle, calm expression. Years of hard work and worry show in thick hands and a pleated brow. At least she's making a good living here, I think. But when the bargaining gets serious the Maya starts shooting anxious glances between blankets hanging on the back wall. Behind her, in a small storehouse, there's another pair of eyes, predatory, avaricious, signaling with haughty puckers and stiff little shakes of the head. The owner of the enterprise is a Ladina: the Indian attracts and charms the visitors, the Ladina takes the profit—Guatemala.

Afternoon. Up Temple III, the most gracile of them all: a sixty-degree scramble up loose stones, mortar, and mud.

Between the outer room and the sharp vault of the inner chamber a carved wooden lintel shows Chitam, the last ruler of Tikal to be commemorated. He was immensely fat. A jaguar-skin robe is stretched like a beer drinker's T-shirt over his paunch; his arms seem puny and undersized, barely able to span the colossal gut; and the buckle of his jade belt hangs in front of his private parts (which were not so private for Maya kings)—an older, fatter version of the already corpulent Chitam shown on Stela 22. There he had celebrated the first katun ending in his reign with the following text, translated by Christopher Jones:

The day 13 Ahau
Eighteenth day of the month, Cumku,
End of the seventeenth katun [of Baktun 9: i.e., January 22, 771].
The completion of its period.
Chitam
In the dynastic line, lord of Tikal,
The ninth plus twenty,
In the count of the rulers . . .[14]

Chitam's swelling form, which must have increased by at least fifty pounds per katun, seems symbolic of his age; and the soaring "art deco" roofline of his mortuary temple strikes one as a desperate declaration of false confidence in troubled times. This is all very ethnocentric, of course. Maya lords were expected to be plump, and the monuments they built were seen as essential to the well-being of the world. But there's little doubt that the theocracy had become dangerously top-heavy by the late eighth century, and resources at Tikal's disposal were starting to shrink.

By 9. 19. 0. 0. 0 (June 26, 810), the probable date of Temple III's dedication, Palenque, Copán, and Yaxchilán had already fallen silent. Quiriguá and Piedras Negras erected their last monuments on the same day. Only one later inscription has been found at Tikal. A few minor centers flowered brightly and briefly after the great cities had died. A century later, on 10. 4. 0. 0. 0, or January 18, 909, the very last Long Count stela went up, at Toniná;[15] but the heyday of the Classic Maya had effectively ended with the completion of Baktun 9 in our year 830. Scrub invaded the streets and fields; palmettoes, logwood, and crocodiles returned to the swamps. As the katuns and the forgotten baktuns passed, the bush evolved into the majestic forest that envelops the ruins today.

Sunset. Looking east from the top of Temple III. The limestone towers of I and II are liquid gold above the embossed copper of the canopy. Human voices fade from the ruins, and roosting howler monkeys, wheezing like asthmatics, begin to bark and roar from the tall trees on the South Acropolis.

Part III

South: Highland Guatemala

Chapter 5

2 Eb *The day generally called Grass in most of Meso-america, though in many Maya languages eb means "point" or "tooth." Eb has a sharp little face with a hard jaw, and is associated with rain and storms.*

Noon. At the Flores airport they tell me there'll be a flight to Guatemala City "midafternoon." I'll be flying on the army airline—the cheapest one.

4:00 P.M. Aloft in an old Fokker airliner of the 1950s. There are pleated gray curtains in the windows, and the plane wags its tail as it flies.

From the air only Guatemala's beauty shows. A view of the lake, gunmetal beneath the overcast, a few minutes of bottle-green jungle; then the aircraft struggles through vapor into the sun, as if waking from a somber dream. A glacier of cloud stretches to north, west, and east, but to the south the highlands climb above the weather, revealing a mysterious country of cones, khaki hills, and red ravines filling with purple shadow.

We fly low, through the mountains, not above them. Thin white lines wriggle like tapeworms into valleys that must have been inaccessible until the army began bulldozing these strategic roads during the civil war. Along them are occasional clusters of tin roofs, winking like heliographs in the sunlight. Are these the "model villages," often described as concentration camps? Other valleys look unchanged in centuries. Isolated huts roofed with pine shingles and tile stray over the landscape—the settlement pattern usually favored by Maya when free from "reductions," colonial or modern. I see two dead towns—roofless churches, thickets bearding the fields—two of the 440 destroyed.

There's little hint of Guatemala City's imminence: a plateau suddenly appears, like the deck of an aircraft carrier plowing a tumultuous ocean of volcanoes. The sun has just gone down; a fluid gloom pours into the surrounding valleys, hiding the slums and rubbish tips that ring the capital. We pass low over outlying neighborhoods; pools of illumination glow on plastered walls and dusty streets.

The runway is dark but still warm when I climb down the ladder, leaving the turgid lowland air behind on the plane. A wispy aureole flames at the tip of the Agua volcano, a perfect black cone against a bloody sky.

There have been four Guatemala Cities since the Spanish conquest. In 1524 Pedro de Alvarado, most dashing and brutal of all the conquistadors, endowed Iximché, capital of the Cakchiquel Maya, with the resounding title Santiago de los Caballeros de Guatemala: St. James of the Knights of Guatemala. (Guatemala was a Spanish corruption of Quauhtlemallan, the Aztec rendering of Iximché, which means "Land of Many Trees.") In 1526 the Cakchiquels rebelled. Alvarado burned the first Guatemala, and founded the second, now known as Ciudad Vieja, in the Almolonga Valley. In September 1541, two days after Alvarado's widow had been installed as governor, the Agua volcano buried the city under mud and water, an event recorded with terse glee in the Maya *Annals of the Cakchiquels*:

On the day 2 Knife the volcano Hunahpú [Agua] swept down; the water gushed ... the Castilians perished and died.[1]

A third Guatemala, nowadays called Antigua, was then built five miles to the north; it was shattered by earthquakes in

1773. In 1776 Guatemala City was moved to its present site, still within sight of the volcanoes Water and Fire. This city was badly damaged by earthquakes in 1917, 1918, and 1976, but it's unlikely that Guatemala will again be moved: there is simply no safe place in the highlands.

GUATEMALA CITY

Mick and Lucy of Chaa Creek recommended the Posada Belén in the old downtown district, a few blocks south of the cathedral and presidential palace. The streets are narrow here, and the single-story houses rise straight from narrow sidewalks, trapping an atmosphere of exhaust, greasy cooking, and urine pissed against the stucco walls. But once past the iron front door of the Posada you enter a spotless old Spanish house with rooms arranged around a patio full of flowers and pottery urns. There's a thick woven blanket on my bed, and an information sheet advising how to work the hot shower (one of those tricky in-pipe heating elements).

From this haven it's three or four blocks to Sixth Avenue, once the heart of the city, now fading as the upper class gravitates to the southern suburbs. The expensive shops have abandoned the area to discount clothing and television repairs; old clubs and offices are being turned into chicken restaurants and cinemas. Enormous neon signs, hanging from wires and rusty brackets, nuzzle each other above the street. Beneath these triumphal arches of capitalism pass the evening crowds, buses trailing pennants of smoke, and the cars of rich kids cruising the avenue as if it were Sunset Strip. Philips rubs noses with Farmacia Klee; Wrangler with a prosperous proctologist. (Dr. Enrique Orellana, ILLNESSES OF THE COLON, RECTUM, AND ANUS, in red letters a foot high on a yellow background.) Wrangler does well in Guatemala—perhaps the tight fit favored by plump Ladina girls helps to keep Dr. Orellana in business. The girls teeter down the street like ninepins on spiked heels, canvased bottoms billowing, red lips pouting, sheer blouses exposing the fuselage of elaborate brassieres.

In front of beauty salons and fast-food joints are people

selling cheap clothes, costume jewelry, candles, hairy puppets that walk and squeak—all laid out on the sidewalk on little cloths. The crowd flows around and through the pedlars; past the beggars on doorsteps—mostly young Indian widows, babies on their backs, faces upturned, the hand held out diffidently because the Maya despise begging and do it only in desperation.

3 Ben  *Ben: Reed; who fosters the growth of corn and man. One of four days who "carry" the year. The tzolkin system was shared by all Mesoamericans, and the solar years were named for the days on which they began.*

A year 1 Reed was the year foretold by the Aztecs for the return of Quetzalcóatl, the pale-skinned Feathered Serpent, from across the eastern ocean. By an extraordinary coincidence, 1519, when Cortés reached Mexico, was a year 1 Reed.

The tzolkin and the year arrive at the same combination every 52 years ($365 \times 52 = 260 \times 73$), so Cortés, who could not have known his luck, won a psychological advantage at odds of 52:1. Because of the relationship between 365 and 20, only four of the tzolkin *names* can fall at the beginning of a year. These four, known as the "Year-Bearers," hold this honor in sequence. For the Classic Maya and the Aztecs, they were Reed, Knife, House, and Rabbit. Since 13 goes into 365 with a remainder of one, the *number* of the Year-Bearer advances by one each year: 2 Reed is followed by 3 Knife, 4 House, 5 Rabbit, 6 Reed, 7 Knife, and so on. The number system is remarkably similar to a pack of 52 playing cards. If you consider each Year-Bearer as a suit, and order the pack as follows: 2 of clubs, 3 of diamonds, 4 of spades, 5 of hearts, 6 of clubs, and so on, you have an exact analogy of the system. This 52-year period, known as the Calendar Round, was of tremendous religious significance. To the highland Mexican peoples, who lacked both the Long Count and the Short Count kept by the Maya, the Calendar Round was *the* calendar—an all-encompassing destiny. The Aztecs counted their 52-year cycle from the day (and year) 2 Reed, and believed that the world was in danger of ending every time a Calendar Round completed its course.

10:00 A.M. The Canadian embassy occupies the upper stories of an office building in fashionable Zone 9. You walk past a security guard and board an elevator that stops at no other floors. At the top there are two more guards and a heavy steel door unlocked from within by a buzzer. You have to shout your business into an intercom, and when you get as far as the booth occupied by a very pretty but very junior Guatemalan employee, two inches of laminated plate glass make conversation difficult. (Secretaries are *always* very pretty in Latin America: lots of nail polish and mascara, frilly see-through tops, and silly shoes.)

"Sí, señorita: W-R-I-G-H-T." (The mantra is second nature by now.) I'm hoping to find a message from David, a journalist friend who's supposed to be flying down from Canada. We're planning to meet in a few days' time and rent a vehicle for a trip through the highlands. David is as reckless as I'm cautious. Last time he was in Guatemala he narrowly escaped with his life after trying to contact the guerrillas.

"No hay nada, señor."

Just like David to be late and like me to be early. I ask if there's someone senior I could speak to. But the letter of introduction I sent from Canada is nowhere to be found; the person I wrote to has been reassigned to a desk in Ottawa; all the senior staff are out of the country—in Honduras to observe "democratic" elections favored by the United States. I read something recently about the Honduran campaigns: one candidate showered the republic with leaflets claiming that his opponent was a sodomite riddled with AIDS. The Americans were embarrassed when it came out that the leaflets were dropped from a U.S. Marines helicopter.

Eventually I'm granted an interview with the only Canadian left in the place. Myron Blatherwycke has a pale complexion, white wavy hair, and the see-no-evil eyes of a career diplomat. . .

"I wonder if you could fill me in on the situation in the countryside—where I should go, and where I shouldn't?"

"Where have you been so far?"

"I just flew up from the Petén."

"If you'd come to me first, I would have told you not to go there."

"What about the highlands?"

"The government has recently had great success in pacifying many areas. Antigua is okay, and I gather tourists are returning to Panajachel and Chichicastenango. You should go there, everyone does, it's beautiful. However, I'd advise you not to travel anywhere after dark."

"I was thinking about northern Quiché and Huehuetenango."

"Those are two areas I would strongly advise you not to go to. I can't stop you, but I would ask you not to go."

I have some other questions—about Canada's policy toward Guatemalan refugees. In March 1984, the Canadian government imposed a visa restriction on all Guatemalans, making it difficult for them to enter Canada on their own initiative. At the same time the Canadian embassy here began "processing" refugees internally. Surely this exposed them to scrutiny from informers watching foreign embassies?

"What about these guards outside the door," I ask, "are they embassy employees or members of a private security firm?"

"They're officers of the Guatemalan police. Why?"

"If I feel intimidated by them—and I do—what's it like for the refugees who try to seek asylum here?"

Mr. Blatherwycke opens a packet of Marlboros, taps out two, and offers me one. He leans forward and lowers his voice: "I can assure you that Canada is quietly helping hundreds of political refugees get out of Guatemala. But for obvious reasons we don't want that spread around."

I tell him about a Guatemalan woman I met in Toronto. Before escaping Guatemala, she and her husband had been organizing homeless people like themselves to settle as squatters in the capital's wastelands and garbage dumps. One day they saw three men loading a machine gun on the bank behind their shack. They grabbed their two babies and ran. Somehow they got as far as the embassy's steel door, but were roughly turned away by the guards. Luckily for them a Mexican diplomat happened to arrive, and he personally ushered them through. They were given a special permit to enter Canada— but what if the Mexican had not been there?

"Well," says Mr. Blatherwycke, a weary smile tugging at his cheek, "we could argue individual cases all day." His cigarette is at an end; and so, clearly, is my interview. "Guards or no guards we get about seventy people a day coming in here."

"I didn't see a soul in the waiting room."

"You hit a slow day."

(Months later, I discover that 382 Guatemalan refugees received visas and permits to enter Canada in 1985.[2] Even if all came through this embassy, it would amount to an average of only one and a half successful applications per working day.)

I leave a note for David with the girl in the glass case. Then out through the steel door and past the raptorial gaze of the guards. Mr. Blatherwycke is right about one thing: Embassies in Guatemala have good reason for elaborate security. They remember what happened on January 31, 1980, when a group of Quiché and Ixil Maya and some student supporters staged a peaceful sit-in at the Spanish embassy.

For months the Indians had been fruitlessly petitioning the government to halt army atrocities in northern Quiché Department. In August a deputation had visited the national congress to protest the kidnapping of seven village leaders, only to be told that the Guatemalan parliament was "no place for *indios.*"[3] Some of the deputation were arrested on the spot and beaten up; others returned to northern Quiché, where they were greeted by the corpses of the seven missing men.

At about 11:00 A.M. on the morning of January 31, the Indians entered the Spanish embassy (which they chose because Spanish priests in the villages had been sympathetic to their plight). They presented the ambassador with a letter:

We ... direct ourselves to you because we know you are honourable people who will tell the truth about the criminal repression suffered by the peasants of Guatemala. ... To a long history of kidnappings, torture, assassinations, theft, rapes, and burning of buildings and crops, the National Army has added the massacre at Chajul. ... We have come to the capital to denounce this injustice. ...[4]

The ambassador contacted the authorities and asked them to keep well away because the protest showed no signs of turning violent, but by 2:00 P.M. hundreds of police had gathered outside. They broke down the doors with axes, undeterred by the ambassador's shouts that they were violating international law. Guns were fired; a bomb or Molotov cocktail set the building alight. Thirty-nine people were shot or burnt to death. Only the ambassador and one Indian survived. Next day the Indian was kidnapped from his hospital bed; his mutilated body appeared later at the university campus, a favorite death squad dumping ground. Spain broke off diplomatic relations with Guatemala. No one was ever charged in the affair.

Later. Houses in the upper-class neighborhoods of Guatemala City are elegantly barred. Wrought-iron grilles, sheets of steel with brass knobs, and bars welded in diamond patterns confront the sidewalk or lurk behind riots of magnolia and bougainvillea: the defenses of the rich against the society they have made.

Servants, some of them Indian women in the mysteriously intricate costumes of their villages, are watering lawns. Other Indians pad along the sidewalk trying to sell potted plants and homemade brooms. A hopeful face looks up from beneath a tumpline across the forehead and a cascade of vegetation carried on a back bent almost parallel with the ground. There is a brief exchange between vendor and servant through a barred gate, a responsorial chant in the shushes and clicks of a highland Maya tongue that sounds like two cooks chopping celery. Then the face bends again to the sidewalk, and the mobile garden glides away on feet so burdened that they spread beneath their load like camel hoofs on sand.

You can tell a lot about a country from its cars. Motor vehicles will one day prove as useful to archaeologists as potsherds and inscriptions. Their rapidly changing styles make them superb chronological markers. But they are more than that: they reflect the social pyramid; and when you add some statistics as to who owns what kind of car, you have a steel allegory of the human world. In social democratic countries cars tend to be small and cheap: proletarian Fiats, egalitarian Volkswagens. In most of Africa there are two kinds of car—decrepit Japanese taxis for the hoi polloi, and smart Mercedes-Benzes belonging to those government men known as the "Wabenzi" tribe. In Guatemala, as in Africa, most of the people have no cars. You must climb the pyramid at least as far as the lower middle class to discover the most archaic and feeble members of the mechanical race—American pickup trucks and finned dragons from the 1950s. A step or two higher up come Toyotas and Datsuns, so patched, welded, and improvised that in North America a scrap dealer would demand money to tow them away.

In Guatemala, where about 2 percent of the landowners own 70 percent of the land, the mechanical oligarchy of Range-Rovers, BMWs, and Mercedes-Benzes is exclusive. These are cars you don't see in Mexico or most other Latin American republics that have a rational import policy and a tax structure aimed at luxury goods. The telling thing about Guatemalan wheeled fauna is that there are so few species between the vermin and the exotica. If you are rich, you're filthy rich; if you're not, well, a '58 Chevy or a '66 Datsun is as close as you'll get to wheels. The fincas, which cannot afford to pay their peons more than about $1.20 a day, support flamboyant jeeps equipped with magnesium wheels, balloon tires, roll bars, extra lamps, and bucket seats in the truck box, filled with giggling señoritas. Urban businesses—coffee and cotton brokerage firms, soft-drink bottling plants, arms suppliers—nurture Cadillacs and luxury German sedans with smoked bulletproof windows, as dark as the faces behind them are pale. The army officers who make all this possible seem to have rather adolescent tastes: Blazers and Broncos with chromium rams and prancing horses. Similar vehicles, devoid of ornaments and license plates, prowl the streets at night, looking for *subversivos* to "disappear." (A Guatemalan I know claims that *disappear* was first used as a transitive verb in his country.)

Afternoon. An odd thing is happening: the quetzal, in a dive for the past three years, has begun to soar. Guatemala's currency is named after the national bird, whose habits, mythic significance, and doubtful prospects were recently explored by Jonathan Evan Maslow in *Bird of Life, Bird of Death*. The emerald tail feathers of the male quetzal adorned the heads and thrones of Mesoamerican kings, and the very word was an adjective for anything of great price. In modern Guatemala the paper quetzal is identified with another precious green commodity: the yanqui dollar. For years the currency stood at par—a ridiculously large unit for all but the rich. When you tried to buy oranges with a half-quetzal note, or even a twenty-five-cent coin, the seller might have to cancel the sale for lack of change or offer you more fruit than you could carry. It was a measure of Guatemala's economic and political integration with the United States that quetzal and dollar held parity for decades. Only in the last few years, when the cost of maintaining the system became utterly ruinous, has the paper bird begun to fall.

I got a good rate for the U.S. dollars I changed at the Belize border—more than three to one—but my quetzals are running out. This morning I tried the banks but none would change any dollars, even in cash, and traveler's checks were laughed away like Monopoly money. The excuse was the same everywhere: "We don't know the exchange rate; come back later." I learned the truth from some black-market money changers behind the post office: the quetzal is rising.

"Traveler's checks? No thanks. Cash, two-fifty."

"Two-fifty! But it was almost three-fifty a week ago."

"Two-fifty today. Tomorrow, two. And next week"—the

money changers could hardly restrain their glee—"*uno por uno*. One for one!"

 ¡*Uno por uno!* It was a battle cry, like "One man, one vote!" or "Today Europe, tomorrow the world!" The revenge of the quetzal, the return of national pride, a revival of the salad days when coffee and cotton were kings. But why? Some claim that Guatemala's impending return to democracy has stimulated a surge of investor confidence. Cynics say that big coffee brokers have just sold the bulk of this year's crop for cash: Guatemala City is awash with dollars; until they're salted away in Switzerland and Miami there won't be much demand for gringo folding stuff.

Eventually someone revealed that the bank at the airport was still buying. I hopped a bus for ten cents and rode for half an hour. There was a line, but I saw with relief that the advertised rate was still above three. When my turn came the bank teller wanted to see my passport. "But you entered Guatemala a week ago," he said gravely. "I'm sorry. Our service here is only for incoming passengers."

"But I just flew up from Petén!" I raised my voice enough to show that I wasn't going to be fobbed off without a fuss. He changed two hundred dollars, which should last me about ten days if I can stick to my budget. As I rode back to the hotel, it occurred to me that I had in my pocket about twice the annual income of a Guatemalan Indian. The pretty notes, with their sailing bird and Maya numerals, seemed somehow unclean. Almost all denominations have the heads of generals on them; but there *is* one Indian—on the fifty-cent note, the one of smallest value.

4 Ix *Ix: Jaguar; the night sun. The dots on his hiero-glyph are jaguar spots.*

Sunny again today, though the mornings and evenings are cool here—"Guate," as locals abbreviate the name, is at five thousand feet.

The Posada Belén at breakfast might be an English guest
house. There's a long dining table in a room heavily furnished
with dark china cabinets containing ancient Maya pots and
figurines. A hatch in the middle of one wall connects with the
kitchen. The opposite wall has a tall window giving on to a
patio; climbing plants filter the light and add leafy borders to
images refracted by the rustic panes.

Most guests eat here every morning: the bacon and eggs,
tea, coffee, and toast with homemade jam are irresistible.
Today there are two journalists from Boston (covering the elections), a British honeymoon couple, a German anthropologist,
an Italian student, and an elderly man with small sparkling
eyes in a reddish turnip face. A moustache wriggles above his
disappearing breakfast. His English is Mayfair mixed with a
mid-European accent I can't identify.

"What are your plens today?" the German asks him.

"I'm going to look at some things. Like those"—he points
at a cabinet of Maya pots—"only bettah."

"Be careful of fakes," I say, hoping to discourage him.
"Some of them are very good."

"I know these things. In New York there's only one man for
the Maya. I'm going there tomorrow. He will authenticate."

"Is this your business, collecting?"

"No, it's not my business. I don't need to work. It's only for
fun. I've been doing this for years. You must know the Hittite
collection at the_____Museum? I bought the whole thing for
them from an old man who could no longer keep it."

I think: He doesn't need to work, he's an international art
dealer, yet he's staying in a six-dollar-a-night guest house with
quirky showers?

"I suppose you realize what you're doing here is illegal?"

"What is illegal? I know these countries. In Guatemala
nothing is illegal if you know what to do, and whom to see."

"I imagine you're right; but surely you're aware of the
looting?"

"You must have been listening to archaeologists." On his
lips the word is full of contempt. "The archaeologists want
everything for themselves. They're so terribly dry. I know some
of them. They're very dry."

"What exactly do you mean by *dry?*"

"No appreciation of artistic value."

"You must know that looters break up Maya stelae with hammers and saws to sell individual glyphs to collectors. Is this what you mean by appreciating artistic value?"

The Collector returns to his plate. He likes his eggs very raw; he soaks up the albumen with small pieces of white bread and feeds himself the way one might feed a baby. Others in the room are quiet, waiting for the next move.

The Collector: "With architectural things I think that is another matter. Perhaps you have a point. But it does little harm to dig up grave goods."

I point out that the plundering of grave goods destroys context, and therefore all the information surrounding the circumstances of the burial—to say nothing of the attendant destruction to buildings and artifacts of no commercial, but often much scientific, value. The Collector pours himself another cup of tea, and looks at me the way a prostitute might regard a nun.

"It always happens. You can never stop it, except perhaps at the source."

"If there were no market there would be no source."

"That's an old argument. And one I personally find unconvincing."

Guatemala's national museum is a neobaroque structure of consoles and broken pediments: an overripe European mausoleum for the differently baroque treasures of the Maya. It has a fine scale model of the center of Tikal, and a timely display on the looting problem.

One of the best exhibits is a replica of the tomb found beneath Temple I at Tikal. It holds the skeleton of Ah Cacau, stretched out on his back beneath a heavy mail of jade necklaces and pectorals. (Like the Chinese, the Maya believed that jade wards off the corruption of death.) I wonder what we'd know of Ah Cacau if his grave had been found by looters, and his temple damaged or destroyed in pursuit of "artistic value"?

In the ethnology section there's a demographic chart of the

departments of the republic. In each case the percentage of Ladinos is given. You must work out the Indian percentage for yourself, but the twenty-two main language groups of the Maya are named. In general, Indians live high, Ladinos low. The coastal departments and those bordering El Salvador are all more than 80 percent Hispanic; the highland departments are conversely Indian. The histogram is probably too old to have been influenced by recent politics. In Guatemala today, the total proportion of Indians varies according to whether the figures come from Left or Right.

The guerrillas and their supporters claim that the population is 70 or 80 percent *indígena* (the polite word for Indian: *indio* has become a word like *nigger*); the government and the army reckon about 40 percent. Why? Because if Indians are a minority it excuses somewhat their total lack of representation, and mitigates the appalling statistics on their poverty and ill health. For example, life expectancy is sixty-one years for Ladinos and forty-five years for Indians. The difference in infant mortality is even worse: about 80 per 1,000 live births and 160, respectively.[5] (The United States, by no means the healthiest country in the world, has an infant mortality rate of 12.) In the Western Hemisphere only Haiti's social statistics are worse; but Guatemala is very far from being among the poorest countries: the problem is the way its wealth is distributed.

The Left, originally a purely Ladino movement, now seeks to associate itself with Indians for the purpose of gaining peasant support and international sympathy. How many Indians are there really? No one can say, but a figure of 60 percent seems a good compromise. One reason Indians are hard to count is because under certain circumstances they become Ladinos. In Guatemala, as in other Latin American countries, "race" is more a matter of culture than genetics: one is an Indian because one defines oneself as such by wearing the clothes, speaking the language, and keeping to the values and traditions that symbolize Indian ethnicity. Many, perhaps most, Ladinos have the copper skin, high cheekbones, straight hair, and black eyes of the Indian, but they are non-Indians because they or their forebears chose—or were forced—to integrate into the dominant Hispanic society. This metamorphosis is known as "Ladinoization," an ugly word for what is frequently an ugly process.

Some Indians choose to become Ladinos for social and economic reasons. Recognizing that almost all doors for advancement are closed to the Indian majority, personally ambitious individuals discard the carapace of tradition that is at once the Indian's shelter and burden. The price they pay is loss of identity, and the resulting insecurity may provoke exaggerated displays of Ladino behavior. Like a religious convert, the new Ladino often scorns all things belonging to his Indian past.

Ladinoization is also brought about by overt racism and persecution. The Hispanic elite correctly perceives wanting to be Indian as wanting to be different. At best this is seen as quaintly ignorant—why should anyone wish to go on living in the past when the future has so much to offer?—but at worst it is downright subversive: Indians are not real Guatemalans; therefore they are not good citizens; therefore they must be made to change. This thinking rises to the surface whenever Indians try to make any kind of collective protest.

In neighboring El Salvador there used to be many Indians until fifty years ago; now there are virtually none. What happened to them is instructive. In 1932, a year after Maximiliano Hernández Martínez was installed as dictator by the military, there was a peasant uprising in which Indians were prominent. They tried to recover lands stolen from them in the past and to set up communal local governments. Hernández (who became a great admirer of Franco) ordered his troops to destroy every Indian village and shoot every man in Indian dress they could find. An estimated thirty thousand died in what is now known simply as The Massacre. Those Indians who survived became Ladinos for obvious reasons. Their children and grandchildren may remember that once they were *indígena*, but their language, dress, and customs have become extinct.

Latin Americans have enormous trouble with the idea that cultural diversity and national unity need not be incompatible. Their attitude seems to be rooted in the medieval Spanish past, when Iberia was the battleground of rival cultures and religions. For seven hundred years, Spaniard and Moor were locked in a contest that could end only when one had completely absorbed the other. The battle was not a simple race war—neither side was very interested in the genetic makeup of the adversary—mind and soul mattered much more than skin color. The infidel had either to be killed or transformed into a believer; coexistence with him as different but equal was out of the question.

Spain applied the same model in America. The aim of the Spanish Crown was not to exterminate Indians but to turn them into good Spaniards. Genocide was largely incidental, resulting from Old World plagues and the excesses of brutal, ignorant colonists. Only when Indians apostatized and rebelled—in other words, rejected European civilization—were they deliberately destroyed. Spain was convinced it held the keys to the world; like the great powers of today, it could neither understand nor tolerate those who wished to live by other rules.

Despite all the cant surrounding the vaunted independence in the 1820s, no part of Spanish America became decolonized. The external colonialism of Spain was replaced by the internal colonialism of the *criollos*—the American-born whites. Hispanic minorities continued to rule Indian majorities. As in southern Africa, exploitation got worse once the white settlers were free of the metropolitan power. The criollos began to attack and dispossess the "backward" Indian in the name of nation building. They offered their indigenous citizens the old choice of the Iberian wars: Become like us or perish. Some countries (Mexico and, briefly, Peru) have tried to break this vicious circle; but not Guatemala. As recently as 1982, a wealthy Ladino told an American journalist: "The massacre of Indians is simply the continuation of the work of the conquest. You finished off the Indians in your country nearly 100 years ago."[6]

5 Men *Men: Eagle; the wise one.*

Back to the embassy this morning; still no word from David. I asked if he picked up my note, and it seems that he has—at least, the secretary couldn't find it. If he hasn't, things will have to wait until after the weekend.

Afternoon. Carlos sits beneath a map of Guatemala stuck with four little blue flags. He wears glasses and a trim beard— insignia of the radical and intellectual throughout Latin America—and his shirt is well pressed. The office is in a prosperous residential neighborhood with big trees and high walls. A whiff of pine resin blows in through the window, and I can see a soldier in camouflage fatigues standing at the end of the street. Is he there to guard the rich, or to observe who visits this building? Carlos seems nervous: the parchment skin of his face and hands glistens with a film of moisture; but the room is not hot.

"Who did you say gave you my name? I'm sorry I didn't catch . . ."

He has that mixture of politeness and suspicion that is typical of Guatemalans. I repeat the name of someone I know in Canada who works for a charitable organization with international connections. He suggested I visit the sister agency in Guatemala, of which "Carlos" is in charge. (I have changed all names and personal details of my informants in Guatemala.) Carlos offers me his hand.

"Any friend of his is welcome here. But you will excuse me if I ask you a few questions? We have to be very careful whom we talk to." He quizzes me closely about the purpose of my visit.

"The situation has improved during this election campaign. People like yourself from outside can go anywhere and talk to anyone. Nothing will happen to you. But please remember that things may happen to those you talk to after you have left. We are one of very few organizations still operating. Some people in Guatemala interpret any kind of help for the poor and destitute as a subversive act. Colleagues in other agencies have been disappeared."

He asks what contacts I have in Guatemala. I give no names. I say I hope to talk to people in different social positions—from Anglo-Guatemalan members of the landowning class to peasants and human rights activists. I ask if we can talk about the strategic hamlets.

"*Polos de desarrollo*," Carlos corrects me, with a wry but very guarded pucker about the mouth. ("Poles of development!"—Orwell might have made up that.)

"I've heard that they're herding together people from different ethnic groups, and that this is breaking down the indigenous culture."

"Yes, it's true, some *polos* contain people from several ethnic groups, but I don't know what effect this will have on the culture. Some of the military themselves don't approve of the practice, because they fear it will help the Indians to organize as a group—across their ethnic boundaries." He turns toward the map, and sighs.

"Guatemala is much more complex than foreigners imagine. I wish you would not speak only of the Indians. There are many poor people in Guatemala besides Indians. We try to think of all the disadvantaged as *campesinos*—as peasants. Foreigners are always concerned about the Indians, as if all that matters is folklore. Justice should not be reserved for those with pretty clothes and quaint customs." I take his point as a mild, perhaps merited rebuke. The Indians do attract romantic interest, but I sense in Carlos a denial of ethnicity, a refusal to see the conquered Maya as a valid constituency with special needs, problems, and rights.

"Surely," I say, "to regard the Indians merely as a class is to deny their right of self-determination as a people?"

"You are right," Carlos says. I can see he isn't convinced. I turn to specifics.

"Two years ago, there were reports of four hundred and forty villages destroyed by the army and about one million displaced persons in the country. Do you have any information on what's happened to those people?"

"Some are in Mexico, some are still in the mountains. Some have returned to their villages and begun to rebuild their lives, but it is difficult. There are many broken families. In just one of our projects in the highlands we are helping fifteen hundred widows. ¡Mil quinientas viudas, hombre! Many have been raped and mutilated; some have had their breasts cut off; many have soldiers' babies that they do not want to care for."

"When they return are their lands still there for them, or have other people moved in and taken them over?"

"Sometimes it's all right, but abandoned land is often taken over by the military or people connected with the military."

I have one more question—the question about Guatemala that is on everyone's mind: Is the return to democracy real? Does it mean that things can improve, or is it simply window dressing? Since 1977, when the repression in Guatemala began to draw worldwide attention, the United States Congress has banned direct military aid. Although the Reagan administration managed to circumvent this by classifying jeep and helicopter parts as "nonmilitary," and by using proxies—Israel, Argentina, South Africa, and other international pariahs—to provide hardware and "advisers," the Guatemalan armed forces pride themselves on beating communism without American help. But the economy is now collapsing under the burden of constant war, and the generals would like the massive support that their colleagues in El Salvador and Honduras are getting. To do that they need a "democratic" front man, a Guatemalan Duarte.

"Those of us who are trying to produce change peacefully have some hope now," Carlos replies. "A lot will depend on you in other countries. If we can get the right kind of aid at the right time, the military option may little by little become less important." He looks me in the eye. He is pleading, not only with me but to himself. He wants to believe what he wants me to believe. "We know it is a slender hope, but it's the only one we have."

6 Cib 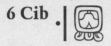 *Day of the Owl or the Vulture—death birds of night and day. There's a saying:* Cuando el tecolote llora, el indio muere: *When the owl cries, the Indian dies.*

Bad weather. I spend the day reading at the hotel. David said he'd be arriving this weekend, but with David you never know.

7 Caban *Caban: Earthquake; a formidable, powerful day.*

Sunday is a big day for fireworks. A notice in my room explains (in English) that the detonations are not the start of revolution. Guatemalan rockets are locally made. Noise is the desired end, with smoke a close second. On any clear day or night you see sudden white dandelions in the sky, followed by earsplitting cracks. Sometimes the noise *is* gunfire, but who can tell?

7:00 P.M. The nightly food quest. I've taken a strong dislike to Sixth Avenue, but it's the only place near the hotel to look for a meal. The restaurants are all the same: large, noisy places with plastic tables and the air hazy with grease and smoke. About the only thing to eat is fried chicken or hamburgers, though the decor varies from Bauhaus chrome to Disney kitsch. One looks in vain for the sort of place that exists in Mexico—small family-run cafés serving delicious local food. In Mexico everyone eats Mexican food; in Guatemala local food is Indian food; nobody who doesn't want to be an Indian eats it, and not many Indians can afford to eat in restaurants.

At night the neon signs and young Ladinos come out and fill Guatemala City with that shabby imitation-gringo fantasy that passes for a national culture. Guatemala is full of sinister jokes, some intended, others not. No one sees anything funny in the slogan of a bridal shop: *Cásese hoy y pague después* (Marry now and pay later). No one detects irony in the undertaker's flickering neon sign—*FUNERALES* ... *REFORMA* ... *FUNERALES*—that amounts to a concise history of the country. Guatemala has gone through many cycles of timid liberalization followed by bloody repression. After each wave of political killing the national conscience awakes enough to seek another way—as it is doing just now—but every time the lid is lifted from four centuries of injustice the social ferment begins to bubble over and a further wave of brutality is the only way to restore "order." Guatemala allows the grass roots to sprout and then mows the lawn. Revolution is continually aborted.

Chapter 6

8 Etz'nab *Etz'nab: Knife; day of the obsidian sacrificial blade.*

No message for me at the embassy. But what about the message I left? The secretary stopped polishing her nails and picked at a few papers on the desk. "Here it is—I forgot to file it. Silly me!"

After lunch, I decide to make an overnight trip to the ruins of Quiriguá, a place I've never seen. Maybe when I get back David will have arrived. The local Budget rental car franchise fixes me up with a Mitsubishi Colt for twenty dollars a day. Only sixteen thousand kilometers on the clock; a few pieces of trim are missing and two tires are prematurely bald: cars have a hard life here.

The highway down toward Guatemala's corner of the Caribbean, wedged between Belize and Honduras, is straight and riddled with holes. So many roads have been built in the highlands for military purposes that there's little money left to repair the country's arteries. Old men with wheelbarrows are shoveling clay into potholes the size of bomb craters. They have to dodge the traffic, hopping to the shoulder, then darting back onto the tarmac between each convoy of roaring trucks—a dance they share with the vultures feeding on flattened iguanas. Sometimes they're guarded by a cardboard cutout policeman, propped in the middle of the road with right arm raised. Cardboard cops in a police state? Another of Guatemala's jokes.

This is the road the British were supposed to build in the 1860s in return for recognition of Belize, but it wasn't completed until almost a century later, when Presidents Arévalo and Arbenz tried to break the monopoly of the International Railways of Central America, owned by United Fruit. The railway had been started during the "Liberal" dictatorship of Justo Rufino Barrios (1873–1885). Barrios is the great hero of Ladino Guatemala: his genius was to make the mestizos (those of mixed Spanish and Indian blood) honorary whites and therefore allies of the upper class against the Indians. Until then, there had been three main strata in Guatemalan society: the small but powerful criollo (white) elite; the Indians, at least three-quarters of the total population; and the mestizos, perhaps one-fifth. The mestizos were pulled both ways; some, like Rafael Carrera, still felt attachments to the Indian society. By expanding the army, the state, and the urban professions, and making them open to anyone who was *not* an Indian, Barrios created the catchall Ladino (Latin) sector and pitted it irrevocably against the Maya.

His "reforms"—the very reforms celebrated in the name of Funerales Reforma and countless other private and public monuments—were a recipe for all the horrors that followed. A contemporary British consul described his regime as "one of the most cruel despotisms the world has ever seen."[1] A Nicaraguan visitor wrote:

> The secret police is a veritable institution. . . . One is always afraid . . . even drunk men are prudent here. . . .
>
> But it must not be forgotten that the author of *progress* is General Barrios; the supporter of *liberty*, General Barrios; the son of the people, father of the people, the grandfather of the people, General Barrios; and finally, the man of democracy.[2]

Barrios and his fellow Liberals decided that the Indians were the root of Guatemala's problems: Indians were backward, ignorant, lazy, and held far too much land for their own good. Their self-sufficiency was a threat to the state, a crime against the future. Barrios had seen the future, and the future was industry and cash crops. German planters were brought in to grow coffee—part of a general policy to encourage white immigration as a remedy for the "clogged blood" of native Guatemala—but these good Teutons needed land and the labor to work it. The solution was simple: the state systematically dispossessed Indian communities, mainly by abolishing ancient communal title—which the Spanish Crown had recognized for centuries and Rafael Carrera had confirmed. Much of the coffee was grown in Verapaz on land stolen from the Kekchí and Pocomchí Maya. (Three centuries before, this had been the land of "True Peace," the short-lived ecclesiastical utopia founded by Bartolomé de Las Casas.) Between 1871 and 1883 almost a million acres of common land were declared "empty," taken by the government, and sold to Ladinos or foreigners.[3] Indians were removed from positions of power in local government and rural militias. At the same time, forced labor laws and debt peonage obliged them to work away from their communities. And when they objected to these quasi-legal methods, the newly modernized and "Ladinoized" army was ready to take action.

On September 4, 1884, troops shot every Indian official in the Quiché Maya village of Cantel.[4] The reason? The Indians had tried to prevent a newly founded textile factory from taking over their land. There were dozens of other incidents like that in 1884; and in 1984 it was much the same: Barrios had founded modern Guatemala.

3:00 P.M. The road meets the Motagua River near El Progreso, of which Aldous Huxley remarked, "I can detect an irony without having it underlined for me."[5] River and road then run straight northeast between the Sierra de las Minas (Range of the Mines) and the low, arid Sierra del Gallinero, which divides Guatemala from Honduras. The moisture of the Petén and the highlands never comes this way, and the valley resembles a worked-out gravel pit that threatens to absorb the river before it finds the sea. The mountains are muddy purple, the air hazy with dust and a pall of diesel that lingers above the road.

Every few miles you come to a little truckstop town, a parody of the North American West: motels and "Drive-Inns" for the rich; tin shacks selling soft drinks and coconuts for the poor. I paused at one of these places, just beyond the turning for Zacapa, where "Butcher" Arana was based. One can't even have a Coke in Guatemala with a clear conscience: the bottlers' union was culled by death squads, and the survivors circulate leaflets saying, *This product contains human blood.* I buy a coconut for ten cents. "Meat or water?" the vendor shouts, machete poised. I opt for "water" (a green nut for drinking) and in three cuts he scalps the tender sac without spilling a drop.

Beyond Zacapa the floodplain widens and becomes less arid. Soon the road is fringed by mile after mile of banana plantations. The trees stand in endless ranks, some heavy with fruit cased in plastic bags, others dangling their lotus-shaped flower at the end of a stem as limp as a cow's tail. Banana trees have an impermanent look; they don't seem sturdy enough to support the clutches of fruit, and I've often wondered how their fleshy leaves, tattered like broken feathers, resist the insects and rot that prey on them. The answer is that they're drenched in chemicals.

Not enough time to visit Quiriguá today: I stop for the night at a wooden motel a few miles from the ruins. The nearest town is aptly named Mestizo; one certainly sees no Indians here. The men have straw hats and baggy cotton trousers with long machetes at their belts; the women wear figure-hugging calico dresses that reveal every sag and bulge on their child-ravaged bodies. They could be peasants from any tropical republic in the world. Gone are the dazzling blouses and saronglike skirts of the highland women, and with the loss of the clothes there seems a corresponding loss of poise. These poor Ladinos—Indians themselves perhaps until a few generations ago—have as a substitute for their ethnic integrity only the economic envy that Hispanic Guatemala exalts as its national aspiration, an envy that in their case will never be requited.

*   *   *

The vulnerability of Latin America to the worst forms of capital penetration lies in the Spanish conquest and the kind of society the Spaniards brought to the New World. The conquistadors came to fight, not to work. Most of them were poor and desperate men, eager to get rich quick and live extravagantly for the rest of their lives. They aimed to recreate in the New World the feudalism that was crumbling in the Old—with themselves as its lords. In short, they had much more in common with the soldier of fortune than the capitalist. Unlike the Anglo-Saxon invaders of America, they didn't want to remove the indigenous society and replace it with one of their own: they wanted to bend the Indian states to their service, to place themselves at the summits of the economic pyramids that had sustained Aztec, Inca, and Maya glory. The Crown and the clerics may have had ideas about transforming those empires into new Spains, but the hard, illiterate conquerors and their criollo descendants were far more interested in squeezing every last drop of wealth from Indian hands into their own. In this they were often frustrated by the laws of the Spanish Crown.

For three hundred years Spain insisted on sending all but the most junior administrators from the mother country, at once denying the criollos any experience in government while sharpening their thirst for independence. Like Afrikaners and white Rhodesians, the criollos longed for the day when they would be free of the fuddy-duddy paternalism that stood between them and whatever was left of the Indians' wealth. *"We did not become free in order to pay taxes!"* they shouted after liberating Peru, and promptly reimposed Indian tribute to pay for their feuding armies and disorderly parliaments.

But the nineteenth century was not the same as the sixteenth: its challenges required sustained energy and expertise, not the crude power to extort tribute from Indians. So they encouraged the immigration of foreign technicians, entrepreneurs, and capital, with the idea that these would build a modern society whose benefits the criollos could enjoy. They were prepared to do what their ancestors had done: use their armies and laws to embark on a second conquest of the Indians, to deliver the lands and bodies of those captive nations for the use of foreign enterprise.

Everywhere in Latin America it was the same. Bolivia gave its tin and its Aymara miners to Europe for a song; Peru handed over its guano and its irrigated coast; Brazil and other Amazonian countries sold their forest Indians into the slavery and genocide of the rubber boom; Mexico's modernizer, Porfirio Díaz, presided over the worst oppression of Indians and the poor in three hundred years.

Having taken this course, the criollo republics became dependent on foreign capitalism to survive. Without the weapons and technology of the gringos some of them might not have been able to defeat the Indian insurrectionary movements that began with Inca Tupaq Amaru in late colonial Peru, continued throughout the nineteenth century, and still smolder today.

To the powerful criollo families, several of which are directly descended from conquistadors, Guatemala is a private fief. The Indians and lower classes are not fellow citizens but raw material to be worked for maximum profit. This *ancien régime* received fresh ideological transfusions from the white-supremacist coffee planters who came in the nineteenth century, and social Darwinist investors who came in the twentieth. The resulting blend of feudalism and fascism is presented, especially to Washington, as a staunch belief in freedom.

If Guatemala's economic and political ties with the outside world were somehow severed, if the umbilical cord of guns and machines and investment were cut, the Ladino minority, like the whites of Rhodesia, might eventually be forced to come to some *modus vivendi* with the Maya. But that day of reckoning is endlessly postponed by the symbiosis between foreign interests and the Guatemalan elite. The most notorious case is that of the United Fruit Company (UFCo), by no means the worst concern to operate in Guatemala but the biggest. United Fruit's inability to accept legal reform led directly to the pivotal event of modern Guatemalan history: the CIA coup of 1954.

The heyday of UFCo was the first half of this century,

when Guatemala was dominated by the dictators Manuel
Estrada Cabrera (1898–1920) and Jorge Ubico (1931–1944). In
1929 UFCo achieved a monopoly by buying out its main com-
petitor, Cuyamel Fruit. (In the 1920s, rivalry between United
and Cuyamel had gone as far as the sponsoring of revolutions in
Nicaragua and Honduras.[6]) By 1952 it held more than half a
million acres in Guatemala alone.[7] Its prodigious size and
ownership of almost all Guatemala's railway, radio, telegraph,
and electricity companies earned it the nickname of *El Pulpo,*
"The Octopus."

The Octopus's firm grasp on strategic industry in Guatemala was expedited by Ubico, who, like the tyrant in García
Márquez's *Autumn of the Patriarch,* sold his country to the
gringos. A ruthless and energetic man, he apparently believed
himself to be a reincarnation of Napoleon. Later he became a
great admirer of the Nazis, and made himself the third largest
landowner in the country through a series of "donations" voted
him by a grateful nation.[8] Upon Ubico's inauguration in 1931,
the American ambassador had declared, "Guatemala is as
friendly with the U.S. as any Latin American republic, and
perhaps is the friendliest."[9] But when Ubico fell in 1944, the
friendship was to go through a decade of estrangement, known
by those who favored genuine reform in Guatemala as the "ten
years of spring."

The thaw was hastened, ironically, by America's own
antifascist propaganda during the war years. Too many
Guatemalans saw parallels between Ubico and the more conspicuous enemies of freedom in Europe and Asia. Demonstra-
tions led to a cycle of repression and unrest. In 1944 Ubico
resigned after handing over power to a junta of conservative
generals, which was in turn overthrown by progressive officers
and cadets. A triumvirate of two army men and a civilian then
drew up a new constitution, modeled closely on Mexico's, and
oversaw elections.

Juan José Arévalo, a forty-year-old schoolteacher, won in
what was probably the fairest vote ever held in Guatemala
before or since. He took office early in 1945. In his inaugural
address he said: "There has been in the past a fundamental lack
of sympathy for the working man and the faintest cry for

justice was avoided and punished as if one were trying to eradicate the beginnings of a frightful epidemic."[10]

For the exploiters in Guatemala social justice was indeed a plague whose outbreak they had every cause to fear. In 1945, as in 1985, the lid had been weighted down on the social pressure cooker for so long that any attempt to lift it might set off an explosion. Arévalo and his colleagues were young, idealistic, and inexperienced. There was no tradition of genuine democracy that could be nurtured or revived, and there were no homegrown political movements that could provide models for popular involvement. Guatemala had nothing like Peru's APRA or Mexico's clever oxymoron, the Institutional Revolutionary Party.

Arévalo himself was an admirer of Franklin D. Roosevelt and the New Deal. He founded the Guatemalan Institute of Social Security and began building rural health clinics and drinking water plants. Spending on education dramatically increased; labor laws were passed; urban and rural wages rose. Recognizing unfair land tenure as both the greatest and the toughest problem in Guatemala, Arévalo proceeded cautiously. He appointed an Agrarian Studies Commission in 1947, but no recommendations were implemented for five years. He was aware how fragile the "revolution" was, and wanted to leave its greatest test until after the 1950 elections, in which Arévalo himself was barred from running by the new constitution.

Despite this caution, the extremism that bedevils Central American politics conspired against the government from Right and Left. Although the Communist party remained officially illegal for most of Arévalo's term, communists rapidly became prominent in unions and other popular organizations. This was only to be expected: Guatemala was a political vacuum, and the communists were one of the few groups with any organization and coherent ideology. They were probably never more of a threat in Guatemala than in postwar France or Italy, but their very existence was anathema to conservative elements. In his five years of office Arévalo survived almost thirty attempted coups, all of them from the Right. The army had been the defender of big landowners and foreign investors since the time of Barrios, and many officers remained loyal to their old paymasters. As Arévalo put it: "In Guatemala there are two presidents, and one of them has a machine gun with which he is always threatening the other."[11]

The turbulent 1950 election was won by Jacobo Arbenz, who headed a broad alliance of moderate and leftist parties. In his inaugural speech Arbenz stressed his commitment to turn Guatemala "from a dependent nation with a semi-colonial economy ... into a modern capitalist state."[12] He tried to follow a report prepared by the International Bank for Reconstruction and Development. Recommendations included crop diversification and raising Indian living standards so as to stimulate an internal market for Guatemalan industry. Arbenz himself—a career army officer of Swiss extraction—was certainly no communist, but he recognized that the survival of his government depended on cooperation with organized labor, which might act as a counterweight to the conservative forces arrayed against him. He also found communists relatively hardworking and personally honest, qualities not noted for abundance in the criollo value system. Unfortunately, his willingness to include some Marxists in his government provided enemies of reform with the very excuse they needed.

Long before the hysteria of the McCarthy era, Ubico had used the word *communist* as a slur upon all who opposed extreme right-wing policies and repression, a usage still current in the region today. (Central American hard-liners have often accused the United States Congress of being communist infiltrated whenever the activities of death squads are criticized; and President Carter's human rights policy earned him the nickname "Jimmy Castro.")

Arbenz was ready to implement land reform in 1952, the year the Eisenhower administration came to power in Washington. Even so, Guatemala might not have attracted American intervention had the United Fruit Company not been among the first targets of the reform. United Fruit had close connections with the Dulles brothers. John Foster (once described by Churchill as "a bull who carries his china shop with him"[13]) was secretary of state, and Allen was director of the CIA. Like other Republicans of that day and this, they presented Guatemala as a test case in the Manichaean struggle between East and West.

Arbenz's reform was aimed at idle lands, and was fundamentally capitalist in conception. His aim was to create a nation of small, hardworking private landowners. Farms of less than 220 acres were exempt.[14] Large estates, whether Guatemalan or foreign, were required to surrender only their unused land, for which they would be paid the declared tax value. The United Fruit Company kept only about 15 percent of its land in production at any one time; arguing that the nature of banana cultivation required large "fallow" reserves, but its holdings clearly exceeded reasonable needs.

Opening up the question of land ownership in Guatemala was rather like trying to break down a dam and ensure that everyone got enough water for a fishpond. The law of 1952 encouraged involvement from the bottom of the socioeconomic pyramid. Peasant unions and local committees sprang up to make claims on land and press for its redistribution. Land was sometimes seized unlawfully, and Arbenz occasionally used heavy-handed tactics in overruling landowner protests. Though there were some cases of favoritism, Arbenz himself surrendered seventeen hundred acres of his family estate.[15] As in Peru's land reform twenty years later, there emerged an insoluble conflict between workers living permanently on an estate, and surrounding Indian communities from whom much of the estate had been stolen.

Despite all these problems the program went remarkably well. Only 16 percent of Guatemala's privately owned arable land was ever touched by the reform, but about half a million people (one-sixth of the population at the time) benefited. Food production did not suffer the massive decline that usually follows such an upheaval, and the figures for Guatemala's overall economic performance during the ten years of spring were equally impressive. GNP per capita rose from $55 to $180; the value of public and internal private investment increased tenfold; and exports rose more than 500 percent.[16]

The United Fruit Company objected to the land reform in principle, and it was outraged by the terms of compensation offered. Like other landowners it had kept its tax declaration as low as possible, and did not regard those values as realistic. The government offered almost $3.00 per acre for land on the Pacific coast that the company had bought twenty years earlier for $1.46. This land was still unimproved and empty except for free-range cattle. The government offered $3.21 for unused Atlantic and Motagua Valley land that had been granted to the company fifty years earlier for nothing. United Fruit regarded these terms as expropriation without proper compensation. The company used its Dulles connections to full effect; the Guatemalan government found itself bargaining not with UFCo but with the U.S. State Department, which demanded $75.00 per acre.

No agreement was possible, and it's unlikely that the State Department ever sought one in good faith. The United Fruit issue became both the cause and the smokescreen for "Operation Success," as the CIA, flushed with their recent victory in Iran, called the plan to overthrow the Guatemalan government. Looking back now, after Cuba (1961), Bolivia (1971), Chile (1973), Grenada (1983), and the present contra war, the events of 1954 have the wearisome familiarity of a formula novel. "The Reds are in control [in Guatemala]," Eisenhower told Congress; and John Foster Dulles spoke darkly of "a network of Soviet agents serving the most ruthless empire of modern times." Even respectable newspapers got caught up in the paranoia: "There can be no battle more decisive than the battle for the Western Hemisphere," trumpeted the New York Times in March 1954, "... the loss to our cause of the Republics next door would be fatal, for then we would be ringed by hostile nations in our own vicinity." By then Anastasio Somoza (Senior) had already made it clear to the United States how to act: "Just give me the guns," he said, "and I will clean up Guatemala in no time."[17]

Accordingly, Operation Success was based in Honduras and Nicaragua. A ragtag "Liberation Army" of mercenaries and Guatemalan exiles was rounded up and supplied with weapons and planes through a CIA "charity" called the Medical Institute. A leader was sought, and found in the person of Colonel Carlos Castillo Armas, who had left Guatemala after heading a failed coup against Arévalo in 1950. He was a pliable little man of limited intelligence, working at the time as a furniture salesman in Honduras.

Beginning on June 18, 1954, Guatemala was strafed by unmarked planes. The pilots were mostly American mercenaries. On the first day they showered the capital with leaflets threatening to bomb the main arsenal and the National Palace if Arbenz did not resign immediately. Later they dropped dynamite and hand grenades on Puerto Barrios and elsewhere. Unsure of his own armed forces, and afraid that retaliation might aggravate matters, Arbenz protested to the United Nations Security Council. The United States insisted that the matter was simply a revolt of Guatemalans against Guatemalans, and a matter for the Organization of American States. American U.N. ambassador Henry Cabot Lodge—a big shareholder in United Fruit and a long-standing lobbyist for that company—browbeat Dag Hammarskjöld to the point that the secretary general considered resigning.[18]

Meanwhile, Castillo Armas and a few hundred followers crossed into Guatemala from Honduras and occupied Esquipulas, where they stayed awaiting CIA orders. This pilgrimage town is the home of a miraculous Black Christ revered throughout Central America. It had the added merit of being only six miles from the Honduran border—close enough for a quick retreat if Guatemala's armed forces chose to support the government. But they did not.

By skillful use of its "Voice of Liberation" broadcasts, the CIA inflated a few armed skirmishes on the ground into a massive invasion. As in Grenada thirty years later, newsmen were kept away from the events; a spiral of disinformation ensured that the United States version circulated not only abroad but within Guatemala itself. The rumor mill and the big lie were perhaps more effective than Eisenhower's planes. Even Arbenz's advisers came to believe that Castillo's force was being swelled by thousands, when in fact the rebels never numbered more than four hundred men.[19]

On June 27 Arbenz resigned, after being given an ultimatum by senior commanders. Unable to get the military to defend him personally, he handed power to an army junta in exchange for guarantees that it would drive out Castillo Armas and respect the reforms so far achieved. His only alternative was to arm the peasants and trades unionists, as he had done in 1950. Arbenz has often been criticized for failing to do this, not least by an obscure Argentine doctor, Ernesto "Che" Guevara, who was in Guatemala at the time.[20] Guevara later called Guatemala "the democracy that gave way," and applied lessons learned there in consolidating the Cuban Revolution.[21]

Before Arbenz walked out of the national palace to asylum in the Mexican embassy, he was allowed to make a farewell speech to the nation. In it he expressed a belief that by stepping down he had saved the essence of the 1944 revolution and avoided a civil war:

> A government different from mine, but always inspired by our October revolution, is preferable to twenty years of fascist bloody tyranny under the rule of the bands which Castillo Armas has brought into the country. . . . Perhaps many people will believe I am making a mistake. . . . Only history will decide.[22]

History decided very quickly. The moderate Colonel Díaz who had given promises to Arbenz was quickly ousted when the Americans made it clear that aerial bombing would continue until he left. Within a few days, Castillo Armas entered Guatemala City—not at the head of columns of victorious troops, but ignominiously from El Salvador in the American ambassador's private plane.

In the following year Vice President Richard Nixon visited Castillo Armas and declared: "This is the first instance in history when a Communist government has been replaced by a free one. The whole world is watching to see which does the better job."[23]

9 Cauac

Cauac: Rain or Storm; the day of the celestial dragon-serpents and the Chacs, the gods of thunder and lightning.

QUIRIGUÁ

Just over two hundred kilometers from "Guate," a rusty sign announces the ruins. Large acacias shade the intersection; a dozen people are waiting for a bus. You turn right down a strip of white dust bisecting the banana trees. After a mile or two you bump across the single track of Barrios's railway, begun in the 1870s and not finished until United Fruit took it over in 1904.[24] The ruins hide in a rectangle of forest imprisoned by miles of orderly bananas.

The Motagua Valley was cultivated in Quiriguá's heyday, but not like this. The city grew cacao for trade but also raised the wide range of food crops that sustained Mesoamerican civilization. Quiriguá's emblem glyph is a stylized avocado. Presumably, enough forest was left to provide a source of wood, nuts, medicinal plants, and game. At the end of the Classic period the bush overran the fields, scaled the walls, and crept into the plazas. There it remained for a thousand years, until swept away by United Fruit's bulldozers. By the time of the Spanish invasion, some small Maya settlements had started to expand in the area again, but the arrival of malaria, yellow fever, and other gifts of the Old World devastated the native population throughout lowland tropical America and made places such as the Motagua Valley virtually uninhabitable before the rise of medical science.

Historians have often spoken of differences in weapons technology and worldview when trying to explain the rapid conquest and colonization of the Aztecs, Mayas, and Incas by tiny bands of Spaniards. Europeans have always rather enjoyed the idea that the Indians took them for gods. (In a new variation on this theme, the French writer Tzvetan Todorov has suggested that the American civilizations caved in because of their failure to conceptualize the "Other.") Only in recent years has the impact of disease been fully appreciated. It's now known that within two or three generations of contact, Mexico and Peru suffered some fifteen major epidemics caused by Old World pathogens to which New World peoples had little or no immunity;[25] between 1520 and 1600 their populations fell by about 90 percent. At least 40 or 50 million people must have died, equivalent in today's terms to the loss of more than half a billion. It was the greatest demographic collapse in human history: proportionally three times more severe than the Black Death, which severely disrupted late medieval Europe—without an accompanying invasion. "Great was the stench of the dead," recalled the *Annals of the Cakchiquels:*

> After our fathers and grandfathers succumbed, half of the people fled to the fields. The dogs and the vultures devoured the bodies. The mortality was terrible. Your grandfathers died, and with them died the son of the king and his brothers and kinsmen. So it was that we became orphans, oh, my sons! . . . We were born to die![26]

The plague referred to here was probably smallpox, which spread through Mexico, catastrophically weakening the Aztecs at their time of need. (Todorov gives scant attention to the fact that the Aztecs had won the first round—soundly defeating the "Other" on the Noche Triste in 1520.) The same plague entered highland Guatemala early in 1521, and then worked its way down to Peru, where it killed between a third and a half of the people in the Inca Empire *before* the Spaniards got there. Among its victims were the emperor and his chosen heir, whose untimely deaths led to a civil war that Pizarro was later able to exploit. Small wonder the Spaniards thought they had God on their side; and small wonder the books of Chilam Balam looked back on the pre-Columbian age as a paradise free from suffering:

> There was then no sickness;
> They had then no aching bones;
> They had then no high fever;

They had then no smallpox;
They had then no burning chest . . .
They had then no consumption . . .
At that time the course of humanity was orderly.
The foreigners made it otherwise when they arrived
 here.[27]

On the edge of the jungle there's a small parking lot, a man
selling tickets at a desk, and some surprisingly clean toilets. A
tunnel lined with giant trees and filled with perpetual twilight
leads to the ruins. Vines hang like bell ropes from a fan vault
flecked with starry chips of sunlight. It is hard to believe that
this cathedral of dripping trees has sprung from the same dusty,
prostrate earth that must be irrigated, fertilized, and sprayed to
yield its tonnage of yellow fruit. I feel submerged in the sultry
air. Sweat mingled with insect repellent runs into my eyes. For
a moment I'm blind, and the darkness fills with brittle birdcalls
that echo and trill as if beneath a dome.

Quiriguá is small compared to Tikal. The ceremonial core
covers only eighty acres; and the surrounding residential areas,
now buried under centuries of river silt, once extended over
one and a half square miles.[28] The city's glory is its tall and
extravagantly carved stelae, displayed to good effect in the
Great Plaza, like columns in a forum. They stand, in Huxley's
fine phrase, "obscurely commemorating man's triumph over
time and matter and the triumph of time and matter over
man."[29] These monuments were first described by Stephens
and Catherwood, and if Mr. Stephens had had his way they
would have been "transported bodily and set up in New
York."[30] Luckily the stones themselves were never removed,
but in the 1880s Alfred Maudslay made casts which he took to
England. These ended up at Cambridge University's Museum
of Archaeology and Ethnology. They were the first Maya sculptures I ever saw.

You enter the plaza at its northwest corner, a long mound
on your left. Other low mounds, half engaged by the forest,
form a border down the eastern side, and Quiriguá's largest
buildings bound the plaza on the south. Even these last are not
high; in contrast with Tikal they emphasize the horizontal

dimension, imparting to the plaza the look of a long playing field viewed by gentle banks of seats. On the west side, as far as I can tell, there are only trees: cohune and coconut palms, ceiba, Spanish cedars, some young mahogany, and a guanacaste hung with oropendola nests, which look like string bags with croquet balls inside. A few outposts of the forest have been left standing among the monuments, adding to the stateliness of the sculptures, and providing welcome pools of shade. The plaza is almost a thousand feet long and five hundred in width, the largest known in the Maya area.[31] Nine stelae and two carved boulders are disposed in three small groups across this space. There is nothing at the center. One has the impression of a giant chessboard during a circuitous endgame.

Only 54 years separate the earliest and latest stelae in the plaza; of the other dated monuments and inscriptions at Quir-iguá, all but one fall between A.D. 672 and 810, a span of 138 years. This near-unity of time and place underlines the brief-ness of Quiriguá's career as an important Maya center. It seems that the city was founded in the early Classic, possibly by a splinter group from Tikal. At that time the Motagua Valley was already dominated by the great city of Copán, which lies on a tributary thirty miles south of here, just inside what is now Honduras. Copán prospered by controlling the rich trade in obsidian, jade, cacao, and quetzal feathers that went down the river to the Bay of Honduras and then by oceangoing canoe up the coasts of Belize and Yucatán. Quiriguá was almost cer-tainly a satellite or client state of Copán until the beginning of the eighth century. Then, after a remarkable ruler came to power in 724, the satellite began to challenge its luminary. This person is most often called "Cauac Sky" because his name shows a sky glyph with elements of the dayname Cauac. In 731 Quiriguá audaciously acquired its own emblem glyph—always a sign of political ambitions—and in 738 Cauac Sky claims to have captured the ruler of Copán. The date 9. 15. 6. 14.6 (May 1, 738) is mentioned several times on stelae, and may be taken as Quiriguá's independence day.

The building and adornment with sculpture of the Great Plaza began thirteen years after this event. From 751 until 805 a monument or pair of monuments was set up every five years.

The series reached its climax with the tremendous Stela E, celebrating the completion of the seventeenth katun of Baktun 9 on 9. 17. 0. 0. 0 13 Ahau 18 Cumku, or January 22, 771. Besides contemporary dates, there are the famous inscriptions on Stelae F and D, harking back to events 90 million and 400 million years in the past—obscure commemorations indeed.

Stela E, with a height of thirty-five feet (counting the buried shaft) and a weight of sixty-five tons, is probably the largest block of stone ever quarried by the Maya. The material is a hard reddish sandstone of high quality brought from about three miles away. Unlike the flat slabs at Tikal and most other sites, the stelae here are approximately square in cross section and carved on all four sides. The glyphs, costume elements, and limbs remain relatively flat, but the faces are cut in deep relief, staring haughtily across the plaza above the mortal plane. The heavy-lidded eyes seem to watch you disdainfully wherever you stand. All but two of the stelae in the plaza were erected during Cauac Sky's sixty-year reign and so bear his face, sometimes adorned with a goatee beard. With one dubious exception his successors were all members of the same Sky dynasty, though their reigns were short. Jade Sky, the last, rebuilt the palace-acropolis to the south of the Great Plaza, and his sculptors carved the last known date at Quiriguá on its facade, in 810.

Somewhere in the middle of the ninth century, Quiriguá fell. The upstart city-state had endured less than a century as a major power. Its ambitions may well have contributed to the political disintegration of the Classic Maya world; certainly they were characteristic of the scramble for power and resources that agitated Maya civilization at its height and eventually shook it apart.

The style of Quiriguá's stelae, as one might expect, is strongly influenced by Copán. Indeed, it's likely that sculptors from that city were pressed into service here after their king's defeat. Copán's sculpture is considered, by our rules of taste, the finest in the Maya area. Figures are carved almost in the full round, engaged only by their backs to panels of exquisite glyphs and cascades of quetzal plumes. The monoliths, wrote Huxley, were treated "as a Chinese craftsman might treat a piece of ivory." Faces are so sensitively modeled that you feel you would recognize these ancient kings if they suddenly appeared in life. At Quiriguá the sculptural technique is still superb; some of the glyphs, especially those on Stela F, and the full-figure ones on D, have been called the finest ever carved; but the overall composition subordinates realism to a cubistic statement of mass and might. The pieces are bigger than Copán's, but one has the feeling that Quiriguá wasn't aware that to exceed is not necessarily to excel.

There is, however, one kind of monument in which Quiriguá does both: the zoomorphs, among the most baffling and impressive sculptures created anywhere. They are large boulders, very free in shape but bilaterally symmetrical, and their outline suggests the model of an animal—perhaps a toad, turtle, or a serpent coiled in a knot. At one end or at both, a human figure emerges from reptilian jaws, and the coils and bulges of the creature's body are adorned with complex inscriptions in cartouches, difficult to decipher because the order of reading is far from clear. In 9. 17. 10. 0. 0 (780) Cauac Sky erected the first of these at the northwest corner of the plaza, beside the modern entrance. It shows him framed by the jaws of the celestial serpent, and surmounted by a sun god mask. The great reptile is most likely the Classic equivalent of the god later known as Itzamná, Lizard House, who is the physical matter of the universe conceived of in animal form. He is shown here with imagery of the day, life, and upper world. Zoomorph G, on the center line of the plaza, was set up in 785 to commemorate the recent death of Cauac Sky. Here the ruler is embraced by the fleshless jaws of the earth-monster, or Itzamná in his night/death/underworld role. The finest of all is P, set up at the foot of the south acropolis stairs after Sky Xul's death in 795. Like the others it defies description, but shows the dead ruler crosslegged in a Buddha pose, surrounded by jaws of exceptional size and flexibility. Oval glyph cartouches dot the body of the monster like heraldic seals.

Zoomorph P was among the Quiriguá monuments at the Cambridge museum when I was an undergraduate. It dominated an upstairs room filled with ethnographic collections. Intricate basketry and primitive weapons were stacked to the

roof in mahogany cabinets. Faceless manikins wore bead
tunics from Hudson's Bay and feather mosaic cloaks from Peru.
A Haida totem pole thrust up into the cupola, where it seemed
to absorb the feeble glow of foggy fenland days. There was never
enough light; you could see what was in the rest of the hall
only after staying there a while. Slowly the tall stelae and
primordial mass of Zoomorph P would assert themselves, the
mysterious surface detail resolving into the writhen figures
and dice of Maya writing. It was the perfect setting for the
sculptures, gloomy as the jungle in which Maudslay had
worked. But this was a dead jungle; the mahogany here was
dried, sawn, and polished; the bows and arrows were brittle,
the blowpipes choked with spiders' nests. The great casts rang
hollow when you touched them. One or two naked mummies
watched from the shadows. It was an abode of the dead, as
perfect as any imagined by the ancient Maya; it smelled of
dried wax and the stale cigars of the Nine Lords of the Night.

Not long ago my wife and I were in Cambridge and I took
her to see the museum: a terrible disappointment. The red
mahogany, green felt, and curved panes had been ripped out
and replaced by sheets of Perspex and plywood boxes covered in
burlap. Fluorescent tubes illuminated introductory displays
with a coarse blue light.

"Where are Maudslay's casts?" I asked the man on duty.

"Oh those," he said. "The British Museum took one or
two. We had to cut up the rest to get them out of here. They
took up an awful lot of space, you see, sir." He seemed quite
unmoved by the loss—their removal had, after all, made room
for a cutaway model of a Bronze Age farmhouse, and several
rows of arrowheads, or some such clichés. I asked if he understood their value to scholars. (The originals have suffered a
century of weathering that the casts have not.) "We did keep
the pieces," he admitted. "They're all stacked away somewhere
if anyone wants to study them."

A woman selling books at a nearby desk seemed a possible
ally. "What happened to all the old cabinets?" I said.

"We kept one. They had to break up the rest. Pity, really.
When they smashed them you could see all the beautiful join-
ery. You can't get work like that done nowadays. But, we had to

move with the times, I suppose. I'd have taken some home, but I've got no room for things like that in my house."

Quiriguá has also suffered an aesthetic loss, however justified: most of the stelae now wear straw hats. These are no doubt necessary to protect them from the acid rains that fall in the last katuns of Baktun 12, but their effect on the plaza's grand design is devastating. No chiaroscuro plays each day across the many stone faces and regalia of Cauac Sky; it's impossible to get good photographs. Ideally, replicas should be put in the plaza, and the originals in a museum. This might cost a million dollars or so—a sum easily found for weapons in Central America, but beyond the wildest dreams of archaeologists.

Chapter 7

The drive back from Quiriguá was quick and uneventful. This part of the country is firmly in government hands; there were no checkpoints. It is often said of nations in Latin America that there are always two countries: a paper country and a real one. More than any other state in the hemisphere, Guatemala exemplifies this. The *paper* Guatemala has a constitution, a system of justice, and regular free elections. In the *real* Guatemala, selfish interests seize power and hold it by corruption and terror. The contrast I've seen between the Motagua Valley and the Petén indicates another dichotomy: center and periphery—two countries that interpenetrate but pull in opposite directions. The one belongs to the military regime; the other to the insurgents; one is urban, the other rural; one depends on infrastructure—roads, airstrips, open fields—the other thrives in the wilderness. This is not a new pattern: it has been the fundamental structure of the Guatemalan conquest-state since 1524.

The *Oxford English Dictionary* defines a nation as a "large number of people of mainly common descent, language, history, etc., usually inhabiting a territory bounded by defined limits and forming a society under one government."[1] Guatemala has never been a nation in this sense. It is a map line drawn around a collection of rival ethnic groups and fiercely antagonistic social classes; an enterprise run by and for the rulers. When the state is weak, the hinterland expands; when strong, the state cuts ruthlessly into the periphery with a new wave of conquest. At present it is almost impossible, and certainly very dangerous, to visit the other country, which has shrunk to a few embattled pockets. I must travel within the tentacles emanating from the center, and must deduce what it is that those arms of the state are so bloodily embracing.

GUATEMALA CITY

6:00 P.M. The man has rubber pads cut from tires on his knees, and blocks of wood with crude handles in his hands; he lacks only a band of padding around the waist to be attired in a parody of an ancient Maya ballplayer's equipment. His court is not the I-shaped precinct used for the ceremonial game of *pok-ta-pok*, in which teams contested the struggle of night and day (though his game is equally a game of life and death), but a small concrete island between lanes of traffic at a junction near the Civic Center. His face is flung back, a mask carved by years of agony; vestigial legs flap behind him like flightless, featherless wings. He pauses, searching the eyes of drivers waiting at the lights, then responds suddenly to the ping of a thrown coin. When he finds one he bends his head to the road with a strange dignity born of pain, seizes it in his lips from beneath a wheel or a smoking engine, and flounders back onto his island where he drops it in a tin.

I've seen the Ballplayer twice before in the same place— not far from the Social Security Institute of Guatemala (starved for funds since 1954[2]). He comes out only at rush hour. His is truly a twilight world, the medieval realm of the *pordioseros*, those who cry, "*¡Por Dios! ¡por Dios!*" and bless you in exchange for your infinitesimal charity. It's the world of Miguel Angel Asturias's great bleak novel, *El Señor Presidente:* a Guatemala that Guatemala tries to banish by decree, just as it has banned most of Asturias's books, despite his Nobel Prize for literature.

Guatemala can't live with its own culture, and perhaps can't even recognize it. One example is the banning of the country's greatest writer. Another is the ceaseless desire of the Ladinos to erect an imitation Europe or United States on the backs and ruins of the Indians. This was realized in its purest form by Estrada Cabrera (the model for Asturias's tyrant), who built temples to the Greek goddess Minerva all over the country. A few still stand: horrid little concrete Parthenons with roofs of corrugated iron.

It was nearly dark when I reached the Posada Belén. I parked in a guarded yard nearby and walked north toward the main plaza to stretch my legs. The din of the traffic was being answered by cracked church bells and crisp detonations.

The Central Park, like most in Guatemala, is devoid of the life one normally finds in the plazas of Latin American cities. During working hours it is busy enough, but at night there is nobody here except policemen and a few worshipers at the cathedral door. The cathedral's design is oddly Wrennish— Ionic columns along the facade and a blue tiled dome. Inside it is tasteful and restrained—white walls and ceilings with stone cornices—almost Anglican were it not for the purple hangings and portraits of apostles in gilt frames.

Three Indian women in the dress of the Ixil people of northern Quiché enter as I leave. They wear brick-red *cortes* and white cotton blouses covered in brilliant lozenges and triangles of embroidery representing stylized birds. Their region was notorious for heavy fighting in the recent war; I wonder what is left for them at home.

The National Palace dominates the north side of the plaza. At first glance it is imposing and appears to be made of stone, but as you go closer you see it's really a concrete fortress, dyed a pale lime green and disguised with French architectural flourishes of doubtful pedigree. Grim-faced little soldiers in flak jackets glance shyly at me as I pass. They have Uzi submachine guns. With all the soldiers and police about, I can't see the need for the signs in the flowerbed along the palace wall: PROHIBIDO CORTAR FLORES (DO NOT PICK FLOWERS). Another of Guatemala's jokes?

10 Ahau

Last time I saw Ahau (Lord, and completer of the series) was in Belmopan, when I started playing with the tzolkin. The calendar's rhythms are beginning to make some sense to me: every time the same dayname comes around, three weeks less a day have passed: every time the same number returns, a fortnight less a day has gone.
Still no David.

Noon. Jenny and Jim live in Zone 13. Big houses are set back from the street among pines and eucalyptus—a menthol smell in the air; you could be in a luxurious suburb anywhere in the Western world. But if you approach the entrance to a property, armed guards appear and large dogs bark behind iron gates. The apartment block is easy to find (because of earthquakes there are few tall buildings in Guatemala). The guard questions me, hand on holster, and talks with Jenny by intercom, then he smiles and opens the steel door in the twelve-foot concrete wall surrounding the grounds. Inside are several new BMWs.

"Jim isn't here yet," Jenny says. "Come in, I'm dying to hear Julia's news." She has the pale complexion of England, blond hair, hazel eyes, translucent skin revealing delicate blue veins on her hands and neck.

We sit in a living room furnished with leather chairs and glass tables. There are some framed weavings on the walls and a fine primitive painting by the Cakchiquel artist Andrés Curuchich. The balcony looks out beyond the ragged edge of the city to pine-covered hills beneath a roiling sky. I tell her about Julia, our mutual friend in London (I've not met Jenny or Jim before), and the purpose of my trip.

"Are you going to write something nasty about Guatemala? Most people who come here do. Remember, I'm a Guatemalan." A brittle laugh. It's easy to forget that her family has lived here for generations until she calls to the maid in the shrill and lispy tones of upper-class Spanish. Her English is so

different: open, soft, the accent and idiom of expensive board-
ing schools.

"I've asked Eusebia to make us a special Guatemalan
lunch; it's a kind of stew with corncobs, and beans, and chunks
of meat."

Jim arrives. He's a tanned American, with a tidy moustache, white cotton shirt, and a pair of jeans. He is jubilant.

"I've sold the finca! Let's have a drink, darling. Let's have a
whole bunch of drinks!"

"I suppose we might as well tell you," Jenny says. "We're
getting out. I don't want to, of course, but Jim was nearly killed
last week." Their eyes meet: *Should we say more?* Then: "The
guerrillas blew up a plane a friend of ours was in. Jim was
supposed to be on board himself. They also got a diplomat.
They've apologized in today's paper."

She hands me a copy of *Prensa Libre (Free Press)*: society
photos; a full-page ad for the Porsche 944 Turbo ("the pleasure
of driving a Porsche . . . 245 km/h, acceleration to 100km/h in
6.3 seconds, leather seats, electric windows . . . everything is
spectacular); and this:

> The attack on a light plane in which the honorary
> consul of Norway, Norman Lynd, was traveling was
> due to a mistake; the intended target was the owner of
> the Finca Panamá, according to a communiqué of the
> outlawed Organization of the People in Arms [ORPA],
> which took responsibility for the tragic occurrence.[3]

The article explains that the guerrillas believed counterinsurgency attacks were being launched against them from the
airstrip of the Finca Panamá, and had therefore been waiting to
down the owner's plane. The aircraft carrying the Norwegian
had stopped there at the wrong moment. The piece ends with a
quotation from the guerrillas' message: "ORPA deeply regrets
the mistake and the death of Señor Lynd, a respected individual
who took a courageous stand against oppression."

"You're not the owner of the Finca Panamá, are you?" I
ask Jim.

"No, thank Christ. Our finca's in the Petén. But I do know

the Panamá—I was planning to visit there, like Jenny said. It's a beautiful place on the southern slopes of the Atitlán Volcano. ORPA has a stronghold in the mountains around there."

"Was it true about the airfield?"

"I've no idea. There's not much you can do to stop the army using your airstrip if they want to."

Jenny and Jim are probably more liberal than most people of their class, but the lunch conversation reminds me of what I used to hear from relatives in Rhodesia: the trouble with Guatemala is political agitation; there's plenty of land for the Indians but they don't want to pay for it. Jim: "If you give a guy something for nothing he won't value it. We've got these Kekchí living on our finca—all they have to do to get twenty acres is register with the government and pay ten quetzals or whatever a year. But they won't pay ten quetzals, they'd rather spend their cash on fiestas."

"I've heard that small homesteaders keep getting evicted from their land by landowners' thugs."

"I guess that happens once in a while, but it's blown out of all proportion. There hasn't been so much of that since old Ríos Montt came to power."

"The Mad Baptist?"

"Yeah, that's the one. A little crazy—had religion all right—but crazy like a fox. Too bad he didn't last. I kinda liked the guy."

"He wasn't exactly marvelous," Jenny adds, "but he was a *lot* better than some of the other ones we've had."

It seems safer to talk about farming. I mention I've read reports about Guatemalan cotton growers using vast amounts of pesticides—sometimes at levels fifty times the recommended maximum. Whole rivers and even the waters of the Pacific have been heavily polluted. DDT levels in Guatemalan mothers' milk are the highest in the Western world.[4]

"Sometimes you gotta. You should see the bugs we get down here. You've just gotta spray the shit out of 'em."

11 Imix

Jenny, who is a connoisseur of Indian art and weaving, told me I'd find more of the remarkable paintings of Andrés Curuchich at the Ixchel Museum, founded by another Anglo-Guatemalan woman and devoted mainly to weaving.

Ixchel, "She-of-the-Rainbow," is the Yucatec name for the female principle in the Maya pantheon. She was the Moon, wife of the Sun, patroness of weaving, childbirth, and medicine. In modern Maya belief Ixchel is inextricably mixed up with the Virgin Mary, even though her virtue was rather questionable. One myth tells of how she left her husband and ran off with the king vulture. To get her back the Sun dressed himself in a smelly deerskin and lay on the ground, sending a blowfly to lure the vultures; when the birds came the Sun seized one and made it carry him to the king vulture's palace, where he retrieved his faithless wife.[5]

The Ixchel has superb textiles, cleverly displayed on stick figures with earthenware pots for heads. Some of the older ceremonial costumes are rarely seen in Maya villages nowadays, but the museum does help contemporary weavers by selling their best work to the public. Even with a commission, the prices asked are extremely low: each tag speaks of the cheapness of Indian labor.

The Cakchiquels, who number about six hundred thousand, are the third largest Maya group in Guatemala (after the Quichés and the Mams). They were originally part of the Quiché kingdom, but broke away and founded their own state about fifty years before the Spanish conquest. The ancient Cakchiquels had a deep sense of history, expressed in their *Annals*, which read much like England's Anglo-Saxon *Chronicle*. The nobles who survived the conquest, the plagues, and Alvarado's terrible extortions kept up the record, writing Maya in the Spanish alphabet and dating events in both the Christian calendar and the tzolkin, until "the month of April, the day 4 Knife . . . the year 1604."[6] The manuscript ends with a prophetic statement: "This is our genealogy, which shall not be lost, because we know our beginning and shall not forget our ancestors."[7]

The paintings of Curuchich (1891–1969) and his descendants have the same defiantly historical quality. Curuchich began painting in the 1930s and was "discovered" during the Arbenz years. Art connoisseurs called his style "primitive" in the usual artistic sense of naïveté and candor; but the Cakchiquel painters applied their own meaning to the word: for them *primitivismo* is nothing less than the evocation and recapture of their past.[8]

The paintings portray Cakchiquel life as it was before the recent upheavals. Curuchich lived in the town of Comalapa, about forty miles west of Guatemala City. Even the latest work by his heirs shows Comalapa as it was before the 1976 earthquake and subsequent violence. Adobe walls and neat tiled roofs that fell are still there in the pictures; men and women still wear styles of dress and adornment that have disappeared with modern influence. Elaborate religious and community rituals are frequent themes—some of them seldom performed since all things Indian became suspect in the eyes of the authorities.

One canvas at the museum shows the archetypal event of the conquest. On top of a great volcano the king of Quiché and the hero Tecún Umán are slain by Pedro de Alvarado. Another figure is weeping; there is a simple caption, misspelled in childish letters: *Brujo Yorando*, "the Sorcerer Weeps." Indeed he weeps: he weeps for the failure of the old religion—the intricate spells, the impeccable astrology, the appropriate garments, the powers of the *nawales* (animal guardians)—to save the Maya from the sharp blades of the Cross.

Not long afterward, Pedro de Alvarado burned the Cakchiquels' capital and pursued them to Comalapa:

One year and one month had passed since [Alvarado] razed [our city], when the Castilians came to Chij Xot [Comalapa]. On the day 1 Rain [April 8, 1527] our slaughter by the Castilians began. They were fought

by the people, and they made war against us for a long
time. Death struck us again, but not one of the towns
paid the tribute.[9]

Almost exactly 453 years later, in March 1980, there was
again killing at Comalapa: the bodies of thirty-nine Indians
were found in a mass grave in a ravine.[10]

12 Ik

At the Popol Vuh Museum (which has little to do with the
famous Quiché book of that name) the conquest is remembered in a different way. At one end of the gallery there's a room
occupied by the characters of the Quiché *Conquest Dance*, an
Indian musical drama that tells the story of Maya defeat in
highland Guatemala. As in the Cakchiquel paintings, events
are represented with the symmetry of myth, and the characters are not historical personages so much as archetypes.

The room is dark, twinkling with sequins and coins sewn
on dusty fabrics the colors of blood, earth, sky, and fire. The
papier-mâché bodies are hidden by the costumes, but their
attitudes, meant to convey movement, are cretinous and
pained, as if stunted by four centuries of malnutrition and
suffering. This is presumably unconscious, the work of a
Ladino curator presenting Indians as his people see them: little
brown automata driven by obscure instincts and obsessions.
The figures remind one of Belsen victims, somehow mum-
mified and covered with their ethnic finery for the amusement
of the master race.

The masks are vivid, rigid with expressions of Maya valor
and Spanish greed, as if the dominant emotions of a lifetime
have been bared in rigor mortis. This characterization is inten-
tional—the work of Indian mask makers—and what a tale
these faces tell. Here are the Maya heroes, King Quiché and
Tecún Umán, attired in their splendid battledress and backed

by personified forces of the Mesoamerican pantheon: Ahitz the
Wizard; Balam the Jaguar; Huitzilzil Dzunún the Humming-
bird.

> Tecún: For I do not wish to turn Christian,
>   Nor to be baptized,
>   And I would rather die
>   Than renounce my faith.
>   Tell all this to Don Pedro de Alvarado. . . .
>   Oh! Wake, my country, wake,
>   And from your volcanoes hurl fire,
>   Burn and destroy the conqueror
>   Who comes to put us in chains. . . .[11]

Against them are Pedro de Alvarado and his men: gargoyle
faces of cruelty and lust. In the background meekly stand the
daughters of the Quiché king, known as Malinches. Their
name comes from Malintzin, Cortés's Indian mistress, interpreter, and spy in the conquest of Mexico. But here the meaning is somewhat different: these women are not voluntary
quislings but victims of war, soon to be raped and impregnated
by Alvarado and his men, to become the dishonored mothers of
mestizo Guatemala.

The *Conquest Dance* is still performed each year in many
highland towns and villages, especially around Quetzaltenango, where the first major battles took place. There are different versions, but the portrayal of the duel between Alvarado and
Tecún Umán, which is the core of all the plays, is astonishingly
similar to a Quiché history written down circa 1550 and not
rediscovered until modern times:

> In the year one thousand five hundred and twenty-four
> there came the Adelantado Don Pedro Alvarado, after
> having conquered Mexico and all those lands. . . .
>   And on the next day a great captain called Tecum
> [Tecún Umán] was sent . . . and the Spaniards began
> fighting the ten thousand Indians which this Captain
> Tecum brought with him. . . . They fought for three
> hours and the Spaniards killed many Indians. . . .
>   Then Captain Tecum launched himself into the

air, for he had come transformed into an eagle, covered in [quetzal] plumes that grew from within himself. . . . He had wings that also sprouted from his body and he wore three crowns, one of gold, one of pearls, and one of diamonds and emeralds. Captain Tecum charged intending to kill the Adelantado, who came on horse-back, and he lunged at the horse to strike the Adelantado, and he cut off the horse's head with a lance. It was not a lance of steel, but of little [obsidian] mirrors, and the captain did this by sorcery.

And when he saw that it was not the Adelantado who had died but the horse, he turned and flew up, so as to swoop down and kill the Adelantado. But then the Adelantado guarded himself with his lance and he speared Captain Tecum through the middle. . . .

And afterwards the Adelantado called all his soldiers to come and see the beauty of the Quetzal Indian. And he told his soldiers then that he had never seen an Indian so gallant, so lordly, and so bedecked in such beautiful quetzal plumes, not in Mexico, nor in Tlaxcala, nor in any part of the nations he had conquered. And for that reason the Adelantado declared that this town should henceforth be called Quetzaltenango [Quetzal Citadel].[12]

Evening. David arrives, trailing bags and boxes and camera equipment. He's a big man, unconscious of his boundaries, like an overgrown toddler—smudged glasses on askew, balding wisps of hair all over his face.

"Good to see you, mate." (He was educated in England and speaks an odd mixture of Canadian and London East End.) He opens a bag; a cascade of papers, books, and underwear spills over the bed and onto the floor.

"Somewhere in this lot there's a letter for you from Janice." David fumbles in another bag; out falls a bottle of Jack Daniel's whisky, a shaving kit in a plastic bag, some socks, and rolls of film. "Let me see those . . . damn, they're already exposed. Must have left the new film behind. No, here it is." Finally, the letter. "Why don't you read that while I get sorted out." He finds glasses in the bathroom and pours us each a large shot of whisky.

"I've got it all planned out," he says. "We'll rent a car and drive up to northern Quiché and Huehuetenango. I'm doing a project on the Maya—you know, cultural survival and all that. I want to meet a daykeeper."

"A what?"

"You mean, here you are, a lapsed archaeologist and you don't know what a daykeeper is? It's all in these books." He starts rummaging in the pile of reading material.

"How did you get hold of these? These are University of Toronto library books."

"Of course they are. We have an arrangement—we can take stuff out for research. I just went in there to the Guatemala shelves and took everything that looked interesting."

It's quite a collection: several recent titles by prominent anthropologists, a decrepit original edition of Stephens and Catherwood that should have been put in the rare book room fifty years ago, the new translation of the *Popol Vuh* by Dennis Tedlock, which I haven't yet seen. In fact there's a lot I haven't seen. David continues:

"There are these guys who keep the old Maya calendar—days and numbers and what-have-you—they're sort of astrologers." He picks up one of the books and waves it triumphantly. "This fellow here, Tedlock, he got one of them to help him make a new translation of the *Popol Vuh*, in fact he became an apprentice and learned to be a daykeeper himself!" David is excited, gesturing wildly, glass in one hand, *Popol Vuh* in the other, like a Bible thumper conducting a mass baptism. Drops of whisky are flying all over the room. "I want to find one of these chaps and ask him if he's passing his knowledge along."

"But, David, people don't just gab about stuff like that. It probably took Tedlock months of painstaking ethnological research—living in a Maya village, eating their food, learning their language, drinking gallons of *aguardiente*—before he got any hard information. Anyway, I've been told these calendar experts are getting rare; the whole thing was on the verge of dying out even before the civil war."

"We'll see, I have amazing luck whenever I go on a field

trip. I have a feeling I'm going to be lucky. Did I ever tell you it was me who broke that scandal about cooking oil in Spain? Sold it to the *Guardian* and the *New York Times*. Soon as you've finished with your lady wife's letter, let's get something to eat and then check out some bars. I'm sure there won't be much nightlife up in the Quiché."

8:00 P.M. David flags down a taxi. "How much to take us around, show us a bit of the city, and leave us in a good bar?" The taxi driver quotes a surprisingly low price, then adds as an explanation: "*¡Mi taxi es feo*"—he laughs uproariously, exposing two gold teeth and one black one—"*pero barato!*" ("My taxi is rotten, but cheap.") He's driving possibly the last Austin in Guatemala City. David sprawls in the front seat; the cabbie has trouble changing gears around his knee.

"What do you think about Belize?" David asks in his interviewer's voice. (Lord! Not *that* question.)

"*¡Belice es nuestro!*" ("Belize is ours!") says the cabbie, repeating a formula learned by rote in all Guatemalan schools.

"What if the British gave Guatemala some money for the road they should have built and left it at that?"

"*¡Belice es nuestro!*"

"Yes, but Belize has been independent three years now. Don't you think it's a bit late? Couldn't Guatemala pursue its claim with Britain and leave Belize alone?"

"You are right, señores, but the answer will still be no!"

"Why do you say that?"

"Because we Guatemalans love a fight!"

"But you're driving a British car."

"*¡Sí, mi taxi es feo!*"

13 Akbal

Akbal: Darkness; a bad day; and I'm not feeling well.

Last night I drank something called "Guatemalan scotch," and we ate hamburgers at a dive called, I think, *La Caverna de la Carne* (The Meat Cave). It was highly recommended by the taxi driver: "This is a good place, a fine place, señores. Excellent food, beautiful girls—you've made a very good choice." I remember an absurdly fat woman dancing naked on a stage in the middle of a basement room, her cellulite illuminated like a gibbous moon.

We staggered to several other places in Zones 9 and 10. The young rich were there: expensive cars and motorcycles, extravagant clothes, fistfuls of uncounted quetzals for drinks and admissions to discos. (Carelessness with money is an essential element of macho display.) Beggars—cripples, young Indian women with babies on their backs, old men, boys—formed a ragged semicircle in the shadows beyond each bright and frantic doorway. Sometimes someone would throw them a coin; most often they were ignored.

1 Kan

Sunday. The hangover has gone, but an upset stomach remains. David goes out to take photographs. I stay in with the *Popol Vuh*.

2 Chicchan

Afternoon. A brief tour of Guatemala City.

Near the airport there's a curious monument which, if the

inscription (in Spanish and Quiché) can be believed, was "erected by the indigenous race to commemorate their liberation by Decree Law 1995." It has an oval platform with a flat roof supported on plain tubular columns: closer in spirit to concrete Parthenons than anything in the native architectural tradition. Decree 1995 was the abolition of debt peonage by Ubico in 1934, on the face of it a worthy deed. But it was followed immediately by enactment of Decree 1996, a vagrancy law compelling peasants with little or no land to work for employers a minimum of 100 or 150 days per year.[13] Yet again, coercion, not fair wages, was used to extract labor from the Indians; the "liberated" indigenous race now had to carry passbooks, regularly checked by the police. And in 1943 Ubico gave landlords the right to shoot poachers and trespassers—a good way to get rid of Indians with ancient rights on the property.

There's a statue to Tecún Umán at a traffic junction. No one knows what the Quiché hero looked like, but I doubt whether this expressionist blend of Achilles and Buck Rogers does him justice.

Outside the Camino Real Hotel, where rooms cost U.S.$100 a night, a singing, flag-waving, firework-throwing crowd has gathered. It's a very well dressed crowd, strictly Ladino: a rally for Jorge Carpio Nicolle, owner of the newspaper *El Gráfico* and presidential candidate of the UCN (Union of the National Center). Girls in tight T-shirts and baseball caps are chanting the name displayed on their chests: "*¡Carpio! ¡Carpio! ¡Carpio!*" He still hopes to win the presidency despite coming a poor second to Vinicio Cerezo in the first round held earlier this month. The word is that he *must* win or be ruined— he's mortgaged his newspaper building to the Army Bank for election funds.

The options were in fact little more than a choice between Center Right and Far Right, but from the viewpoint of the latter, Cerezo's Christian Democrats—roughly equivalent to Britain's "wet" Tories or the American Democratic party—are dangerous radicals on the fringe of the political spectrum. This is, in a way, perfectly true: the half of the political spectrum that in most countries exists to the left of Christian Democrats

is exiled, or dead, or fighting in the mountains. Three hundred
CD officials and countless ordinary party members have been
murdered since 1954. Cerezo himself has survived several
attempts on his life. For years he never slept two consecutive
nights in the same house. On one occasion he was attacked in
his car outside party headquarters; afterward he counted
thirty-seven bullet holes; luckily the car was armored. Cerezo
admits that his main ambition is to finish his term and hand
over power to an elected successor: something achieved only
once before in Guatemalan history. Like Arévalo, he is well
aware that there will be a shadow president holding a machine
gun to his head; and like Méndez Montenegro, who headed the
so-called "third government of the revolution" from 1966 to
1970, he will have to strike a deal with the military, a deal that
may make him impotent. (Poor Méndez Montenegro ended up
being satirized as *El Adobe*, "The Mud Brick," for the vigor of
his democratic opening. The would-be revolutionary presided
helplessly over the bloody campaigns of Arana, who then succeeded him.) "If I get elected I must do many things," Cerezo
said recently. "Each will provoke a coup."[14]

This election is a study in the art of the possible. The army
and extreme Right have been discredited abroad by the crescendo of repression, and at home by an economy beggared to
win the war and line the pockets of corrupt generals. They hope
to elect someone who will cloak the status quo in enough
respectability that American aid and arms can flow in. They
think Carpio might be that person; they are less sure about
Cerezo. The populace (insofar as one can generalize in such a
divided nation) hopes to elect the most liberal candidate who
has a chance of survival. In the first round there was a Social
Democrat—recently returned from Costa Rica, where he fled
after his party's founder was killed in 1979—but he received
few votes because Guatemalans have learned the futility of
electing dead men.

Also eliminated in the first round, but far from a spent
force, was the sinister figure of Mario Sandoval, candidate of
the National Liberation Movement (MLN), founded by himself
and other Castillo Armas cohorts in Honduras before the coup
of 1954. Sandoval has always represented the landed oligarchy,

the military hard-liners, and fanatical anti-communists. He has openly boasted of founding La Mano Blanca, first of the systematic death squads. (White hands were painted on the doors of suspected leftists; within a few days the suspect would be killed, tortured, and/or disappeared.)[15] Sandoval once said he thought it might be necessary to kill half a million Guatemalans (more than 6 percent of the population) to "pacify" the country.[16] He is equally frank about his ideology: "I am a Fascist, and I have modelled my party on the Spanish Falange."[17] His extremism apparently began when he was beaten up by left-wing police during the heated Arbenz years. Such attacks were relatively rare then, but Sandoval has been exacting revenge ever since, perpetuating the cycle of violence in which Guatemala, like a victim of child abuse, seems hopelessly trapped.

"¡Carpio! ¡Carpio! ¡Carpio!" the crowd chants, but Guatemala is hung with posters of Cerezo's face and the words ¡YA TENEMOS PRESIDENTE! (WE ALREADY HAVE A PRESIDENT!) As it turns out, they are right.

Chapter 8

3 Cimi

We went to Budget this morning and were given the same Mitsubishi I took to Quiriguá—better the devil you know.

Cimi: Death. For the first time on this journey, I'll be entering Guatemala's Indian heartland, where the recent fighting was most intense. In these highlands stretching north and west of Guatemala City to the borders of Mexico live approximately four million Indians—half the population of Guatemala and about three-quarters of all the Maya in the modern world.

I have many questions about the war. How much was it a genuine Maya uprising; how much a Ladino conflict with Indians dragooned into fighting on both sides? Did the Guatemalan military follow a deliberate policy of genocide? How far were the interests of the Indians and the revolutionary Left compatible? How far can one assume that the many different Maya groups even share a common interest? Has the failure of the insurrection seriously damaged the Maya, as many believe; or has it brought a new Indian awareness, transcending ancient rivalry and isolation?

Generalizations (mine included) about what Indians want, or how they behave, and about Guatemalan culture and politics, must be taken as broad impressions that resolve themselves into coherent images only when viewed from afar. The closer one gets to any problem in Guatemala, the more one's

162

analysis begins to crack and shatter into fragments of irreconcilable detail. There is little consistency in the interpretations of others: each has seen what he wanted to see. One historian confessed to me that he no longer thought there was any such thing as reality in Guatemala: "People ask me what my sources are and I tell them rumor. You listen to rumors and you pick the one you like best." It wasn't merely a joke.

On our way out of town we had a quick look at Kaminalhuyú, "Hill of the Dead." These ruins, the most important Maya city in Preclassic times, are now a forlorn collection of adobe mounds rapidly disappearing beneath a suburb of Guatemala City. You turn off Roosevelt Boulevard and find them behind a Burger King. Here the early highland Maya developed styles in architecture and sculpture that were later transplanted to Tikal. There was strong influence from Teotihuacán: Kaminalhuyú thrived and depended on the Mexican axis, and soon faded after the fall of that first great city in the Valley of Mexico.

The location of the modern Mexican and Guatemalan capitals within walking distance of these two ancient ones says a lot about enduring patterns in Mesoamerican politics. Those in Washington who suffer from domino nightmares should be comforted by this: Mexico has four times been united by imperial cities in its central highlands; Central America has always been a region of squabbling city-states. The political current flows south not north. The idea that Nicaragua, or El Salvador, or Guatemala might spread some ideological contagion northward through Mexico to the gringo empire is the most ludicrous paranoia. Unfortunately for Central America, the United States suffers from what Carlos Fuentes has called "unabashed historical amnesia."[1]

It was about eleven o'clock when we left the Hill of the Dead and began climbing the serpentine Pan American Highway. David was driving. I felt vulnerable in the passenger seat, which has no belts.

He said, "What I like about these rental cars is that you can drive the hell out of them. I feel so"—he took both hands from the wheel and made expansive gestures in the limited space— "so *free* down here, away from all those petty regulations up in Canada."

Guatemalan traffic obeys no lanes: the vehicles follow anarchic trajectories like strands in a loosely woven belt. Cars build up behind each overloaded lorry and bus, the knots, as it were, in the weave. David passed them all.

"You have to watch out for these Latin drivers," he shouted above a braying of angry horns, "they're highly capricious."

The road slices through cliffs of volcanic ash and aggregate; the smooth canyon walls are neatly painted with the propaganda of recent regimes: ¡TRABAJEMOS! NO CRITIQUEMOS A GUATEMALA. (WE SHALL WORK! WE SHALL NOT CRITICIZE GUATEMALA.)

"That means *you'll* work," David said, taking his hands from the wheel again to point like Lord Kitchener at peasants walking on both sides of the road, "and *you* won't criticize Guatemala."

After a long climb, the road straightens and runs along the bottom of a vee between wooded hills. At the end of the vee rears the perfect cone of Volcan Agua, framed like the foresight of a rifle, with a gun barrel of straight black tarmac running toward it. The sky is clear, a deep steel blue, and the volcano wears a wreath of vapor that forms at the summit and streams from its leeward side the way a comet's tail flees from the sun. Add to this the bottle green fields of the plateau to which we are descending, and you have a composition that no artist could possibly get away with. In oils, watercolor, or even a photograph it would be the most overwrought cliché; in reality it is pure exaltation.

We stop the car and get out. The squalor and pain and menace of human Guatemala now seem far behind, as if they belonged to an unhappy childhood. I think of what someone once offered as a reason, or at least an excuse, for human life: consciousness is the universe contemplating itself. And for a moment of unmeasured length the cruel experiment of man seems worthwhile, and I feel thankful to someone or something for enlarging the brains of apes.

We bypass Antigua, where we plan to spend the night, and follow the *panamericana* to Tecpan Guatemala, Alvarado's first capital.

The 1976 earthquake and subsequent man-made violence have given Tecpan a mean, dirty look. Not even the rainbow colors of a wedding procession can dispel an air of hopelessness in the town; the Cakchiquel inhabitants still seem sunk in the despair that overtook them when they realized their mistake in allying themselves with the Spaniards against the Quichés and Tzutuhils. The disunity of the Maya is at once their greatest strength and greatest weakness. They could not be subdued like the Aztecs by the destruction of a single city, nor paralyzed like the Incas by the ransom of a god-king. But their internecine squabbles blinded them to the Spanish threat until it was too late.

A gravel road leads through some wheat fields, and then climbs a mile or two into pine woods where the ruins of Iximché, the Cakchiquels' original city, still stand. The squalor and heat of the town are washed away by the resinous mountain air, and we forget the harshness of life in Guatemala until we meet an Indian family on the road. Walking in front is a boy who looks about twelve, though he's probably sixteen. He has a huge bundle of firewood on his back, secured by a *mecapal,* the forehead tumpline that was the only harness of ancient Mesoamerica. Behind the boy are his mother and father, each with a tree trunk balanced on the head. The timbers must weigh a hundred pounds apiece, but the woman and man both find the energy to change their grimaces to smiles, and wish us *buenos días.*

IXIMCHÉ

Noon. The altitude is almost seven thousand feet. A Cakchiquel family in charge of the ruins lives beside the entrance to
the parking lot. A little girl of five or six laboriously opens the
heavy gates. Her mother sells us tickets through the window of
their home, and her father walks with us to the edge of the
ruins, scanning the ground for litter. The site is spotlessly
clean. No other visitors are here.

Iximché is a tranquil park, about a mile long and up to a
quarter mile wide. Remains of temples, palace platforms, and
two ballcourts stand whitely among well-mown lawns. Stands
of ocote and Caribbean pine cover what were once suburbs and
the steep cliffs protecting the Cakchiquel stronghold. A raven's
croak echoes in the woods. The architecture, dating from
shortly before the Spanish conquest, bears little resemblance
to that of the Classic period. The pyramids here are only about
thirty feet high; there are no vaulted rooms, no stelae recording
dynastic history and the ponderous turning of the wheels of
time. Instead one has a succession of courtyards, where the
head families of three or four important lineages lived. Their
palaces were built of wood, plaster, and thatch on top of stone-
faced platforms covered in painted stucco. Walls between these
quadrangles reflect the constant power struggles mentioned in
the *Annals of the Cakchiquels:* palace revolts and military
coups were apparently as common in ancient Guatemala as
they are today. The total population was about ten thousand
people, a tenth the size of Tikal or Teotihuacán, and possibly
only a twentieth of Aztec Mexico City.[2]

If one forbears making comparisons with the Classic
period, Iximché in its heyday was still a striking place. The
whole hilltop was paved with lime plaster. Jaguars, monkeys,
serpents, gods, and warriors paraded in bright colors along the
walls of the principal buildings, inside and out. To judge from
fragments that survive, the mural style was not very different
from that of the Mexican painted books: stiff but energetic,
with costume detail, iconography, and symbolic use of color
taking precedence over realism.

Highland Guatemala, now the richest repository of living Maya culture, had been a backwater during late Classic times. Then, as the Petén cities were being claimed by moss and trees, warrior groups from the Gulf lowlands moved into highland Guatemala and Yucatán. The process was undoubtedly complex, similar to the movement of "barbarian" peoples in Europe after the fall of Rome. And as in Europe, the incursions eventually left a pattern of small nationalities that has endured to this day. The analogy can be taken further: from genealogies in the *Popol Vuh* and other records it is clear that the invaders considered themselves to be wholly or partly of Toltec—i.e., Mexican—origin. But after they had staked out their conquest-states they gradually absorbed the culture of their subjects, just as the Franks, Visigoths, and Lombards became Latinized by the remnants of Rome.

Toltec forebears of the Quiché ruling class probably entered Guatemala about A.D. 1250, and quickly imposed themselves as warlords on Maya-speaking groups.[3] Like the Norman conquerors of England, they spoke a different language, but gradually forgot it and learned Quiché. Under an energetic ruler named K'ucumatz (an alias of the ubiquitous god-hero, Quetzalcóatl) the Quiché state began to expand. By 1450 it covered most of what is now highland Guatemala and parts of the Pacific coast.[4] It was a loose imperial confederation, held together by marriage alliances, religious ties, and military threats. But such Mexican-style imperialism didn't triumph over Maya Balkanism for long: local patterns reasserted themselves, and dissident groups began to drift away. Only fifty years before the Spanish invasion, the Cakchiquels seceded and founded their own state here at Iximché, with the bitter words of Quicab, the Quiché king, ringing in their ears: "May my curse go with you in your triumph."[5]

The Cakchiquels and Quichés fought minor battles right up to the eve of the Spanish conquest. The situation was further complicated by the rise of the Aztecs. The expanding empire of Mexico had established a garrison on the Pacific coast by the year 1500; and in 1510 the embattled Quiché king—faced with endless revolts and a large delegation of threatening Aztec diplomats—decided to put himself under the tutelage of Moctezuma.

In 1521 the Mesoamerican balance of power was overturned by Cortés's conquest of Mexico and by the smallpox plague, which killed many of the Maya leaders:

> On the day 12 Death [April 26, 1521] the king Hunyg, your great-grandfather, died. Two days later died also our father, the Ahpop Achí Balam, your grandfather, oh, my sons! Our grandfathers and fathers died together. . . . We were children and we were alone; none of our fathers had been spared.[6]

The Quichés, well informed of events in Mexico, began trying to organize a united front against the impending Spanish invasion. Many groups joined them for the disastrous series of battles near Quetzaltenango, but the Cakchiquels declined, having already sent messengers to Cortés.[7] After the death of Tecún Umán the Quichés lured Alvarado and his men to their capital, K'umarcaah, with the alleged intent of trapping them there and setting fire to the city. Alvarado discovered the "plot," if such it was, and burned three of the Quiché rulers alive. After that he called on the Cakchiquels to help in a mopping-up campaign. In April 1524, Alvarado moved to Iximché and made it the capital of Spanish Guatemala.

The Cakchiquels soon discovered the true nature of the incubus they had allowed into their midst. Within days Alvarado was threatening them with the same atrocities he had used against their enemies:

> Tonatiuh [Alvarado] then asked for one of the daughters of the king and the lords gave her to Tonatiuh. Later Tonatiuh asked the kings for riches. He wanted them to give him heaps of [precious] metal, their vessels and their crowns. And as they did not bring them immediately, Tonatiuh became angry with the kings and said to them:
> "Why have you not brought me the metal? If you

do not bring all the wealth of the lineages, I will burn
you and I will hang you. . . ."[8]

Rather than submit to this extortion, the Cakchiquels
fled: "On the day 4 Death . . . we scattered beneath the trees,
under the vines, oh! my sons."[9]

So began five years of guerrilla war against the Spaniards.
In 1526 Alvarado burned Iximché, and soon afterward abandoned Tecpan Guatemala. But by 1530 all the Cakchiquel lords
had surrendered, and the horrors of war were replaced by those
of slavery:

> During this year terrible tributes were imposed. Gold
> was delivered to Tonatiuh; four hundred men and four
> hundred women were delivered to go and wash for
> gold. All the people extracted gold. Four hundred men
> and four hundred women were delivered by order of
> Tonatiuh to work at Pangán [Ciudad Vieja] in building
> the city of the Lord. All these things, all this, we saw,
> oh! my sons. . . .[10]

These things have not been forgotten by Guatemala's
Indians. In February 1980, just two weeks after the Spanish
embassy massacre, a predominantly Indian organization called
the Peasant Unity Committee (CUC) convened a meeting here
at these ruins and issued an extraordinary document called the
Declaration of Iximché.

> We the indigenous peoples of Guatemala declare and
> denounce before the world: more than four centuries
> of discrimination, denial, repression, exploitation,
> and massacres committed by the foreign invaders and
> continued by their most savage and criminal descen-
> dants to the present day. . . . The massacre at the Span-
> ish embassy is not an isolated case but part of a chain
> of killings. The suffering of our people has come down
> through the centuries, since 1524, when there arrived
> in these lands the assassin and criminal Pedro de
> Alvarado.

The declaration then lists the slaying of Indians during the conquest, the burning alive of the Quiché kings, the massacre at Comalapa in 1527, and a rash of hangings in 1540–41. It continues with the slavery and exploitation, remembering the Cakchiquel king, Belehé Qat, who dropped dead while being forced to wash for gold. It cites the principal Maya uprisings from early colonial times to the present, and gives the Indian view of the Guatemalan "nation":

> And so came 1821; the sons of the invaders say they achieved independence. . . . But what happened on that date was that the wealth and the dominion were no longer shared with the kings of Spain. . . . And to be able to carry on stealing lands and manpower from the Indians, those rich criminals created the national army. . . .
>
> And they go on killing our people in so many ways, by keeping us hungry, by paying us miserable wages in the factories, on the farms; by cheating us in the weighing of coffee and cotton [in piecework], and by poisoning us in the cotton fields [with pesticides]. . . .
>
> And they still go on trying to fool us with folklore festivals, like the Day of Tecún Umán, the Day of the [Native] Race . . . giving little medals, diplomas, little handshakes and smiles to professional performers and Indian beauty queens. . . .[11]

The origins of the most recent cycle of violence go back to the aftermath of the 1954 coup. As soon as Castillo Armas was firmly in command of the country he began to undo the reforms of the previous ten years. He returned the land distributed by Arbenz to its former owners, repealed the 1946 constitution, and took away the vote from illiterates, thus disenfranchising three-quarters of the electorate, especially Indians.[12] He banned all existing political parties, peasant leagues, and labor confederations. And he put Ubico's infamous secret police chief back in his old job.[13] This was the nature of the "free" government extolled by Richard Nixon, a government that had promised to "do more for the people in two years, than the communists were able to do in ten."

The Americans poured in hundreds of millions of dollars in aid and investment, trying to make that hollow promise come true. The economy did well enough, continuing the progress of the Arévalo and Arbenz years. Between 1960 and 1980, Guatemala had the highest GNP in Central America and the third-highest per capita income (behind Panama and Costa Rica). But little if any of this trickled down to the base of the social pyramid. Guatemala continued to have the highest rate of infant mortality in Central America; four out of five peasant children were (and are) malnourished.[14]

To maintain this "showcase of capitalist development"[15] the United States gave more and more military aid. In return the CIA used Guatemala as the training ground for the Bay of Pigs fiasco and other ventures. A revolutionary Left emerged in the 1960s. Like the Right, it ignored the Indian population as apathetic, politically naïve, and largely irrelevant to Guatemalan politics. The guerrilla bands operating in the mainly Ladino departments of Izabal and Petén were of the Guevara *foco* school; and, as in Bolivia, they were easily destroyed with help from the Green Berets.

That failure taught the Ladino Left that the Right could only be challenged with help from the Indian majority. In the 1970s, remnants of the old guerrilla groups moved into the highlands and began forging social links with Indians for the first time. They learned to overcome their disdain for the conquered race, and brought the message that class struggle should transcend ethnic boundaries. They spoke of a new Guatemala where there would be enough land for all and an end to discrimination. The Indians might not have been receptive to these overtures had they not been suffering from greater land hunger and repression than ever before.

During the 1960s and early 1970s, Indians had been forming cooperatives and community organizations with help from foreign aid workers and progressive priests. These movements, largely innocent of wider politics, attracted the attention of right-wing death squads, who saw them as a communist challenge to the power of Ladino landowners. In 1975 the MANO death squad sent the following letter to leaders of cooperatives in Guatemala City:

> We know of your PROCOMMUNIST attitude. . . . We know by experience that all labour organizations and cooperatives always fall into the power of the Communist Leaders infiltrated into them. We have the organization and the force to prevent this from occurring again. . . . There are THIRTY THOUSAND CLANDESTINE PEASANT GRAVES TO BEAR WITNESS. . . .[16]

Priests and co-op leaders began to disappear; Indians active in local politics were killed or run out of town. After the 1976 earthquake, reconstruction organizations also became death squad targets. It was in this climate that the Peasant Unity Committee emerged, attracting a large membership under mainly Indian leaders. For the first time Indians were able to transcend the linguistic, ethnic, and historical divisions among themselves; they also began to work on an equal footing with poor Ladinos. Many took part in strikes, marches, and meetings such as the one at Iximché. As all avenues for peaceful change seemed blocked, some began to consider joining or supporting the guerrillas.

ANTIGUA

At its height, when it was second only to Mexico and Lima, this "Very Noble and Very Loyal City of Santiago of the Knights of Guatemala" had sixty thousand inhabitants and forty churches. Now it has the look of a partly inhabited museum: chunks of earthquake-shattered masonry lie like cubist sculptures among ornamental flowerbeds. The highland Maya had wisely avoided using masonry vaults; even the kings lived in wooden palaces. But the Spaniards' belief in the superiority of their gods and civilization prevented them from making any concession to local conditions. Wood wasn't good enough for the Knights of Santiago: they built their Moorish colonnades and Roman arches, usually of brick and rubble hidden by stucco facades, and they doggedly rebuilt them after every quake. Gradually, however, they made the towers less lofty, the vaults less spacious, the columns thicker and shorter, until they arrived at a species of dwarf architecture. The features of the full-sized adult remain but they are compressed and coarsened. The result is strangely anachronistic: Norman proportions encrusted with baroque conceits.

Supper in a café named after Doña Luisa Xicotencatl, Alvarado's Tlaxcalan "wife," who gave birth to Guatemala's first mestiza while her husband was burning the Quiché kings at K'umarcaah. The Spaniards' Mexican auxiliaries appear, if at all, as a footnote in history, but it's clear from the tremendous impact of Nahuatl on Guatemalan placenames that the early Spanish conquest-state was really a hybrid Ibero-Mexican enterprise—a continuation, in native eyes, of Mexican interventions in the Maya area since the time of the Toltecs and Teotihuacán. All these -tenangos, and -tlans, and -tepeques and -tecas are Nahuatl words.

Antigua today is full of gringos. Language schools and foreign missionary organizations base themselves here to avoid the noise and dirt of Guatemala City. You see large blond gringas, huipiles tucked into bulging blue jeans, drinking beer and enjoying the relentless courtship of Ladino men half their size.

A pale man with hairy ears sits hunched over a copy of the *Miami Herald*. There's a missionary *type*, as conspicuous as any hippie. His polyester shirt and complete lack of physical grace mark him as some sort of American fundamentalist. I wonder how the Church of the Word is doing since the fall of Ríos Montt. Guatemalans are bold enough now to put signs in their windows: WE ARE CATHOLICS. WE DO NOT ACCEPT PROTESTANT HOUSE CALLS AND PROPAGANDA.

4 Manik :

10:00 A.M. To Lake Atitlán today, another tourist resort. We'll spend the night at Panajachel, sometimes called "Gringo-tenango"—one of the few good jokes in Guatemala.

We turn off the main road at Patzicía, a Cakchiquel town, and take the old route through the hills. Forty-seven Indians were massacred here by the army in 1944, an event recalled in the Declaration of Iximché. At Patzún, another Cakchiquel town farther down the road, the wounds are more recent. In the first seven months of this year the army or a death squad (probably "off-duty" army and police officers) has been practicing here the less dramatic technique of "serial massacre." Sixty Indians have disappeared, a few at a time. Two were found floating in the town well with their throats cut. The killings have left 45 widows and 146 orphans.[17]

The road joins a paved highway from the coast. We pick up speed and emerge from behind a chain of mountains. The lake appears suddenly, far below, kidney shaped, silver and finely rippled, with dark cloud shadows sailing across it. The water is twelve miles long and six wide, and the walls that surround it are themselves volcanoes—some still active—joined by old lava flows and sweeping hills. The Indians consider the Atitlán basin the navel of earth *and* sky, for as one enters it the sky becomes defined by its rim of smoking cones.[18]

The magnificence disappears behind the restaurants and concrete hotels of Panajachel. At the beach, plump Gua-temalans from the city are struggling in and out of bathing costumes. There's even a blond windsurfer on the lake. Hip-pies, like remnants of an archaic tribe, congregate with guitars and flutes beneath a tree, so bedizened in native costume that it would be hard to distinguish them from Cakchiquels and Tzutuhils, were it not for the men wearing women's blouses, and the women in men's pantaloons. Where do you see hippies now but in the Third World?

This is clearly no place to linger. David and I strike a bargain with a young Cakchiquel boatman to take us across the lake to Santiago Atitlán, a Tzutuhil town on the south shore. Basilio Chicbal is about twenty-five with a broad smile and good Spanish. He wears rubber boots, jeans, a red shirt, and a cowboy hat; the only ethnic item in his dress is a broad woven belt. Basilio used to be a fisherman, but now he makes most of his living from tourism.

At the height of the war in 1982, the Organization of the People in Arms (ORPA) controlled much of Lake Atitlán and other rural areas in the Cakchiquel departments of Sololá and Chimaltenango. But the Guatemalan army's harrowing of villages suspected of "subversion," and Ríos Montt's cynical but effective strategy of sending poorly armed Indian militias (under Ladino commanders) into the front line, has succeeded in driving the insurgents back to strongholds on the Pacific side of the volcanoes. ORPA claims to be 90 percent Indian in its membership; its commander-in-chief, however, is a white man—the son of Miguel Angel Asturias, Guatemala's Nobel laureate. Its continuing presence near here has prompted fears that the Tzutuhils are in danger of brutal reprisals. Shortly before I left home, Survival International, a London-based organization for the defense of indigenous peoples, reported that the government had plans to "clean out" Santiago Atitlán and resettle the people in a fortified strategic village.[19] When we're safely on the water I ask Basilio Chicbal if there's been any recent trouble.

"There are still a few boys in the mountains, but down here it's fairly quiet now." His face gives nothing away.

"Have people been moved from Santiago?"

"Not as far as I know. It is *tranquilo* now."

Tranquilo: calm, quiet, peaceful—everywhere you go in Guatemala this is the word you hear. It's peace, but the peace of military occupation, the *pax Ladina*. The war was fought to change the structure of power and ownership in Guatemala. Now, after all the killing and destruction, the best that can be hoped for is a return to the *status quo ante*. That is what *tranquilo* means.

The water is clear and dark, and more than a thousand feet deep. A brisk wind flicks spray from the waves and dashes it in our faces. The midday sun has leached color from the landscape and tarnished the volcanoes with a haze. Anyone who's lived near mountains knows how they approach at dawn and dusk, and hang imminent on moonlit nights. The sun as it climbs humbles them, and they draw away, to wait on the horizon for longer shadows and the flattery of evening light. Here, where one is wholly enclosed, their daily retreat dilates the world. Itzamná of the sky lords it over Itzamná of the earth: the reptilian world-creature loosens his coils and flattens himself to bask beneath his heavenly counterpart.

It takes about forty minutes to cross the open water and then run into a tiny gulf where the town is hidden. We pass some rocky islands.

"There used to be ruins there," Basilio says, "but not since the chalets were built." Among the trees are several holiday cottages that wouldn't look out of place on Lake Huron—the Tzutuhils have sold some of their lakefront to rich Guatemalans and gringos. Holidaymakers water-ski around men fishing from dugout canoes.

"Do you still fish?" I ask Basilio.

"*Ya no vale la pena.*" ("It's not worth the trouble anymore.") He explains that a few years ago some government agency had the bright idea of stocking the lake with black bass. They ate all the crabs and small fish on which the Indians depended for protein, but didn't do well enough to become a substitute.

As soon as we set foot on the rickety jetty, children surround us and begin chanting in soft yet insistent voices, "*Saca foto, un quetzal.*" ("Take a picture, one quetzal.") Spanish from Tzutuhil lips sounds like a languid Italian; and when the kids drop their price to fifty centavos they pronounce *cincuenta* as *chincuenta*. They're all dressed in the local *traje*, girls and boys in purple and white. I try buying peanuts, but this only causes half a dozen other peanut vendors to come running. It's impossible to get free of them. Basilio stays with his boat, not too confident of the treatment a Cakchiquel's property might get if he left it. (Basilio's ancestors destroyed the Tzutuhil fortress and ceremonial center with the help of Pedro de Alvarado.)

Santiago is a terraced town with stone walls and cobbled

streets, roofs of thatch and tile, climbing like a heap of books from the clear black water to a whitewashed church. The adult women wear a long ribbon of narrow handwoven cloth wound round and round the head so that it forms a halo like a reel of tape. (Very similar turbans were the fashion for men at Copán in the Classic period.) The older people are reserved and sullen. They don't approve of the youngsters' behavior and chide them, to little effect. One child, very poor and dirty, asks me for five centavos, and as soon as I reach into my pocket, a dozen others press around until I can hardly move. A little girl is even bold enough to keep patting the pocket where my money is. In desperation we teeter into the church. I take out all my change and hand it to a young Indian woman in charge of the visitors' book; she agrees to share it out among the ones who need it most.

Santiago Atitlán may be far from Panajachel, but the worst effects of tourism are only too apparent. One wonders what can be done. These people are short of land: weavings, peanuts, and photograph opportunities are among the few things they can sell. Nobody wants to see his children begging from gringos, but no one wants his children to go hungry. Tourism exploits the Indian, but the Indian suffers when tourism is withdrawn. The dilemma is one of control, and it will remain unresolved until the larger question of Indian rights in Guatemala is addressed.

When electricity was introduced in 1974, a revealing myth took hold: many Tzutuhils feared that the generators ran on people, and that employees of the electrical company roamed the streets at night looking for Indians to feed the machines. A silly supersition? Or a way of expressing the destructive effect of modernization imposed without local control?[20] Electricity is usually the first—and often the last—development project in rural Latin America. Governments consider it more modern, progressive, and important than things like safe drinking water and sanitation. With it come radios, record players, and television sets; the pace of acculturation and indoctrination accelerates, the attractions of the city and the Ladino way of life are advertized, but infant mortality and disease continue as before.

* * *

The church, built in 1568, is full of ancient and bizarre wooden saints propped against the walls. They are not static or serene, but stooping, writhing, dancing, oozing a glutinous blend of sanctity and pain.

In the Indian towns of Guatemala, saints are cared for by organizations called *cofradías,* or "brotherhoods," which until recently were also the framework of local government. Particular saints were associated with lineages and districts, much like the gods of pre-Columbian times. Though superficially Catholic, the practice was a form of ancestor worship: through the cofradía hierarchies the dead upheld the power of the living elders. Men rose in the cofradías by sponsoring religious festivals at great personal sacrifice and expense; prestige was gained by giving away wealth—the very antithesis of the capitalist ethic. With the reforms of Barrios and subsequent meddlers, Ladino officials were imposed on Indian communities. The cofradías became subordinate to the Ladino state, and were exploited as an unpaid level of government responsible for menial duties and control of Indians.

Even those shreds of authority have since been torn by the onslaught of new religions. The old conservative Catholic church of Guatemala had been quite happy to ignore the idiosyncrasies of the Indians; the archbishop and bishops served the rich, and showed an indifferent tolerance toward the poor. But with the reforms of the 1940s and early 1950s came a desire to purge the church of medieval torpor and put an end to its role as the ideology of the status quo. Energetic young priests were brought from Europe and North America by the Catholic Action movement. As soon as they settled into the villages and learned a bit of Maya, they began to discover that the conversion of the Indians, supposedly concluded in the sixteenth century, had not been a success. Candles were still being burned in caves, stone "idols" were being worshiped on hilltops, prayers were being offered to mountains, and the most important Maya god was not Jehovah or Jesus, but a figure enigmatically called Tiox Mundo or Santo Mundo, "World God" or "Holy Earth."

If these priests had known some archaeology they might have recognized Mundo as Itzamná, the great Lizard House, in his earthly form. He had been given a Spanish title but in other respects he was thoroughly Maya. The idols, caves, rocks, peaks, and springs were manifestations of Mundo/Itzamná, just as they had been in ancient times. Moreover, the shaman-priests—usually the same old men who devoutly looked after the saints and organized the fiestas of the Catholic year—were keeping what they called the Calendar of Mundo, the ancient count of the tzolkin.

Catholic Action was interested in saving souls as well as filling collection boxes; heathen beliefs could no longer be tolerated. "Idols" were smashed, customs denounced, irregular "saints" demoted or expelled. Chief of these in Santiago Atitlán was one called Maximón. The new Catholics said he was merely an effigy of Judas Iscariot, because he resembled the straw Judas figures burned during Holy Week. Experts on the Indians said his name meant San Simón mixed up with *max*, a Maya word for tobacco. (Maximón usually appeared in public with a big cigar between his wooden lips—just like the ancient Death Lords.) To his followers, Maximón was a great many things. He was Saint Andrew; he was Saint Michael, captain of the angels; he was perhaps also Saint Peter, keeper of the keys of heaven (or was he called "Don Pedro" after Pedro de Alvarado?). Maximón was lord of diviners and daykeepers, those who spoke to Holy Earth. He was the lord of sexual matters, and could make barren wombs bear. Maximón watched over wives when husbands were away, but sometimes he slept with them himself. Maximón was the *Mam*, "Grandfather," a name for the Year-Bearer. He was the meeting of opposites, the soul of ambiguity.[21] One thing was clear to Catholic Action: Maximón was not very Christian.

Until 1950 Maximón lived in the cofradía chapel of the Holy Cross. Between fiestas he was kept dismantled, his wooden torso, limbs, masks, and fine clothing all carefully wrapped and stored in a bundle in the roof. But one night a visiting priest and two accomplices broke into the chapel, intent on putting an end to the Tzutuhil "heresy." They

smashed Maximón's head and stole two of his masks or faces—
one of which later turned up in Paris, at the Musée de
l'Homme.[22]

The people of Santiago Atitlán couldn't believe that Maximón had disappeared. Some held that the pope, impressed with
Maximón's power, had summoned him for an audience, but
soon it became clear that there had been foul play. Telegrams
were sent to President Arbenz; the president intervened and a
compromise was found.

Today Maximón seldom enters the church but still lives in
the cofradía of the Holy Cross, where he is served by the most
powerful and respected shaman-priests in Santiago Atitlán. The
church may have become more Christian, but Maximón has
become a rival church.

Chapter 9

5 Lamat

The good weather we've had in the highlands broke today. We left late in the morning from Panajachel and made the steep climb out of the Atitlán basin to Sololá, the department capital. The sky was a gloomy whirlpool and the lake a stippled crucible of molten lead.

CHICHICASTENANGO, Department of El Quiché

Late afternoon. This town has many names. In Quiché it is called Chuwilá, "Above the Nettles," or Tziguan Tinamit, which means "Town Surrounded by Canyons." It may also have been ancient Chaviar, where the Cakchiquels lived before they left the Quiché kingdom.

We get a room at the Hotel Santo Tomás, the finest in town, for about sixteen dollars. There's hot water, colonial-style furniture, even a corner fireplace and a stack of logs. The rooms are arranged around patios full of flowers, stone fountains, and parrots on perches. There are only three or four guests besides ourselves. It should be a delightful place, but now it feels tainted. According to human rights organizations there were fifty-four massacres in El Quiché during 1982 alone; more than three thousand civilians were killed.[1]

Our room looks out on the canyons and the magnificent pine-bristled hills that climb out of them and stride toward the horizon. The cloud has lifted from the western mountains, allowing the sun to throw a weak coppery light on the dark trees. Bright green clearings glow on the hillside wherever a farmer has a patch of young corn. From one of these, on a bluff about a quarter of a mile away, rises a dense coil of smoke that stands like a charmed snake in the chill air. At first I thought it was a fire but as I watch, the bottom of the snake swishes vigorously from side to side, its body gains substance, and it climbs higher and higher until its head is lost in a drift of mist. There is a man amid the coils, swinging a censer and performing odd little steps as he turns to address the directions and the mountaintops: what could he be but a Maya shaman-priest, worshiping at a family shrine, asking the World for a good crop? I notice other plumes of smoke, blue against the dirty clouds, rising from small fields higher up the mountains. Apart from the worshipers, everything is still; one has the feeling of being in an enchanted place, a land of ancient numina.

Supper. They try to cater to the gringo palate. I've ordered shish kebab; it doesn't taste like beef to me, but David insists it's "standard Central American cow."

The waiters are among the few Quiché men who still wear traditional dress. Even the headwaiter, who is Ladino, wears it, but with the bad grace of an Orangeman forced to dress as a bishop. They look strangely like eighteenth-century pirates: black woolen knee britches with slit seams; jackets of the same material embroidered with sunbursts and rich flower designs resembling Canadian Métis work; and a colorful *tzut*, a headcloth like an Afghan turban, with long tassles down the back. The wearers seem to resent this display of ethnicity: the Quichés because they're obliged to prostitute something archaic that should be reserved for solemn occasions; the headwaiter because dressing as an Indian is a daily mortification to his Ladino pride. He is a fat, dyspeptic Falstaff, wearily obsequious to gringos and domineering with subordinates. The real Indians ignore him and speak only Quiché among themselves;

luckily for them he can be heard approaching by his stertorous breath and his leather sandals creaking on the tile floor.

After supper an old man, dressed like the others, comes to play marimba in the patio. These large xylophones are believed by most Guatemalans to be a native instrument, but they probably came from Africa with early slaves. The poor old fellow plays in much the same way that the waiters wear their clothes. He has no audience but us and a large red macaw that heckles him unmercifully.

Relics of foreign influence on the Indians during colonial times—such as the Quiché men's costume and the marimba—have led some people to argue that the modern Maya culture of Guatemala is actually not Maya at all, but rather a product of Spanish domination. This argument, by offering a doctrinaire basis for denial of the Indian, appeals to the insidious racism in Ladino political thinking of both Right and Left. It is particularly attractive to orthodox Marxists who dislike the idea of ethnic identity because ethnicity often conflicts with analyses limited to class struggle and economics.

La Patria del Criollo, an influential book by Guatemalan historian Severo Martínez Peláez, is deeply flawed in this way. Martínez sees postconquest Indian culture as somehow inauthentic—not a survival or development of Maya society but "the historical consequence of colonial oppression. . . ."[2] He attacks the romanticism and "cultural fetishism"[3] of those who think otherwise, and sets out to "explain scientifically"[4] the "Indian phenomenon." Thus, the Indians' hierarchies, cofradías, dances, clothes, and religion are all "Spanish," forced on them to facilitate their exploitation. (Martínez is blind to the Maya structures artfully hidden behind European façades.) Furthermore, he argues, those elements of ancient Maya culture that have survived—languages, for example—did so only because they too were useful to the criollo exploiter. The Indians kept nothing, adopted nothing, rejected nothing themselves: they were putty in the hands of the colonists. The long and courageous history of Maya resistance is set at naught. For Martínez, the Indians' very survival is proof of their defeat.

Even worse, he believes that Indians can be liberated only by being culturally destroyed. In his futurist dithyramb: "The colonial [i.e., Maya] languages will be spontaneously abandoned. . . . The gaudy and elaborate colonial Indian costumes will be incompatible with machines. . . ."5 and "deindigenization [his word for Ladinoization] will bring about the abandonment of fearful and servile attitudes."6 Martínez cannot conceive that the Maya might wish to become modern without ceasing to be Maya; that their languages and customs might have some intrinsic meaning and validity to them; in short, that they might be possessors of a culture with as much right to exist as his own.7

One wonders how he would react if a North American told him that Latin Americans should abandon Spanish because English is the universal language of science; that Guatemalan women must wear trousers at all times because dresses are incompatible with machines; that Hispanic taste is meretricious; that the "de-Hispanicization" of Latin Americans is the only way to end their oppression by the gringo.

6 Muluc

A day of Water, and it's still raining.

Chichicastenango could be an Andean town: it has the same adobe walls, red at the bottom where rain has eroded the whitewash, the same Spanish tile, cobbled streets, raw light, and fresh thin air. Women in bright clothes, bundles on their backs, long black braids tied together with bright ribbons, and small children following, pad silently along the streets. Ladino Guatemala intrudes in the form of beauty salons called Unisex (meaningless, for no Latin man would be caught dead in one) and the ponderous neon sign of the Banco del Ejército, the Army Bank.

The square is already starting to fill with wooden stalls and canvas awnings for the weekend market. Blankets and huipiles for tourists are piled beneath sheets of plastic, and Indian families are getting ready to spend a night or two amongst their merchandise. But not everything is for gringos; over by the Calvario chapel you see piles of pottery and rustic furniture, and next to the church there are flower stands and dark, mysterious kiosks crammed with herbs, leaf-wrapped packets of incense, and homemade fireworks.

The church of Santo Tomás, one of Guatemala's chief tourist attractions, stands in the southeast corner of the plaza. It was built about 1540, and despite the white colonial façade of columns and cornices, it is a Maya place. A large semicircular flight of stone steps leads to the front door; and these steps are a sacred stage like the huge stairways of the ancient pyramids. Here the senior shaman-priests burn clouds of incense and arrangements of candles to Mundo and the ancestors. These men are *chuchkahau*, "mother-fathers," heads of their lineages, guardians of calendrical knowledge, and rememberers of the dead. Many of their forebears are buried beneath this church: every portion of the steps and the floor inside is dedicated to the founders of families, going back in some cases to the ancient Quiché kings.

Next to the church is the Dominican monastery where, in 1702 or thereabouts, a friar named Francisco Ximénez found the manuscript of the *Popol Vuh*. Fortunately Ximénez was a freethinking man who recognized the value of the work, now considered one of the world's great books. He copied the Quiché text (written in the Roman alphabet) word for word and added his own rendering into Spanish. The original has since disappeared, but internal evidence and archaic language show that it dates from the late 1550s. The alphabetic text was apparently based on a codex kept hidden from the Spaniards and now lost. As the royal Quiché authors say in their foreword: "There is the original book and ancient writing, but he who reads and ponders it hides his face."[8]

They had good reason to be secretive: all "ancient writing" was regarded by the Spaniards as rife with the Devil's falsehoods, and its eradication was a principal reason that Maya nobility and scribes were taught to read and write their own languages in Roman script. The friars hoped the Indians would confine this new literacy to the religion and culture that came with it, but the Maya seized upon it as a way to preserve old knowledge. Dennis Tedlock, the *Popol Vuh*'s latest translator, says: "Just as Mayan peoples learned to use the symbolism of Christian saints as a mask for ancient gods, so they learned to use the Roman alphabet as a mask for ancient texts."[9]

The *Popol Vuh*, or "Council Book," is in some ways a highland Maya counterpart to the books of Chilam Balam, but broader in scope and less overtly structured by the Maya calendar. It tells the Quiché creation myth and the history of the world. It has often been compared to the Old Testament, and there's been a great deal of largely circular argument as to how much its authors might have been influenced by the biblical model. Is it really a faithful rendition of a pre-Columbian book, or a digest of Quiché cosmogony and history defiantly intended to compete with the invaders' Bible on their own turf? The authors make explicit reference to the new religion: "We shall write . . . amid the preaching of God, in Christendom now";[10] but this doesn't stop them, in their magnificent opening lines, from naming the creator as Quetzalcóatl (K'ucumatz in Quiché), the Plumed Serpent:

> Now it still ripples, now it still murmurs, ripples, it still sighs, still hums, and it is empty under the sky.
> Here follow the first words, the first eloquence:
> There is not yet one person, one animal, bird, fish, crab, tree, rock, hollow, canyon, meadow, forest. . . . The face of the earth is not clear. . . .
> Only the Maker, Modeler alone, Sovereign Plumed Serpent, the Bearers, Begetters are in the water, a glittering light.[11]

Creation is the work of many gods, who are all aspects of one god: "Heart of Earth, & Heart of Sky"—Quiché names for the Itzamná duality. As in most American Indian mythologies, the world is made and destroyed several times. The first living things disappoint their makers by failing to speak and—mark this—failing to learn the days of the sacred calendar. They become the animals, who eventually pay for their stupidity by allowing their flesh to be eaten by man. In the second attempt the gods make a man of mud (a parody of Adam?), but he is too soft and washes away. Thirdly they make a race of wooden people, but these are mechanical, avaricious, and ungodly. The wooden folk are drowned, scorched, and devoured by jaguars. Even their tools, cooking pots, and domestic animals rebel against them: a warning, possibly unique in ancient literature, against the dangers of technology, as Alejo Carpentier has pointed out.[12] A few survivors become the monkeys of the forest.

Lastly the gods discover yellow and white maize, the perfect substances from which to fashion mankind. But this creation is a little too successful; the corn people have perfect sight and perfect understanding—godlike powers that alarm their makers. So the gift of sight is partly revoked: "They were blinded as the face of a mirror is breathed upon. Their eyes were weakened. Now it was only when they looked nearby that things were clear."[13] These first men are four in number, and after they have been humbled they are given four women: "And this is our root, we who are the Quiché people."

The creation story is punctuated by the deeds of gods and heroes, who represent elemental forces and astronomical bodies in allegorical form. The action is complex, skipping back and forth between generations and events above and below the surface of the world—a nonlinear progression of time apparently expressing the movements of Venus (hidden for long periods) and Mars (which has periods of retrograde motion relative to Earth). The book culminates with a long and devious struggle between two generations of hero Twins and the Death Lords. The Twins spend perilous nights in a series of underworld houses filled with darkness, hail, hungry jaguars, fire, carnivorous bats, and slashing obsidian razors.

Having survived or escaped the lodgings provided by the Death Lords, they are challenged to a ball game series, a contest between life and death. The games are played with trickery on both sides, but the Twins emerge victorious. After further twists in the plot, they defeat Xibalbá, the Underworld, and rise into the sky as sun and full moon. Henceforth the Death Lords will receive only offerings of resin (the blood of trees:

incense and rubber) and broken pottery, and they will be allowed to prey only upon wicked and worthless people. Blood sacrifice will be reserved for the sun.

As more has become known about ancient Maya iconography and religion, scholars have uncovered more and more of the *Popol Vuh*'s content in Classic period art, vindicating those who argue that the book is thoroughly indigenous. Scenes from the Twins' exploits in the underworld are painted so faithfully on polychrome funerary vases that these amount almost to another codex—a Maya "Book of the Dead." There they are in exquisite brushstrokes: the Twins, Hunahpu and Xbalanqué; and the arrogant, rather louche Lords of Xibalbá, puffing on big cigars and surrounded by beautiful girls. The Twins' victory was Mesoamerica's Resurrection, reified each time a Maya ruler offered his blood or the blood of captives to keep the World and the ancestors alive.

The *Popol Vuh* heroes also distribute the first maize and show their grandmother how to ensure its fertility by burning incense before consecrated ears of seed corn, a rite still practiced by Maya today. At this point in the book comes the final, successful creation. The Quiché and other peoples appear, worshiping their creator with these words:

> Heart of Sky, Heart of Earth,
> give us our sign, our word,
> as long as there is day, as long as there is light.
> When it comes to the sowing, the dawning,
> will it be a greening road, a greening path?
> Give us a steady light, a level place,
> a good light, a good place,
> a good life and beginning.[14]

The rest of the book deals with the history and genealogy of the royal Quiché lineages from the time they left the Toltec city of Tula, through the days of their greatness at K'umarcaah, to the Spanish conquest. Many Postclassic rulers traced their descent from Tula, the Rome and Thebes of Mesoamerican civilization. But Tula's location is far from clear; or maybe we should ask, which Tula? It seems unlikely to have been the

Tula ruins about fifty miles north of Mexico City, shown by excavation to be a small and rather shoddy place. Quite possibly the tradition comes down from much remoter times: an echo of Teotihuacán.

7 Oc

A Dog day. The weather clears in the afternoon. We'll stay for the mass and market tomorrow morning, and then move on to Santa Cruz del Quiché.

2:00 P.M. David returns from one of his camera forays with a loud blanket and a small boy:

"This kid says he can take us to see an 'idol' up on a hill near here. Want to go?" And turning to the boy, "*¿Cómo se llama?*"

"*Me llamo Pedro, señor.*"

"*Sí, pero el ídolo—¿cómo se llama este ídolo?*"

"*Pascual Abah, señor.*"

Pascual Abah—I've heard of him. An old Maya god on a hilltop, quite popular with tourists, I gather. We set off behind Pedro. He's a bright Ladino kid, about eleven years old; and guiding tourists to the idol is a good source of pocket money. It's a short walk, past the church, down a narrow cobbled street lined with dark doorways, and out along a sandy road beside a ravine. The air is cool and damp. David, wrapped in his blanket, looks like a Blackfoot Indian at a trading post.

The boy leaves the road and begins to climb a muddy footpath beneath big pines. The ground is slippery—wet clay with a layer of loose needles. We begin to feel the seven-thousand-foot altitude—especially David, who's spent the last year at a news desk. He's panting like an old horse, his breath visible in the cool of the woods. "You might not think so, but five years ago I passed the Canadian army's arduous training course."

"Whatever for?"

"Oh, I was planning to go down to Nicaragua and travel

with the Sandinista forces. I was in lovely condition—fifty push-ups, no sweat. Don't know if I could do five now."

It's really only a climb of 150 feet but it takes us half an hour. As we get near the shrine the air is tinged with the smell of wet ashes, incense, and gunpowder. The sun is battling with a cloud, throwing a timid light among the upper branches and casting shadows in a small clearing of trodden clay. It takes a moment to make out the blackened, rather phallic stone, about a yard long, standing up from a semicircular rubble wall. Its front is carved with a crude human face—rather like very early Preclassic work, though it's probably much more recent. The figure's hybrid name means the "Sacrifice Stone," and he is considered to be a manifestation or agent of Huyup Tak'ah, "Mountain-Plain," a Quiché title for the Earth deity.[15] To Pascual Abah's right a spherical rock resembling a cannonball is set into the wall, and on his left there are two flat altars with squat stone crosses above them. Two more crosses preside over small altars opposite and there is a fifth altar positioned farther away which has no cross. The crosses are stubby with arms of equal lengths—like the old symbol of Quetzalcóatl[16] and the Maya hieroglyph for *kin:* sun, day, or time itself. A cross can be many things among the Maya: besides these associations and its Christian ones, it represents the four directions, the world-tree, and the eye of God; it has specific connections with water, earth, crop fertility, and the dead. Small wonder that so many Maya chose the patronage of the Holy Cross for the "Spanish" towns in which they were forced to live.

There is nobody here at the moment, but a lingering reek of incense and alcohol tells of a recent ritual, perhaps this morning. Behind Pascual Abah himself I find a freshly severed chicken head and a large pile of tawny feathers. The leaf wrappings of incense packets are scattered around. Two altars are still smoldering. They are little stone fireplaces, in which ocote chips (shaved from a pitch pine nearby) are burned with a mixture of incense, candles, and the blood of sacrificial fowls. These things—alcohol, wax, incense, chickens, and above all the accompanying prayers and recitations of days—are given as payment to Earth for fertility, and to establish a reciprocal relationship by which Earth will be obliged to continue rewarding his worshipers.

Not surprisingly, Pascual Abah offended Catholic Action every bit as much as Maximón. One night in 1957 the reformers attacked the idol with a fanaticism reminiscent of Padre Orbita at Tayasal. They broke the stone in two and hurled it down the canyon. Thinking he could dispose of heathenism at a stroke, the Chichicastenango priest even went so far as to decree abolition of the cofradía saint cults. This was too much for the Quiché traditionalists. They took up arms and attacked the monastery beside the church. The priest was lucky to escape with his life. Pascual Abah was repaired with cement and reinstated on his hilltop.[17]

8 Chuen

Sunday morning comes with a whooshing and popping of rockets, as if Chichicastenango were under mortar fire. We get up early and walk down to the square. Mass is to be held at eight o'clock but already the cofradías are gathering around the church to the sound of a drum and a small flute.

One-one-one-one; one-two-three, one-two-three, one-two-three; one-one-one-one; one-two, one-two, one-two. The music sounds elemental and immeasurably ancient, played on the *tun*, a two-tone wooden slit drum of pre-Columbian design. The pace quickens on the duple beat, and the flute follows, playing the same four notes over and over, up and down an alien scale, its very monotony an opiate engaging some receptor in the brain. This is sacred music, archaic even when the Spanish came, an artifact untouched by church hymns or the marimba music that the Maya have since made their own.

The Maya do not so much transform their culture as add to it: new ramifications are grafted on but the old roots and trunk remain its fundamental structure. The strange beat of the tun, like the 260-day "Calendar of the World," keeps to its own time—a foundation on which later, more elaborate structures were raised; and like all foundations it has endured beyond the fall or disfigurement of what was built above.

By now the semicircular flight of steps is full of people, some performing rituals there, others making their way through the cloud of incense to the front door. Candles glow like fireflies through the smoke. Women on the lower steps are selling arum lilies and other flowers, as bright as their striped huipiles; silent babies stare wide-eyed from brilliant carrying cloths on their mothers' backs. Most of the Quiché men wear straw Stetsons and cheap manufactured clothes, but at the top of the platform there are half a dozen chuchkahau dressed in the outfit we've seen on the hotel staff. Here the strange blend of Mesoamerica and Europe seems appropriate, adding dignity to the lined, fervent faces swinging censers, calling on ancestors, kneeling in quiet supplication, oblivious of the orderly turmoil all around them.

Visitors may enter the church by the side door from the old monastery. Pews occupy about half the nave; the rest is kept free at the back for arrangements of candles and private devotions to ancestors and saints. The cold air is sharp with candlewax and *pom* incense. Gray morning light from small, high windows struggles to push back the smoke. The ornate altarpiece bristling with candles looks like a distant town on fire. There are hundreds of Indians in the pews, men on the right, women on the left. The priest comes; the church fills with hymns in Quiché. How different they sound, these hymns—not merely because the half-familiar tunes are influenced by Maya melody but because the hundreds of worshipers believe every word they sing.

When the service ends, traditionally dressed elders of a cofradía gather briefly on the platform at the top of the steps. They carry ebony staffs bound with silver, two of which are topped with silver repoussé images of a crucifix and sunburst. The old men come down the steps and set off at a brisk pace in the direction of our hotel.

"Well, we're going that way too," David says. "Let's follow them."

Eventually they disappear through a door in a blank adobe wall. David is bolder than I:

"Let's see if they'll allow us to pay our respects to the saints."

A young man in modern clothes answers our knock.

"Come in, come in," he says. "Please wait here."

We enter a small patio surrounded by dilapidated adobe buildings with sagging tile roofs. This is clearly a private house, but a room in the corner is reserved for the saints and their brotherhood. The young man goes inside and talks quietly with the elders. Two of them come out, and shake our hands. We introduce ourselves; they are Don Jorge Uquín and Don Apolinario Chinic. In their ceremonial dress and headcloths they look much alike: both seem to be about sixty, wrinkled by the mountain wind and sun; their hands feel like briar roots. They smile and invite us in. They seem pleased that their saints have visitors.

The chapel is small and dark, and filled with color. Red, yellow, and green paper flags hang in rows from the ceiling like heraldic banners. The floor is strewn with pine needles; their scent blends agreeably with the sacred atmosphere of candlewax and incense, and the woodsmoke lingering on the men's clothes. The *cofrades* (brotherhood members) are seated on a wooden bench along the back wall, holding their staffs. They rise one by one and shake our hands. Don Jorge, who is the head of the cofradía, explains that the silver staff tips, now detached and placed on the table, belong to Santo Tomás, the patron of Chichicastenango, and San Miguel the Archangel. The sunbursts are mobile "representatives" of the saints, whose main images reside here.

In the gloom Saint Michael and Saint Thomas regard us from two glass cabinets against the far wall. They are almost hidden by an offering table covered in brass candlesticks and bouquets of arum lilies. Pine boughs are bent above the table to form a kind of celestial arch. The flowers stand in powdered-milk tins that must have come to Guatemala as earthquake relief. DONATED BY THE PEOPLE OF THE UNITED STATES OF AMERICA, says a faded label in English, NOT FOR RESALE. (A futile warning:

much of the earthquake relief was fenced by corrupt merchants and politicians.)

"May we make an offering?" I ask.

Don Jorge squeezes past the table and invites us to approach the saints. He opens the doors of the glass cases, revealing two figures about four feet high, richly dressed in jewelry, velvet, and brocade. The faces are pink and doll-like. Bank notes protrude from folds and pockets in their attire. He takes our offered quetzals and tucks them under the saints' silver necklaces, murmuring a prayer in Quiché.

When we leave, the Guatemalan farewell *Que les vaya bien* (May it go well with you) seems almost a benediction.

Chapter 10

Noon. The twelve-mile drive to Santa Cruz del Quiché takes us through heavily wooded hills like crumpled velvet. Clouds appear below us as we climb, lying motionless in canyons and brimming against the hills. Beauty cloaks Guatemala the way music hides screams. The only clues to the cruel political landscape beneath this scenery are electoral signs painted on rocks and trees beside the road. The signs become more frequent as we approach an army camp and roadblock on the outskirts of the department capital.

SANTA CRUZ DEL QUICHÉ

There's a striped pole across the road and a watchtower, a stork's nest of rough lumber with a protruding machine-gun barrel. Santa Cruz del Quiché fills today much the same role it filled four centuries ago: the center of non-Indian penetration into the heart of the Quiché realm. The town itself is about half Ladino, a far higher proportion than Chichicastenango, and the non-Quiché numbers have been swelled recently by Ladino army officers and Indian levies from other Maya groups.

Even in peacetime, the Ladino republic uses recruitment into the army as a powerful tool for breaking down Indian identity. Teenage boys are rounded up from their villages by press gangs and taken far away to training camps. They are made to chant that they have no mother, no father, no home: their father is the president, their home Guatemala, and the gun is their bride. They are sometimes encouraged to commit "Ladino" crimes such as rape and theft from peasants, for the very reason that these things are abhorred so deeply by Maya that an Indian who does them will feel alienated from his people. At the same time the army gives them *castellanización* (basic Spanish and literacy), which may be a help in later life, but is taught in such a way that it further undermines their self-esteem. For their time in the army the young Indians are transformed into fake Ladinos, a process that exacerbates the brutalization inherent in all military training, and helps explain how Indian troops have been made to commit atrocities against their own race.

We pass the checkpoint with no trouble and drive through narrow streets to the plaza. It's an unremarkable place, less picturesque than Chichicastenango. Santa Cruz is an obviously occupied town in a nation occupied since 1524.

Not long ago the *Wall Street Journal* published a profile of the military commander of El Quiché.[1] It described Colonel Byron Disrael Lima as a man of autocratic powers and the certainty of mind to use them. His heroes in history are Hitler and Napoleon. He admires conquerors, including the Israelis who, besides supplying the Guatemalan army with weapons and advisers, train and equip G2, the infamous military intelligence unit. They also give expert advice on the control of dissident ethnic groups. There has been talk of "Palestinianizing" the Maya.[2]

In some ways Colonel Lima is predictable: his hobbies are playing dominoes and washing his pedigree dogs; in others he is not: he sees poverty as the root of insurgency, and appears to be sincere in applying the "hearts and minds" policy intended to woo peasants with medical care, food, and education. Yet when asked about atrocities he insists that they were done by guerrillas posing as soldiers to incriminate the army. He despises civilians, especially politicians, for their ineffectuality and corruption, but is blind to the fact that army paramountcy helps to make the breed.

Politicians in Guatemala must be very corrupt, very conservative, or very brave. For the past twenty years, each crop of public men has been culled of reformers by the death squads. In 1979 Santa Cruz del Quiché elected its first Quiché mayor in centuries.[3] (There have always been Indian mayors in highland Guatemalan towns, but this man held the civic post usually occupied by a Ladino.) During his brief term an international conference on the *Popol Vuh* was held here, the place where the great book was first written in the Roman alphabet. One year later the mayor was assassinated as he was riding home on his bicycle. The gunmen were seen speeding away in an army jeep.

K'UMARCAAH

The ruins of the ancient Quiché capital (also known by its Mexican name, Utatlán) sit on a plateau about two miles west of the modern town. A muddy road drops down into a ravine, past the remains of one of Estrada Cabrera's Minerva temples, and then climbs up to the quiet pine woods that cover the site. At the entrance there's a ticket office and a small museum containing a model of the city as it once looked.

The custodian is a man of about thirty, with shiny black hair, a broad aquiline face, and confident manner. In fluent Spanish he begins to explain the model of the city, or rather the city as represented by the model. He identifies major building complexes as the residences of Rey Quiché (the Quiché king) and two sons.

"The sons of the king were called Oxib Queh, and Beleheb Tz'i; they lived here, and here." His pronunciation sounds crisp and authentic.

"Do you speak Quiché yourself?"

"Of course, I *am* Quiché. My name is Eulogio Rokché." He adds that the king's sons were named for the calendar days on which they were born—a routine practice in ancient Mesoamerica.

"Do people still keep the Maya calendar around here?" David asks.

"Yes they do. People come here on certain days to make offerings. They come on 12 Ah, 8 K'anil, 13 Tzikin, and many other days. The days also govern a person's fate. For example, Hun Tihax [1 Knife] is a very bad day. When a child is born on that day the parents usually have a ceremony to ask Mundo, the god of the earth, to change it."

David is bubbling with excitement: "You mean, you know the Maya calendar!?"

"Well I don't know exactly how it works. It's a cycle, I think it runs for six months. . . . A man once told me some of the days. If you can wait a moment I have the notes he gave me in my office." Rokché goes to look.

"This is absolutely bloody fantastic!" says David. "What did I tell you about my luck? If we can find out from this bloke what day today is, maybe we can correlate that calendar you've been keeping in your diary with the one they have here. You see there's a special day—I was reading about it on the plane, it's called 8 Monkey—they have a huge ceremony in Momostenango, for the ancestors and all that. If we can figure out when it is we might see something amazing."

I tell David that 8 Monkey, in my reckoning, is today.

"Why the hell didn't you say so before? What are we waiting for? If we leave now and drive like pricks we could still get there."

It's a long time since I studied the correlation problem, but as I remember it, the modern calendars are out of synchronization with one another. I explain to David that my 8 Monkey is counted forward from Thompson's correlation for the Classic period: "It doesn't necessarily mean anything. I'd be very surprised if the local tradition corresponds."

Rokché comes back with a list written in ballpoint on a scrap of lined notepaper. In my journal I've been using the Yucatec daynames, which Mayanists take as a standard. They vary from one Maya language to another, though their meanings are much the same. Here's Rokché's list; I've added the Yucatec equivalents in brackets:

7 Cawuk	—Saturday	[Cauac]
8 Hunahpu	—Sunday	[Ahau]
9 Imox	—Monday	[Imix]
10 Ik'	—Tuesday	[Ik]

11 Ak'abal	—Wednesday	[Akbal]
12 C'at	—Thursday	[Kan]
13 Can	—Friday	[Chicchan]

The list is obviously incomplete, and whoever wrote it appeared to think that the cycle was meshed with the week.

"Are there any more?"

"I believe there are more. But this is all I've got so far."

"What about today?" David says, his voice booming in the small concrete room. "Have you any idea what today is?"

"Well, since today's Sunday, it might be 8 Hunahpu," says Rokché, consulting the list.

"That's it—Monkey! Is Hunahpu Monkey?"

"No, Monkey in Quiché language is Batz', señor."

As there are no other visitors to K'umarcaah, Rokché offers to show us round the grass-covered mounds and small plazas. Much of the cut stone was taken for building in Santa Cruz, and the ruins are not nearly as well preserved as at Iximché. There seems to have been a similar pattern of compounds containing "palaces" (possibly semipublic buildings for council meetings and ceremonies) built on masonry platforms. At the time of the conquest four royal lineages occupied the city center. The *Ahpop*, or King, came from the senior Cawek line, directly descended from Balam Quitzé, first of the four ancestors named in the *Popol Vuh*. He ruled as *primus inter pares* with a deputy and two other lords. Each major lineage comprised a number of lesser ones that had hived off through the generations. By 1524, K'umarcaah was a crowded city of narrow streets and high walls, inhabited by a total of twenty-four chiefly lineages, their vassals, servants, and artisans. Beyond the core city lay satellite towns, one in each of the four directions.

We come to the ceremonial precinct, which has been cleared of trees. Two mounds face each other, identified as the temples of Tohil and Awilix, the first a solar, masculine, rain and sky god; the second (about whom less is known) lunar, feminine, and nocturnal. Between these, in the middle of the exposed cement floor of the plaza, there's a circular foundation: all that remains of the temple of K'ucumatz.[4] It must have been similar to the Quetzalcóatl temple in Aztec Mexico—built round so as not to bruise the Feathered Serpent in his role as god of winds.

Tohil's temple today is merely a rubble core with almost vertical sides, rising to a height of about thirty feet. John Lloyd Stephens saw it in 1840, when the stone facing was still intact:

> It is a quadrangular stone structure, sixty-six feet on each side at the base, and rising in a pyramidal form to the height . . . of thirty-three feet. On three sides there is a range of steps in the middle, each step seventeen inches high, and but eight inches on the upper surface, which makes the range so steep that in descending some caution is necessary. At the corners are four buttresses [pyramid terraces] of cut stone. . . . On the side facing the west there are no steps, but the surface is smooth and covered with stucco. . . . By breaking a little at the corners we saw that there were different layers of stucco, doubtless put on at different times, and all had been ornamented with painted figures. In one place we made out the body of a leopard [jaguar], well drawn and coloured.[5]

Stephens would fain have done a little more breaking and digging, but he was warned off by the priest of Santa Cruz—the Quichés were restless since an earlier treasure hunt, ordered by a Guatemalan president, had destroyed the main palace. The Indians, Stephens wrote, "were in a state of universal excitement . . . at swords' points with the Mestitzoes, ready to cut their throats." Later in the century, Ladinos regained the upper hand in Quiché and managed to strip the Tohil temple of its steps and façades. According to Rokché, the stone was used for the clock tower in Santa Cruz.

Sketches made by Stephens's artist, Catherwood, show a typical Toltec design, with balustrades flanking the precipitous stairs. A much older drawing in a Quiché document reveals that the building had a tall conical roof comb of phallic appearance supported on four masonry pillars. Under this open-sided shelter war captives were sacrificed in full view of the public. The victim was first intoxicated, tied down to the altar, and given a merciful blow to the head. His heart was then removed with an obsidian knife known as the "Hand of God."[6] The body was most likely slid down the smooth western side of the pyramid in imitation of the setting sun.

Although the Classic Maya had practiced various forms of blood sacrifice, large-scale heart extraction was a highland Mexican custom spread by the Toltecs and continued enthusiastically by their successors in the Maya area and central Mexico. Tohil of the Quichés was clearly a war god similar in function to the Aztecs' Huitzilopochtli—an apotheosis of the state's divine right to feed the sun with battle captives.

Gruesome though these gods may seem, they were not far removed in spirit from the Spaniards' own war deity, Santiago. That Christian made frequent bloody appearances on the battlefield to smite the heathen. In Spain he was known by such nicknames as Matamoros, the "Moor Slayer," and in the New World he became Mata-indios, "Killer of Indians."

The gods of Mesoamerica were not discrete personages like those of ancient Greece or Rome. They were nodes on a divine continuum, titles given to the multitudinous God in whom all opposites were balanced. Their interrelationship was every bit as esoteric as the Christian Trinity, and their manifestations as numerous as the Hindu pantheon. The more one examines Tohil the harder he becomes to categorize, the broader his powers and associations. Among other things, he was a giver of fire, which the *Popol Vuh* says he made by spinning on his heel in his sandal. Besides his Toltec connections, he appears as Tahil in Classic inscriptions at Palenque; and his name even survives today as T'o'ohil, title of the religious leader of the last openly pagan Maya, the Nahá Lacandon.[7] At Palenque he is shown with a smoking mirror—another fire-making device—later attributed by the Aztecs to Tezcatlipoca, whom the Spaniards called Jupiter, Lucifer, and the god of hell.

Lucifer was never expelled from the Mesoamerican

heaven: war and peace, life and death, heaven and underworld, good and bad, were all in the nature of God. And so they remain for Maya traditionalists to this day. Modern Quiché daykeepers told anthropologists Barbara and Dennis Tedlock that what worried them most about non-Maya Christianity, whether Catholic or Protestant, was its denial of the earth's divinity and confusion of the world with evil: "He who makes an enemy of the Earth makes an enemy of his own body."[8]

The Maya shaman-priest who said that put his finger squarely on the force that animates and will probably destroy our civilization. The Judeo-Christian (and Muslim) tradition is founded on the belief that the earth is a kind of machine put here by God for the use and testing of man. Animals are little machines without souls over whom Adam and Noah were given dominion, to treat as they saw fit. No moral obligations or reverence are owed to the beasts of the field, much less to the forests and grasslands, lakes, rivers, and the earth itself. In their attitude to the physical world, and the denial of the old nature gods, Judaism, Christianity, and Islam are the first material-ism. The planet is a vale of tears, necessary for man's suste-nance but potentially hazardous to his soul. He can use it but he must not love it. In the words of the gospel singer, "This world is not my home."

The ruins seem to animate Rokché; he strides from building to building, his eyes filled by what he sees in his mind. Recita-tions of myth and history burst from him with the bardic rhythm of ancient texts:

"In this plaza Don Pedro de Alvarado burned Oxib Queh and Beleheb Tz'i alive. This is what happened. When the lords heard that Tecún Umán had fallen, mortally wounded, in hand-to-hand combat with Pedro de Alvarado, they decided to invite the Spaniards to come here, to the capital of the Quiché kingdom, to make peace. They had a secret plan to ambush Pedro de Alvarado when he came into the city. But the Span-iards discovered the plot, they captured the lords, Oxib Queh and Beleheb Tz'i, and burned them here, in the middle of the plaza, in the year 1524."

This version agrees closely with what Alvarado himself wrote. David asks whether there really was a plan for an ambush, and how the Spaniards found out about it.

"Ah," says Rokché. "What happened was this. When the principal lords, Oxib Queh and Beleheb Tz'i, knew that the Spaniards were already on their way, they decided to dig a cavern in which to hide the women and children so as not to spill tender tears and innocent blood. Only warriors remained in the Quiché city. When Pedro de Alvarado saw this he became suspicious."

"Does this cave still exist," I ask, "or is it just a legend?"

"No, it exists—right beneath where we are standing. Have you got flashlights?"

I pull out my tiny pocket torch. Rokché isn't sure it will do, but he leads us down a path on the north side of the plateau, until we stand in a small clearing about seventy-five feet below the level of the buildings. The dark mouth of a cave enters the cliff and appears to run in the direction of the plaza above.

As soon as we go in I can smell the sharp fragrance of pom incense, and when I turn to look back, the daylight spilling into the tunnel is fogged with a diffuse residue of smoke. The tunnel is indeed man-made—you can see tool marks on the walls, and the roof is hewn in the shape of a corbeled arch. I ask where the smoke has come from.

"*Costumbristas, zahorines*—they come here to say prayers." He uses the Guatemalan Spanish terms for Maya traditionalists. The first refers to those who practice the "customs" dedicated to the ancestors, hills, and Earth. *Zahorín* is an old Moorish word for "diviner."

"In this place the Quiché kingdom and the Quiché king disappeared. And in his memory and to thank him for good crops they come here. They burn incense and aguardiente, and they call on Rey Quiché. They also call Pascual Abah, Tecún Umán, Hunahpu, Xbalanqué, Wahxakib K'anil, Caplahuh Queh, Oxlahuh Tz'ikin. These are the gods they call on here."

After about fifty feet we come to an alcove in the tunnel wall. There's evidence of a recent ritual: wax, incense wrappings, soot, ash.

"This is the first altar," Rokché says. "There are nine in all."

Most of the gods he's mentioned are tzolkin days—evidently still regarded as deities, as they were in ancient times; Hunahpu and Xbalanqué are one of the sets of Twins in the *Popol Vuh*. But *nine* altars! The same number as the Lords of the Night and the levels of the underworld.

We come to a small side passage with a shaft descending from it. Rokché says it's about ten meters deep and can be entered only with ropes; the Quiché princess was hidden and later buried here, but her spirit emerged as a gift of music:

"When the princess disappeared and began to hide here, that was when there grew the first tree whose wood is used for making the keys of the marimba. And that is why sometimes when we dance to the marimba we are filled with sadness."

So this is how the Maya made that instrument their own.

We go farther and farther into the hill. It's dark as a mine. Rokché shows us each of the "altars." Some are small niches just large enough for a fire; others branch off like fingers for several yards. At last—perhaps three hundred feet from the entrance—we come to the end. A small chamber has been hollowed in the aggregate: this is the principal altar, the ninth. There are signs of many fires.

I've since read what I could find on this tunnel. Dennis Tedlock believes it may have been dug during the reign of the great King Quicab, and that it represents the Seven Caves of Tula, mentioned in the *Popol Vuh* and other Mesoamerican texts.[9] These traditions were confirmed when a cave with seven branches was recently found beneath the colossal Pyramid of the Sun at Teotihuacán.

As for more recent legend, the tunnel is too small to have held all the women and children of K'umarcaah, but it's possible that some hid here from Alvarado. I think Rokché's story is more likely to be symbolic. The tunnel was probably associated with female aspects of the Earth deity. If there were originally seven branches, the number may have been increased to nine after the Quiché state fell to the Spaniards. As an entrance to Xibalbá, the underworld, it would also be associated with death and the past. Modern daykeepers regard the cave as a mouth of Mundo, capable of swallowing people—much like the fleshless jaws of Itzamná shown on the monuments of Quiriguá and other Classic sites. Above all, it is now regarded as the place where the old social order—the Quiché kingdom, personified by the king and princess—has become entombed.

In Peru there are similar beliefs about the Inca king, known in modern myths as Inkarí. Inkarí is said to be hiding in the underworld—not dead exactly, but slowly restoring himself for a triumphal return and victory over the "Spaniards," or Euro-Peruvians. Modern Quichés do not seem to share the idea of a messianic return of the past order; but they do believe the past is not irrevocably lost, and that it can act upon the present. Rey Quiché, the Quiché princess, and Tecún Umán have joined the world of the hero Twins and the first ancestors. They have left the earthly stage but remain accessible to those upon it. For their descendants, as Dennis Tedlock nicely puts it, "it is not that the time of Mayan civilization has passed, to be followed by the time of European civilization, but that the two have begun to run alongside one another."[10] The Quiché kingdom has gone from the surface of the earth and is now below in Xibalbá; but every Quiché traditionalist carries it with him in his blood and in his head. It will exist for as long as it is remembered, which is much the same thing as saying while there are still Quichés. Contact with the past defines the present and the future; the mechanism for such contact is the calendar. As a daykeeper once eloquently replied to Catholic Action supporters who advocated replacing the feasts of the ancient day count with Christian ones, "One cannot erase time."[11]

We are about to leave the tunnel mouth when two Indians arrive and speak to Eulogio Rokché in Maya. One is dressed traditionally in pink and red striped shirt and britches; the other has modern clothes.

"These gentlemen are from Sololá," he tells us. "They have come here to make an offering to Holy Earth. They have come to ask for his help with their vegetable crop—their carrots, cabbages, tomatoes—and they're going to ask also for help in buying a small truck so they can market their produce."

"So people don't come here only from the local area?"

"No, they come from all Quiché, and from Totonicapán, Tecpan Guatemala, even from the capital."

"Is it only Quichés who come?"

"No. One of these señores is Cakchiquel, but we understand each other's language."

David asks if they might let us stay and attend the rite. Rokché inquires—they will, provided we give them time to make preparations alone and agree to make a contribution to their costs.

After stopping at the site office, where the custodian checks to see if there are any other visitors, we go back to the tunnel. Rokché enters first, asking us to wait outside. A few minutes later he returns and tells us to follow him. Soft voices drift from the darkness ahead like echoes from the bottom of a well. At last we see flames at the tunnel's end: the costumbristas are busy at the main altar. Tapers are stuck to the walls for light. The elder man is instructing the younger to unwrap leaf packets of incense. All the time he is chanting in Cakchiquel or Quiché sprinkled with a few Spanish religious terms and the name for the earth god, *Santo Mundo*, "Holy World." Rokché explains the meaning of the opening prayers:

"This is the first time they have come here, so they must ask permission to approach Mundo, the supreme creator of this place. If they are granted permission they will come back again with a gift, with offerings of the vegetables they grow. The young man is the son-in-law, and as he has arrived in the new house of his father-in-law, he has come to ask permission to learn the office of his new father. This place is very powerful, so for that reason they have come here to ask the permission of Holy World."

Rokché falls silent as the older man chants rhythmically, imploringly, his voice rising and falling in pitch and strength. Most of the oration is in Quiché; I catch only fragments in Spanish:

Capitán del reino	Commander of the
Quiché,	Quiché kingdom,
Tecún Umán . . .	Tecún Umán . . .
Ay, Dios Mundo . . .	Oh, God of World . . .
Nana María Tecún . . .	Lady María Tecún . . .
Ciudad de las santas	City of the holy ruins
ruinas del reino Quiché. . .	of the Quiché realm . . .
Ay, Dios Mundo,	Oh, God of World,
Alcalde Mundo,	Mayor of World,
Presidente Mundo,	President of World,
Juez Mundo	Judge of World

What to make of these names and titles? María Tecún is perhaps the wife of Tecún Umán with attributes of the Virgin Mary. The "Mayor of World" is a title given to the Year-Bearer—the tzolkin day on which the current 365-day solar year began. Because of the permutations of 260 and 365, only four days can take this role and they do so in strict rotation, though their associated numbers run from one to thirteen and repeat. One Year-Bearer in each set of thirteen is called the President.[12] Lesser days are assigned to the Year-Bearers as "secretaries," "treasurers," "scribes," and so on: modern titles for ancient duties. The Maya regard public office and the "carrying" of time as burdens, both honorable and onerous. In the beautiful full-figure glyphs from Classic Copán, the time lords are shown setting down and taking up bundles of katuns, tuns, and kins, as one leaves office and another takes over. Thompson wrote:

> The life of the community and the acts of the individual were rigidly adjusted to the succession of days with their varying aspects. Each day belonged to a god who took a lively interest in his duties. . . . The day ended; the officer of the day was relieved. The one next in charge might be of a very different nature . . . the mood changed as abruptly as in a Tschaikowsky symphony.[13]

Each Year-Bearer represents a cardinal direction, and in some communities actual mayors are chosen from the corresponding quarter of town. Emphasis is on the harmony between celestial and human worlds. The Spanish titles conferred on the days are not a sign that European modes have ousted native ones. Quite the contrary: the foreign hierarchy has been made to fit into and "run alongside" the preexisting structure. The Maya have added; not replaced. Spanish words have been invested with meanings as old as Mesoamerican civilization.

The elder man is now perfuming his apprentice by passing a bundle of incense over his body, around the arms, above the head, down his back, while quietly intoning his name and introducing him to Mundo. Next he kindles a fire with candles and handfuls of incense. The flames flare up, casting an orange glow on the faces of the worshipers. David and I keep to the fringe of the light; Rokché was behind us, but at some stage in the ceremony he returned to his duties in the world above.

Ay, Dios Mundo,	Oh, World God, Mayor
Alcalde Mundo,	of World,
Rey Quiché, Tecún	King Quiché, Tecún
Umán,	Umán,
Principal, General de	Leader and General of
los Indianos [sic],	the Indians,
Nuestra raza Maya-	Our Maya-Quiché
Quiché . . .	race . . .
Santas ruinas K'umar-	Holy ruins of K'umar-
caah . . .	caah . . .
ayuda . . . permiso . . .	help [us. . . . give] per-
	mission . . .

Now the daykeeper recites the days of the calendar, but so quietly and privately behind the crackle of the raging fire that I cannot hear them all. The power of the days and their influence increases with the size of the number with which they occur. It is not only the daynames who are gods, the numbers too are divine, ranked according to their quantity and numerological associations. In his chanting the daykeeper starts with *Hun*

(One) in a small, timid voice, rising in a steady crescendo until the triumphant shout of *Oxlahuh*, the auspicious and powerful Thirteen:

Wakib Tihax	Six Knife
Wucub Cawuk	Seven Rain
Wahxakib Hunahpu	Eight Lord
Beleheb Imox	Nine Crocodile
Lahuh Ik'	Ten Wind
Hulahuh Ak'abal	Eleven House
Caplahuh C'at	Twelve Lizard
OXLAHUH Can	THIRTEEN Snake
Hun Camé. . .	One Death. . .

More candles and incense are added. The faces of the men are lost in a sooty fog at whose heart burns a ball of flame like the sun watched through dark glass. We go nearer and their faces reappear, red-gold, absorbed, the first men gazing at the first dawn. Warm above, cold below, heat in our faces, subterranean chill behind; no light but the fire, no air but the perfumed breath of the fire; a great roaring and the ancient words rising and falling, completing the cycle—*OXLAHUH*—and running on with the next. Suddenly a different scent, the reek of distillation, as the young man kneels and the elder sprinkles him with alcohol from a tiny bottle; the liquor is given to the fire, blue-green flames dart among the red: a hissing joins the roar and the endless names of the day lords. The vault has filled and the smoke lowers itself like a locust sky. We must crouch to breathe, snatching drinks from a small cool river of air that flows along the floor and rushes past us to feed the blaze. More incense, more candles—the red Heart of Sky ardent within the black Heart of Earth. The Maya men stand over the fire, faces bent toward its center. The daykeeper's hand throws a powder; a sparkling serpent writhes in the flames and crackles like a meteor shower through the black pall; he throws another, and both men reach out to grasp the starry creature and anoint themselves with handfuls of its scales. Now the cave is a tempest of black and red, and burning air. The daykeeper's mouth

still moves with the sacred names and supplication, but I hear
only the roar and the crackle, and I hear the words of the *Popol
Vuh:*

> On this blessed day,
> thou Hurricane, thou Heart of the Sky-Earth,
> thou giver of ripeness and freshness,
> and thou giver of daughters and sons,
> spread thy stain, spill thy drops
> of green and yellow;
> give life and beginning . . .
> thou, Heart of Sky; thou, Heart of Earth;
> thou, Bundle of Flames . . .[14]

We are lying on the floor gasping at the little oxygen that
remains in the tunnel, and can take no more. After groping
back only a couple of yards I turn to look at the men and the
flames, but there is nothing to see, not even a glow, so black is
this darkness filled with darkness, this double night. The flash-
light is invisible unless shone into one's face, and no daylight
can be seen until the moment we burst from the cave into the
afternoon. The world seems impossibly rich and clear; I feel
like a blind man miraculously given sight. The trees, the
plants, the soil, pebbles, and leaves, the sky—a blue lake, stirred by branches and filled with astonishing white patterns—all
are for a moment incomprehensible. Senses focused for so long
on elemental dualities of light and dark, heat and cold, air and
smoke, are overwhelmed by such a multitude of shapes, hues,
and sensations, such a confusion of distance and proximity,
substance, and detail. It is as if I see with the clarity the gods
took back from the first human beings: the world is new.

Smoke is pouring from the tunnel like diesel from the exhaust
pipe of a Guatemalan bus. Our next thought is for the daykeeper and apprentice. How long can they survive in there?
The respiratory system has limits, no matter how enthused.
We wait at the tunnel mouth, resolving to go back in if they
don't come out in ten minutes.

But they do, all smiles at the beauty of the world and because the gringos haven't managed to stay until the end. They introduce themselves: Juan Iztayul, in his late thirties with a frank and wise face, and his son-in-law, Max Vinak, not long past twenty, with a bewildered look that I can well understand. We walk together up to the ruins and exchange information on their significance. For them the Tohil temple is the temple of Tecún Umán (the Quiché war hero has evidently attained the status of his god). On Tohil's rubble mound there's a small niche of recent date, blackened by candlesmoke, a sign that his cult is not yet dead. Iztayul and Vinak ask us to take their picture in front of it, and give us their address so that we can send them prints. Iztayul speaks a clear, straightforward Spanish purged of its irregularities. Like many Maya, he says, for example, *"Yo no sabo"* for "I don't know" (instead of *"Yo no sé"*). This comes in answer to our questions about the tzolkin. We still don't know what day it is, and he isn't going to divulge professional secrets. When I produce Rokché's list of seven days, he says, "Oh, you've pretty well got the whole thing there." And when I ask what *today* is, he replies inscrutably, "If it's Sunday, then it must be 13 Noh."

The sun is now slanting through the pines, bathing the grassy mounds and the hills beyond in a pure, saturated light. We stop to say goodbye to Eulogio Rokché. Like all Guatemalans he's extremely polite, but a crinkle of amusement chases across his face. He unlocks the public washroom behind his office. "You might want to compose yourselves, señores."

Two chimney sweeps peer at us from the mirror: sooty faces streaked with sweat, black rings around red eyes. Our pale jackets look as though they've been used to smother a bonfire.

4:00 P.M. We offer the costumbristas a lift as far as the Los Encuentros crossroads, where we turn west to Quetzaltenango. The Santa Cruz checkpoint makes me nervous. What will the soldiers think of a car with two gringos and two Indians in it?

"They'll probably take us for preachers," David says. "No problem."

The soot wasn't easy to remove, especially round the eyes; I wonder how many evangelical preachers wear mascara.

I ask Iztayul if he knows the *Popol Vuh*—he might because a senior chuchkahau from Momostenango helped Dennis Tedlock make his English translation, and daykeepers from all over Guatemala go to that town for training.

"Here," David says, handing him the Toronto library copy, "this is a new translation into English."

Iztayul looks closely at the photograph of a page from the Quiché original. "This is Cakchiquel, isn't it?" he says, amazed. In Guatemala it's very rare to see anything written in Maya.

"Actually it's ancient Quiché, but Cakchiquel and Quiché were almost the same at that time."

"Where can one get this book? Is it available in Quiché or Spanish?" On an impulse we stop at the hotel in Chichicastenango, and buy him a copy of the Spanish edition by Adrián Recinos.

"Better be careful with that," David warns them. "Indigenous people in Guatemala have been killed for owning any book, even the Bible."

"Yes, we know. We'll keep it hidden."

Chapter 11

The road cuts through woods, undulates over hills, and winds between impeccably contoured wheat fields. Beyond Nahualá the Pan American Highway reaches ten thousand feet, its highest point on the continent. In this cold country there are few Ladinos. The Quiché men wear somber checkered kilts and overshirts of black wool. Many are daykeepers and shamans. The antiquity of their profession in these places is attested by the names: Momostenango, "Citadel of Altars"; and Nahualá, "Land of the Nawal."

The view at the pass is overpowering: a row of volcanic cones to the west, with the sun's last rays streaming between them; to the north a horizon of older, softer mountains; and, in the middle distance an immense basin rippled with lesser hills and a flock of purple and magenta clouds.

QUETZALTENANGO

Dusk. The scene of Tecún Umán's defeat is a rather dismal city whose provincialism is emphasized, not dispelled as the citizens imagine, by neo-Classical facades and colonnades. The town is redeemed somewhat by its setting: a dinosaur's back of volcanoes between here and the Pacific. The population is about half Ladino, half Quiché. Some Indians have become wealthy by trading in crafts or managing to penetrate the urban professions. A Canadian who knows Guatemala well told me he's seen Quiché women in native dress driving their own Mercedes-Benzes here. However rare a sight, it shows that Indians can sometimes prosper without repudiating their ethnicity. Rich Indians are anathema to the Guatemalan Left, not only because they are seen as traitors to their "class" but because their very existence undermines the doctrinaire assessment of Indians *as* a class, not a people.

We spend the night at the Pensión Bonifaz, which despite its cozy name is a large, impersonal hotel. Hot water! I'm busy scrubbing the mixture of soot, incense, and candlewax from my hair and skin when, above the hiss of the shower and through the bathroom door, I hear an oath escape from David like the bay of a large hound.

"Jesus Christ! You idiot!"

I emerge, dripping. "What's the matter?"

"You're the matter. Why did I listen to you about the bloody calendar? Today *was* 8 Monkey, and we missed going to Momostenango! All because you thought you knew what you were talking about." David uncorks his Jack Daniel's and takes a long pull. He hands me the bottle and throws a book down on my bed. "Have a drink and take a look at this."

The book is *Time and the Highland Maya* by Barbara Tedlock (wife of Dennis, translator of the *Popol Vuh*). The book wasn't in the university library when I was reading up on the Maya before I left, and all the time I was poring over the *Popol Vuh* in Chichicastenango it was sitting in David's suitcase with the information we needed. The upshot is that the tzolkin *is* still consistent. All the day counts in modern highland Guatemala agree not only with each other but with Thompson's correlation—in fact, he changed his calculations by a couple of days to agree with them.

What led me astray was that the starting point of the 365-day year varies from place to place, an irregularity that had already begun before the Spanish conquest. The situation in Postclassic Mesoamerica resembled that of Europe after Pope Gregory XIII corrected the Julian calendar by removing ten days from 1582.[1] Protestant England didn't accept the change until 1751, by which time the discrepancy had grown to eleven days, and Russia didn't follow suit until after 1917. When the correction was made in England, rioters shouted, "Give us back our eleven days of life!" The Maya, however, took the change in their stride: "On the 2nd of February [1584], on which fell the day of Saint Mary of the Purification," wrote the Cakchiquel annalist, "they blessed the candles and changed ten days, which should not be counted because the order came from the Great Pope, the Holy Father of Rome. . . . Sixty years [have passed] since the Castilians arrived."[2]

Although the Mesoamerican New Year and the Year-Bearers fell out of synchronization soon after the Classic collapse, the tzolkin—the calendar's fundamental cycle—remained the same everywhere, just as the days of our week are the same throughout the world. When it was 8 Monkey in the Quiché kingdom, it was also 8 Monkey for the Itzá, the Yucatec Maya, the Cakchiquels, and the Aztecs. The Tedlocks' work confirms that the tzolkin is *still* perfectly consistent. It has not missed a beat since before Europeans invaded the New World; and has almost certainly turned over every 260 days without a break since its invention at the dawn of Mesoamerican civilization, a thousand, perhaps two thousand, years before the birth of Christ.

9 Eb ⦙ 🔲

At breakfast I read more of *Time and the Highland Maya*, a superb study that reveals not only the sophistication and importance of modern Maya attitudes to time but at a stroke confounds anyone who doubts that the modern Maya are truly the heirs of their ancient culture.

I've worked out the day of my birth: it is 6 Kan (C'at in Quiché), the day called Lizard, Maize, or Net. According to Tedlock, "a person whose birthday is C'at . . . will be a fornicator or debtor or both."[3] Furthermore, such a person is useless as a daykeeper.

* * *

11:00 A.M. We rejoin the *panamericana* at Cuatro Caminos and make a quick detour to Totonicapán. I suggested going on by dirt road to Momostenango, but David is keen to reach Huehuetenango today. 8 Monkey has been and gone, and won't come back for 259 days.

TOTONICAPÁN

On the edge of town there's a public *lavadero* (a place with basins and stone slabs for washing clothes), its columns and circular form apparently inspired by the Tholos at Delphi. It is almost as ruinous. The plaza is formal, dominated by the inevitable neo-Classical town hall with pink Corinthian columns and a baby blue facade.

It's generally believed that an Indian mayor named Atanasio Tzul had himself and his wife, Felipa Soc, crowned king and queen of the Quichés here in 1820. Guatemalan historians have tried to interpret these events as an Indian contribution to the criollo independence movement that was brewing at the same time; and Atanasio Tzul has been compared with Tupaq Amaru II, who led the great Inca rebellion of 1780. But none of this will really wash. The troubles seem to have been little more than a tax revolt that began with the proclamation of the new Spanish constitution of 1812, its subsequent repeal and reinstatement. Indian tribute was abolished, reimposed in 1814, and abolished again in 1816. Because of the lag in communications, and the tendency of corrupt officials to continue collecting tributes and pocketing the proceeds, a great deal of unrest was stirred up, especially among the Quichés. Tzul's supposed "coronation" didn't take place until late in the dispute, and it may well have been exaggerated by the authorities to justify repression. There were few points of similarity with the great Andean rebellion of forty years before, which cost two hundred thousand lives and came very close to restoring

Inca rule in the Andes. A general Quiché uprising seems to have existed only in the minds of Hispanics, guiltily aware that there were indeed grounds for such a war.[4]

The Indian movement took other forms in Guatemala. In 1824 the western Quichés, including those of Totonicapán and Momostenango, tried to annex themselves to Mexico, as Chiapas had done. They had correctly judged the criollos' new Central American federation to be a threat. Then came Rafael Carrera, and by backing him they saw a way to protect their lands and theocratic hierarchies. But there was always the problem of Maya disunity and pragmatism. In the 1870s, some Momostenango Quichés actually fought *for* Barrios and gained land as a reward—becoming practically the only Indians to benefit under his regime. Later they formed an elite palace guard for Estrada Cabrera and Ubico; they were even allowed to build altars in the grounds of the National Palace and make sacrifices there to the rhythms of the tzolkin.[5]

The Pan American Highway passes about twenty miles to the west of Momostenango and strikes north. It follows, more or less, the old boundary between the Quiché kingdom and that of the Mam people, who were partly taken over by the Quichés in the mid-fifteenth century. The Department of Huehuetenango, the extreme northwest corner of the Guatemalan highlands, roughly conforms to the ancient Mam state. Ladinos predominate in the fertile plains and the city of Huehuetenango (Old Citadel), but 70 percent of the department's population is Indian.

The country is dry and hot, torn by deep canyons. At the bottom of one we see the wreckage of a bridge, a twisted piece of Meccano guarded by an army patrol. The rusty girders are festooned with dead trees, bits of plastic, and clumps of grass washed down by sudden floods. The civil war was severe in this department: from 1981 to 1982, there were twenty-six known massacres of civilians;[6] 399 schools were destroyed in three years.[7]

HUEHUETENANGO

Six thousand feet. The city stands at the foot of the Cuchumatanes, the highest and most remote mountain range in Guatemala. The Mexican border is only fifty or sixty miles to the west, and its presence shows. Instead of the gray facades of Quetzaltenango, the plaza here is surrounded by brightly painted shops and filled with flowers. Music pours onto the street from a cantina. There's a breath of levity that I've not found anywhere else in Guatemala. Oh, to be in Mexico, where the bookshops are full, the army no more seen nor mentioned than in Canada, and people will tell you loudly over a beer that the president is a *cabrón* and the ruling party a gang of thieves.

3:00 P.M. The Hotel Zaculeu, a ramshackle colonial structure with high beamed ceilings, plank floors that smell of kerosene, and a patio overgrown with trees and thorns, takes its name from the nearby ruins, capital of the Mams for almost a thousand years before the Spanish conquest.

David has "had it with ruins" for now. I leave him taking a beery siesta, and drive up to the site.

ZACULEU

The ruins were excavated and restored by the United Fruit Company in the late 1940s as a public relations exercise. The main buildings were squared off, plastered with cement, and then whitewashed. When I was here in 1970 the place still had the clinical appearance of a movie set, but now it has mellowed. The pyramids are larger than those of Iximché and K'umarcaah, and the view to the north is magnificent. The bulwark of the Cuchumatanes broods over Huehuetenango like an immense black tidal wave petrified in the act of breaking, with a layer of spray hanging permanently along its crest.

The Mams did not capitulate to the Spaniards with the

burning of K'umarcaah, and Alvarado delegated their conquest to his brother Gonzalo. The *casus belli* (as if the Alvarados ever needed one) was that the Mam leader, Kaibil Balam (Double Jaguar), had had a hand in the plot to trap and burn the Spaniards in the Quiché capital. In July 1525, Gonzalo de Alvarado set out from Iximché with forty horse, eighty Spanish foot, and two thousand Mexican and Maya troops. The Mam capital consisted of the fortified center at Zaculeu and an extensive commoners' town where Huehuetenango stands. The Spaniards found the lower town deserted and the Mams barricaded inside Zaculeu. Alvarado sent a message to Kaibil Balam:

> Let it be known that our coming is beneficial ... because we bring tidings of the true God and Christian Religion, sent by the Pope—the Vicar of Jesus Christ, God and Man—and the Emperor King of Spain, so that you may become Christians peacefully, of your own free will; but should you refuse the peace we offer, then the death and destruction that will follow will be entirely of your own account.[8]

This was of course a précis of the infamous Requirement, contrived by wily legal minds to ease the conscience and absolve the mortal soul of the Spanish king. Kaibil Balam ignored it. Three days later the Spaniards and their allies attacked.

The ruins are surrounded on all sides but one by ravines. The attackers tried a frontal assault where a narrow neck of land joins the city to the surrounding plain. The Mam forces sallied out, only to be cut down by cavalry. But even though the ground was soon strewn with "green crests covered in Mam blood" the Spaniards were unable to make a breach.[9] While Alvarado was preparing for siege, a second Mam army came down from the Cuchumatan highlands. Again there was a bloody battle, and only the cavalry saved the Spaniards from defeat. Alvarado now settled down for a siege that lasted six weeks and brought both sides close to starvation. Eventually relief supplies arrived at the Spanish camp, and a weeping Kaibil Balam surrendered.

*   *   *

It is one of Guatemala's sinister ironies that the Mam leader's name has been appropriated by the crack counterinsurgency troops. Since Indians are regarded by the elite of Guatemala as (1) quaint subhuman mental defectives, or (2) potentially rebellious savages, the Kaibiles are solidly Ladino. The atrocities allegedly committed by them and other army units, like the early accounts of Nazi horrors, strain the belief of anyone living far from the social climate in which they took place. But reports are many and detailed, often mutually consistent, gathered from priests, anthropologists, foreign aid workers, diplomats, and many of the 150,000 refugees who fled through the mountains and jungles to Mexico. I will cite here only one:

> On the 18th of April [1982], soldiers entered the village of Chichupac, telling the people not to be afraid. "We are defending the country," they said. "You must trust us. . . . The government we have now is good. We will return tomorrow, but we want everyone to gather together in the church. If you have old people who are sick, take them to church tomorrow, because we will bring two doctors with us. . . ."
>
> Some people believed the soldiers, and they went to church. Many soldiers arrived and they passed out used plastic toys. There was no doctor . . . the soldiers did not respect the statue of Christ that the catechists had put on the altar. They began to destroy the statue with their machetes. The people were surrounded and could not leave the church. Then the soldiers called out people's names, including children, and took them to the clinic nearby. All the names were of people who had learned to read and write. . . .
>
> The women were raped before the eyes of the men and the children in the clinic. The men and the boys had their testicles cut off. Everybody's tongues were cut out. Their eyes were gouged out with nails. Their arms were twisted off. Their legs were cut off. The little girls were raped and tortured. The women had their breasts cut off. . . .[10]

There was a strong anticlerical element to the repression because Catholic Action had turned from smashing idols to educating peasants and protesting injustice. The very church that had welcomed the overthrow of Arbenz was now a victim of the reactionary forces it had helped to unleash. Even Protestant sects were not always immune, especially before Ríos Montt took power. People were sometimes shot for the crime of owning Bibles. Thirteen Catholic priests were killed between 1978 and 1983, and more than one hundred fled the country.[11]

The army routinely denies the atrocities, claiming they are lies or the work of guerrillas disguised as soldiers. But witnesses have often reported the presence of helicopters and trucks—possessed only by the army.

Stephens described Zaculeu as "a confused heap of grass-grown fragments,"[12] but this didn't discourage him from some frenzied digging: "We were not strong enough to pull down a pyramid, and lost the morning in endeavouring to make a breach in one of the sides. . . . We discovered no treasure, but our day's work was most interesting, and we only regretted that we had not time to explore more thoroughly."[13] Thank goodness he didn't.

I search in vain for signs of costumbre—candles, incense, or the broken pottery still offered the lords of Xibalbá—but the Mams have been driven from the rich land of the Huehuetenango Valley, and the only visitors to their ancient capital are tourists. According to Stephens the site passed out of Indian hands shortly before his visit; he describes the ruthless extinction of the Indians' ancient rights with little compassion. (For all his admiration of the ancient Maya, his sympathies lay with the Liberals and progress, not the "lawless chief" Carrera.[14])

The owner of the ground, a Mestitzo, whose house was nearby, and who accompanied us to the ruins, told us that he had bought the land from Indians, and that, for some time after his purchase, he was annoyed by their periodical visits to celebrate some of their ancient rites on top of [the main pyramid]. This annoyance continued until he whipped two or three of the principal men and drove them away.[15]

10 Ben ‖ 😊

11:00 A.M. A day trip high up into the mountains to Todos Santos Cuchumatán, the main town of the modern Mams.

A few miles of pavement to the small town of Chiantla, then gravel. The Mitsubishi, well behaved until now, shudders and clanks; I wonder how far we'll get before one of its balding tires bursts, or the crankcase is cracked by a rock. Every now and again we are forced to the ditch and bathed in white dust and black smoke by army trucks and buses. After an hour we come to a curious *mirador*, or lookout spot, with a parking lot, a fine view of the valley, and nine concrete cones inscribed with extravagant verses to the Cuchumatanes:

¡Oh cielo de mi Patria!	Oh heaven of my fatherland!
¡Oh caros horizontes!	Oh precious horizons!
¡Oh azules altos	Oh high blue
montes. . . .	mountains. . . .
La alma mía os saluda,	My soul salutes you,
Cumbres de la alta Sierra,	Peaks of the high range,
Murallas de esta tierra	Ramparts of this land
Donde la luz yo ví!	Where first I saw the light of day![16]

This is the last sight of the valley before climbing onto the bleak *páramo*, or plateau.

It becomes colder and grimmer. Seen from below, the battlements of the Cuchumatanes were capped with cloud, and these clouds now lour above our heads and brush the hillsides with mist. We're stopped several times at checkpoints manned by civil patrols. Cold, sullen young men surround the car, fingering their weapons—mostly Mauser rifles from World War II; our passports are scrutinized minutely, as if by experts in forgery. Then the barricade, a pole on a pivot, weighted at one end with a sackful of stones, is parsimoniously lifted just enough to let us through.

These patrols make me nervous. All male peasants between the ages of eighteen and fifty—almost a million men—have been forced to enroll. (To refuse is to risk being deemed a *subversivo* and summarily shot.) They are unpaid, minimally trained, and pitifully armed. Some have only machetes and sticks, and those with rifles are given few bullets. The civil patrol must guard bridges, power lines, and roads; and whenever there's a report of guerrilla activity, it is sent to investigate. The Indians have been placed on the front line, with guns at their backs.

For the first years of the patrol scheme (1982–83) the peasants were in an impossible position: neither side could protect them but both sides held them responsible for wavering allegiances. The new patrols actually drew guerrilla attacks on villages considered to have "gone over" to the army. And for these very reasons the scheme worked. Several observers have suggested that at this time army and guerrillas largely exchanged tactics: the insurgents were forced to use terror or abandon areas they had controlled, while the army began to curb its own indiscriminate killing. Demoralized and confused, the Indians were left with little but the "hearts and minds" campaign—the food handouts, school repairs, and resettlement in strategic villages. Even a wooden shack in a barbed-wire compound was better than being hunted by Right *and* Left.

We turn west onto a smaller, rougher road across the plateau. A sign gives the altitude at more than fourteen thousand feet, but this seems too high; I'd guess eleven or twelve. The landscape reminds me of the Peruvian altiplano. You see the same dirty sheep, the same people, suspicious in their isolation, stupefied by a poor diet and the cold. Even the women's clothes—a long blue skirt, shawl, and battered felt hat—could belong to Ecuador or northern Peru. The flat land is carefully demarcated with barbed-wire fences and stone walls. Most of this good grazing belongs to Huehuetenango Ladinos; the wild rock outcrops that break suddenly through the plain

like stony islands in a lake are left to the dispossessed indi-
genes. The walls that separate the lands of the two races have a
shaggy coping of some kind of epiphyte. The leaves hang
almost to the ground, but rows of scarlet flowers on long stems
run down the tops of the walls and give the only color to this
somber landscape of military grays and greens.

There's another patrol where the barbed-wire fences end.
Beneath their bandoliers and leather jackets the men wear the
pajamalike Mam trousers with broad red stripes. Once again
the careful puckered scrutiny and usual questions:

"¿De qué país son ustedes?"	"What country are you from?"
"Canadá."	"Canada."
"¿Adónde van?"	"Where are you going?"
"A Todos Santos."	"To Todos Santos."
"¿Para qué?"	"For what purpose?"
"Para conocer, no más."	"Just to see it."
"Pasen, pues. Que les vaya bien."	"Go ahead. Farewell."

We fork left through a small village. Another civil patrol; a
football field; an evangelical chapel boarded up. The houses are
made of pine beams chinked with clay, and roofed with hand-
split shingles. They look oddly like Brueghel homesteads: pigs,
chickens, turkeys, and scattered garbage. David gets out at an
isolated shack beside the road and begins switching lenses,
aiming for the best shot. An old man rolls out of the front door,
his limited Spanish hampered by swigs of aguardiente from a
green plastic canteen. He has a shrewd, dissolute face, covered
in a sparse beard like the hair on a coconut. *"¡Cada foto, un
quetzal!"* he shouts. David pays up. His nephew, a shy and sober
lad, asks us for a lift to Todos Santos.

2:00 P.M. If the road gets any worse the Mitsubishi won't make
it. Rocks are scraping underneath. The nephew reckons we

have about fifteen kilometers still to go, and that we're almost at the *cumbre,* or crest of the pass. I carry on for another mile or two, weaving to avoid the biggest rocks and deepest holes. We decide to content ourselves with the view from the top and turn back if the road doesn't improve. But when we reach the pass there is nothing to be seen. A solid mass of white cloud, flat and utterly opaque, starts at our feet and stretches away until it mingles with the leaden sky. Down there somewhere is All Saints.

I've wanted to come here since reading *The Two Crosses of Todos Santos* by Maud Oakes, one of the earliest studies to reveal that the ancient Maya calendar had survived into modern times. She also delved into the ethnic conflict between Indians and Ladinos, symbolized by crosses in front of the church. From time immemorial a tall wooden cross had stood there. For the Mam "prayermen," or daykeepers, it was the cross of Holy Earth, as old as time itself. But a new Ladino *intendente* (administrator) decided the time had come to modernize Todos Santos; he ordered that the old cross be replaced with a new one made of concrete. The daykeepers begged him to change his mind, but they were brushed aside and the old cross was thrown down in the weeds. "Soon after a wind came up, and this wind never stopped. The weather became cold, very cold, the coldest in many years. The sheep died.... No rain fell and all the corn dried up."[17] The prayermen went to the mountaintops and through divination asked the lord of the hills what had happened, and he told them: "You have cast down the big cross, the cross that was born long ago when Santo Mundo was born, the big cross that came with the creation of the world.... Put the big cross up again in the same place. Otherwise all the people and all the animals will die." Eventually a new intendente (also a Ladino) took the place of the first, and the prayermen were able to convince him that the warning had to be obeyed. The great wooden tree, almost thirty feet high, was set up again beside the cement cross of the Ladinos, and from that day there were two crosses in front of the church in Todos Santos.

I once met an American who had lived recently in Todos Santos. According to him the old wooden cross was again taken down in the late fifties during the height of the Catholic Action campaign against costumbre. Again disasters visited the village, culminating in the horrors of the war. In March 1982, 156 houses in the village were burned and fourteen people strangled in the church, apparently by the army. On another occasion almost one hundred people were killed, apparently by the guerrillas. According to my informant, the local commander of the EGP (Guerrilla Army of the Poor) was an Indian, but used his position to settle old scores with personal enemies, further dividing the shattered community. At first the Indians had been attracted by the guerrillas' promises of land and an end to Ladino oppression, but the war brought only destruction and anarchy.

"It was absolute chaos," the American said. "People were being killed merely because they had the same name as somebody wanted by one side or the other. In an odd way the troubles brought a revival in the ancient customs. At the worst period in the war they put back the old wooden cross in front of the church—it must have been gone for at least twenty years—and people told me that from then on things began to improve."

I would like to see if the wooden cross of Mundo is still there, but it is not to be. The road, difficult at the best of times, is impossible in the fog. There are only two hours to sunset, and we've been warned more than once never to drive at night in Guatemala.

When we get back to the lookout with the nine verses, the sun is about to drop off the edge of the world. Silver light pours from a chink in the overcast, painting fans between tiers of charcoal cloud. David gets out for a photograph. I walk to the edge and absorb the view. Suddenly there comes a sense of renewed clarity, as if I had woken from a daydream or finished an absorbing book: oxygen returning to the brain.

11 Ix

The car had a flat tire this morning. I took the wheel to Reparación Robles. Sr. Robles was a brawny Ladino with an easy laugh and an optimistic outlook. " ¡'tá buenísima la llanta!" he said, regarding the vestigial tread: "A very, very good tire!"

1:00 P.M. We follow a straight, sandy road east from Huehuetenango toward northern Quiché, the very region least recommended by Mr. Blatherwycke of the Canadian embassy. The country here is open and flat: fields of corn and wheat neatly bordered with maguey cactus and dry stone walls, the land pale and prostrate beneath the midday sun. David drives with his usual manic insouciance.

"Have you ever thought of competing in a rally?" he says. "I'd like to. I think I might be rather good."

The Cuchumatanes lay on our left, dappled with cloud shadows and shimmering in the day's warmth. Gradually they closed in and lifted us, and brought us down again above the Río Chixoy, which cuts across the center of El Quiché, then curves northward to form the border with Alta Verapaz. From there it drops down to divide Petén from Mexico, and joins with other rivers to become the Usumacinta. In a few days this dark, clear water twinkling below us will flow red and brown, freighted with topsoil, past the ruined Classic cities of Yaxchilán and Piedras Negras before emptying into the Gulf of Mexico, five hundred sinuous miles from here.

In early afternoon we reach Sacapulas, where salt has been extracted since the time of the Quiché kings. There's a Bailey bridge across the river guarded by some bored but friendly soldiers. One of them is having his hair cut beside the water. Women are selling oranges and avocados. The climb and descent have used almost half a tank of fuel—far more than we anticipated—but there's none to be had in town. We fork left and begin to climb northward, back into the high country. Here the Cuchumatán range is broken and gouged by valley after valley—a vertical land of rocky peaks and pines, with warm and tidy valleys far below.

Both our maps agree that Nebaj is only eighteen kilometers from Sacapulas. Our anxiety over fuel subsides for an hour—the time it takes to negotiate that distance over roads almost as stony and narrow as the one to Todos Santos—then returns when we realize we still have to cross from this watershed to the next before we can expect even a sight of our goal. Is Nebaj any bigger than Sacapulas? What if it has no *gasolina?*

"We'll worry about that when we get there," says David. "Nebaj's got a huge army base—maybe they'll sell us some helicopter fuel."

Far above Cunén we give a lift to a young Indian. He speaks Quiché and very little Spanish, but understands enough to confirm that Nebaj is "still very far," maybe four hours, maybe six. Even allowing for the slower pace of Guatemalan trucks and buses, this is not good news. He rides with us for about twenty minutes and gets out at a small village perched on a ridge. Two or three abandoned adobe houses, now full of weeds, look as if their roofs were burned. The war feels close again.

3:00 P.M. The road has become narrower, cut into the side of a steep precipice as we approach the pass, and it's blocked by a tanker truck. The driver explains how he stopped for a piss and can't get the engine to start: the battery is dead. Can we give a push?

"I don't think the front of the car will take it."

"No, no. Not with the car. Just the three of us. If we can get it rolling it'll start."

It seems utterly hopeless—three men against a twenty-ton truck. Perhaps the urgency of the situation gives us what is known as hysterical strength, a surge of superhuman force. We push and the truck moves. The driver jumps in, pops the clutch, and the engine crackles into life.

"Are you carrying any *gasolina?*"

"Sorry. Only diesel."

Nebaj is visible from the top of the pass: a web of human settlement radiating from the white cusp of a colonial church. The town, tiny yet pivotal, lies at the center of a wide green basin rimmed with dark mountains. The late-afternoon sun is casting spears of shadow from eucalyptus, pines, and hog-plum trees beside the road.

NEBAJ

Six thousand five hundred feet. This is the largest of three towns that make up the Ixil Triangle, a region of northern Quiché that gained infamy as a killing field in the early 1980s. The Ixil, who numbered about fifty thousand, are one of the smallest and most distinctive highland Maya groups. In November 1982 Americas Watch reported that they had been "all but wiped out as a cultural entity."[18] In this and other reports, Indians throughout Guatemala were said to be discarding traditional dress and trying to pass as Ladinos to avoid drawing fire. It was feared that the ethnocide of the 1932 Salvadorean *Matanza* was being reenacted in Guatemala, the last predominantly Indian country north of the Panama Canal. It's a relief to see the striking Ixil huipil on almost every woman we pass. The bold kaleidoscopic designs stand out at a distance, instantly appealing, like stained glass.

The Ixil are an ancient branch of the Maya, with roots in the Classic period. Although they may have fallen briefly under the hegemony of the Quichés in the fifteenth century, they were independent at the time of the Spanish invasion. They helped the neighboring Uspanteca inflict a stinging defeat on a Spanish army, and were not fully conquered until 1530. Like all native Americans, they suffered a catastrophic decline in numbers during colonial times, but the great rampart of the Cuchumatanes isolated them from the worst of Spanish rule and the first excesses of the republic. It wasn't until the very end of the last century that Ladinos came to live amongst them.

In the streets of Nebaj, the radiant women are outnumbered by soldiers wearing mottled green and brown. There's a machine-gun nest at the edge of town, at the end of every major street, and at the four corners of the square. I've read that the Guatemalan countryside has been turned into an armed camp, but even in Petén and Santa Cruz del Quiché there was nothing like this. Images of inquisitive gringos found dead in ditches come to mind. (Mr. Blatherwycke doesn't seem quite such a stuffed shirt now.) I remember a promise I made to my wife: last time we spoke on the phone she said, "You won't let David talk you into going anywhere you shouldn't, will you?" "Of course not," I said; but here I am.

David, however, is an old Central America hand. He drives straight up to the police station in the main square, and asks two officers where we can find a place to stay. I hope they aren't going to suggest the jail.

The officers direct us to a large courtyard on a corner a couple of blocks away. "Gringos always stay at Las Tres Hermanas."

The Three Sisters has a pretty patio containing several fruit trees and turkeys; there's another Budget car much like ours in the driveway. We're met by a very old Ladina woman with iron gray hair and parchment skin cracked by a kindly expression. Yes, she has rooms, and she charges one and a half quetzals a night (about fifty U.S. cents); is that all right? When she produces the register I see what the police meant. Almost all recent guests have been gringos. Among the names are several journalists who have been highly critical of Guatemala. If the death squads haven't bothered them, they're not likely to take an interest in David and me.

The owners really are three sisters, indistinguishable except that the one I take to be the eldest has a few whiskers on her chin. Two Ixil girls work for them, washing sheets in a stone basin next to the well in the middle of the courtyard. One of the girls shows us to our rooms. It's the barest accommodation I've seen since northern Peru, windowless, with a stick to prop shut the door. The bed is a spartan product of local carpentry and the mattress is made from flour sacks stuffed with kapok from ceiba trees. The sheets are flour sacks sewn together. I drop my things and go back outside. The thin evening air smells of smoky fires and tortillas. I ask the elder girl, who must be about thirteen, whether the three sisters offer meals, but she shakes her head.

"She doesn't know how to talk," the younger one says. I wonder whether her condition is the result of psychological trauma.

The girls take us into a dining room at the corner of the patio. The last light of the day filters in through a small window high up beneath a beamed ceiling that sags like the rib cage of a cow.

We've just finished our supper of chicken, black beans, and tortillas when other guests arrive—a German film crew, and a Canadian volunteer with a weaving project for orphans. A solitary bulb illuminates the hairy faces and deep tans of the Germans. We introduce ourselves; cigarettes and beers are passed around. The Canadian woman begins telling jokes about Lucas García, the brutal and reputedly dense military president overthrown by Ríos Montt. (The U.S. State Department estimated that death squad murders ran at three hundred per month during his last year in power.[19])

"One day Lucas García decided he was going to go out and meet the people—so he goes down to the park outside the National Palace to have his shoes shined. And the shoeshine boy says to him, 'Hey, señor, would you like to hear a Lucas García joke?' And Lucas Garcia looks down and says, 'But I *am* Lucas García!' And the shoeshine boy says, 'Oh, well, in that case I'll tell it to you *very, very slowly.*' "

"Where did you hear this?" asks one of the Germans.

"I went dancing last night up at the base with the colonel. He loves to entertain you with his jokes."

"He's also one of those who founded the Kaibiles. Be careful."

By now word has got around that there are some new gringos in town. We're already being shadowed by a small boy who wears a pair of rubber boots and smells strongly of urine. He wants to be our guide. He has a testimonial written in English on a scrap of dirty paper: "This boy's name is Armando. His mother and father are dead. He will be a very good guide. I can recommend his services. Please reward him well." Armando waits outside in the patio, sitting on a shoeshine box. Also outside the room are three Ixil women who hold up beautiful woven huipiles and headcloths whenever we glance in their direction. A man of about thirty pushes past them into the room and shakes our hands obsequiously. He too wants to be our guide.

"Don't hire this man," one of the Germans says. "This man is the biggest arsehole in town. If you want to see burned houses, he will show you. If you want to see human bones, he will take you. He is the sleaziest arsehole. And he's probably a spy. Take the little boy if you need."

Chapter 12

12 Men •|| 🗿 *Men: Eagle; day of wisdom.*

It was cold in the night; my feet stuck out of the tiny, hard bed with its single blanket. At half past five I surfaced from an improbable dream to hear a man in the next room praying aloud in Ixil.

After breakfast, Armando is waiting. He takes us down narrow grassy streets on the edge of town, past concrete basins where girls are washing clothes. Some of the older ones wear the magnificent Ixil headcloth, a seven-foot scarf wrapped in a spiral with their long black hair and piled on the head. A fringe of large pom-poms frames the face, giving a rich and regal effect like that of an ancient Maya headdress.

We follow Armando across the flat land that attracted the Ladinos. The corn is twelve feet high, brown and ready for harvest, morning-glory and squash vines spiraling up the stems. It's impossible to see anything until we climb a small hill, squeezing between the plants, our jeans covered in burrs. From the top, all becomes clear. We are standing on an ancient pyramid and can see six or seven more of about the same size; some long low mounds could be palace platforms or the sides of a ballcourt. The Nebaj ruins are thought to be Postclassic in date. The ancestors of the Ixil do not seem to have built much in the Classic period, though they were industrious makers of carved jade and fine polychrome pottery. Vases from the Nebaj

233

and Chixoy regions have been found in the royal tombs of lowland cities, including Tikal. With a deft sense of line and caricature, the artists portrayed underworld deeds that would be written seven centuries later in the *Popol Vuh*.[1]

A ceiling of clouds is resting on the mountains; one feels contained in a dark green bowl spread with a cloth of white and gray. To the northeast the hills are lower, beginning their descent to the Petén, and there the cloth has been lifted, revealing a corner of pale blue sky. We climb four of the mounds, and even though they're eroded and overgrown, each has a shrine and little wooden cross. As we turn to walk back into town, a column of incense rises from the top of a pyramid beside the path. We linger a few moments, and hear a soft voice reciting the names of the day lords.

A padre told Stephens and Catherwood that from the uplands just east of here he once caught sight of a thriving Maya city, "occupied by Indians, precisely in the same state as before the discovery of America":

> He looked out over an immense plain extending to Yucatán and the Gulf of Mexico, and saw at a great distance a large city spread over a great space, and with turrets white and glittering in the sun. The traditionary account . . . is, that no white man has ever reached this city; that the inhabitants speak the Maya language, are aware that a race of strangers has conquered the whole country around, and murder any white man who attempts to enter their territory. . . .
>
> The interest awakened in us was the most thrilling I ever experienced. One look at that city was worth ten years of an everyday life. If he is right . . . there are living men who can solve the mystery that hangs over the ruined cities of America; perhaps who can go to Copán and read the inscriptions on its monuments.[2]

Stephens did not have time to follow this chimera, but in any case he was 150 years too late. I believe the story recalled the Itzá kingdom of Tayasal. There probably *were* men there as recently as 1700 who could have gone to Copán and, with difficulty, read the writing of a thousand years before. For the Ixil, the memory of Tayasal had mingled with older echoes of the Classic period, and the lowlands had become a mythic place where the order of the past existed in all its purity and magnificence. It was their equivalent of Paititi—the legendary Peruvian city, deep in the jungle, where it is said the Inca king still reigns.

The first Ladino arrived in Nebaj about 1895, one Don Isaías Palacios, who is said to have fathered more than fifty children by raping and seducing local women.[3] With the assault on the Indians' wives and daughters went a similar attack on their property and labor. Robert Burkitt, who traveled here in 1913, wrote:

> The rum business and the coffee business work together in this country automatically. The planta- tion advances money to the Indian and the rum seller takes it away from him.... Work leads to rum and rum leads to work.... I used to think that Chi- chicastenango was the drunkenest town in the coun- try, but now I think it is Nebaj.[4]

The more land the Ladinos were able to alienate from Indians, the more vulnerable the Indians became to debt peonage. Many Ixiles began to depend on the yearly trek to the coastal estates; others responded by moving northward and colonizing the foothills. After 1954, such enterprise was encouraged by the government as a substitute for genuine land reform, and Indian homesteaders were given titles. But unfor- tunately for the Ixil, for the Kanjobal to the west and the Kekchí to the east, oil and minerals were discovered in the Petén piedmont. The military named the area the Northern Development Belt and began building roads and airstrips. Cat- tle barons, coffee growers, and speculators moved in. Among those profiting were Arana Osorio (the "Butcher"), General

Kjell Laugerud, and General Romeo Lucas García—each a president of Guatemala during the 1970s. The army and private militias drove away Indian settlers or reduced them to serfdom; courts were bribed to ignore appeals; the Northern Development Belt became notorious as the "Land of the Generals."

Correctly judging the Ixil and Ixcán regions as fertile revolutionary soil, the Guerrilla Army of the Poor (EGP) began to infiltrate. One of their first actions was the 1975 assassination of a rapacious landowner, Luis Arenas Barrera, known as the "Jaguar of Ixcán."

> His home base, La Perla, was a fortress. It was perched on a high promontory, impossible to reach unseen. . . . It was always in contact with the outside world by radio. . . .
>
> June 7 was pay day, which made it easier for us to approach the offices where the workers were . . . clustered in front of the manager's office waiting for their money. Standing in front of the manager and looking like a bird of prey, the lord of the land was counting his coins and unfolding some crumpled bills. When we ordered him to raise his hands, his eyes rested for a second on his assailants and he instinctively reached for his gun. A quick burst of gunfire killed him just as he was pressing the trigger of his revolver. . . . [5]

The death of Arenas gave local Ladinos an excuse for systematic attacks on cooperatives and other organizations that threatened their control of Indian labor. Between February 1976 and the end of 1977, a total of 168 co-op leaders were killed in the Ixil Triangle and the Ixcán.[6] As all peaceful avenues for redress were blocked, the hitherto conservative and unpolitical Ixil became receptive to insurgent propaganda.

Early in the morning of January 21, 1979, the Guerrilla Army of the Poor invaded Nebaj and held it for several hours. They executed Enrique Brol, another landowner, and expounded their cause to townsfolk assembled at the market. Even the hippies at the Pensión Las Tres Hermanas were brought to the meeting and ridiculed for "imitating poor people when in reality they lived on their rich parents' money."[7] The guerrilla leader was Ladino, but the other speakers were Nebaj Indians who had joined the EGP. A young man spoke of Ladino exploitation, and two women denounced the sexual slavery practiced by such men as Brol.

In the evening the Guatemalan army arrived; next morning they gave a lecture of their own. "Those people who came yesterday are tools of foreigners," the commander said, "because those people are communists, and we in the army have already proved that communism is no good for Guatemala." One old Ixil man had the courage to answer back:

> The only thing we ask is that you respect our people, that you respect our town; that you respect our women, and do not beat people up. Because I was a soldier myself . . . and the [army] made me rob people, they made me hit people, and since the army has come to Nebaj they have raped women and kidnapped men. . . . We are Indians, but we are not animals.[8]

11:00 A.M. The German film crew have told us that it's possible to visit Acul, one of the "model villages" into which displaced persons and other suspect civilians have been herded under military supervision. But first we need to find gasoline. We're directed to a local landowner, who sells us a few gallons at an exorbitant price.

It takes us several tries to find the right street leading out of town, and when we finally do so, two Ixil women ask if we can give them a lift to Acul. They climb in the back seat, and bury themselves under baskets of food and gifts.

"*Voy a visitar a mi hija* [I'm going to visit my daughter]," says the older woman in very broken Spanish. The rest of the conversation is one of labored misunderstandings and broad smiles.

The road quickly becomes a wide gravel thoroughfare, big enough for three or four trucks abreast. After experiencing the main road to Nebaj it seems utterly pointless, like a stretch of superhighway at the end of a farm track. This road is not marked on our maps—it must be part of the network carving up the Northern Belt.

A much smaller road branches off to Acul, up a cleft between steep mountainsides. After a mile or so it becomes too rough for the Mitsubishi. We park and continue on foot. A narrow river runs headlong beside us; butterflies flutter from the moist ground and play about our heads. We tramp on with a sense of curiosity and foreboding, wondering when a barbed-wire perimeter and tin-roofed watchtower will loom out of this pastoral landscape. The Ixil women trot along with the rapid and serene gait of people accustomed to walking everywhere. After fifteen minutes the track levels out and enters a small valley. There's a fenced pasture with two ponies in it, and a cluster of finca buildings beyond: a house with a veranda, a barn, and some sort of shed. About five minutes later we come to Acul. Two young Indians, resting in the long grass, raise the pole to let us pass. They tell us to check with the soldiers in the village center.

ACUL

Houses in quadrangular blocks climb up the hillside to our left, surrounded by stands of maize about twelve feet high: tin roofs glinting above a sea of silvery tassels. It's good to see corn—I've read reports that the Indians in these places are forbidden to grow their traditional crops for fear that the food will find its way to the guerrillas.

The center of the village is a muddy triangle with a stand-pipe where women are filling the water containers you see all over Guatemala—green and white striped jars that look gourdlike and rather African, especially as they are always carried on the head. They're made of plastic. There's a small whitewashed church—apparently the only adobe building—and a watchtower of thick timbers. I watch the women: no sign of uneasiness on their faces; they take no interest in the soldiers and the soldiers take no interest in them. Evidently local people can come and go as they please. The older of our companions asks how long we plan to stay here, measuring an arc of sky with her hand. She points out her daughter's house, and asks us to stop there before we leave.

Three soldiers scrutinize our passports and tell us we must wait for the commander; one of them goes to fetch him from a long building where a throng of women and small children has gathered. David takes out his camera and begins snapping pictures.

"I'd feel a lot better if you'd put that away until we get permission. You never know what might provoke these people."

He gives me a weary look, but he stops.

The commander is a young, refined man with bad acne and bookish gold-rimmed spectacles (mirror sunglasses are usually de rigueur among Latin American military). He looks more like a medical student than a captain in the Guatemalan army.

"Journalists?" he says. "You can go anywhere, and talk to anyone you like, and you're welcome to come down to the clinic here and see what we're doing for the people."

"What are you doing?"

"We give them food and medical help, free of charge." Then a frown crosses his face and he points to the wall of mountains surrounding Acul.

"You must promise me not to go walking in the hills. There are still some *subversivos* out there and we cannot be held responsible for your safety. I'm sure you understand." We certainly do: an American journalist and his companion disappeared while hiking near Huehuetenango about eight months ago. I note the word *subversivos:* it's the official term for insurgents throughout Central America. *Guerrilleros* is thought too glamorous and politically unsound.

"How many guerrillas are there?" David asks.

"How many *subversivos?*" say I.

"I can't give you that information. There are not many, but they turn up when you least expect them. Go anywhere, but please stay out of the hills."

Acul's street names, painted on wooden boards, are explicitly political: Calzada de Libertad, Avenida República de China, Avenida Soldado Guatemalteco—Boulevard of Free-

dom, Avenue of the Republic of China (Taiwan), Avenue of the
Guatemalan Soldier. The houses are almost all of thick planking, sawn from jungle hardwoods and notched together at the
corners. Development is in the Latin American order of priori-
ties: electric light but no sewer or latrines. Streets of mud and
stones; pigs and dogs investigating corncobs and scraps of plastic; knots of women walking home from the standpipe under
the gaze of the watchtower. It has been said that Indians from
many different ethnic groups are congregated in these villages,
and that this is destructive of their identity. But here, judging
from the dress of the women, there are only Quichés and
Ixiles—two groups who have lived amongst each other since
the time of the Quiché state. There seems no animosity
between them: the brilliant Ixil brocade and the striped woven
huipil of the Quichés walk side by side.

We climb to the edge of town below the mountain and look
down on a world of corn, with small huts and streetlamps
poking out. Before leaving Canada I saw an article about model
villages; there was a photograph of a grim, scorched area with
nothing but barbed wire, corrugated iron, and a watchtower. It
looked like a cross between a concentration camp and a shanty-
town. It was Acul. Acul has mellowed, but these tiny kitchen
gardens are not enough, and the women must queue every day
at the army post. The army is indeed handing out food and
medicine—but in return for work on roads, reconstruction,
and the civil patrols. The people are not starving, but they are
entirely under military control. A building marked "Agrarian
Cooperative" is boarded up.

The worst years in the Ixil Triangle seem to have been
1980–81, with aerial bombing and dozens of civilian deaths
every day.[9] In March 1982 the evangelist general, Ríos Montt,
took power. He was among those officers who realized that the
wholesale terror presided over by men like Arana and Lucas
García won recruits for the guerrillas. What happened next is
not clear. Some Guatemalan journalists claimed that during
the first two months of Ríos Montt's regime more than four
thousand peasants were killed in a systematic scorched-earth
campaign; other sources blamed these killings on army splin-

ter groups loyal to Lucas García and the MLN fascist party.[10] As so often in Guatemala, the "truth" is a matter of choice.

According to an eyewitness, this is what happened on April 20, 1982, here at Acul—the original Acul, a village of which nothing remains but the adobe church:

> They searched the houses and pulled the people out, and took us to the churchyard. The lieutenant walked up and down pointing at people, saying, "These will go to hell, these will go to heaven." The ones he said would go to hell they took . . . to the cemetery with their hands tied behind their backs. They dug a big ditch and lined them up at the edge. We all had to come and watch. . . . They shot each one with a bullet in the face from about a meter away.[11]

Twenty-four were killed that day; twenty-two the next day. On several other occasions the soldiers returned. A witness reported that they burned houses in September 1982, and again the following June. The survivors fled either to the mountains, to Mexico, or to burgeoning camps on the edge of Nebaj. In December 1983 Acul was rebuilt and officially repopulated under army supervision; two thousand former inhabitants returned, as well as eight hundred people from another destroyed village.

3:00 P.M. We call at the house the Ixil woman pointed out. She introduces us to a strapping man of twenty-five. "This is my *hija* [daughter]," she says. (Ixil speakers evidently have as much trouble with Spanish gender as the average gringo. She means *hijo*, son.) How does he like living here? we ask.

"It is fine," he says, "It is *tranquilo*." Calm, peaceful: the simple goal of the war-weary populace. Is there enough land?

"There is very little, señor. All this"—he sweeps his hand around the looming hills shaved here and there into vertiginous cornfields—"has its owner. There is no free land."

"Who is the owner, does most of it belong to the Ladino of the finca on the edge of town?"

"No, that Ladino has only the pasture, and he gives very little employment. The rest belongs to Indians who have always owned it, from the time of the grandfathers, for hundreds of years. Some have a little land, others have more. Everything has its owner."

"So how do you make a living here?"

"I go to the coast twice a year to work."

"For how long?"

"About forty days each time if I'm lucky. There's very little work."

"And what are they paying there?"

"Now it's about three quetzals a day—without food. We have to pay for our food. That takes about half our wages."

"So when you come back from the coast, how much do you have left?"

"Very little—about sixty quetzals, something like that. It's very little." Very little indeed—the equivalent of twenty American dollars.

What future is there for the inhabitants of this "model village" without land? And as for its positive aspects—the absence of barbed wire, the apparently decent behavior of the army—how typical are these of the other forty or fifty settlements? Is Acul a Potemkin village, a facade built for the steady trickle of foreign journalists attracted to Nebaj by its reputation for genocide? And even if all is just as it seems, what will happen when the army withdraws its food and medicine? These people have become wholly dependent; refugees on their own soil. Even the unsavory option of plantation work is not as available as it once was. Some estate owners began to mechanize when the war disrupted their supply of Indians; others have found a ready labor pool in the thousands of displaced persons who fled to the coast.

The Ixil women chatter and joke all the way back to Nebaj, animated by their visit. From time to time a tassled turban flashes in the mirror like a tropical bird; their laughter helps dispel the gloom welling in my mind.

"¡Dios se lo pague!" they call when they leave us: "May God repay!"

Evening. A supper of rice, beans, and tortillas. Afterward we call on the priest. Two soldiers appear at the corner and watch while we knock. A nun invites us in. The father is away, but we might be able to catch him in the morning.

"Do you want to see what we're doing?" she asks. She takes us through the hall to a patio filled with Ixil children, mostly girls between the ages of five and fifteen. All are quietly sitting at backstrap looms—the simple weaving device of pre-Columbian America that has produced the dazzling textiles of ancient and modern times. The girls shyly glance up for a second, their busy fingers never stopping.

"We have seventy orphans living here at present. We are trying to arrange markets for their handicrafts in North America."

David wants to ask more questions but the nun says it would be better if we talk to the priest. We ask if there are any cofradías still functioning in Nebaj.

"I wouldn't know about that, but if you go to the house of Don Arcadio, he may be able to help you." She turns to Armando. *"¿Tú sabes dónde está la casa de Don Arcadio?"* *"¡Sí!"* the boy says with professional pride.

Armando leads us back through the plaza, past two gun emplacements, to a dark street half overgrown with grass. We knock and repeat the name we have been given by the nun. A middle-aged Ixil man greets us in good Spanish. He confirms that he is a prominent member of one of Nebaj's twelve cofradías, and invites us in.

Because the Ixil were largely isolated and self-governing until the turn of the century, their society retains some of the social stratification of preconquest times. Though *Ixil* itself means "People of Maize," many Indians have lived in the towns of Nebaj, Chajul, and Cotzal for generations and do not rely on farming. There are Ixil shopkeepers, barbers, butchers, bakers, even professional soldiers—trades usually dominated by Ladinos elsewhere in Guatemala. In Nebaj, Indians and Ladinos live in the same neighborhoods. Indians generally have older houses of a hybrid Maya-colonial design with two or three rooms and a wood-pillared veranda on the patio; Ladinos favor modern stucco facades in pastel colors, with windows giving onto the street; but there is no residential segregation and little visible difference in wealth between upper-class Ixiles and middle-class Ladinos.

Don Arcadio's house is neither poor nor rich. It's actually a collection of separate one-room buildings—a typical Maya arrangement—some of adobe, others of wood. It has electric light, locally made pine furniture, and a muddy courtyard containing chickens and a small black pig. His wife and daughters wear the Ixil huipil, wraparound red skirt, and headcloth. Only Maya is spoken among the family. Commercial calendars and cigarette advertisements decorate the walls of the room we're in; most of the floor is occupied by two large beds with woven blankets. A radio in the kitchen (a separate hut) is playing Mexican music, drifting on and off the signal.

"In the foreign press," David explains, "it was reported that the Ixiles were almost destroyed by the war. We heard that many were scattered and demoralized, that many were abandoning their way of life; and we also wonder whether Protestantism and Catholic Action have divided the community."

"There were some ... excesses ... here a few years ago, some people were killed, some houses were burned. But then God sent us Ríos Montt and things began to get better."

David and I look at each other. The rabid evangelist Ríos Montt praised as a savior by a traditional cofrade! Again we are confronted by the complexity of Guatemala. Ríos Montt has been described as the worst and best of the generals. Only one thing seems certain: neither Right nor Left, Ladinos nor Indians are monolithic; the guerrillas are divided into three or four "armies," loosely coordinated by an umbrella organization; the army is riddled with political differences, personal feuds, and Byzantine intrigues. Guatemala seems almost a Central American Lebanon.

I wonder if we're being fed a line by Don Arcadio, but he

goes on to criticize the government and the economic conditions that force so many Ixiles to seek work on the plantations:

"You know they go and work for sixty days and the landlord offers them thirty or forty quetzals. How can they live on that?"

"Isn't there a minimum wage of more than three quetzals per day?"

"Yes there is, but nobody pays it. They deduct for transport, for the food—which is always very bad—for any time off, even for sickness, for broken tools, and anything the men may buy in the finca store."

He makes no attempt to lower his voice, even though the room we are in has a small window overlooking the street and there are probably soldiers outside. I press him no further on politics, remembering what Carlos said: We can ask questions, but what might happen to those who give us answers? We turn to religion. Do the Evangelicals pose a threat to Ixil traditions?

"There are many who are now evangélicos. They don't want to follow the customs anymore, they don't want to do anything. It gives me much pain because we must honor our ancestors and the fiestas are very expensive. Just an ordinary marimba costs fifty quetzals a day, and for the big one we bring for the great fiesta in August it costs ninety. Then there is the incense, the costumes, the food—all of it has to be paid for. It makes me sad that many younger people no longer support the cofradía." He pauses; a lively grunting comes from outside as the pig is fed some scraps. "Christmas Eve is approaching, and for that I'm fattening up my pig, to make tamales for the members."

"How many evangélicos are there in Nebaj?"

"The majority. There are more now than Catholics. They have no respect for the old customs, the images. They say the images are just bits of wood. They say they have no heart."

He stops for a moment, seeming to reflect. Then comes another surprise:

"Many have heard the call of Jesus Christ. But I believe it doesn't matter, everything belongs to God. I myself have sometimes thought of hearing Jesus Christ, to be born again, but I would not give up the cofradía."

"Could you do both?"

"Why not?"

He brightens a bit—adding that the Protestants are not as strong as before; some of them are even starting to participate in fiestas. It seems that religious matters are endlessly renegotiable to the Maya.

"Has the army attacked the costumbres in any way?"

"No, not the army. They are not concerned with that."

"Are there people who still keep the days of the Ixil calendar?"

"Oh, yes. You must ask my uncle, he is a daykeeper himself."

He calls to another part of the compound. An elderly man comes in, shakes our hands, and sits down on one of the beds. His Spanish is broken, and occasionally Don Arcadio has to translate. Unlike the Quiché shaman-priest at K'umarcaah, this man is eager to talk about the calendar. He seems pleased by our interest. I ask if he can tell me the names of the days. He closes his eyes and begins to recite. And in front of the names he puts a title, Kub'aal—Ixil for "God," "Lord," or "Father." This is not abstract calendrical nomenclature, but the evocation of deities, endlessly bearing their quanta of time.

Here are the days, with their Quiché and Yucatec equivalents. I've also included possible translations, but bear in mind that the associations of a day are not confined to the obvious meaning of its name, and that these vary in different Maya languages.

Ixil	Quiché	Yucatec	English
Imux	Imox	Imix	Earth Being, World, Crocodile
Iiq'	Ik'	Ik	Wind, Life, Breath
Aq'b'al	Ak'abal	Akbal	Night-House, Evil
K'ach	C'at	Kan	Maize, Lizard, Net, Ripeness
Kan	Can	Chicchan	Snake
Kamel	Camé	Cimi	Death
Chee	Queh	Manik	Deer
Q'anil	K'anil	Lamat	Venus, Sunset, Rabbit

Choo	Toh	Muluc	Water, Fish
Ch'ii	Tz'i	Oc	Dog
B'aatz	Batz'	Chuen	Monkey, Thread
Ee	E	Eb	Grass, Tooth
Aa	Ah	Ben	Cane, Reed
Ix	Ix	Ix	Jaguar, Maize
Tz'ikin	Tz'iquin	Men	Eagle, Bird, Moon
Aama	Ahmac	Cib	Vulture, Soul, Wax, Insect
Noq	No'h	Caban	Earthquake, Season, Thought
Tiax	Tihax	Etz'nab	Knife, Sacrifice
Kaoo	Cawuk	Cauac	Rain, Storm
Hunaapu	Hunahpu	Ahau	Lord, Sun

I ask whether some days are better than others.

"Kub'aal Aa is a good day, so is Lord B'aatz, and Lord Tz'ikin. There are other good days, and some bad ones." The old man pauses, then adds, as if reading my thoughts, "The name of today is Twelve—Twelve Lord Tz'ikin. In Ixil, *Caplabal Tachbal Kub'aal Tz'ikin.* Tomorrow will be Thirteen Lord Aama."

Evidently we have arrived on a good day. I wonder if this is why they are so forthcoming. For the Maya nothing happens purely by chance. There are influences at work in everything: the weight of the number; the character of the day; the character of the year in which the day falls. Added to these are the positions of the planets, the phase of the moon, the earthly seasons of rain and heat. I am about to ask about the Year-Bearers, when the old man again anticipates my question.

"Four days," he says, "carry the year. They are Lord Chee, Lord Iiq', Lord Noq, and Lord Ee."

"When will you celebrate the New Year?" I ask. Uncle and nephew debate a little in Ixil; I hear the Spanish words *marzo* and *febrero*. Don Arcadio explains:

"The Ixil new year used to begin in March, but because 1984 was a leap year, it now falls on the last day of February. Next year it will be Lord Thirteen Chee."

(Later, I sort this information out. It confirms that not only is the tzolkin here in perfect step with all the others, but the relationship of solar year and tzolkin is the same for the Ixiles and Quichés. Thus, both have the same Year-Bearers, and both start the Maya new year together. So we are currently in a year 12 Wind, to be followed, on February 28, 1986, by 13 Deer. The year after that will be 1 Grass—a "President of World," because he is first in a number sequence. After him comes 2 Earthquake; and 1989 will be a year 3 Wind.)

We ask if we may make an offering to the saints. The daykeeper agrees to do this in the proper way, with what he calls a "twenty-candle" ceremony. David goes out shopping and comes back with about twice that number of slim handmade candles. Don Arcadio and his uncle take us into their small cofradía chapel across the patio.

The ceiling is hung with plastic flags, cut like doilies. (Plastic starts out as a wrapping or bag in a well-to-do household, gets thrown away, is plucked from the cargo of the garbage trucks, washed, hung up to dry, cut into patterns, and used to adorn chapels and churches all over Guatemala.) The floor is of earth and the walls of adobe. There's a poster for Vinicio Cerezo and the Christian Democrats beside the images of the saints.

The altar is a simple wooden table supporting two magnificent brass candlesticks and two pottery ones. In front of these there's a flat pottery candle-holder, shaped rather like an ice tray with a single row of fourteen sockets. The daykeeper fills this, and then kneels down, sticking seven more candles on the ground by melting their bases. It puzzles me that a "twenty-candle" ceremony should have twenty-one, but then I remember how he recited the names of the days, repeating the first again at the end. This also explains the fourteen sockets in the candle-holder: a full sequence of thirteen, plus one—the way we count an octave.

On the altar beside the saint there's a great wooden crucifix, swaddled in bright Ixil cloth. The Christ wears a halo of bronze sun rays, as well he might—*Kub'aal Q'ii*, Lord Sun, and *Kub'aal Cristo* are one and the same.[12] The twenty day lords are, among other things, manifestations of Lord Sun. The Mexican scholar Miguel León-Portilla has pointed out that the word for "sun" also means "day" and "time" in all Maya languages: "The Maya conceived of time in close association with the solar deity, something divine in itself, limitless and ubiquitous."[13] Time animates, and is indivisible from, space: "All the deities present and acting in space are the changing countenances of time. Isolated from time, space becomes inconceivable. In the absence of time-cycles, there is no life, nothing happens, not even death."[14]

When all the candles are burning, the daykeeper lights a pottery brazier full of pine chips and copal incense. A blue cloud rises before the altar and wreathes the images. Oily flames light up his old, wise face as he chants the names of the day lords.

A sense of elation overtakes me. Here among the very people we feared destroyed, a Maya calendar priest has made us a gift of knowledge. His gift is also a statement: politics and the calendar have always been linked for the Maya; by telling us the names of the days and the years, the daykeeper has answered our larger question—he has affirmed that the Ixil survive.

While he chants, I think of a passage in the *Chilam Balam of Chumayel* that cannot be very different from what we are hearing now. It tells of the creation of time and the world—in that order—the creation of the first *uinal*, or twenty-day period. *Uinal* is cognate with *uinic*, meaning "man," or "person": twenty is the number of our digits and of our destiny; and in twenty days God made the Maya universe. This translation by Gordon Brotherston conveys the Maya fondness for wordplay:

1 Chuen, the day [the Creator] rose to be a day-ity and made the sky and earth.
2 Eb, he made the first stairway. It ebbs from heaven's heart, the heart of water, before there was earth, stone, and wood.
3 Ben, the day for making everything, all there is. . . .
4 Ix, he fixed the tilt of the sky and earth.
5 Men, he made everything.
6 Cib, he made the number one candle and there was light in the absence of sun and moon.

7 Caban, honey was conceived. . . .

8 Etz'nab, his hands and feet were set. . . .

9 Cauac, the first deliberation of hell.

10 Ahau, evil men were assigned to hell. . . .

11 Imix, he construed stone and wood; he did this within the face of the day.

12 Ik, occurred the first breath. . . .

13 Akbal, he poured water on the ground; this he worked into man.

1 Kan, he "canned" the first anger because of the evil he had created.

2 Chicchan, he uncovered the evil he saw within the town.

3 Cimi, he invented death. . . .

[4 Manik missing]

5 Lamat, he invented the seven great seas.

6 Muluc, came the deluge and the submersion of everything before the dawning. . . .

Then the twenty deities came to consider themselves in summation and said:

Oxlahun tuc: uuc tuc, hun

Thirteen units plus seven units equals one.[15]

Chapter 13

13 Cib ⁝‖ 🐢   *Day of the Vulture.*

Noon. We begin the hundred-mile journey eastward across northern Quiché to a place called Tactic, where the road joins a paved highway to Guatemala City.

We climb out of the Nebaj Valley and cross back over the mountain range. In early afternoon the Río Chixoy comes in sight, a dark thread shot with white rapids in a canyon far below. From here the road runs east through Cunén to Uspantán.

USPANTÁN

In 1529, four years after the defeat of the Mams, a Spanish force was soundly beaten here by the Uspanteca and their Ixil allies. Nebaj and Chajul had apparently offered little resistance, but Uspantán was fortified and prepared for war. An inexperienced Spanish commander tried a frontal assault, and was simultaneously ambushed from behind. It was the greatest Indian victory in the Guatemalan wars. The Spaniards and their auxiliaries were routed; and, as in the first European defeat at Mexico City in 1519, Spanish hearts were torn out and offered to the local war god.

At the end of 1530 the Spaniards returned, this time better equipped and led by a seasoned commander. They stormed

251

Nebaj and set it on fire, then destroyed the Uspantán forces by skillful deployment of cavalry. Since the Spaniards regarded the Ixil and Uspanteca as "rebels," all captives were branded and sold into slavery.[1]

Modern Uspantán is equally tragic. The town was hit badly by the 1976 earthquake, and has since been shaken by other tremors. Men are working on the church facade, still split by a vertical crack. But the cruelty of nature has been nothing compared to that of man. From villages near here came many of those burned in the Spanish embassy massacre of January 1980, and that was merely the culmination of a long series of atrocities.

I have found it difficult to judge to what extent the Indian population of Guatemala actively supported the guerrillas; and equally difficult to evaluate how far the guerrillas held the interests of the Indians at heart. The political spectrum has been clouded by the issue of race; and race has become part of the rhetoric of politics. Ladinos of every stripe, from oligarchs to communists, wave the banner of Maya culture in foreign contexts while they trample it at home. I have yet to meet, or read, a non-Indian revolutionary with any clear idea of what self-determination for the Maya might mean.

Fortunately, a young Quiché woman who took part in the recent events has dictated and published her memoirs in exile. Her story is of an Indian family that did indeed side with the rebels—not because of foreign infiltration or Marxist inclinations, but because their experience of the status quo became intolerable. Rigoberta Menchú Tum was born about 1959 in a small village near Uspantán. Her father, Vicente Menchú, was a community leader. (Their surname reveals descent from the ancient Menchú lineage of the Quichés.[2]) She did not learn Spanish until an adult because her parents didn't want to send her to school. "My children," her father said, "don't aspire to go to school, because schools take our customs away from us." The teachers taught "that the arrival of the Spaniards was a conquest, a victory, while we knew that in practice it was just the opposite."[3]

(It is revealing to compare this unschooled Quiché's deep understanding of her people and their past with what Severo

Martínez Peláez has written in a recent article: "The Indians do not know their history," he asserts. "They do not know where they come from . . . they do not possess a definition of themselves. . . ."[4] How little he must know the Maya.)

Menchú is explicit about Quiché culture and religion. "We have kept our identity hidden because we know how to resist, we have hidden whatever governments have tried to take away from us."[5] In language worthy of the *Popol Vuh* she describes the fundamentals of modern Quiché belief: "The one father is the heart of the sky, that is, the sun. The sun is the father and the mother is the moon. . . . They are the pillars of the universe."[6]

From an early age Rigoberta traveled to the coast with her parents and siblings to work on the plantations:

> Two of my brothers died in the *finca*. The first . . .
> Felipe . . . died when my mother started working.
> They'd sprayed the coffee with pesticide by plane
> while we were working, as they usually did, and my
> brother couldn't stand the fumes and died of intoxica-
> tion. The second one . . . was Nicolás. He died when I
> was eight. . . . [from] malnutrition. . . .[7]

When Rigoberta was about fourteen, her best friend María also died from being sprayed in a cotton field.

In the early seventies Rigoberta's father became embroiled in a long dispute with powerful Ladinos over the ownership of some land. After spending the family savings on lawyers' bills, surveyors, and trips to the departmental capital, Vicente Menchú was imprisoned; upon his release he was kidnapped by the landowners' thugs, tortured, and left for dead. He was never able to walk or work properly again, but he became increasingly active in peasant unions. In 1977 Menchú was imprisoned once more, as a *subversivo*. There he met another Indian who talked about the formation of the CUC, the Peasant Unity Committee. After he got out for the second time, Vicente Menchú went underground.

On the ninth of September, 1979, Rigoberta's younger brother was kidnapped and tortured. His sexual organs were mutilated, skin was flayed from his face, but he did not die. Two weeks later the army paraded him and several other victims before their relatives at the Ixil town of Chajul; the captives were then doused with gasoline and burned alive. Four months after this, Vicente Menchú and other Indians from northern Quiché, together with some Ladino sympathizers, staged the occupation of the Spanish embassy that ended in death for them all on January 31, 1980.

On the nineteenth of April, Rigoberta's mother was kidnapped, tortured, and killed near Uspantán. Rigoberta then went into hiding, and later fled Guatemala to bring her story to the outside world. She acted as narrator for the film *When the Mountains Tremble*[8] and dictated her book, *I, Rigoberta Menchú*, in Paris.

It must be said that hers is not the only Indian story in Guatemala. In this compressed and broken land you can find whatever you seek. If you want to find army massacres they are everywhere; if you seek guerrilla atrocities they, too, have happened. If you want to find rich and abusive Indians, you can do so, though they are rare. But the weight of evil falls heavily to one side: there are far more cruel and exploitive Ladinos than Indians; and there is far more innocent blood on the hands of the national army than on the hands of the insurgents.

Whether Guatemala's state terror amounted to genocide is largely a matter of semantics. In the strict sense it was not: there was no governmental policy of killing Indians simply because they were Indians. But Indian life has always been cheap—as cheap to Ladino army officers as it is to Ladino cotton growers. If ten or twenty innocent Indians were killed so as to kill one guerrilla, it mattered little to many commanders. And at the individual level there was indeed genocide: the civil war enabled every racist to practice his own personal pogrom. Those Ladinos who feared the modest political and economic gains that Indians had made during the late sixties and early seventies, who found that they could no longer force an Indian to get off the sidewalk, give up a bus seat, work without pay, provide sexual services, surrender a piece of land, or put up with insults—many of those insecure and violent men found themselves with the chance to do whatever they wished. The government did not order genocide, but it presided over a reign of terror directed mainly against Indians. In this sense there was a race war, and the Ladinos once again conquered the Maya.

What would have happened if the Left had won? Would the Indians have been adequately rewarded for their participation? Would discrimination have been purged from the new Guatemala? Would Indian desires for the preservation of their languages and culture have been met with the creation of suitable institutions—bilingual education, for example, and official multiculturalism? Might there perhaps have been an Indian head of state? Would presidents Arana, Laugerud, and Lucas have been followed by a President Balam, K'anil, or Tzul? The very idea seems absurd, especially to Ladino Guatemalans. But since the majority of Guatemala's population is Indian, why should it be any more absurd than a President Nyerere or Prime Minister Gandhi?

I think it unlikely that four hundred years of structural inequality and ethnic competition would end with the victory of one nonindigenous ideology (Marxism) over another (social Darwinist capitalism). Though numerically the minority, the Ladino sector has such superiority in the skills needed to run a modern economy and state that the Indians would have a very difficult struggle to gain their rightful share of national power. They would also be in direct competition with the mass of poor Ladinos for reallocation of the land and resources of the deposed oligarchy. The Ladinos are members (albeit junior ones) of a culture that is globally dominant, and they speak a language that links them with almost every other country in Latin America. As in Peru, Bolivia, or Ecuador, it is hard to see how the indigenous nations trapped within these Hispanic republics can emerge and regain autonomy while the present world order endures.

A leftist victory in Guatemala might improve the lot of the Indians considerably—especially in matters of health, nutrition, and education—but it would not bring them to power. The malignant Ladino tyranny of the Right would be followed by a better-intentioned Ladino rule of the Left. For Martínez, "socialist Indianism [indigenismo] is a contradiction in terms."[9] If the ideologues of the new Guatemala were of his stamp—and many would be—the Maya could expect scant respect for their identity and culture.

But whether doctrinaire Marxists like it or not, there are two sets of polarities in Guatemala: rich/poor and Ladino/Indian. A just society cannot be built without addressing both. Leveling differences may be the solution for the first, but in the case of the second it is tantamount to destruction of a people who have always made it very clear that they wish to remain as Maya, to preserve cultural systems and values that are uniquely theirs. A historical wrong must be put right: a people has been subjugated; a Maya nation, or group of Maya nations, lies submerged but still vital within a republic called Guatemala, created by and for the invaders and their international connections.

Guatemala is a white settler colony masquerading as a nation, more insidious and far more brutal than South Africa. If a true Guatemalan nation is ever to be built, it must be founded on the principle that Indians and Ladinos are equal, but different. Only in this way will the war that began in 1524 be brought to a just conclusion.

TACTIC

We reached the pavement an hour after nightfall. It was an anxious drive, the tank almost dry and loose rocks bombarding the crankcase, but the late-afternoon views were magnificent. The border of El Quiché and Alta Verapaz is defined by the immense canyon of the Chixoy, here running north. Its western walls were already sunk in twilight when we reached it, but the eastern side was a folded rampart of endlessly varying gilded greens. Beyond, with a shelf of cloud clinging to it like a bracket fungus, lay the Sierra de Chamá, the last wall between highlands and Petén.

After days of jolting over rocks the tarmac seemed a bed of air; we floated into the Texaco station at Tactic, tired, relieved, and hungry. The name of this town (pronounced Tak-TEEK) has nothing to do with generalship: it's the mating call of the male quetzal as he flies, his yard-long emerald plumes trailing behind him.[10] The village stands at the edge of the Biotopo del Quetzal, a shrunken remnant of cloud forest where Guatemala's national bird, symbol of beauty and freedom, battles with extinction.

The pump boy recommended a chicken restaurant just down the road, a place of *"categoría"* in his opinion, a classy spot.

In the shadows of a few naked bulbs and the smoke from the kitchen, it takes a moment for the categoría to evaporate before our eyes. Here is a washbasin and a mirror by the door! But as you approach you see that the mirror is corroded beyond use, there's no soap, and when you turn on the tap no water runs out. Used paper napkins, cigarette ends, and chicken bones cover the floor and tabletops. In one corner a half-naked female statuette holds up a red light bulb among some plastic flowers: Lady Liberty peddling her virtue.

Gabriel García Márquez once said that the Latin American writer's great problem is not to create fantasy from what is real, but to make Latin America's reality believable—a much more difficult task. What temerity a writer needs to say anything about a place like Guatemala; or even a place like this restaurant. You turn from Liberty under the red light to see a safari-suited man stalking a Bengal tiger on the plywood wall that hides the kitchen; the jungle is straight from a Tarzan comic, and the hunter from *Soldier of Fortune*. I step up to the jukebox and find a song called *"Martes Me Fusilan,"* "On Tuesday They Will Shoot Me."

A door in the jungle opens and a slovenly girl comes out to take our order. She has bare feet and traces of purple nail polish on her cuticles. Do we want a leg, wing, or breast? I order breast and chips.

"Yo quiero un pollo entero," David says. "A whole chicken. I want a whole chicken, and I'll pay whatever it costs."

David's chicken arrives—a greasy pile of avian body parts—and he begins to eat. One by one the dogs slink in: friendly, humble, diseased, pathetic dogs. They surround David like disciples at the feet of a saint, tails wagging, noses sniffing; soulful looks at me, at David, at the pile of chicken. A piebald dog, a beige dog, a collieish dog, a black dog, a dog with a withered leg.

"I hate dogs," David says. "But at least it isn't people watching us eat."

1 Caban .

GUATEMALA CITY

The Posada Belén feels almost like home.

The hotel's owner, a plump and cheerful man of Swiss extraction, tells me of a custom observed by the inhabitants of Guatemala City each December: *La Quema del Diablo*, the Burning of the Devil.

"Everybody makes a little bonfire outside his front door. They burn old newspapers, rubbish, and little figures of the Devil. If you go outside early on this day the whole city is thick with smoke. They believe all the evil of the year is destroyed and a new beginning comes. It happens on the seventh."

"That's the day before next week's elections. Did they choose the date deliberately?"

"It was just a coincidence. When the government realized it, they wanted to ban *La Quema del Diablo*—they don't like the custom."

2 Etz'nab •

David leaves for Tikal, Belize; then Canada via Miami. I wish I could stay for the Devil's roast and the elections, but I'd better head for Mexico tomorrow. As the Maya would say, December is being counted, and I must visit Chiapas before meeting my wife at Cozumel in a fortnight's time.

3 Cauac

Morning. Time to pack and send home books (an involved procedure at the post office).

Afternoon. I catch a first-class bus for the Mexican border—an old Greyhound coach. I have a ticket with a numbered seat; there are no standing passengers; and I think I'm in for a comfortable trip. But at the edge of the city the driver opens the door and a dozen people with baskets and cardboard suitcases pile in. The conductor makes them sit on the floor with their heads down whenever we pass a police or military checkpoint. Presumably their fares go into the driver's and conductor's pockets.

The bus descends rapidly into the hotlands of the Pacific coast. Pines and eucalyptus give way to sugarcane, mile after mile of it. Most of the canes are in flower, crowned by tassles undulating in the wind. An occasional ceiba, rising like a tall mushroom above this glaucous sea, is all that's left of the primeval forest. To Indians the ceiba is the world-tree, to Ladinos it's Guatemala's national plant; neither race lightly cuts it down.

ESCUINTLA

The name of the town means "Place of Dogs," and it's full of the mangy creatures scavenging in empty lots. The zinc-roofed wooden shanties are reminiscent of Belize. A lone Ixil woman stands resplendent and poised amid the squalor. On the horizon, where the highlands begin, a few patches of bush cling to the crevices of eroded mesa-like hills, red and purple in the hazy air. The rivers we cross are black and dead—killed by abuse of pesticides.

* * *

After dark the journey becomes a mystery tour through a hot, moist country I have never seen by day. Only the heavy atmosphere conveys the essence of each town and junction: rotting mangoes, burning rubbish, mud flats, cane alcohol, a greasy meal, a latrine; from plantations the deadly fragrance of chemical sprays, from the road diesel and gasoline—the foul breath of our civilization. The conductor sheds all caution in stuffing the bus. At each stop he walks along outside, shouting and stabbing his finger through the windows: "*Usted señor, usted señora, pase más atras.* [You sir, you madam, move farther back.] *¡Toditos, toditos, tienen que subir!* [Everyone, absolutely everyone, must get on!]" He becomes increasingly manic as the night wears on. Nine o'clock—the promised time of arrival at the frontier—comes and goes. The conductor's shouts draw heckles from the human millipede along the aisle. "*¡Aquí nos asfixiamos!* [We're suffocating here!]"—a murmur of agreement; "*¡Cuidado con la mano!* [Watch it with the hand!]"—a roar of laughter. I think: It's all right for the conductor, he has the doorway to stand in. But eventually he fills even that, and rides for half an hour attached to the side of the bus like a rock climber, toes in the handles of the luggage hold and fingers gripping a windowsill.

11:00 P.M. At last, the frontier. It takes another hour to get through the Guatemalan side: the power keeps failing and the passport officer hasn't got a candle.

At midnight I walk across the international bridge. A small boy changes the last of my quetzals for pesos. Mexico! Suddenly I realize I've been holding my breath for weeks.

Part IV

West: Chiapas

Chapter 14

4 Ahau : 🔲   *Day of the Sun Lord*

SAN CRISTÓBAL DE LAS CASAS, MEXICO

The big bells of the cathedral are tolling for mass with the *chang, chang* of a railwayman striking carriage wheels—a nostalgic sound. I feel very tired. The hotels in Tapachula (the first town inside Mexico) were full last night. I went back to the bus station and caught an express for San Cristóbal at half past twelve. We drove for hours through the thick dark air of Soconusco, the Pacific littoral conquered by Moctczuma a decade before the Mesoamerican world abruptly collapsed. I may have slept a bit there, but it was the kind of sleep in which you think yourself awake; images swam in my mind like fish in a bowl; they seemed to have some logical connection that vanished whenever a jolt brought intrusion from normal consciousness. Then the bus climbed over the continental divide, and whenever it met another vehicle, headlights shone into my eyes like a midnight arrest. I drank sweet black coffee in a gray dawn at Tuxtla, and two hours later arrived here and took a room in the first hotel I saw, right on the plaza. I had a shower and tried to nap but it was futile. The maids carried a radio around with them and banged their mops against the furniture; three large parrots in the hall squawked every twenty minutes, as if trained to keep a narcolept awake.

The colonial heart of the city was destroyed by Ladino

civil wars in the 1860s. Only the cathedral is original, and it
turns its side to the square.[1] But the arcades and gardens are a
pleasant change from Guatemala's sterile and pretentious Hel-
lenism. There's life here: balloon sellers, ice cream men, a
couple of buskers, children running, Chamula women hawk-
ing dolls—and not a soldier in sight.

The first time I was here, almost ten years ago, the Indians
seemed repressed and desperately poor. The city—culturally
and historically closer to Guatemala than to the rest of Mexico—felt racially tense. Chamula women followed you everywhere with their pathetic woolen dolls, whining, "*Cómprame,
señor, cómprame,*" like tedious brats. One was irritated and
stirred to pity in equal amounts, but how many dolls could one
buy? The Chamulas are still here but they seem changed: their
faces are brighter, their clothes cleaner, their approach is more
direct and dignified. Has their life really improved, or do things
just look better after coming from Guatemala?

I go to a long-distance telephone in a pharmacy and spend
an hour getting through to my wife. The chemist, a sour man
with a bulldog's face, dials incessantly and gestures at me
through the glass door of the soundproof box. Cables were
broken in the Mexico City earthquake, and it's hard to get a
line. It was much easier to call from Guatemala, but one had to
be careful what one said: "All international calls are tapped," I
was warned.

The city's name is composed, oddly, of Columbus's patron saint
and the man who became Spain's conscience for what he called
"the destruction of the Indies." Bartolomé de Las Casas was
born in Seville in 1474; his father sailed with Columbus in
1492. Bartolomé arrived in Hispaniola just before the turn of
the century and soon began to denounce injustices committed
by his countrymen against the rapidly dwindling natives of the
Caribbean. He was ordained in 1510, and returned several
times to Spain to lobby the king. His idealism earned him
hatred and the official title Protector of the Indians.

Like many who have played Utopia in America, Las Casas
tried to establish model colonies. The first, on the Venezuelan

coast, was destroyed by hostile natives; the second, in the land
he called Verapaz (True Peace) had some success among the
Guatemalan Maya but was soon wrecked by those of his com-
patriots who wanted no such example to thrive—a familiar
fate of social experiments in Latin America then and now.

In 1543 the Spanish king named Las Casas bishop of
Cusco, the old capital of Inca Peru, but Bartolomé declined,
preferring an appointment to a territory without riches.
Instead he became first bishop of Chiapas, a "new," poor province on the frontier of Spanish Mesoamerica. In 1544, at the age
of seventy, Las Casas left Spain for the post; it was his thirteenth crossing of the Atlantic.[2] Three years later he was recalled to answer charges brought against him and his ideas by
enemies and interest groups. There followed the famous
"debate" (never actually face-to-face) between Las Casas and
Sepúlveda before the Council of the Indies. It was an extraordinary occasion, perhaps the first time in history that an imperial power formally examined its own conscience and
questioned its moral right to rule. Sepúlveda, who nowadays
reads like a more erudite Hitler or Khomeini, set out to prove
that the American Indians were, like Africans, not really
human beings, and that everything done by the Spanish conquistadors was justified by the famous papal bull that divided
the New World between Portugal and Spain; Christianity was
allowed any means to its end. Las Casas argued that Europe
had been granted only the right to evangelize without the use
of force, and that native American governments were under no
obligation to accept the political hegemony of Christendom
against their will. He presented horrifying figures—fifteen
million dead because of Spanish greed—which at the time
seemed the most flagrant hyperbole but are now known to have
been close to the truth.

Las Casas won his battle, but of course the wars were lost.
The Arawaks, Aztecs, Incas, and most of the Mayas were
ruined. Spain tried to prevent further conquest, but there was
little left to conquer; and the Crown was in any case quite
unable to restrain those Johnny-come-latelies who tore
through South America's jungles searching for El Dorado,
which was nothing but a memory of what had already been

destroyed. Yet the New World would have been a worse place without Las Casas; the very fact that Spain produced and listened to such a man is one of history's marvels.

The present bishop of Chiapas was wearing a gray suit and tartan shirt without a tie. A jovial personality bubbled to the surface at his eyes, magnified by heavy glasses. I explained why I'd come. Would he have time for an interview?

I had been shown into an anteroom with a lofty ceiling and high-backed wooden chairs around the wall. The building had the cavernous smell of a church: damp mortar and flagstones vaguely spiced with incense. The sun came in through tall barred windows, clothing a picture of the pope in stripes. I'd never met a Catholic bishop before. I wondered how to address him. Not *señor*, surely—perhaps *monseñor?* At this moment the bishop appeared.

"Samuel Ruíz," he said, holding out his hand. "Could you come back at four? There's a gentleman coming to see me from Austrian television. He has interests similar to yours—perhaps we could do both interviews together?"

When I return, the television crew—an Austrian interviewer and Mexican cameraman—has already arrived.

"How about this room?" the bishop is saying. He opens double doors to a long chamber resembling a baronial dining hall. Former bishops in full regalia glare sanctimoniously from the walls.

"Too formal?"

"Yes, too formal," the Austrian says. "What about out here in the passage? Is there enough light, Hernán?" The cameraman peers through his camera and nods. The passage is separated from a neglected patio by a glass partition. (At seven thousand feet, San Cristóbal is often cold and wet.) On the end wall hangs a large oil painting of a modern martyr: Bishop Oscar Romero, gunned down at his cathedral in San Salvador by a right-wing death squad.

"Could you sit below Monseñor Romero?" the Austrian asks.

"Of course," says the bishop. "Is this chair all right, or shall

we look for something more, er, *underdeveloped?*" He
chuckles. The Austrian chooses an ugly steel chair with a
plastic seat. The interview begins:

"What can the church of today offer the Indians?"

"I believe that the church can offer—*must* offer—the
same thing that it has always offered the poor since its foundation: total liberation; liberation from all oppression, from all
mistreatment."

"Does this lead you to contradictions with the Vatican?"

"With Vatican Two there are no contradictions."

The bishop is a liberal man, conscious of his delicate political position. Delicate not only in Mexico, where the church
officially does not exist, but also with regard to the present
Vatican, where the word *liberation* has become suspect. Liberation clerics hold that spiritual freedom requires a climate of
physical freedom; that the church must concern itself with
hunger, injustice, and exploitation as well as with the needs of
the soul. Unhappily for them, Pope John Paul II doesn't like
priests to get involved in politics, except in Poland.

The interviewer asks next about involvement of the Chiapas church with Guatemalan refugees. (Bishop Ruíz gave
sanctuary to Rigoberta Menchú when she fled her country, but
he doesn't mention it.)

"We don't see the action we have taken for the refugees as
any different from the pastoral care we provide for all Indians
and poor people within the diocese."

Again the perfect diplomat. The refugees have been a
source of embarrassment for the Mexican government. Their
presence just inside the border led to bloody incursions by
Guatemalan forces in claimed "hot pursuit." Mexico did not
want to encourage the refugees, and has since moved most of
them far away to Campeche and Quintana Roo.

"We think the best solution might have been to relocate
them in the interior of Chiapas, away from the Guatemalan
border but still in an environment similar to the one they left
and among peoples who have a closely related culture. Our
position is really to support whatever the refugees have told us
themselves. Those who wanted to move received our support;
those who decided to go back to Guatemala received our sup-

port; and those who want to stay here in Chiapas have also got whatever support we could offer them."

"How many went back to Guatemala?" I ask.

"It wouldn't be more than a hundred families. Others may have left the camps in Campeche and Quintana Roo and crossed back into Guatemala secretly, but of course there are no figures on that."

"*Muchas gracias,*" the Austrian says. Television interviews are short, and he's got as much as he needs. I move on to Indian culture and religion:

"What is the attitude of the Catholic church now to the so-called costumbres that have come down from ancient Maya times?"

"Nowadays we speak, in Latin America, of a *religiosidad popular.* We have learned to reevaluate the popular expressions of belief. We see now that each people lives its religion within its own historical experience. We feel that the path by which each people seeks God—in other words, their native religion—is a legitimate path. In short, there are many ways to God. What we are trying to do is to incorporate the insights of sociology, of anthropology into the way in which we bring the church to the indigenous people. Until very recently the process of Christianization was too often the same as Westernization. We no longer think it has to be that way."

The tradition of Bartolomé de Las Casas seems well served.

5 Imix

The sun is out, after a cold wet night. *Huevos rancheros* for breakfast; then off to find the New World Archaeological Foundation, a Mormon-funded research group based in San Cristóbal.

Away from the plaza, the conquerors' buildings remain: a Moorish architecture that turns inward, sheltering a garden patio, a well, the family's women, showing only its perimeter to the world. Nowadays the outer walls are washed in white or blue or red and faced with a cement dado, but the windows are still barred, the doors still bound and studded with iron. Tile roofs give postage-stamp edges to the shadows. I pass a *tlapalería*. Ah, Mexico, with its singsong Spanish full of Nahuatl. Ancient Mexicans loved color *(tlapalli)* and that love survives, not only in the murals of Rivera and Orozco but in the humble word for paint shop.

I find Susanna Ekholm almost hidden by papers and potsherds. She's a small, cheerful woman with clear eyes and salt-and-pepper hair. She stands up and draws a cardigan around her.

"Welcome to my nightmare!" I follow her eyes: cabinets from floor to ceiling; drawers labeled Heads, Torsos, Legs, Dog Bodies, and Spare Parts. The night's chill has not left; a small electric fire beside Ekholm's desk is struggling against the length and height of the room. On the wall behind her a political poster gives a concise history of the nation:

> *Hace un chingo de años los indios éramos bien chingones, y Cuauhtémoc era el gran chingón! Pero llegaron un chingo de gachupines y los muy hijos de la chingada hicieron mil chingaderos y chingaron a los indios ... y nos llevaron a todos a la chingada!*
>
> *Y para que no nos sigan chingando, éntrale al Partido Mexicano de Trabajadores!*

· Mexican slang gets a lot of work from the root *chingar*, which means, basically, "to fuck." From it are derived unguessable meanings. A *chingo* is a large quantity or number; a *chingón* is an intelligent or valiant person, an *hijo de la chingada* is a bastard or a son-of-a-bitch; a *chingadero* is a thing; to send or take someone *a la chingada* is to tell him to go to hell or dispatch him to a sticky end. The poster is untranslatable, but here goes:

Many many years ago we Indians were clever and powerful, and Cuauhtémoc [Moctezuma's successor and Mexico's great Aztec hero] was the smartest of all. But there came a shitload of *Gachupines* [derog. for

"Spaniards"] and those bastards did a thousand fucking things . . . and took us all to hell!

And to stop them fucking us over, join the Mexican
Workers' Party!

"I take it not everyone here is a Mormon?"

"Some are and some aren't, and there's a few, you know,
jack Mormons in between."

"I've always wanted to know how it is that the Mormons
keep on supporting archaeology when the more they learn the
less it must support their ideas. Do they still think American
Indians are the lost tribes of Israel?"

"God, I feel like a cigarette before we get into that one!"
Ekholm rolls her eyes. "But I'd better not push my luck—we do
try to observe Mormon taboos while on the premises. As I
understand it, there was a crisis in this organization about
twenty years ago. The archaeologists—not all of whom were
Mormons, even then—threatened to resign en masse unless
academic freedom was guaranteed. The church eventually
backed down. So we publish our findings, and the people in Salt
Lake City can do what they want with them."

"So if they want to think that Maya pyramids are variations on Solomon's temple, it's up to them?"

"You've got it."

Susanna Ekholm's "nightmare" is specifically a wealth of
late Classic Maya pottery from a find she made at a place called
Lagartero, near the Guatemalan border. Dozens of fine polychrome plates and vases are laid out on tables. The colors are
almost as fresh as when new, but every vessel has been assembled from shards.

"What you see here is only a fraction of it—wait till I show
you the storeroom—I've got dinner settings for eight hundred
just in the flower pattern alone. And little me had to stumble
on it by accident. All because of a ceiba tree."

During some very hot weather Ekholm decided to dig in
the shade of a silk-cotton tree growing among the ancient
mounds at Lagartero. There she discovered a huge pit filled
with broken pottery.

"A lot of the artwork is conventional, but there are some

pieces by an obvious master." On her choicest specimens the brushstrokes have the economy and assurance of Japanese caricature. "This artist had the genius to defy convention. He or she left out iconographic details whenever they threatened to clutter the design. The lesser painters didn't fool around like that."

The intricate compositions in reds, yellows, browns, and blacks are portraits of Maya ceremonial life. One shows a rustic temple—like those that probably stood on top of the modest pyramids at Lagartero—painted wooden pillars, thatched roof, a dais covered in jaguar skin. The building is flanked by giant supernatural birds, but there's also startling realism: even the pegs stretching the skin are visible.

The pottery was first broken and then deliberately scattered as it was thrown into the pit. Ekholm found pieces of the same vessel up to thirty feet apart. Some pots show signs of use, but many were brand-new; all were very similar in style, locally made. About 90 percent of the vessels bear the glyph of Chuen (or Batz), the day sign of the Monkey. Clearly this was no ordinary rubbish dump.

"It's my guess," she says, "that a sacrifice of this size would have been made only at a major calendrical event—possibly the end of Baktun 9 in A.D. 830."

Scenes from the *Popol Vuh* come to mind. The first pair of hero Twins, called Hun Batz and Hun Chuen, are both simian deities; their names can be translated as One Spider Monkey and One Howler Monkey, respectively.[3] When the Death Lords were finally humbled by Hunahpu and Xbalanqué (the younger half brothers of the Monkey Twins) they were told that blood sacrifice would thenceforth be reserved to the Sun: "There will be no cleanly blotted blood for you, just griddles, just gourds, just brittle things broken to pieces."[4] Nowadays, at Momostenango and many other places, the altars of the ancestors are heaps of broken pots, added to regularly on the day 8 Monkey.

"See this monkey wearing red scarves on his head and wrists?" Susanna Ekholm is excited now. Showing her nightmare to someone else has dispelled the weariness of an endless project. "Today in the Chamula monkey dance, the people dressed as monkeys wear red bandanas. We also found a lot of pebbles in the pit, and pebbles are still used today in Chamula New Year ceremonies. Also, on this pot there's a bound Maya lord who strongly resembles a figure associated with the New Year in the codices."

All of these things point to a ceremony associated with calendrical cycles, but which ones? A recurrence of a specific Monkey day, such as 8 Batz, in the tzolkin? The beginning of a new 365-day year? The rare and momentous completion of a baktun? Or the less rare but equally momentous completion of the Mexican 52-year Calendar Round? Possibly the pit was dug and filled during a period that spanned all four. Later I played around with calendar tables and came up with these figures: a new solar year began just 57 days before the end of Baktun 9; and in the highland Mexican system, a new Calendar Round began in A.D. 831. From the glyphs on the Lagartero pots it's clear that a Monkey day was important, but the associated number is not given. There is really no hard evidence for thinking that it must have been 8; but, for what it's worth, 8 Batz fell 130 days—exactly half a tzolkin—into the new Baktun 10.

Susanna gave me free run of the NWAF library and left me there this afternoon. It smelled of damp books mingled with kerosene (used on floorboards) and some arums in a vase by the window. I had a view of the city's roofs and wooded hills beyond, dark and furry in a woodsmoke haze, of sagging tiles and telegraph poles like weathered crosses with a cat's cradle of wiring strung between them. I dipped into several books, including a facsimile edition of all surviving Maya codices— the Dresden, Paris, and Madrid (named for the cities where the originals are kept), and fragments of a recently discovered fourth. I found Robert Laughlin's *The Great Tzotzil Dictionary of San Lorenzo Zinacantán*, a landmark of modern Maya linguistics published by the Smithsonian and given Senator William Proxmire's Golden Fleece Award as an example of how government money is "wasted" by academics. Pollen spilled from the arums and left a powdering of spent fertility on my pile of books. Sunlight leaked across the floor.

I've missed the Mexican lunch hours (noon to three) and it's too early for supper. I have a beer and sandwich at the Diego de Mazariegos, the best hotel in town, named after the conqueror of Chiapas. Nostalgia for the Spanish past is not encouraged in Mexico, but Chiapas occupies a cultural and historical position distinct from the rest of the country. In the colonial period it was part of Guatemala, but when the Central American federation was formed after the collapse of the Mexican Empire in 1823, Chiapas voted to stay with Mexico. The *mestizaje*, or mingling of races and cultures that took place between Aztecs and Spaniards, ultimately producing a new nation, did not happen here or in Yucatán, although both regions have experienced increasing Mexicanization since the Revolution and the socialist reforms of the 1920s and 1930s. *Mestizaje* is a dangerous word. It is often extolled by non-Indian ideologues in countries with large Indian populations as a sort of gloss to justify depriving the natives of their culture, a euphemism for Ladinoization, Westernization, or ethnocide. But true *mestizaje* implies a meeting in the middle, a genuine blend of cultural forms, not the triumph of European culture over the indigenous.

Of all the American and European nations that clashed in the sixteenth century, the Aztecs (who usually called themselves the *Mexica*) and the Spaniards had the most in common. Both were ruthless warriors and plunderers intent on living luxuriously at the expense of others. Both had predatory religions that justified sacrificing infidels and foreigners to their ends. Huitzilopochtli and Saint James the Indian Slayer deserved each other.

Denied their own state, the Mexica aristocracy joined in building that of their conquerors—a common pattern in history; witness the Scots. Even though the weight of political power lay with Europeans, the Indian/Spanish dichotomy never became as polarized in central Mexico as in the lands of the Inca and the Maya. An authentic hybrid culture emerged. The Aztec elements in that culture have since been diluted; but a new people had been engendered, and this new people formed the popular base of the Mexican Revolution and the modern nation born from that bloodletting.

6 Ik  *Today's sign is Wind, Air, the breath of life. Ik is also a day of violence; a bad day to travel. I decide to put off visiting the Maya villages until I've done most of my work in San Cristóbal.*

Ricardo is in his late twenties. He wears jeans and a T-shirt, and the way he speaks has a softness and sensitivity often hidden in Mexican men, burdened as they are by Aztec and Spanish *machismo.* He uses the familiar *tú*—a pleasant change from the old-fashioned courtesies of Guatemala, which seem now like an ornate facade on a rotten building, the crisp uniform of a police state. Ricardo has spent three years working with children in border refugee camps; his small office is crammed to the ceiling with Guatemalan weaving and handicrafts.

"One of our projects is to make materials available so they can continue working. In January we'll be having a textile exhibit in Cancún. That way they can find markets in the United States and overseas." I ask him for statistics on the refugees; the figures he gives agree with what the bishop told me: about fifty thousand registered; perhaps twice that many in all; and half the registered refugees already moved to the Yucatán Peninsula.

"They had to be moved somewhere," he says bleakly. "I was there myself in Las Margaritas—one of the largest border camps—during the bombing in 1983. I have photographs. The Guatemalans came over in helicopters. You can imagine. The people started to move northward, about fifteen kilometers from the frontier. Then, in 1984, there was an attack on El Chupadero—*twenty kilometers* inside Mexico." He swings his chair around and glances out the window, as if he half expects to see Kaibiles marching down the street. "Those camps are more or less empty now. In 1984 the government began taking people to less sensitive areas."

He looks me in the eye, a wan smile struggling to break cover from his moustache. "In my view the relocation was necessary, but there were many problems with the way it was done. As usual, politics overruled humanitarian concerns. You know that many Tzotzil and Tzeltal have begun to colonize the jungle? Well, those settlers began to help the refugees a lot. It was a sort of Maya reunion, something very beautiful to see. They began sharing their languages, their textiles—it was a Maya cultural interaction. In one little camp where we worked there were people from six language groups, and the children were learning to speak all six, as well as Spanish. The powers-that-be didn't like this solidarity between the *indios* of Mexico and Guatemala. Not long afterward I was at the United Nations. I happened to see a recommendation from the United States government to our government demanding that even the local Mexican Indians be cleared from the border area to create a 'clean zone,' a kind of—what did they call it in Vietnam?"

"DMZ?"

"Yes, a DMZ! The U.S. wanted a line of defense against 'communist subversion.' "

"Can I keep that on the record?"

Ricardo pauses; then says quietly, *"Sí, puedes usar eso—* you can use that."

7 Akbal

The Tzotzil and Tzeltal of Chiapas not only survive but retain a typically Maya diversity within their shared cultural system. Each village has its own variety of speech and style of dress reaching back to the pre-Columbian past, gradually altered by evolution and necessity. The plumed headdresses have been replaced by hats hung with colored ribbons; shorts or trousers have ousted the breechclout; cloaks and ponchos are made from sheep's wool instead of native cotton and rabbit fur. But the patterns remain: a particular ribbon may represent a jaguar penis; dreams and mythology are woven into cloth; suns and feathered serpents inhabit geometric designs.

Walter Morris, an expert on Chiapas textiles, has written:

The hieroglyphic books have been destroyed. The
great pyramids and palaces of stone have fallen into
ruin . . . weaving alone has given artistic expression to
the profound wisdom of Maya culture. . . . Through
repeated cycles of birth and decline, conquest and
revival, weaving has preserved the design of the Maya
universe.[5]

He and other enthusiasts have helped the Chiapas Maya
set up a cooperative called Sna Holobil, "The Weavers' House."
I saw the shop this morning, its walls glowing with rich colors
and reticulated motifs. The craftsmanship seemed to resonate
with the plateresque facade of the sixteenth-century church
next door. However little else they have in common, Maya and
Spanish are two cultures that have always loved the baroque.

I was invited to attend one of Sna Holobil's business meetings. A tiny patio with yellow walls was thronged with women
in indigo skirts, broad belts, and white huipiles richly brocaded
in countless shades of magenta, yellow, orange, and blue.
Caterina, a Tzeltal from Tenejapa, sat behind a desk issuing
receipts for pieces that will be sold in the shop. She shook my
hand and smiled up at me, a wide, warm face beneath a wreath
of black hair formed from two glossy braids wound around her
head in Grecian style. An old man from Zinacantán leaned,
arms folded, against the wall. He wore a pink poncho edged
with crimson and scarlet thread; streamers from a straw hat
fell to his waist, below which he had on jeans and leather
sandals. His wife, beside him, was eating an orange. The patio
crackled with the crisp repartee of Tzeltal and Tzotzil, but
quieted to a murmur when the meeting began in a neighboring
room.

Everything was done in Maya. The style was oratorical—
only occasionally did speaker and listeners meet one anothers'
eyes. The speakers were mostly women, and they delivered
what they had to say forcefully and with immense poise,
whether seated at the table or on the palm mats covering the
floor. The gathering reminded me powerfully of scenes in
ancient Maya sculpture, of cross-legged figures inclined toward
each other with the chin raised and the hands striking elegant

gestures—a refined yet lively discourse following ancient rules of etiquette and debate.

Afternoon. Susanna has invited me on a picnic in the hills. We stopped to collect a Dutch artist and his wife. There's a colony of gringos here, rather like the ones Lawrence knew at Lake Chapala when he was writing *The Plumed Serpent*. (The Mexicans called them *existencialistas*, which wasn't meant as a compliment.) The artist is building an *existencialista* house in the shape of a serpent with wobbly stone walls and a flat concrete roof. He has a vague expression and two English sheepdogs that look and behave like dirty polar bears. Ray and Liz, students at NWFA, who've joined us in their Volkswagen bus, have another pair.

We follow a smooth tarmac road up into the pine forest, past a village called Crushton. (How English the sign looks, but I think it's Maya for "Stone Cross.") At Romerillo, a hill has three tall crosses dressed in pine boughs and below them rows of graves—mere piles of earth covered by mahogany planks. Many of the houses here are modern brick or concrete block affairs, but there are some of the traditional Tzotzil type: wattle and daub cubes with thatched or shingled hip roofs capped by a small gable resembling in silhouette an ancient roof comb. The village women wear long black skirts, red belts, blue blouses, and blue shawls; the men are in either black or white, depending on the color of the sheep that supplied their hairy, leather-belted cloaks.

We climb above the settlements, leaving behind the aroma of cooking fires, and park near the road in a clearing surrounded by dwarf oaks, madrone trees, and large solitary pines. This is cloud forest and the bromeliads are in flower, sending up blooms like orange asparagus tips.

The Dutch couple flop down on the ground, mobbed by their dogs; Elizabeth and Ray unpack shrimp, salads, bread, and cheese. I produce a dozen Dos Equis beers.

"Good stuff, Dos Equis," says Susanna. "But fattening."

One of the sheepdogs—they all look the same, but their doting owners tell them apart somehow, the way mothers distinguish identical twins—makes a grab for a sandwich already on its way to Susanna's mouth. She gives me an *oh, God!* look and quotes Marx to the shaggy head: "I never forget a face but in your case I'll make an exception."

"Whot was thet?" from the artist.

"Good grief, the dog's drooling in the salad!" from me.

"Jamie! You're an SOB! Git!" from Liz; but Jamie takes no notice.

"Let's take them for a walk," I suggest.

This is not a good idea. The four animals—it's hard to think of them as dogs—tear through the bushes down the hill and into a sheep pasture beside a stream. Liz and I follow, sliding down clay paths, grabbing at shrubs. Excited barks and frantic bleating echo through the woods. Luckily the worst hasn't happened. The dogs are playing in the stream, the sheep racing for cover. Just at this moment two Tzotzil men, probably Chamulas, appear—black ponchos, leather belts, long machetes, and hostile expressions—like villains from a spaghetti western.

"Where are you from?" one asks in good Spanish.

"San Cristóbal," says Liz.

"What are you doing here?"

"Just out for the afternoon. Picnicking."

"Where are your cars?"

"Up there." She waves her hand vaguely toward the hill behind us.

"What are the license plate numbers?"

"I'm afraid I don't know."

I remember some of the things Susanna has told me about the Chamulas. They don't like outsiders, especially on their land. Apparently a tourist was killed recently for making free with his camera in Chamula church.

"What are these animals?"

"They're dogs. English dogs. Sheepdogs."

"They eat sheep?"

"No, they *love* sheep," Liz insists. "They're specially bred to care for sheep. Sheepdogs—*perro pastor.*"

The Chamulas look at the dogs, now panting on the stream

bank. The very idea of a *perro pastor* is clearly the most outrageous gringo lie they've heard in ages. The sheer monstrosity of it seems to impress them, or possibly they're just too dignified to argue.

"You'd better take your dogs and leave immediately."

We do.

8 Kan :|

"Languages," said Samuel Johnson, "are the pedigree of nations." French and Spanish have academies to keep them "pure." English, which sails under many flags and has round heels in the presence of bombastic foreigners, does not. But consider the fate of the world's little tongues. Each language is a unique description of the world, shaping and shaped by culture and environment, imposing categories on inchoate experience; its death is the phonic and gnostic equivalent of extinction of a species. Erse, Maori, Ainu, and Maya survived like rare fauna in their enclaves until hunted by ships, roads, schools, and radios in the service of governments, empires, global economies, and faiths. It's been said that a language (a thriving one) is a dialect with an army behind it; the only guarantee of success is expansion, and the minimum requirement for survival would seem to be a nation-state.

The genetic collapse of indigenous America has been surpassed by a mortality of words. The language that gave us *potato* is dead; the ones that gave us *caucus* and *chocolate* are dying; the future of Maya, from which we got *hurricane* and *shark*, is uncertain, not only because of relentless attack by Spanish but because the ancient fragmentation of the Maya themselves has left not one language but more than twenty. Even in Guatemala, where Maya speakers outnumber Ladinos, no single Maya tongue is spoken by more than a fifth of the population. (In the Andes, by contrast, where the Inca Empire left a legacy of Quechua, state bilingualism is an option.) So

Maya has been condemned by history to the margins of the modern world. But, like the Welsh, the Maya do not give up their culture easily.

Sna Htz'ibahom,[6] a writers' workshop, aims to reverse the erosion of Tzotzil and Tzeltal by publishing booklets and staging theatrical productions in those languages. The office is on the edge of San Cristóbal in a complex belonging to INI, the National Indigenous Institute of Mexico. You cross a muddy stream and walk between whitewashed buildings separated by gravel drives. A sign announces Sna Htz'ibahom and glosses the name as "Writers' House, Culture of the Maya Indians." I notice that they use *indio*, boldly rehabilitating that word and defying, perhaps, any pressure toward assimilation (of which INI is sometimes accused).

"Of course, why not? We are Indians, aren't we?" Maryan (Tzotzil for Mariano) is sitting at a bench by the window, painting a papier-mâché head. He's young, no more than thirty, but his forehead is deeply lined, and his hand rises with a slight hesitation to sweep a lick of black hair from his eyes. He's the head of the group, a Chamula from Chamula Center, capital of the largest Tzotzil township. His Spanish is better than mine, but I can tell it's his second language by the soft cadences and occasional gender confusions in his speech.

"This is for a puppet theater we're developing," he says, holding up the head. "Not just for entertainment, but to instruct—about problems like alcoholism, violence, public health, corruption. A sermon doesn't do any good, but if you amuse people you can teach them something."

"Especially with the more satirical pieces!" Another man, older and obviously Mexican, appears. He's Alfredo, a schoolmaster from Mexico City. "Mainly Aztec and Portuguese in my background. But I help out here because I've had some experience teaching among native communities in the jungle. The biggest problem these people face is the problem of land."

Maryan nods emphatically: "This land we're sitting on, right here in San Cristóbal, used to be part of Chamula!"

Alfredo continues, "Historically, the Indian is the rightful owner of the land. But the *caciques*—the big landlords—have enormous estates while others have nothing. The Indian remains the servant of the rich, working for miserable wages."

I mention that I've just come from Guatemala, and this sounds familiar. What about the Revolution and the land reform begun by President Cárdenas more than fifty years ago?

"In the constitution of this country it states that no individual may own more than a hundred hectares. But what happens?" Alfredo shrugs and rubs his thumb and fingers together. "Simple. The big landowners offer bribes and register their estates in the names of their aunts and uncles, nieces and nephews, brothers and sisters." He laughs, mocking an election slogan: "*¡Así es la revolución en marcha!*"

According to figures I've seen, the Revolution in Chiapas wasn't all in vain. The size of Chamula township, essentially a small Maya city-state relentlessly shorn of its best land during the colonial and prerevolutionary periods, increased from 94 square miles in 1936 to 142 square miles in 1968.[7] This makes it larger than the sovereign nation of Grenada, although its population is less. Even so, the poor, mountainous soil, eroded by centuries of overgrazing, cannot support Chamula's fifty-five thousand inhabitants. Pressure has led to conflict with other Indian townships, and friction within Chamula itself. Many Chamulas have migrated to the city or to *ejidos* (collective homestead lands administered by the Mexican government) in the jungle lowlands, where they are vulnerable to corrupt officials and cattle barons.

The revolutionary land reform decreased the power of traditional elders in Chamula and elevated a new group of ambitious, bilingual Indians ready to cooperate with the federal government. They have now become an entrenched oligarchy, sustained by the ties of patronage that hold together the Mexican corporate state.

"Many people in Chamula are not happy with the *presidente de tierras*, who apportions the communal lands, even though he's a Chamula himself. So we are making a puppet for him." Maryan shows me the head he's working on. It's plump, and suavely corrupt, a closed, forbidding countenance: a modern Chitam of Tikal.

"Nothing too direct," Alfredo adds. "That would be asking for trouble. Just a little satire to raise consciousness, to get the message across, especially to the young."

I ask about the spread of evangelical fundamentalism. Has it become a problem in highland Chiapas?

"Terrible!" says Alfredo. "You know, they come here to divide us—not just the Indians but all of Mexico. It's a new wave of ideological colonization, planned in the United States by the CIA!"

"How many Chamulas have become Evangelicals?"

"Oh, many," says Maryan hotly. "Many!"

"How many? Ten percent, twenty?"

"No, more, far more, about half. And there are so many different kinds. The community is very divided. Chamula Center is one of the few towns that is protecting the customs, the traditional Catholicism. Some of the others—Tenejapa, Oxchuc—their customs are practically finished."

"The Evangelicals do do some good," Alfredo adds. "They stop people wasting money on alcohol and tobacco. But their mentality is so closed. Everything's a sin. They won't take part in civic ceremonies. No dancing—that's a sin. They won't even sing the national anthem. That's a sin, too!"

"They sing it all the time in the United States."

"Of course, of course. It suits their purposes."

The conversation turns to language. Maryan shows me some of the books Sna Htz'ibahom has published: collections of folktales and oral histories.

"How much demand for these books do you find? How many people can read Maya?"

Maryan answers. "It depends on the town. In Chamula the language is still quite pure but in other places they're speaking a mixture, especially the young people. Some of them even make fun of their own language. But in Chamula and Zinacantán they are very keen to learn. Our next project is a school textbook with Tzotzil and Tzeltal grammar and lessons based on the customs of the elders."[8]

In an effort to encourage them, I tell them what happened to English—how it was submerged for three hundred years after the Norman Conquest, but eventually triumphed, albeit greatly changed.

"These little books are a beginning," Alfredo says. "Four hundred years ago Bishop Landa destroyed the codices of Yucatán, and in Mexico they burned the library of Netzahualcóyotl. They say it took three days!"

There's outrage in his voice. For him, the rape of the pre-Columbian world is a wrong keenly felt. Mexicans, as Octavio Paz has said, "relate the present to the past, whereas [North] Americans relate it to the future."[9] The past lies immanent in the landscape and the mind; the present is recognized for what it is: merely the cutting edge of ancient instruments and forces. (Tlaxcalans, whose ancestors helped Cortés, still get beaten up as "traitors" in Mexico City bars.)

Alfredo is here to help redeem the past. It's too late for *his* people: the Aztec nation has lost its language and changed beyond recognition; but here, among the Maya, a corner of the old Mesoamerica can be defended and revitalized; a broken part of himself put back together.

9 Chicchan ⋮ 🔲   *Day of the Snake; a Sunday.*

When I visited Chamula in the mid-seventies, the road was bad and transportation irregular. I remember walking all the way back to San Cristóbal one evening. It took about three hours, though it would have been less if I hadn't stopped to watch two turkeys mating by the roadside (the male aroused the female by walking on her back like a chiropractor). Now there's a fast paved road and a fleet of Volkswagen buses cooperatively owned by Chamulas.

It's nine in the morning; the sky is electric blue, sparsely populated by small clouds of improbable whiteness and solidity, as if painted there by a child. Olive pinewoods, black tarmac, and brick red erosion scars pulsate with the intensity of mountain light. Susanna has brought her Caribe, a Mexican edition of the VW Golf. We follow a truck with Gothic lettering on its bumper: *Se sufre pero se aprende*—"One suffers but one learns." Fatalism mixed with defiance—very Mexican.

ZINACANTÁN

A detour here to see the church. Susanna warns against taking photographs. Her warning is repeated when we buy admission tickets, issued by the Indian municipal government. *"Templo de San Lorenzo Zinacantán,"* says the print in creaky Spanish. "Visitors are not allowed to carry cameras inside the church or outside. Respect the ceremonies of the Officials and Standard Bearers . . . [and] those in charge of the Saints and other traditional fiestas. The person who infringes this decree will be severely castigated."

Near the main church there's a small chapel dedicated to the Lord of Esquipulas. His worshipers are outside, solemnly drinking *pox* (moonshine) from Coke bottles, and listening to doleful music spilling thinly from the chapel door. I look in. A ghetto blaster sits on a table, the chapel's only occupant. Another group of Zinacantán elders is standing nearby. They might have sprung from the pages of a codex: regal and vaguely threatening in long black cloaks trimmed with red; gray head-cloths adorned with brilliant wool pom-poms that spill down their backs; and on their feet, below white cotton shorts and muscular brown calves, high-backed leather sandals identical to those worn by Toltec warriors carved at Tula and Chichén Itzá a thousand years ago.

The San Lorenzo church is remarkable mainly for its saints, many of whom wear Zinacanteco robes. It also has a wooden cross, twenty feet tall, swathed in blue cloth and decked with streamers like the ones on the Indians' hats. When we come out, copal smoke is billowing from the chapel door and the men who were drinking have gone inside. Three musicians on a bench to the right of the altar are playing a harp, a violin, and a guitar. The instruments, like the alcohol, are homemade; they produce a reedy, off-key dirge of fathomless sadness. Three other men in full regalia dance slowly, swaying to the maudlin songs. Hats and bottles are on the table, and behind those you see a dark Christ wreathed in arum lilies, chrysanthemums, and clouds of incense.

CHAMULA CENTER

Last time I was here, Chamula still had the look of a run-down ceremonial center rather than a town—just a church, a hall, and a few half-inhabited houses arranged around the broad, bare plaza. Now the houses have spilled down the approach roads and made them into streets. There are shops and small restaurants with outdoor tables. Three steep hills, topped with wooden crosses, have new flights of steps leading to their summits, giving them the look of ancient pyramids, which in a way they are: each is a mountaintop shrine belonging to one of Chamula's three wards. The god represented by the crosses is the usual Maya amalgam of Sun and Christ, fertility and the four directions.

The plaza is full of the orderly bustle of an Indian market. Indians do not shout at you to buy their wares; a soft entreaty is made if one lingers to look at the clothing, fruit, dried spices, medicinal herbs, and pottery incense braziers on sale. Since the Revolution, Chamula has banned outsiders from living within the Center. All shops, restaurants, and market stalls are owned by Maya.

"There are many rich Chamulas," I hear a taxi driver telling his tourists. "Son muy trabajadores y comerciantes." Very hardworking and businesslike—virtues that San Cristóbal's Ladinos have grudgingly come to respect.

Everyone, even the motorcyclists, wears local dress. Off to one side, on benches facing a bust of Benito Juárez (Latin America's only Indian president), the lords of Chamula are seated in a semicircle. Their wide straw hats, cymbal-shaped and hung with ribbons, give them an Oriental look only partly dispelled by piratical white head scarves with red tassles. Like all Chamula men, they wear the chuh, essentially a woolen poncho sewn together down the sides and smartly gathered at the waist by a leather belt.

Politics and religion are one and the same here, as they have always been for the Maya. Orthodoxy is loyalty, and schism tantamount to secession. Until the turn of this century, the Chiapas Maya deeply resented the control of Catholic religion wielded by Spanish and Ladino officials. They didn't reject Christianity itself, but they wanted the right to run their own church and add to its canon by local revelation. Miraculous appearances of Virgins and saints were common, but every time a new cult came to the attention of the authorities it was ruthlessly suppressed. Early in the eighteenth century, such intolerance led to the so-called Tzeltal Revolt (in which many Tzotzils were also involved). And again in 1869, when some stones fell from heaven and spoke to a Chamula girl who became known as Saint Rose, Ladino authorities, with contemporary Yucatán and their own guilty consciences in mind, saw the cult as the beginning of a "caste war" between races. The whites invented tales of Indian savagery—not omitting a latter-day crucifixion—and achieved a victory for civilization by shooting down hundreds of kneeling Chamula men, women, and children in cold blood.[10]

Eventually anticlericalism triumphed in Mexico and the Indians were left to follow their own inclinations. The appearance of living saints—no longer seen as a threat to church and state—has become almost routine, especially in Zinacantán. They arise, attract followers, prosper or fail, much like mediums and psychics in our own society.

The rise of evangelical sects was quite another matter. Here came rich, powerful foreigners with rigid ideas, out to infiltrate and destroy the Indian power structure by luring away the disaffected. They had little success in Chamula until the 1970s, when overpopulation and deepening corruption in the Maya hierarchy began to throw people their way. Protestantism, like the "heresies" of the past, offered a religious rationale for dissent and appealed to the centrifugal itch so deeply rooted in the Maya soul. Some followers of the new churches went off and founded villages with biblical names. Others took advantage of the education offered by gringo sponsors to become articulate spokesmen against the entrenched alliance of Maya and Mexican *caciques*. This was too much for the traditionalists. They saw the whole, harmonious fabric of Chamula, oriented on the sacred space of the Center, sanctified by the gods of Mesoamerica and Europe, beginning to unravel. It wasn't anything new in Maya history, whether pre- or post-Columbian; but the traditionalists weren't going to give up without a fight. A ban was imposed: Evangelicals, whether gringo or Maya, were expelled from Chamula Center and forbidden to preach there. Those who defied the ban were liable to find that their houses caught fire or that goons waylaid them on mountain trails.

In 1981, Mikel Kashlan, himself a Chamula and leader of the largest Protestant group, was chased into the woods and killed. His supporters called it martyrdom; others claimed that he was involved in a dispute over ownership of a truck. Whatever the truth, his murder displeased the bishop of Chiapas. The Catholic church had finally learned to tolerate all sorts of Maya eccentricities, but the killing of fellow Christians, even Protestants, in defense of the faith went too far. Priestly services were suspended as punishment.

Withdrawal of "foreign" priests has always been considered an ambiguous predicament by the Maya. On the one hand they respect the prestige and expertise of the priesthood, but they resent doctrinal pedantry and unwelcome discipline from pulpit or confessional. During the Yucatán Caste War, they solved the problem by capturing Ladino priests and bending them to their will, but Chiapas in the 1980s was not the time or place for that. The Chamula elders' solution was to secede from the Catholic fold and affiliate themselves with an obscure body called the Mexican Orthodox church of San Pascualito.

This is not, as one might imagine, an offshoot of Byzantium. The Mexican Orthodox church emerged during the Revolution as a nationalized Catholicism. During the heyday of Catholic Action it enjoyed a modest revival by harboring dubious Christs, saints, and Virgins no longer welcome in Rome. Chief of these in Chiapas was San Pascual Rey, also known as San Pascualito Muerte: Saint Paschal King; Saint Paschal Death. His origins are murky and macabre: he seems to have been a pre-Columbian death god, reinforced by medieval traditions of the Grim Reaper, who paradoxically became a specialist in miracle cures. Somehow he acquired the name of Saint Paschal, with whom he had little else in common. Physically, he is a wooden skeleton seated in a wheeled cart. His "remains" (called the Holy Skeletal Replica) are kept in a church in Tuxtla, the state capital, where they are particularly venerated by Zoque Indians and Ladino spirit mediums.

Impressed by the size and fervor of San Pascualito's following, the leader of the "Orthodox" church moved to Tuxtla in 1960, took over the sanctuary, elevated it to a cathedral, and declared himself archbishop and patriarch. There he offers the old Latin mass with prayers in Zoque and marimba music.

This was exactly what the Chamulas were looking for: a suitably Thespian prelate, versed in the Latin mass (which they preferred to Maya mutilated by an earnest padre) and not likely to give them any tedious moralizing so long as the collection plate was full. A few times a year the "archbishop" visits Chamula and performs ornate fiestas, baptisms, and weddings. The rest of the time the church is left to Maya shamans.

The church is an impressive colonial structure surrounded by a whitewashed precinct wall. It stands, Chamulas say, at the navel of the world. Its patron is San Juan, always popular with sun worshipers because his day falls close to the solstice.[11] You enter the precinct through a stone gateway and pass beside a green wooden cross decked with branches and flowers—undoubtedly a world-tree. The Romanesque arch of the church door has recently been painted blue and green with three arcs of brilliant floral rosettes. All this color, set off by the sunlight reflecting from the white facade, dazzles the eyes and closes them against the darkness of the interior. It takes a moment, after entering, to see the Chamula policeman, dressed in white chuh and equipped with a polished club, whose gaze sweeps tourist hands for cameras and their heads for hats. Women must cover the head; men must not.

Gradually my pupils open and I become aware of an enormous cavern fogged with incense, the food of Maya gods. Extravagant candle arrangements glimmer like city lights seen from the air. Shafts of daylight, swirling with smoke, strike down from tiny windows high above. The stone floor is covered with bottles of moonshine and, of all things, Coca-Cola. (Evidently Coke has been adopted as a ritual fluid by those who eschew alcohol.) Before these offerings kneel the sick, while chanting shamans pass eggs over their bodies to absorb the ills. Other individuals and family groups are worshiping in front of saints and crosses wrapped in Maya cloth. We thread our way to the main altar. The vaulted ceiling reverberates with the fricative murmur of Maya prayers, sharp cries from babies on their mothers' backs, muffled groans from those in pain or despair. This seems truly a church of, for, and by the people.

I reach the sanctuary and gaze up at a ceiling painted with silver and gold stars on navy blue, like the vault of a Pharaoh's tomb. Panels at the four corners are occupied by animals: a lion to the left of the altar; a jaguar on the right; and directly above me, a bull on one side and the eagle-and-serpent emblem of Mexico on the other. Some obvious symbolism comes to mind: the animals of Spain and Judah are in the inferior left-hand positions. A jaguar, avatar of God, is on the right.[12] The eagle and serpent are perhaps not merely a patriotic icon but combine to form the plumed serpent, in whom the duality of earth and sky unites. "Quetzalcóatl! They have forgotten thee," cries Christ in *The Plumed Serpent*[13]; but every year Tzotzil dancers still dress up as the old Mesoamerican god.[14]

A gust of aguardiente blows into my face; I hear a torrent of Tzotzil and Spanish ending with *"¡Limosna* [alms] *carajo!"* It's a Chamula policeman, evidently deep in his devotional cups. He is fingering his stave, raised above my head.

"How about an offering for San Juan?" he says.

"An offering? Certainly." I wonder what's expected. Susanna is nowhere in sight. He taps a collection box beside the image of Chamula's patron. I dig in my pocket and trickle some coins into the slot. It is time to leave. I make my way through the crowd and smoke to the door. The policeman keeps reappearing like a figure in a bad dream, his ruddy face alight with drink, faith, and xenophobia.

"What about San Pedro?" comes the voice again. I pay Peter's pence.

"And San Pascualito!" he adds, as I reach the door.

Chapter 15

10 Cimi

The road between San Cristóbal and Palenque is a living thing that shakes its coils and sheds its skin according to the seasons. The pavement is fragile and discontinuous, buried under landslides, cracked by subsidence, held together with strips of gravel and clay. The forest thickens and fills with startling juxtapositions of tropical and temperate species as we wind down into the lowlands: a pine next to a palm; a liana chandelier hanging from an oak; an orchid beside a cactus, one prospering in the wet season, the other in the dry. It has been raining almost every day, and the clifftops dangle waterfalls like horses' tails.

There was a disturbance at the hotel last night. Two youths were fighting, stripped to the waist, evidently drunk. The loser was frog-marched out by the manager, who throws a good half nelson. I sat in the bar and watched the Guatemalan election results on TV. The campaign had sunk pretty low: Cerezo's supporters called Carpio and his colleagues a bunch of filthy *maricones* (queers); Carpio defended himself on television, offering to prove his virility with his opponents' wives and daughters; Cerezo's people said Carpio had insulted Guatemalan womanhood; and so on. Cerezo won, as predicted—the best hope for a country that has little else.

Guatemala: it seems now, after a week away, a microcosm of all the ugliness and beauty in the world; of stupidity and wisdom; evil and good—endless Manichaean opposites, and darkness with the upper hand. Things may not be wonderful in Mexico, especially for Indians, but almost all the people I've met here—the weavers and writers, the Chamulas who cleared us off their land, the Maya officials and policemen, the liberal bishop—if this were Guatemala these people would be dead.

Susanna came round with two friends for a drink—Monique, a French linguist, and Philippe, her brother. We smoked Gitanes and drank tequila, and watched a homage to John Lennon on this the fifth anniversary of his death. The next program, about famine in Africa, was broken by commercials for cat food.

I always seem to be setting off on a Death day; this time to see Palenque and what is left of the Chiapas rain forest before heading north and east to Yucatán. In eight days Janice will arrive at Cozumel. Monique and Philippe want to see Palenque, too, so we're sharing a taxi for the five-hour trip.

Philippe has no Spanish, and his English is as bad as my French, which makes conversation laborious. He's a civil servant from Toulouse, with a cartoonist's gift and sense of humor beneath the resignation in his eyes and shoulders. Monique is the dominant sibling: it's *Philippe!* this and *Philippe!* that, but he doesn't seem to mind. At eighteen she took a teaching job in Mali. The war had just ended, there were no jobs in France, and she had always wanted to go to Africa. The colonial service recruiters showed her a picture of waves crashing on a beach. Not until she got to Dakar did she discover that Mali is a landlocked country. It took a week of arduous travel to reach her posting in the interior. There was so little water she couldn't take a shower; her charges were insolent adolescent boys, who, being Muslims, despised a female teacher.

"They went on strike the day I arrived because they thought they should have been sent a man. They were full of anti-French ideas that they hadn't thought out properly. And the food! The food was the worst I have ever eaten in my life.

Worse than anything we had during the war. When I left that place after two years I was on the point of a nervous break-down!"

Her interest turned to the New World and she came to Mexico to study sixteenth-century Nahuatl and Spanish. Here was the fascination she had been looking for; she stayed.

The *taxista* is a jolly fellow named José Ticayehuatl. He's huge and has wisps of hair swept thinly over a head as smooth and brown as a football. A row of stitches adds to the likeness. "This," he says, tapping the scar. "Some bastard with a beer bottle gave me this."

He and Monique have hit it off. She, delighted with his surname, keeps trying to converse with him in Nahuatl. Unfortunately he doesn't speak *mexicano*, as he calls it. "My grandmother did, but I lost what words I had when we moved away from Puebla."

When it becomes clear that the *señora francesa* is not offended by a good joke, the conversation gets less academic. "This morning I had a very cowardly breakfast!" José announces, grinning gold to see if we can guess the punch line. "*¡Porque desayuné sin huevos!*" He breakfasted without "eggs," i.e., balls.

"Do you know what we call the governor of Chiapas?" José asks. "We call him the Tailor! Do you know why?" We have no idea.

"It's because every time the president asks him about trou-ble in Chiapas—what's the matter with the students? What's the problem with the Indians?—the governor replies, 'I am taking measures.' "

After a couple of hours, small plantations of coffee, fruit, and cacao appear beside the road, the coffee beans spread out in the sun to dry before being hulled. Round a bend comes a pickup truck, its windshield half obscured by an icon of the Virgin Mary. In the back of the truck young people are waving and singing, and behind them comes a procession of runners bear-ing torches. José crosses himself. It is, he says, the pilgrimage in honor of the Guadalupe Virgin.

Soon after the conquest of Mexico a baptized Indian named Juan Diego saw the Virgin Mary hovering above the abandoned temple of Tonantzin, Aztec mother of the gods. As a memento of the encounter, a miraculous painting of the Virgin appeared on the Indian's cloak. In Catholicism the line between heresy and sanctity has always been fine. (Saint Francis of Assisi, for one, very nearly ended on the wrong side of it.) The difference between beatification and the bonfire was usually a political decision. If Juan Diego had happened to see the Virgin, say, at Chamula in the eighteenth or nineteenth century, he and his followers would have been crushed. But in this case the church authorities saw an opportunity for mass "conversion" of skeptical Aztecs. The miracle was given papal approval; the two mother goddesses became one.[1] Her name was changed to the Virgin of Guadalupe, but a few Nahuatl-speakers still call her Tonantzin.

At Agua Azul we stop to see the cataracts: broad cascades of turquoise water pouring from one natural basin to another. In the campground stands a solitary Winnebago (Idaho plates) surrounded by grazing cows; a large Brahma bull is lying in the restaurant doorway, vacantly chewing a banana skin.

PALENQUE

The eight-year-old Hotel Ruinas is almost a ruin itself: the concrete ceiling of the lobby is webbed with cracks and shored up by wooden poles. Despite this it's brightly lit, *"sin vergüenza,"* as Monique puts it—without shame.

I take a shortcut through the forest to see the ancient city at dusk. The woods are so dark I have to wear my glasses. There's a constant insect hum—an electrical sound—among huge trees and crumbling walls half buried by twelve centuries of decay. This part of Mexico is karst country, and water deposits limestone wherever it flows over rock. Here, in a small ravine below the city center, is a series of natural pools that might have been designed for an Edwardian production of *Swan Lake.*

Each basin looks like a giant scallop shell, with stalactites dripping from the level rims like beards of candlewax. For the Maya this was a sacred spot—there are ancient walls and shrines wherever you explore. Several years ago a friend of mine ate magic mushrooms here and claims he saw a procession of Maya gods. His hippie days and mine are gone, but Palenque still has its hairy pilgrims. Two men and a slender dark-haired girl are bathing naked. "Want to smoke a number, man?"

I press on up the slope, reminded of the first time I saw this place. It was 1968 and I was nineteen. I'd been awarded a hundred pounds by Cambridge University as a travel bursary, enough for a cheap flight to New York and a bus to Mexico. I remember the interview with the committee that made the awards: "Mr. Wright, your records show that you passed the first-year Tripos with only a third-class degree; we don't usually give out funds to people with results like that. Can you tell us why we should make an exception?" I said lamely that I thought they would see a substantial improvement in the second-year results (not yet announced) and that a visit to Mexico would provide the stimulus I needed to follow a career in New World archaeology. They believed me.

The ruins are deserted by the time I emerge behind the site museum. Surrounding hills still have dabs of sunlight on their tips, but twilight is flooding the plazas, brimming over the terraces and steps. I know of nowhere in the world that has a setting like Palenque's. Delphi comes close, if you can imagine its hills and its view amplified and clothed in rain forest. The city straddles the geographical boundary between the Maya highlands and the lowlands of the Mexican Gulf. The buildings are cupped by steep hills as if resting in an open palm. To the north they look out over an immense plain, stretching without interruption to the sea some sixty miles away. The ceremonial plazas lie about two hundred feet above the plain, and the buildings rise another hundred feet from that. But there is none of the grandiosity of Tikal. Palenque's structures are buoyant, elegant, harmoniously proportioned to the magnificent hills with which many of them are engaged. In this—their articulation with nature's architecture—they replicate the setting of the city as a whole: its toes on the plain, its back in the mountains, the five doorways of its principal temple gazing out over the flatlands.

At the core of the city are two eminences: a labyrinthine palace with an extraordinary tower; and the Temple of Inscriptions. The palace stands on an artificial platform roughly one hundred yards on a side and thirty feet high; the temple crowns a nine-tier pyramid built against a hill. These buildings have been restored, and now, with the sun gone, their limestone walls glow ivory against the deepening jade of the forest.

In 1968 the road to the ruins had only recently been upgraded from a muddy track; not many visitors came. I'd been told it was possible to camp in the parking lot and had brought a tent and sleeping bag. It was late afternoon when I arrived, after hitchhiking from Villahermosa. An old Chol Maya was in charge. He lived in a wooden hut surrounded by turkeys and chickens in an uncleared corner of the main plaza. My Spanish was very bad then and so was his. But he kept saying, *"Hoy piesta, perigloso,"* until I caught on that there was to be some heavy drinking in a nearby village that night, and that he thought I would be safer if I slept up in the Temple of Inscriptions, out of sight.

It was lucky for me that I did, although not so much because of wandering drunks. I slept very lightly, with my penknife close at hand. I had never traveled outside Europe before and woke at every noise. The temple was far from deserted: there were bats in the roof and bees in the walls; a large rodent kept trying to steal food from my pack. Then there were less rational fears. I began to think of all the people who might have been sacrificed on the very spot where I lay, and about the long vaulted passage that led down from the chamber next to mine to a crypt deep in the bowels of the pyramid. There the Mexican archaeologist Alberto Ruz had made a sensational discovery some years before: a sarcophagus containing an ancient king guarded by the skeletons of several retainers who had accompanied their lord to the afterlife. If I was ever going to see a ghost, this seemed a likely place.

At about two in the morning a tropical storm blew up. First there was an outpouring of the sky, as if a layer of water had suddenly collapsed upon the earth. (It would surely have flattened my cheap tent.) Then came lightning of a brilliance I have never seen before or since. Besides individual bolts arcing down into the jungle, the whole turbulent sky would be illuminated for seconds, like a false ceiling of fluorescent lights. I sat in the doorway of the temple, a curtain of water falling before me, and watched the pale ruins and dark hills appear and vanish as the storm raged over Palenque. The thunder was felt as much as heard, a deafening blast in the heavens followed by a detonation deep within the pyramid, as if the old king and his retinue were trying to blast their way out of the underworld. Directly opposite me was the tower, a slender structure seventy feet high, pierced by large windows where Maya astronomers had once observed the planets. It rose above the mysterious galleries and jagged roof combs of the palace like a campanile, sometimes in black silhouette, sometimes drenched with magnesium light.

Tonight there is merely a chorus of frogs and cicadas, darkness rising to engulf my perch in that same temple doorway, a dying salmon glow over the western hills, and the stars lighting up one by one in the east above the tower.

11 Manik

I returned early to the ruins, entering through the proper gate this time. Monique and Philippe were still having breakfast. They take things slowly. Neither is very fit and both smoke far too much.

The sun is strong this morning; everywhere the skiffle of crickets follows your tread. Now, in broad daylight, I can see the changes that have taken place since my first visit, in 1968, and my last, in 1977. The plazas have been cleared of scrub and converted into smooth lawns dotted with fruit trees. The mosses and epiphytes that were colonizing even the restored buildings have been removed; everything has a white, scrubbed look. Workmen are carrying garbage bags by tumpline to a waiting truck. I hear them speaking Chol, thought by most experts to have been the version of Maya spoken here in the city's heyday. A cheering sound.

Those who doubt that Maya "palaces" were really residences should be convinced by Palenque's palace. It was built late in the Classic period by daring architects who experimented with new variations on the corbeled vault and kept the masonry bulk of the walls, roofs, and roof combs to a minimum. The galleries are lofty and broad, with airy porticoes and small windows in the T shape of Ik, the glyph for wind. The outer galleries look over the city from the palace perimeter; the inner ones enclose private courtyards decorated with sculptured panels and steps. Near the tower are remains of steam baths and lavatories.

If the cramped, ponderous architecture of Tikal's Central Acropolis may be compared in spirit to a Norman castle, then Palenque's palace is an Elizabethan country house. Traces of stucco molding still cling to the doorways—rococo compositions of vegetation and mythological beasts; a band of planetary signs (possibly a Maya zodiac) circles the rooms at the spring of the vault. Perhaps most surprising are the trefoil arches, formally, though not structurally, similar to Arab design. These have intrigued and misled visitors from Caddy's day until our own. I hear a "guide" trying to impress two blond gringas resting in the eastern courtyard:

"Hello, I'm Rafael. Wair jou from? United Stays?"

"Iowa, where the tall corn grows." (Giggles.)

"Look this one here, please. See this arc? This is Arabic arc!" The girls stare at the "arc," evidently baffled; Rafael stares at their breasts.

"Thank you," they say, and start to walk away.

"Hey! Jou now they have been found Arabic and even Hebrew writing in Palenque! I chow you. . . ."

* * *

Thanks to the work of Peter Mathews, Linda Schele, and others, the city has yielded its history over the last fifteen years. Their studies were coordinated in a series of conferences organized by Merle Greene Robertson, an artist who made Palenque her home and devoted herself to recording and publishing all the carved reliefs and modeled stucco. They found that the city was a minor center until shortly after the middle Classic hiatus. Then, during the long and illustrious reign of Pacal (Shield), the king buried beneath the Temple of Inscriptions, Palenque quickly rose to the first rank of Maya states. Women were important here: two queens ruled Palenque in their own right, and Pacal's mother, Lady Zac Kuk, was a power behind the throne.

She gave birth to Pacal on March 6, 603, and he was "crowned" when only twelve years old. An oval tablet, carved in bas relief and set into a palace wall, shows his installation, attended by his mother. The city rapidly extended its control over the western part of the Maya area and diffused its emblem glyph. Pacal died in 683, after ruling for sixty-eight years. At death he left a record of Palenque's dynastic history in the Temple of Inscriptions, which he built to be his mausoleum. It is architecturally more sophisticated than the pyramid-tomb of Ah Cacau, who came to power at Tikal during Pacal's last years. The burial chamber has a cross-vaulted ceiling more than twenty feet high, so well designed that it has survived thirteen centuries without a crack. In it stands a huge sarcophagus carved from a single block of stone, with a stone lid measuring twelve by seven feet.

The scene carved on the lid has been made famous by Erich von Däniken's assertion that it reveals a spaceman taking off in a rocket. Actually, every element in the design is consistent with Maya iconography. Far from ascending to the sky, Pacal is falling back into the fleshless jaws of the earth-monster. Von Däniken's "exhaust flames" are the earth's ophidian teeth, and his "control panel" is a cruciform world-tree rising above the underworld's maw. The same world-tree appears on reliefs in the temples of the Sun, Cross, and Foliated Cross built by Pacal's heir and dedicated to the Palenque Triad a holy trinity ancestral to the city's royal line.[2] If one wants to entertain chimeras, the evidence for wandering Christians is much more compelling than the presence of astronauts. But must we always defame the inventiveness of human beings?

At the top of the four-story tower I find Philippe, coughing and struggling with a crumpled pack of Delicados—his Gitanes have run out and this local brand, popular with Mexican truck drivers, is the nearest thing he's found. He wipes his brow theatrically. "I sink ze Mayá must 'ave been very little people! I find her very difficult, ze stairs." He presses his palms together to emphasize the narrowness of the ascent. "I know now what ze Mayá look like." He hands me a sketch he's done on the back of an envelope. It's a clever pastiche of Maya art—a haughty patrician head with flattened brow and trailing plumes, and below that, instead of a torso, a pair of stocky legs and feet. "Voilà, ze Mayá!" He chuckles like a concrete mixer.

The top of the tower is almost at the level of Pacal's mortuary temple, and on the winter solstice the sun, viewed from here, sets directly above his crypt.[3]

Philippe goes his own way. I climb the Temple of Inscriptions, descend by the vaulted passage to Pacal's dripping tomb, and return to look at the three great tablets that give the temple its name. They contain the longest text of any Maya monument—620 glyph blocks in all, recording the reigns of Pacal's ancestors, astronomical events, and a staggering projection into the future: on the west panel Pacal noted that the eightieth Calendar Round anniversary of his accession (80 × 52 years) would fall eight days after the completion of the current *pictun*, the cycle of twenty baktuns, or 8,000 years. So there they are: the Maya equivalents of October 13 and 21, A.D. 4772. *That's* hubris. And as if the gods were tickled by his numerology, he died when eighty years old.

Pacal's son and successor, Chan Bahlum, looked to the past. His buildings, the three graceful temples in a hilly cul-de-sac east of the Temple of Inscriptions, are monuments to the symmetry of human and mythic time. In every one we see the new king, then forty-eight, receiving the regalia from ghostly Pacal (why this obsession; was there something smelly about his claim?). Not content with this, Chan Bahlum's inscriptions fix precisely the genealogy of the ancestral Palenque Triad, whose members were the Hero Twins (remembered much later in the *Popol Vuh*) and "God K,"[4] patron of royalty, who survived in Aztec times and was aptly named for a politician: Smoking Mirror. Like most gods, they were long-lived. The parents of these three were born in 3122 and 3121 B.C. The children came into the world on October 19, October 23, and November 6, 2360 B.C.[5]

Even these dates are recent compared to others in the temple group. When Chan Bahlum died in 702, after ruling eighteen years, his younger brother and heir erected a fourth shrine to record the apotheosis of the departed king. On these reliefs Chan Bahlum is shown emerging victorious from the underworld exactly three solar years and one tzolkin after his death. He then dances across sacred waters toward his mother, the Lady Ahpo-Hel. The old queen rises and presents Chan Bahlum with the pixielike God K. The text then links Lady Ahpo-Hel to the moon goddess and reminds the reader of God K's first epiphany by the moon, nearly *one million* years before![6]

Chan Bahlum's younger brother, Kan Xul, was fifty-seven when he became king. He devoted himself to enlarging the palace, and apparently built the four-story tower in honor of his father, Pacal. After a reign of about eighteen years he was unlucky enough to be captured—and probably sacrificed—by the upstart city of Toniná, which lies about halfway between Palenque and San Cristóbal de Las Casas. This ominous event revealed the political instability that was beginning to shatter the Classic Maya world. Palenque had a number of fleeting rulers during the rest of the eighth century; the city's last Long Count monument went up in 783. A dated pot suggests that a ruler with the Mexican name of Six Death took over the city in 799. This may have been part of a general movement of aggressive Mexicans up the Usumacinta River. Ironically, Toniná outlived Palenque, and has the distinction of erecting the last Long Count stela known—in 10. 4. 0. 0. 0, or A.D. 909.

* * *

Palenque's great legacy is artistic. Stone suitable for stelae was rare in the area, so the city's sculptors developed bas relief on limestone tablets to a perfection that rivals or surpasses the best Egyptian work. The modeled stucco was equally fine. Outside walls of the palace and temples were covered in life-size reliefs of rulers and deities performing ritual acts. These are now badly damaged, but photographs taken in the last century give an idea of how they once looked. The figures are so graceful, and their attitudes so fluid, that many early travelers assumed they showed women and children dancing. The portrait heads of individual kings modeled in the full round are even more astonishing. Several have been dug up in perfect condition. Medallions on a palace wall show where eight or nine of them were mounted in a row. As with the best Greek marbles and Ife bronzes, one looks at these and feels instantly in the presence of an individual.

But not every visitor is impressed. Graham Greene, who came here in 1938 by mule, had this to say of the temples and their sculpture: "little rooms like lavatories where a few stalactites have formed and on some of the stones are a few faint scratches which they call hicroglyphics."[7]

When I leave the ruins I notice a young man in a long white smock standing by the ticket office. With his mane of wavy black hair he resembles an amiable hippie hospital patient. He's selling spears, bows, and arrows tipped with flint blades. He is evidently a Lacandón, a group who live deep in the Chiapas forest and are thought to be descended from wandering Mayas never conquered or "reduced" by Spain. David left me a copy of The Last Lords of Palenque, a fine book about them by Victor Perera and Robert Bruce; I think I recognize the souvenir seller from a photograph.

"Yes, I'm in the book," he says in Spanish. "My name is K'in García, but my gringo friends call me Louis the Fourteenth."

"Louis the Fourteenth?"

"He was a king of France, across the sea," K'in García

laughs, showing a row of fine white teeth with gold caps. "He looked like me.

"Which gringo friends?"

"The Na Bolom people."

Na Bolom, "Jaguar House," is the old mansion of Frans and Trudi Blom in San Cristóbal. Frans Blom was a Danish archaeologist; Trudi, now over eighty, is a Swiss pastor's daughter who came to Mexico in the 1940s and made herself champion of the Lacandón. Their home became a shrine and safe house. Ethnographic collections and a large library on the Maya are kept there; and any Lacandón who visits highland Chiapas may stay as long as he likes. Artists, photographers, and scholars are also welcomed.

I went to Na Bolom a few days ago. There were no Lacandón; Trudi Blom, now ailing, was not at home. The place seemed to have been colonized by a tribe of young Mexican artists, one of whom showed me around. He hurried through the few rooms that still have Lacandón artifacts and old photographs behind dusty glass, laughing scornfully at the Indians' rude appearance. He dwelt lovingly on wall after wall of paintings (most of them bad) done by himself and other members of the group.

K'in García is a son of Old Chan K'in, patriarch of Nahá and the last Maya priest openly to have resisted Christianity.

"I've read about your father. Is he well and still living at Nahá?"

Louis XIV beams a royal smile. "Yes, he is well. Do you know Nahá?"

"No, but I'd like to go there. Would it be all right if I just turn up?"

"Of course. People can visit Nahá—when the road is good. Do you want to buy a bow?"

"I'm afraid not. Couldn't carry it."

"Would you like to take my photograph?"

K'in García poses with his weapons, a figure from an ancient relief.

"I charge four hundred pesos a picture," he adds, after I've snapped three or four.

Chapter 16

12 Lamat •‖ 💠

This morning I checked out of the Hotel Ruinas and went into modern Palenque, five miles from the ruins. Monique and Philippe left for Mexico City by bus. If I can get a vehicle I may just have time to visit the Lacandón and the ruins of Bonampak and Yaxchilán in the Chiapas forest.

I spend most of the afternoon looking for a jeep—no luck—and end up at the Hotel La Cañada, which sometimes runs tours to the ruins. But the owner is away and his son doesn't think there'll be any trips for at least a week. "There was another gentleman asking," he adds. "There he is, that man with the hat, at the bar."

The man in the hat is drinking rum and Coke and leaning across the bar toward the barmaid, a pretty American blond. He's wearing khaki and a wide-brimmed brown fedora. He looks about fifty—gray hair and a red, boyish face. I hear him saying:

"How does a girl like you manage to stay single?"

"I'm not."

"Who's the lucky guy, then?" She smiles and polishes a glass.

I introduce myself. "Len," he says. "Glad to meet you. So you're from Canada, eh? So am I, and here we are in the Canada Hotel, isn't that something?"

"It's Cañada, actually. It means 'ravine,' " the barmaid says.

"Oh, is that right?" Len takes off his hat and scratches a sunburned bald spot. I buy him another Cuba libre and get a Dos Equis for myself.

"I hear you're thinking of going to Bonampak and Yaxchilán. Perhaps we could join up?" I suggest.

"Let me tell you what I'm doin' here. I'm not a tourist, see. Concrete's my business, and I'm down here for a week collecting samples. I study ancient concretes. I make my living with the modern ones, but the old ones get me out around the world. I've worked in Egypt, Israel, Yucatán, Belize, you name it. Now these ruins you're talkin' about, are they Mayan ruins like the ones here?"

It isn't difficult to persuade him, especially when he hears I'm "not a tourist" either. He has a rented Volkswagen and a tent, but no Spanish; could I contribute half the car costs, some food, and translation? It's a deal.

"You won't mind if we stop along the road for snakes, will you?" he adds. "I'm a bit of a herpetologist, see."

"Oh, do you know the species around here? I'd like to learn."

"Well, not exactly. Last time in Mexico I got this snake rather like a king snake. It was brown. When I was in the Amazon I got a *beautiful* boa constrictor! Someone had run him over but the skin was perfect. I got him all skinned and salted and smuggled back into Canada. Laid it out in my basement—almost fifteen feet long it was—and my darn dogs ate it."

I say I don't mind stopping for snakes as long as they're already dead. Would he mind if we try to visit the Lacandón?

"The what?"

I show him Perera and Bruce's book. It has photographs of the Nahá Lacandón and a jungle lake with a dugout in the foreground.

"Boy! I'd love to go out fishing in a dugout canoe. Never done that. That'd really be something, eh? Let me see that lake again. Boy, I bet there's lots of crocodiles in there. I'd love to see some crocodiles!"

* * *

Evening. We buy tinned sausages, buns, tinned fish, and queue for fuel at the Pemex station. We'll leave tomorrow at seven.

13 Muluc

We drank pretty late last night, planning the trip. Len told everyone we were doing ARCHAEOLOGY. From the way he delivered the word (normally a dusty sound), you could tell he equated it with safari, serendipity.

"You know," he said, "I'm surprised how many *tourists* get this far." (Tourist was the opposite of archaeologist.) "They're willing to go through all that pain just to see some ruins."

"You drive," Len says. "You know, I race powerboats and fast cars, but I don't like to drive down here. Prefer to watch for snakes." He settles back into the passenger seat; then: "What! No hat?"

I explain that my cotton sun hat, bought in Egypt from a man wearing a pile of them, had got so stained and torn that I threw it away.

"The older they get the better I like 'em. But the wife, she threw my old one out. I bought this new for the trip." He takes off his fedora and shows me the label inside. "It's the genuine Indiana Jones model, see?"

Good pavement soon gives way to broken asphalt—much worse than no paving at all—followed after ten miles or so by gravel. The hills and valleys have been devastated by development. Farming, ranching, and logging have conspired to murder the jungle.

"The *jungle* begins at Chancalá!" Len says, consulting a sketch map he made last night (*jungle* is another of his favorite words). "That's what the feller at the Canada told me." But after Chancalá, twenty-five miles from Palenque, the country is almost as threadbare as before. The road gets worse, deeply rippled and rutted by heavy trucks. Like Len, I've always imagined that the Mexican side of the Petén, known as the *selva lacandóna*, was a virgin forest of giant trees. But what we see resembles something from the American West of the 1930s. A very wide, very bad road, down which vehicles approach in a strange sidewinding minuet, trailing boas of dust as they weave between potholes and stones. White powder covers grass and bushes and endless barbed wire. Every few miles we come to big ranch buildings. Between the *ranchos* are *ranchitos*, the tin-and-plank shacks of migrants from other parts of Mexico. These people, who now outnumber the native Lacandón a hundred to one, are clustered in ejido villages as miserable as any Guatemalan "development pole," in appearance if not in intent. Nueva Coahuila, Nuevo Guerrero—the names recall the dustiest, most hopeless parts of the Mexican republic. Men in cowboy hats and leather boots drink beer in roadside bars; ranchero music lopes through the burning air; women with loads on their heads shuffle along the roadside, their cheap gingham dresses as faded as the land at midday; only those new to puberty look young. At such places the musk of the tropics is swamped by gasoline, alcohol, urine, and human shit. Huge logs lie in ditches, fading with neglect. And while the migrants move up the valleys and logging roads, highland Maya are forced down by land hunger, scorching their way through the forest with milpa fires.

At last the road begins to wind upward into heaving limestone hills. This land is poor for farming, but even here wildfires started by the colonists have left acres of blackened skeletons like the blasted woods of the Somme. Slowly new growth is creeping back, and it seems to gain strength as we gain height. Here and there the dark green foliage is relieved by yellow myrtle or purple wigs of morning glory. The road gets narrower; trees begin to touch above it. This forest was felled once before by the Maya and it returned. Perhaps, after a thousand years, it can survive another assault; but such a cycle offers little for those dependent on its fragile bounty.

We pass a turning for New Palestine, a name redolent of fundamentalism. About eighty miles from Palenque we come to another turning and a shack. Lacandón youngsters run out, brandishing strings of beads and toy bows. They look like Victorian slum children dressed for bed. They crowd around, shouting prices and shoving trinkets in our faces. It's impossible to ask directions. I drive on a few hundred yards to a forestry department office; but it's empty and the children run until they catch up with the car. Len purchases some respite with a string of beads. I suppose it had to happen: the natives forcing beads on the explorers.

At last an adult, dressed in shabby Mexican clothes, confirms that this is the fork for Bonampak.

The road goes five miles or so to the village of Lacanhá, where most of the southern Lacandón live. The Lacandón are divided into northern and southern groups, defined by differences in speech and, until the missionaries came, a religious life focused on different ceremonial centers. The southern group made regular offerings in the ruined temples of Bonampak and Yaxchilán, while the northern Lacandón regarded Palenque as the birthplace of the gods. Robert Bruce, coauthor of *The Last Lords of Palenque*, believes that the unknown genealogy of the northern Lacandón "points directly back to the throne of Palenque."[1] (This view isn't widely shared. The Spaniards called any unconquered Maya *lacandónes*, a term derived from a phrase meaning "those who worship stone images.")

The modern Lacandón probably have many ancestors, including Itzá, who fled the fall of Tayasal. They kept their freedom by forsaking their civilization. They abandoned towns and became seminomadic in the forest. The cloaks of feathers and jaguar skins were set aside. They had no temples except thatched god-houses and ancient ruins. They forgot the calendar and hieroglyphic books. What remained to them was the lore of peasant and woodsman, knowledge of seasons, herbs, and wild animals, worship of sun, moon, and natural forces. Maya culture was pared to its essentials, to the foundation upon which the superstructure of civilization had been raised more than three thousand years before. The Lacandón became, as it were, the guerrillas of the Maya heritage, surviving by mobility and the austerity of their needs.

The Spaniards sent a few expeditions against them, and wiped out one or two larger groups, but there were few rewards

for would-be conquistadors. The reduction and indoctrination
of the Lacandón remained for the twentieth century and the
airplane; for those drawn by vulnerable "heathen" souls. How
seldom missionaries tackle their equals: the Lord's work is
most easily done among the defenseless. In the late 1950s,
Philip Baer arrived at the northern Lacandón community of
Nahá. He was with the Summer Institute of Linguistics—a
beguiling name adopted by the American Wycliffe Bible Translators to cloak their activities with an ethnological veneer.
Nahá had had enough experience of white men during the
Travenesque mahogany days to be unimpressed with missionary tactics, but the southern Lacandón at Lacanhá were more
isolated and less prepared. After the death of their spiritual
leader, Baer successfully infiltrated and converted them.

The road to Lacanhá winds whitely between thick walls of
secondary forest. Suddenly, out of the bush comes a brocket
deer, a slight creature with limpid eyes and big ears. It stops,
feet pointed like a ballerina's, and looks at the rattling, bounc-
ing car.

"Stop. Stop!" Len grabs his camera, but the deer skips away.

Soon afterward, the road opens out to reveal a bulldozed
clearing, a makeshift garage, and a few huts—the outskirts
of Lacanhá. There's a sign in English: WELCOME TO BETHEL.
TURNING FOR BONAMPAK RUINS. FOOD, COLD SODA AND SAFE CAR
PARKING.

A young Indian in checked shirt and flared jeans brings us
Cokes from beneath an old Wagoneer; his wife serves two
plates of "pheasant" in a greasy tomato sauce.

"Have you seen the paper today?" he asks, as if it's the most
natural thing in the world to catch up on news in the heart of
the forest. He points to an article on the front page of *El
Excelsior*, recounting the lack of respect shown by young Lacandón to their elders, described as living in the past.

"Is it true?"

"¡Sí!" he replies, as if I've asked a stupid question.

There's a roar of tires on gravel. A blond woman jumps

down from a white jeep before it comes to a complete halt. She's wearing a tight T-shirt, slacks, and her hair is held in a ponytail by a scarf.

"Here comes *el dueño del periódico* [the owner of the newspaper]," our host says weightily, as if we're about to meet Conrad Black. With the woman are two Mexican men—one bare chested except for a pair of suspenders, the other peering from behind dark glasses and a Rasputin beard. The woman produces a sheaf of photographs; our host and his wife go through them laughing and calling out people's names. All are speaking Spanish, but the woman has a slight French accent. She and her companions are anthropologists, she says, working at Nahá.

"You should come and visit us on your way back. This," she adds, squeezing our host's arm, "is Chan K'in the Third. He's from Nahá. Three years ago he wore a long smock and had hair down his back. Then he got religion and moved here to be with the other Evangelicals. He's an important man in the community now."

"What about this article? Is it true?"

"It's not very good. I brought it because I thought they'd like to see themselves in print. The journalist wrote bad things about Chan K'in here. He said he was an opportunist. I don't think he knows what the word means."

So this was one of the many Chan K'ins (the Lacandón have only four common names for men and three for women). The patriarch of Nahá, the spiritual if not the historical last lord of Palenque, is Old Chan K'in; then there are Young Chan K'in, Chan K'in Chico, and several others who have taken Spanish nicknames. Old Chan K'in has had three wives (more or less simultaneously), so it isn't easy to keep track of relationships. Looking at this young man in his shirt and jeans, I remember something Old Chan K'in told Robert Bruce:

Long ago the [southern Lacandón] used to behave correctly in the homes of the gods. They would say, "If a person breaks a stone he dies.". . . But now the young . . . break the stones and shout, "It is not true! See! I break the stones in the house of the gods and I do not die." But they do not see that they die each time they break a stone.[2]

Chan K'in III shows me where to park the Volkswagen and waits while we extract backpacks and get ready for the hike to the ruins. He walks with us to where the Bonampak trail leaves the road. "*¡Mucha vitamina para caminar!*" he says, referring to the pheasant. "Many vitamins for walking! Whenever I have a long walk through the forest I always try to eat pheasant."

At first the trail is easy. One could be tempted to try it with a car, but after about a mile there's a streambed spanned by a makeshift bridge of tree trunks—only a vehicle with a winch would get across that. We advance in a tortoise-and-hare motion. Len likes to hike slowly and steadily; I prefer to march ahead and rest until he catches up. (The Maya have a version of this myth: eclipses are contests between a turtle sun and rabbit moon.)[3] After an hour I sit down on a log and watch a procession of leaf-cutter ants waving chips of greenery aloft like battle standards.

Two hours pass and still no sign of the ruins. The sun was high when we began, striking down on our heads from between the trees, but now we have shade and can appreciate the wild-life: parrots, morpho butterflies, and the inevitable circling, ever-hopeful *zopilote*. Len glares at the vulture:

"I wonder if he knows something we don't know. Six miles is a long way. You know, when you said six miles I thought, I drive that far every day into town and it's nothin', but on foot in this climate it's another matter." He drops his pack and opens his canteen. "We'd better watch our water. Boy, if we run out of water, we're sunk."

BONAMPAK

After two and a half hours comes a smell of woodsmoke. Twenty minutes later the trail ends in a clearing of mown grass. There are three or four thatched huts, an old truck on blocks, a couple of wooden bungalows. A young man stripped to the waist is washing at a tap. He's Mauricio, an epigrapher from INAH (Mexico's anthropological institute), working on conservation of the famous murals. We find we know people in common—Peter Mathews and others I remember from my student days. An elderly man emerges from one of the huts and gazes proprietorially in my direction.

"You'd better have a word with that gentleman there," Mauricio says. "He's one of the site guardians." Len arrives, panting; the guardian agrees to let us camp the night, but he isn't sure we can see the ruins today: it's already four o'clock and the men have knocked off. Other employees appear; one agrees to show us round the site provided we pay him overtime. There's an air of suspicion and resentment of visitors—rather crushing after such a long walk. Len produces a letter given him by a Mexican archaeologist for whom he took samples on an earlier trip. Eventually we convince them we're *gente de confianza*, trustworthy folk.

Local Maya don't seem to be employed here, even though it was a Lacandón, Chan Bor, who first led an outsider, Giles Healey, to the ruins in 1946. Healey claimed that the Lacandón didn't know the frescoes existed, which seems highly unlikely. But it's hard to resist his story that as he entered the painted rooms a black puma wandered out.[4]

You walk down a wide path shaded by colossal buttressed trees to a plaza; on the far side is a steep hill artfully terraced to form a pyramid. Broad steps climb to a row of shrines; dark doorways stare like a gap-toothed mouth beneath a tall brow of rock and exuberant vegetation. The buildings on the plaza are piles of rubble except for a small three-roomed palace containing the only complete set of Maya wall paintings from the Classic period. The odds against their survival are incalculable. First, that they should be here at all: Bonampak was a small center, relatively unimportant, overshadowed by Yaxchilán twenty miles away on the Usumacinta River. Second, that the paintings should be of such quality: far from being provincial, these rank with the finest representational work that has come down to us in any medium used by the ancient Maya. It is as if Michelangelo had chosen to paint the ceiling of a country church instead of the Sistine Chapel. Somehow

these masterpieces behind unguarded doors survived the icon-
oclasm that ravaged several cities at the time of the collapse.
Somehow the invading jungle, which leveled every other structure at Bonampak except the shrines on the hill, spared this
building. And by a happy accident eleven centuries of rain
percolating through the mortar of the vault precipitated a thin
layer of limestone that sealed the murals from Lacandón
incense and the atmosphere.

Since 1946 the murals have not been so lucky. Conservation and study were hampered by political disputes; visitors
were in the habit of throwing water or kerosene on the paintings to bring out the colors. Now the Mexicans have begun
major restoration. The building wears a hat of corrugated iron,
and electric fans stir the damp air inside. Our guide removes
screens from the doors (put there to keep out bats) and shows
us in.

"Absolutely no photographs."

"Even without flash?" asks Len, who has fast film.

"Even without flash."

There's little point in taking pictures with all the scaffolding and paraphernalia anyway. In the first room conservation is
well advanced. The stalactite coating has been scraped back in
neat strips, revealing faces, hands, bright colors, and calligra-
phy. I've seen a replica of this building in Mexico City and am
expecting to be disappointed by the real thing. But within
moments I no longer notice the clutter and whirring fans. The
paintings are able to dominate such intrusions. Immediately I
feel that ineffable tingle famous things can bestow when one is
in their presence for the first time. I felt it in the burial chambers of Egyptian pyramids (though not outside), and again in
the Qorikancha, or "Sun Temple," of the Incas; I felt it in front
of Bosch's paintings in Madrid. It comes from proximity to
something ancient, alien; from being in a space filled with dead
voices and the silent echo of the years.

The murals tell a story, open to differing interpretations,
though the theme is clear. Fourteen Maya lords in white capes
adorn the east gable and south vault of the first room; and on
the triangular west wall the ruling family—the lord, his wife,
and another woman—are sitting in patrician attitudes on a

stone dais. The focus of everyone's attention is a royal child, presumably the heir apparent, held up before the crowd. Below, on the walls beneath the spring of the vault, a musical procession entertains the lords. Some of the musicians are human, wearing breechclouts and elaborate cotton turbans; others are masked as grotesque supernatural beings, some of the earth, others of the sea. A manikin with a vegetal head and the T sign of the wind in his eye is presenting an ear of corn to another; above them on the right rears a character from Pincher Martin's death-dream, snapping lobster claws in place of arms; at his feet sits a man with a crocodile head. This fantasia contrasts with the scene above the door, where the lord of Bonampak is dressing for a great occasion. He is backed by an arc of quetzal plumes, while longer tail feathers of the same bird erupt in a spray from the starched cotton of his headdress, which itself includes fish, bird, and reptile motifs. His head is in profile; an enormous jade spool hides his left ear, and a jade collar covers his shoulders and chest like mail. His torso is bare to the waist, below which he wears a jaguar kilt and a richly embroidered loincloth. All this splendor might be overwhelming were it not for informal touches. A manservant or minor lord is adjusting the jade cuff at the ruler's wrist, attentive as any gentleman's gentleman; another brings something in a bowl—perhaps body powder. A nobleman standing behind the first servant has his arm outstretched and his mouth open in speech. He is about to tug the servant's hair and say, *Just a minute, you.* Other attendants on the right are fussing nervously. *Is everything all right? What have you done with the jades? Let me check that jaguar skin.*

The culminating ceremony is shown in the third room, to the west. Members of the ruling family appear again: four matronly women are sitting on a dais, engaged in the Maya sacrifice of shedding blood from their tongues onto paper sheets; but these rites don't stop them having a lively conversation. Another woman sits cross-legged on the floor with a toddler in her arms, and she is talking over her shoulder to one of those above. Like their modern descendants, these ancient Maya seem relaxed during religious rituals; personal interaction was allowed. Best of all, we see the women.

No female principle was active in the Maya universe; and since Maya sculpture was a religious art, that concerned itself precisely with the divine Nature of Things, no representation of the female form appears among the ruins. . . . Maya art is florid, but invariably austere; a more chaste luxuriance was never imagined. . . . The female form, as we have seen, never appears. . . .[5]

Bonampak had not been discovered when Aldous Huxley wrote that, but even by the lights of 1934 his assertion was wrong. Ixchel, the moon goddess and patroness of weaving, was known from the codices and murals at Tulum; and in the British Museum a lintel from Yaxchilán showed a royal lady drawing blood from her tongue. Unfortunately for Huxley, his "eminent authority" on the Maya was the notorious pothunter, Thomas Gann.

There is something about Latin and pre-Columbian America that brings out the worst in British writers: Graham Greene's philistinism at Palenque; his and Waugh's bigoted diatribes on postrevolutionary Mexico; and Huxley, that great romanticizer of the noble savage, adopting every prejudice of the mestizo and criollo toward the Indian, and managing to sneer at all three. "Frankly, try how I may, I cannot very much like primitive people," he sniffs. "They make me feel uncomfortable. '*La bêtise n'est pas mon fort.*' "[6]

The action in the west room has been interpreted as a sacrificial dance. The preservation is poor, but it's possible to make out richly costumed figures standing on the steps of a pyramid. From their hips protrude gigantic wings, apparently of brocade draped from horizontal poles and edged with feathers. From their heads flare colossal headdresses, as large as the figures themselves, so fluid and fantastic that the plumes rise like smoke and blend with the god masks presiding from a celestial band at the top of the vault.

It is the central room that gives meaning to the whole assemblage, and which, by its startling content, upset scholars' notions of Classic Maya society. As you enter the room you walk into a battle that covers every wall but the one at your back. Grimacing faces are surmounted by heraldic crests and feathered helms. Men clothed in jaguar skin tunics and gaiters are leaping, dodging, grasping enemies by the hair, plunging obsidian-tipped lances through chests. The enemy, an abject group of half-naked barbarians, cringe and die. Realism is achieved by comic-book techniques. The figures are outlined in black and filled with washes of strong color: copper for the skin of the victors, brown for that of the enemy; green for the feathers, yellow with black spots for jaguar pelts. Great attention is paid to the cast of an eye, the pout of lips, the jut of a jaw. The fighters are as mobile as athletes caught in action by a camera. Depth is achieved through bold superimposition and foreshortening. Though there is some stylization, one can agree that "the naturalism is stronger and the drafting more skillful than in any Old World art of the same period."[7] The fetor of the small room becomes the sweat of battle, the reek of blood and intestines spilled in the steaming forest; and, aided by distant parrots and a woodpecker's tattoo, you hear the battle cries, the crash of wood and stone and bone.

The entire room is propaganda of the most blatant and effective kind. White caption boxes filled with hieroglyphs tell the story. Bonampak's troops could be officers of the Reich, and their quarry some despicable non-Aryan breed. But both sides look distinctly Maya. Who is being attacked? Is this an example of a raid to capture sacrificial victims? Or is it, as the fragmentary inscriptions seem to say, a major offensive by the allied forces of Yaxchilán and Bonampak against a rival? The murals are very late, dating from about 790. The lord and lady shown are Chaan Muan, who came to power in 776, and his wife, Lady Rabbit, a Yaxchilán princess. Although Bonampak was inhabited throughout the Classic period, most of its existing monuments date from Chaan Muan's reign, suggesting a brief rise to prominence in the last katuns of Baktun 9.

The battle's aftermath is painted above the door. Humbled captives plead for their lives. To modern eyes there is a gloating cruelty in the scene. Chaan Muan—so lifelike that you recognize his face from previous appearances—stands regally clasping a lance encased with jaguar skin. On either side of him other notables parade in elaborate cloaks and huge animal-head crests. The brilliant colors of these figures stand out against a background of Maya blue. Like the dance in room three, the scene takes place on tiers of red-painted steps—probably the very flight that climbs the hill from the plaza. The butt of the lord's spear rests behind the forehead of a dead captive sprawled backward across three steps in a pose that might have come from the brush of Michelangelo. Nearby are three terrified survivors with blood dripping from their fingernails, and at the sprawled figure's foot rests a head on a bed of leaves, an oddly peaceful smile playing at its lips.

The triumph celebrated on these walls was a brief one. The dates on this building were the last the city inscribed. The murals were never quite finished; caption boxes were left unfilled. As Mary Miller has written in a recent study of the frescoes: "The story of Bonampak ends. The little heir probably never reached the throne. The site was abandoned; the artists were dispersed. Painting of this caliber vanished from ancient Mesoamerica."[8]

I remember a Gahan Wilson cartoon I saw some years ago in *Playboy*. It showed a city devastated by nuclear bombs; a loudspeaker hung from wires among the ruins, mechanically repeating a victory announcement that ended with the refrain *"This is a recorded message."*

When we come out the sun is hovering above the trees to the west. Shrines on the hill are outlined in gold, but the wall of rock and vegetation behind is deeply shadowed. A great carved stela in the middle of the plaza—among the largest ever erected by the Maya—is thrown into sharp relief. Scaffolding surrounds it at the moment, but the fierce eye of Chaan Muan is still able to transfix. I ask our guide if any Lacandón come here with offerings.

"Not for the last few years."

"Why not?"

"Because the young people are either Evangelicals or out of hand."

We retrieve our packs and pitch the tent beside the INAH

camp. After a foul supper of cold tinned frankfurters, Len produces his rum. He talks about earlier trips: how he was eaten by bedbugs in Iraq and stricken by a strange lung ailment in Egypt. "We found a mummy's leg lying on the sand. It's on my basement wall at home. I recovered from whatever it was we caught, but the poor guy that was with me—he wasn't so lucky. It got into his voice box and now he talks like a girl."

There's no moon and no cloud; by eight o'clock the sky is obsidian speckled with the luminous dust of the Milky Way. I lie on my back and watch stars fall whenever a Maya god throws down his spent cigar.

1 Oc .

We were up at first light. I persuaded Len he'd better check with the conservators before helping himself to any concrete samples.

We got back to Bethel by ten and examined the car. It was just as we had left it, but has suffered badly on the road: a front wheel bearing is loose, the exhaust has been hammered flat by stones, and the fan belt has a crack. Chan K'in III lent us a few wrenches but they didn't fit. Still, we set off for Frontera Echeverría—a journey of about an hour—to see if we could get a boat down the Usumacinta River to Yaxchilán. Women were washing clothes and themselves in the water, skirts hiked up around brown thighs, sleek breasts swinging like aubergines. There were a few beached canoes but no boatmen. They were all off cutting down the forest. Len sat in a dugout and got me to take his picture. Across the river was Guatemala, deceptively peaceful and deserted.

At least we were able to buy some fuel. The car gets less than twenty miles per gallon on these roads.

* * *

After waiting all afternoon for a boatman, we drive back down the road a short way and camp for the night.

2 Chuen ⦿ 🔲

We tried once again this morning. Still no boatmen. So much for Yaxchilán. We went back to Chancalá, had lunch there, and took a narrow road up into the hills to Nahá. It climbs so gently that the changes in vegetation due to altitude are very subtle. Lake Nahá appeared below us on the right, a dark mirror set in forest.

NAHÁ

2:00 P.M. Two small boys approach. They are wearing the usual smock and lank hair; unlike those at Lacanhá they don't try to sell us anything. I get out my copy of Perera and Bruce and look up the names of some of the people mentioned. On an impulse I ask for Kayum.

"I'm Kayum," says the first boy.

"So am I," says the second.

"Isn't there an older Kayum?"

"Yes, he's my father," says Kayum One.

Kayum's house is neatly built of hardwood planks with a shiny tin roof. It's surrounded by a grove of orange and avocado trees. A gravel path leads to a veranda with a concrete floor. He shakes my hand shyly. I show him the book. He chuckles at the pictures.

"I paint," he says. "Would you like to see my paintings?" He points to a row of artwork on the wall: an oil painting rich in symbolism—hard to make out—several photographic portraits, and a sensitive pencil sketch of himself, done by someone else. After admiring these I am at a loss what to say. I feel the absurdity of just turning up at the home of a stranger. I ask if it would be all right if Len and I walk down to the lake.

"The little one will take you down," Kayum senior says. "But first you must talk to the *presidente.*"

At this moment a smart Chevrolet four-wheel-drive truck pulls in beside some buildings by the road. Kayum One calls, "There comes the presidente now!"

From the driver's seat climbs a tall Lacandón in his thirties. He is wearing an immaculate white smock, which contrasts vividly with his raven hair. He has a trace of moustache along his upper lip, and quick, intelligent eyes. We introduce ourselves.

"I am Chan K'in," he says. "Where are you from?"

He answers his own question by reading the license plate on our car: "Ah, I see, Quintana Roo." He laughs. (Len rented the car at Cancún). I recognize him from the book: this is Young Chan K'in. I explain that I met K'in García at Palenque, and that the anthropologists we met yesterday at Lacanhá said they would be working here.

"What anthropologists? You mean those three with the white jeep? They've gone. You might find them at Mensabak."

"Aren't they working here?"

"No. That's what they wanted. They arrived this morning and asked if they could stay for two months. We decided against it. We don't mind people coming for visits, to have a look around, but two months is much too long. We told them no."

What I fondly imagined might be an introduction to this community now seems a liability. The Lacandón have had their fill of anthropologists. Who can blame them? I emphasize we've come only for a couple of hours. Is it all right to walk down to the lake and chat with people? I add that I'm writing a book about the Maya, but I see Chan K'in's expression glaze: obviously there have been dozens of visitors who are "writing books"; he's heard it before. I produce *The Last Lords of Palenque* and show the photographs. Chan K'in's family gathers round—his wife, a pretty woman in a pink dress, and some children wearing Lacandón shifts. It's hard to tell whether the younger ones are girls or boys. There is much amusement at the pictures, and it takes me too long to realize that in reading the captions aloud to these people I am patronizing them. Chan K'in has already demonstrated his ability to read, and he is better spoken in Spanish than many Mexicans. His Lacandón clothes disguise a man of the world, one who drives a new Chevrolet, and who once lived for two years with an adventurous Canadian woman when he was in his twenties. His versatility makes him an appropriate community president, a post recognized by the Mexican government. But he is also a traditional leader, next in line to succeed as *T'o'ohil*—an echo of Tohil of the Quichés—by right of being Old Chan K'in's eldest son by the senior wife. Whether he will do so is another matter. Bruce and Perera seem to think that the Lacandón religion will collapse when the old man dies.

Chan K'in asks if I can leave the book at Nahá; I explain that it belongs to the University of Toronto. Instead I give him a packet of cigarettes and a butane lighter, acceptable small gifts according to Perera and Bruce. But I can't help feeling like a missionary or whisky trader, an obnoxious white man handing out trinkets. I only hope it is taken as intended: a small gesture of goodwill.

The two little Kayums take us down toward the lake. We follow the airstrip, seldom used since the opening of the road in 1979, then a narrow trail through tall weeds growing on the dead stalks of last year's corn. Beyond this is a patch of dense bush, maybe seven or eight years old. A thatched hut with open sides stands in the middle of a small clearing surrounded by morning glory and wild sunflowers.

"*La Casa de Trudi,*" say the boys, explaining that the Lacandón keep this house ready for Trudi Blom. It is now the only one left in the old village, which was abandoned as soon as the road came in. It is also one of the few still made of traditional materials: a fitting monument for the woman who dedicated much of her life to defending these Indians and their forest; but in its proud isolation also a sign that the Lacandón, knowing they can no longer turn their backs on the outside world, have moved on.

The boys want to know how much we will give them for the guided tour. In this there is no cravenness or unseemly haste. They make it clear that they are offering us a service and expect a fair price. We agree on five hundred pesos each, expensive by Mexican standards, cheap by Canadian: a satisfactory compromise. This includes photographs.

Between the clearing and the lake lies a ridge of tall trees: ceiba, Spanish cedar, and a curious tree with a smooth red trunk that peels like a cheap cigar.

"That's a tourist tree!" Kayum giggles. "Because it looks like a white person burned by the sun."

"Are there any mahogany left?" I ask.

"You should ask Chan K'in."

Logging of the jungle, mainly for mahogany, has long been of deep concern to the Lacandón and their friends. Through Trudi Blom's efforts the Indians received title to a large area of forest, but timber companies continue to extract wood, now paying a small royalty to the "owners." The money brought consumer goods and, predictably, internal disputes. Most of the royalties were paid to the leader of the Christianized southern Lacandón, who falsely claimed to represent Nahá and other northern communities. The apparent prosperity of Nahá, and the fact that felling has ceased, suggest that a compromise has since been worked out.

The trail rises briefly and then falls to the shore of the lake: deep emerald water ringed by thickly wooded hills. The boys and I go for a swim. Len, imagining crocodiles, stays on the bank. The water is clear and deep and surprisingly cool below the surface. Icy pockets indicate the whereabouts of springs feeding the lake. The dust and heat and destruction of modern Chiapas can be forgotten here, and for a moment it's possible to believe that the Lacandón world is still as it has always been.

Like most forest peoples, the Lacandón understood the limits of their environment and kept their population small. A generation ago there were only about two hundred of them altogether; now there are slightly more than twice that number—one quarter of them at Nahá. Their religion, like that of all American Indians, is built upon the ethic of reciprocity between man and nature. The obligation to the earth for supporting human life is discharged by offerings. The traditional Lacandón, like most Maya, burn large quantities of incense. At

Nahá this is still done in "god-pots," pottery braziers modeled with features of the deities they represent. Until recently the old men performed ritual bloodletting, pricking their ears with a stone point and allowing drops to fall into the incense burners. The Lacandón also offer behavior enjoyed by the gods—and by themselves: music and song, drinking of fermented *balché*, and smoking of fat cigars rolled from home-grown tobacco.

Kayum Two, it turns out, is the youngest son of Old Chan K'in by the patriarch's third wife. He offers to take us to his father—apparently an introduction is included in the tour. I wonder about the propriety of intruding on the old man, but the allure of meeting the last overtly pagan Maya priest is too great.

Back at the road Young Chan K'in has opened the shutter of his store and is deftly tapping out figures on a pocket calculator. The Nahá Lacandón have avoided the usual pattern when a society without money is suddenly invaded: an influx of greedy outsiders extending credit and selling goods at exorbitant prices. There is nothing "primitive" about them; they remind me of back-to-the-landers—people with university degrees who live in tipis and log cabins by choice. Perera calls them "these rude, sophisticated people." It is as if the civilization of their distant ancestors never left them. And when a new civilization comes to their forest they are not overawed—they think nothing of traveling to Mexico City and calling on the president of Mexico with a grievance. They did this recently over the mahogany issue, and those who saw them speaking with López Portillo remarked on how they addressed him as an equal. Of course, these are the strongest here, the ones who have been unimpressed with Jesus Christ regardless of His gifts and airplanes. But even the disunity of the Lacandón as a whole is typically Maya. Some are Adventists, some Baptists, some Catholics, some unchanged in their ancient beliefs, others no doubt syncretic and "heretical." It is the old Maya strategy of strength in diversity: no matter what happens next, some of them will be prepared.

Kayum Two leads us through the main part of the village

to a house on a small knoll. Almost everyone has an orchard surrounded by chicken wire to keep out wandering pigs; I get an impression of tidiness and respect for privacy, as one might expect from people who until recently lived dispersed through the forest. Old Chan K'in's house is no different from the others. Kayum tells us to follow him in, but I hesitate and knock at the door.

"*Adelante!*" calls a man's strong voice within. It is dark inside, there are no windows; daylight and a cooling breeze trickle in between the rough planks of the walls. Two women are grinding corn in a cast-iron mincer and patting out tortillas on a table. These are Koh II and Koh III, Chan K'in's wives. (Koh I, mother of Young Chan K'in, recently died.) The women seem very shy and do not respond to my greeting.

Old Chan K'in is sitting in a hammock strung across the end of the one-room house. He welcomes us with a wide smile and motions us to sit down on a bench beside a table with a plastic cloth. I offer him a cigarette and take one myself. We sit in silence and smoke. His hands are crippled with arthritis. Apart from this there are few signs of his ninety years. (He was six or seven when the first anthropologist visited the Lacandón in 1902.)[9] Not a gray hair streaks his mane, and his eyes, crinkled with age and poised amusement, are very bright; they follow my every gesture from beneath thick, agile brows like those of Groucho Marx.

After meeting him in 1957, Robert Bruce wrote: "When I first saw Chan K'in I felt at once that I must never tell him the smallest lie."[10] I feel it, too: here is a man who can see through facades. Normally I'm uncomfortable with silence, but at this moment I do not grope for words. I do not try to explain why I'm here. I feel as though he knows—not the details perhaps: that kind of mysticism is beyond me—he knows I have a reason, and somehow approves. Most likely this is mere wishful thinking; but his kindly, knowing gaze softens the doubts I have about disturbing him. At least he suffers fools gladly.

Behind him there's an alcove filled with an immense stack of corncobs. It seems, by its position behind Chan K'in, almost a shrine to the god of maize. Also behind him on a shelf is a

hand-rolled Lacandón cigar. Len makes me ask Chan K'in
which he prefers: a filter cigarette or the big stogie.

"The cigar!" he replies, chuckling at the naïveté of the
question. *"Porque esto es muy lápido* [Because this is very
brief]." His Spanish is good. Like many Maya, he confuses *l* and
r. He used the Lacandón word for cigar—*hach k'uuts*—literally "true tobacco." The Lacandón have a similar name for
themselves: they are *Hach Winik*, the "True People."

I ask next about the mahogany cutting.

"No, that is stopped. We want to keep the forest the way
it is."

According to Bruce and Perera this isn't exactly correct.
They say four hundred mahoganies were cut, and that the
logging sent the forest and Nahá itself into irreversible
decline.[11] Bruce believes the great trees were kingpins of the
forest ecology, and he likens the psychological effect of their
loss to the destruction of the North American buffalo a century ago. Even worse, logging roads have made it easy for
colonists to invade and burn the Lacandón's jungle. Many of
these invaders are highland Maya, but they come from groups
that have been enemies of the Lacandón for centuries.

All this has given Chan K'in's thoughts an apocalyptic
turn. He believes that *Xu'tan*—the end of the present world—
is coming soon, and even denies his own priestly role on the
grounds that the age when men could talk directly to the gods
has passed.[12] These ideas fall within a long tradition of Mesoamerican anxiety about the world's end, but the late twentieth
century has certainly given Chan K'in evidence of its
approach. On Victor Perera's most recent visit, the Lacandón
were talking about AIDS and atomic war.[13]

We leave Chan K'in with a pack of cigarettes and a
lighter.

"I smoke a lot," he says, nodding his head.

"They say it's bad for the health."

"Look at me," he answers. "I smoke every day and now I
am very old."

"How old *are* you?"

"One hundred and fifty years. No, more!" He shakes with
laughter.

* * *

The drive back is easier now that I know where to expect the main hazards. The evening sun dapples the trees and illuminates their blossoms—red, white, purple—and tumescent bromeliad spears attached like Christmas decorations. It's after six when we reach Chancalá. The dusty crossroads with its parked trucks, small shop, and restaurant looks busy and urban compared to where we have spent the day. It is twilight now; on the balding hills silhouettes of trees that escaped fire and bulldozer stand out defiantly against a rose-petal sky.

Near Palenque Len sees a snake on the road. He leaps out and prods it with a stick to make sure it's dead. The black and yellow body, eight feet long and thick as a wrist, has no visible wounds. He pries open the jaw and peers in like a dentist examining a reluctant child. The fangs are none too impressive: it seems this is a harmless species. Len hands me his camera and begins striking poses in the headlights.

"I kinda hate to leave a fine specimen like this," he says. "I think I'll bring it along. Promised my boys I'd bring back something if I got the chance."

"Where are you planning to skin it?"

"In my hotel room. Always do."

"What about the blood and guts?"

"You never seen one skinned before? It comes off just like a sock."

Part V

North:
Yucatán
Peninsula

Chapter 17

3 Eb :

CAMPECHE

This is a city I should like. Its eighteenth-century walls (built against British pirates), superb cathedral, and wide promenade all glow in the sun with the bone luminescence of Yucatán limestone. A wide blue sky, clean cobbled streets, seafood—it's a city of attractions but somehow I never seem to hit it off with Campeche.

I once stayed in a villa on the coast with Frank, an American psychologist who was studying octopi. He had dozens of them in little tanks and mazes he had made out of Perspex in an old fish cannery. Seawater constantly flowed through his system of tunnels and boxes, echoing from the metal walls and roof. The octopi lived in earthenware pots like miniature caves. You'd look in and there was nothing to be seen, no evil eye, no exploring tentacle; just a dark hole with something in there. At feeding time Frank would take small crabs and drop them into the maze. It was astonishing how fast an octopus could move. One moment a crab was floating down through the water; then a rubbery Dracula shot out of his castle, enveloped his prey, and shot back in. "An octopus is smarter than people think," Frank said affectionately. "You'd be amazed what I can teach them." They seemed to me like disembodied hands, grasping organs that had become autonomous.

I thought of Frank and his octopi on the way here from Palenque. The bus was second class and there were many hours to fill as the small towns came and went. Ten minutes here, twenty minutes there: women selling soft drinks in plastic bags with straws, like catheters; the half-musical, half-whining refrain of *tamales, tamales, tamales calientitos;* the smell of diesel, hot tarmac, and urine. Emiliano Zapata was an oil town; Escárcega a giant truckstop; Champotón a decaying seaport with a fishy breeze. Champotón may have been the original home of the Itzá, and there in 1517 the Maya inflicted a stinging defeat on the first Spanish force to explore the Gulf coast. The Maya were not in the least overawed, not even by firearms: "Though we fought back with swords and muskets and crossbows they brought us to a bad pass,"[1] wrote Bernal Díaz, who returned two years later with Cortés. The Spaniards fled in disarray to Cuba, where their leader, Hernández de Córdoba, died of his wounds.[2]

Perhaps I've never taken to Campeche because it hasn't got a good hotel. The expensive Baluartes is a soulless concrete box spoiling the prospect of the waterfront and city walls; the only alternatives are places like the America, an old five-story walk-up with blaring TV sets, rusty watercoolers, and scraps of Kleenex in the potted plants. It was nine o'clock when I got there; the room had a stained mattress and a dirty plate containing the shriveled remains of a cucumber; but I was too tired to look for somewhere else.

As compensation I have dinner at the Baluartes. The dining room is large, sparsely populated by local businessmen and upper-middle-class Mexican families on holiday. One sees immediately the truth of the saying "The criollos have always run Mexico." Despite the Revolution and the Aztec revivalism of the 1930s, the people sitting at the tables are several shades paler than the men standing over them: the diners have European faces; the waiters Indian. A fat man across the room is fast asleep: head down on his arms, a bowl of cold soup and several cocktail glasses in front of him: Lowry's Consul to the life. The waiters don't know what to do. Would the señor like to wake up, or is the señor quite happy where he is? Eventually one is brave enough to shake the Consul's shoulder; another comes by for moral support. *Excuse me, sir, your soup is getting cold. . . . Could we perhaps serve you some coffee?* But, oh dear, the hand on the shoulder only produces loud, troubled snores and a ghastly, choking, bubbling sound, as if the snorer were being drowned in treacle. Other patrons start to laugh; their laughter emboldens the waiters, who raise the huge man to a sitting position and put a coffee in front of him. He wakes up like a baby: bewildered and utterly dependent. A minute later he's asleep again.

4 Ben :

8:30 A.M. To the offices of COMAR, the Mexican commission for refugees. I waited an hour to see the *Doctora*, a brusque, attractive woman in charge of the Campeche branch. She told me nothing I didn't know and said that only in Mexico City could I get permission to visit the camps.

"What would happen if I just drove in to one?"

"There are police checkpoints. You will be turned back for sure, and you could be arrested." She suggested I phone COMAR headquarters in Mexico City, and added: "I can't help you at all. If we helped every journalist who comes here wanting to see the refugees, we wouldn't have time to do anything for the refugees themselves. And you haven't even got a press card." She had a point, but I suspect the real reason for all this stonewalling is that the Mexicans fear criticism for having resettled the Guatemalans so far from home. I spent two hours trying to get through to Mexico City but there were no lines. I thought the Doctora might be bluffing about police and considered renting a car and driving to the nearest camp. But I didn't—I have to be in Cozumel tomorrow night and can't risk any trouble with authorities: a sensible decision, perhaps, but it left me feeling cowardly.

* * *

Afternoon. By ADO bus to Mérida, capital of Yucatán.

Mérida has changed from what I remember. The thatched Maya houses with their round ends and whitewashed walls are getting rare. Many have been replaced by concrete bungalows; others are hybrid in style: Maya shape with pink or green walls and wrought-iron window grilles. But it's still a city of windmills—big fans atop steel towers, slowly pumping water with a rhythmic creak from the aquifer beneath the prone, riverless limestone—only now the windmills are outnumbered by TV antennas.

The sidewalk cafés around the plaza have gone; the taxi ranks where men would sidle up to you with *Taxi? taxi? taxi for the Maya rueens?* (in those days a taxi was way beyond my budget) have been cleared away to make room for endlessly circling traffic. And the House of Montejo, in 1970 still occupied by an eighty-year-old scion of the conqueror's family, has been turned into a bank.

There's threadbare elegance at the Posada Toledo, where I spend the night: tall rooms with French doors opening onto a tiled colonnade and patio; stained glass; art nouveau lighting fixtures: the Ladino elegance of the Porfirio Díaz dictatorship, built on the Indian misery of the henequen plantations. You can't look at this overripe and derivative taste, so quaint in our day and so meretricious in its own, without thinking of the Maya, dispossessed and enslaved.

5 Ix

I rent a Renault 5 and drive east across the peninsula. I should have been more suspicious of the good deal they gave me—one of the tires is showing some steel whiskers and if I open my window the exhaust comes in. Luckily Yucatán is having a *norte*—cold northerlies and showers.

The little towns are much the same: apsidal houses in stone-fenced yards; Maya women in gray mantillas and white cotton huipiles with floral embroidery around their stocky necks; men on bicycles, long machetes hanging from their belts like swords; and everywhere the smell of cooking fires and orange trees.

CANCÚN

Fifteen years ago Cancún didn't exist; now it's a city of thirty thousand, created entirely for tourism. So completely has the fantasy Mexico displaced the real one that the "Mexican" food here is American: tacos made of ground beef with processed cheddar and iceberg lettuce. And you can drink the water.

It's a relief to get through the place, past the airport, and on to the fast, straight highway south to Xaman Ha. Tourist Mexico abruptly ends; ranchitos and Maya villages reappear. One of the homesteads is called Rancho La Ley del Monte—Law of the Jungle Ranch. I stop for fuel at Puerto Morelos. The Pemex station has a trilingual sign: NO FUMAR; NO SMOKING; MA DZUDZ.

At Xaman Ha I park the car and catch the evening plane to Cozumel—a ten-minute flight in a twelve-seater.

Cozumel is tourist Mexico again, but an earlier version with a few rough edges left. My taxi from the airport follows a truck piled high with dead dogs—poisoned by the authorities in a purge of the meat market.

6 Men ·

There is nothing like anticipation for slowing time (and fulfillment for spending it). The hours passed like a jail sentence this morning, no matter how I tried to busy myself by riding round the island on a Honda 50 without a front brake.

Cozumel is little more than a coral cay: swampy and windswept, nibbled and chewed by the warm bite of the Caribbean. On promontories and patches of higher ground in the interior there are small ruins—relics of the seafaring Putun or Chontal

Maya who established a maritime trading network from the Gulf, round the Yucatán Peninsula, and down into Honduras during the last centuries before the Spaniards came. Trading and perhaps raiding; for the Putun may have been the Meso-american Vikings and their predations may have begun as far back as the end of the Classic period.[3] The Itzá, the Xiu, the Yucatán "Toltecs"—no one really knows who they all were or exactly where they came from. Most likely they were part of the same process: a complex series of migrations and invasions that began with the fall of Teotihuacán in the seventh century, intensified with the Classic Maya collapse, and were still rever-berating throughout Mesoamerica when Europeans intruded here. Like the Vikings and the Franks, these Gulf peoples—half Maya, half Mexican—absorbed the culture of their victims. The problem of sorting out what happened is comparable to probing the origins of the English without any documents except *Beowulf*, a few yards of the Bayeux Tapestry, and *Sir Gawain and the Green Knight*. First Latin-speaking Romano-British; then Germanic Anglo-Saxons; then Norse-speaking Danes; followed in turn by another kind of Norsemen who had forgotten their Teutonic heritage and taken up a variety of Latin known as French. Something of that complexity hap-pened in Postclassic Yucatán.

I watched Janice come down the ladder from the plane, pale-faced and chic in her city dress. A brusque change from Toronto in midwinter to the soft air and golden light of a Yucatán afternoon.

An evening of margaritas, which she likes and I avoid, and catching up on two months of one another's lives.

7 Cib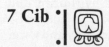

We took the morning plane, retrieved the car, and set off for Chichén via Tulum and Cobá.

TULUM

This small, walled city, built about a century before the Spaniards came, was probably the most important of a string of towns along the Quintana Roo coast occupied by the seafaring Putun. Spaniards of the Grijalva expedition, sailing past in 1518, saw "a bourg, or village, so large that Seville would not have appeared larger or better."[4] From the sea Tulum is indeed impressive, its Castillo towering above a sheer cliff; but the architecture is really rather a minor variation on the Maya theme. The main pyramid—only about thirty feet high—probably contains less cut stone than the mere roof of Temple IV at Tikal. But Tulum charms and intrigues by its state of preservation and its setting. It is a fine thing to climb the Castillo, walk around on a narrow ledge to the back and, like Stephens, who stayed here in 1842, look "out upon the boundless ocean."[5]

The buildings are small and ornate. Some have two stories, and on their corners you see strange stucco faces with screwed-up features and pointy chins like Punch's. There are cramped rooms with traces of mural painting. The great goddess Ixchel is here, seated on a low throne, receiving offerings from worshipers. Unfortunately, one can't linger and appreciate the intricate, codexlike illustrations—impatient tourists from Cancún swarm at each interesting spot, aiming cameras like bazookas. The air is full of suntan oil and insect repellent; and when we go up the main pyramid, a model is posing there in bikini and beach wrap: "Great! Lovely, wet the lips, fantastic, show a bit more tit, lovely . . ." Chichén Itzá and Palenque are big enough to absorb the crowds, but Tulum has become a Florida "theme park," a toy city overrun by half-naked gringos.

When I came here in 1970 a road had only just been opened and there were no facilities for visitors. I ate in a Maya hut (beans, tortillas, and boiled eggs; it was always the same) and slept in the bottom of a lighthouse just south of the ruins. The keeper was a friendly sort who rented hammocks for seven pesos a night. The ruins then were mysterious, still partly overgrown. I remember the night walks back from the "restaurant" to the lighthouse, hermit crabs scuttling across the path, the bush on either side of me alive with cicadas; fireflies like shooting stars.

I didn't know it then, but the Maya who live around here are followers of the Speaking Cross that led their grandparents and great-grandparents through the many victories and defeats of the Caste War. Until the 1920s they kept three crosses in a shrine on the main pyramid. (Even before the Caste War, Stephens had seen an altar "which seemed to bear marks of not very distant use.")[6] Then Thomas Gann of all people—the Indiana Jones of Belize—heard about the cult and decided he would like to lay hands on what he imagined was the original Speaking Cross.[7] He failed, but his activities, and those of more respectable archaeologists, prompted the priesthood to move the Tulum crosses to X-Cacal Guardia, where they remain today.

COBÁ

We got here by a new road cut through what was, a century ago, the jungle no-man's-land between white-controlled Yucatán and the Maya free state.

Cobá, like Lamanai, is a Classic city that continued in partial use during Postclassic times. Apart from two large pyramids, preservation of the buildings is poor, but remarkable inscriptions have been found. On three stelae one finds the extraordinary date 13. 13. 13. 13. 13. 13. 13. 13. 13. 13. 13. 13. 13. 13. 13. 13. 13. 13. 13. 13. 0. 0. 0. 0. This *could* be taken to mean that twenty cycles (each ascending by a factor of twenty) had been counted to a total of thirteen before the current Long Count era began. But it's more likely that the thirteens are functionally zeros, chosen for the religious import of the Mayas' favorite number. In this case they await the future rather than record the past. Perhaps they hint at both. Whatever the correct interpretation, the temporal scale implied is staggering—billions of times greater than our estimates for the age of the universe.[8]

* * *

We stop for dinner at Valladolid, just half an hour from Chichén Itzá. It used to be a rather abandoned colonial town, still sunk in the century of Hispanic despair that began when Maya troops sacked it in 1847, but over the last fifteen years the location (roughly halfway between Mérida and Cancún) has made it a tourist stop.

The Caste War began here in 1847. Valladolid had been a bastion of racism and exploitation for three hundred years. Even after independence from Spain, Indians and mestizos were forbidden from using the plaza and better streets. However, the whites' racial disdain didn't stop them from exercising *droit du seigneur* with Maya girls and keeping the prettiest ones as concubines. Indian men were regarded as beasts of burden—a drunken priest even saddled a Maya and lacerated him with spurs.[9] As usual, repression got worse once the criollos were free of the metropolitan Crown. The Yucatán bush, long used by the Maya for milpa farming, was declared "empty" state land. Much of it was sold to cattle ranchers and sugar planters. The Indians either became serfs or were violently driven away; when they resorted to the courts, ancient title deeds and genealogies were likely to get "lost."

Outbreak of the Caste War was hastened, ironically, by internal strife among Ladinos. They were divided into liberals and conservatives, federalists and centralists, those who favored union with Mexico and separatists who thought Yucatán should go it alone. For twenty-five years following independence in 1821, the various factions had fought each other and the armies sent from Mexico City. The population of Yucatán at the time was about half a million, of which Ladinos amounted to 130,000. To raise enough troops the whites had had to recruit Indians. The Maya proved adept at learning the arts of modern war, and many of them were organized for this purpose by their own *batabs*—native leaders descended from ancient aristocracy.

Unknown to Ladinos, the old enmities, alliances, and political hierarchies of pre-Columbian Yucatán had survived beneath a facade of submission to Spanish rule, especially in the eastern area around Valladolid and Chichén Itzá. Ruined cities were still collecting ceremonial tribute and vying with each other for the prestigious right to "seat the katun" every 20 years, and to seat the *may*—the Short Count cycle of thirteen katuns—every 260.

The Maya calendar not only recorded the past and predicted the future; it organized the world and sanctioned earthly power. Throughout the Classic period, rulers edited their lives and genealogies to resonate with the deeds of mythology and the great procession of the ages. In Postclassic Yucatán, fourteen or fifteen petty states cemented shaky alliances and confederations by sharing out "custodianship" of calendrical periods in much the same way that municipal office is rotated in step with the Year-Bearers by Guatemalan Maya today. Needless to say, disputes arose about protocol and correct interpretation of the time machine. Ambitious politicians began challenging their rivals' calendrical systems and setting up their own. Different counts and eras proliferated, especially after the Spanish invasion.

Munro Edmonson, who has made new translations of Chilam Balam books written mainly during the colonial period, believes that sixteenth-century Yucatán had been divided into western and eastern camps, controlled by the Xiu (who lived near Mérida) and the Itzá, respectively. These differed on the thorny question of when to "start" the Short Count. (This may seem an esoteric *casus belli*, but medieval Europeans went to war over the computation of Easter, and the powers of the modern world are willing to toy with extinction over the meaning of liberty.) The Xiu allied themselves with the Spaniards, promptly became Christians, and seated a cycle of thirteen katuns at Mérida at about the time the Spaniards settled there.[10] They hoped this would ensure their ascendancy under the new order. The Itzá remained pagan much longer and did their own fiddling with the calendar. At Valladolid in 1752, they adopted a new count of twenty-four katuns containing twenty-four years each. This had the virtue of stretching their cycle well beyond its appointed end.[11] Life began to imitate art: the Itzá must have been impressed when, under their revised cycle, Spanish rule ended after lasting exactly thirteen katuns.

And it was perhaps no coincidence that the Caste War broke out, here in the Itzá heartland, exactly one katun after that.

The dress rehearsal came in January 1847 when Indian troops rioted and sacked Valladolid, killing about eighty whites and raping the women of the landlords who had for so long made free with Maya girls. Later that year a separatist colonel began canvassing Indian support in the Valladolid area for yet another revolt against the government in Mérida. Among the batabs he spoke to were Manuel Ay, Jacinto Pat, and Cecilio Chi, all Mayas of substance and education.

The position of these privileged batabs was ambiguous. They were bilingual and bicultural, loyal to Maya traditions, yet responsible for fulfilling white demands for Indian labor and taxes. Many dreamed of a day when they would no longer have to exploit their own people for the *dzul*. They resented the way the Ladinos had stolen the rewards of independence. By 1847 they had fought too many white battles and got nothing in return but broken promises of land and freedom. Nothing, that is, except modern weapons and military training.

While the colonel was negotiating with the three batabs, an informer betrayed Manuel Ay to the Valladolid authorities. Evidence against Ay was flimsy but whites wanted revenge for the Indian rampage in January. He was shot by firing squad on July 26. His execution polarized the races. The colonel withdrew; Chi and Pat continued planning rebellion, but of a different kind. This time, they decided, they would fight no more white men's wars: they would reconquer Yucatán from the dzul and put a Maya government in Mérida. Not only was the time ripe according to the prophecies of Chilam Balam but external circumstances favored the Indians. Yucatán was at war with Mexico, and Mexico with the United States; the Maya had guns and knew they could get more from the British in Belize. They also had the example of the Indian-Carrera alliance in Guatemala. It looked as though the criollo independence of the 1820s would be followed by Maya independence in the 1840s.

8 Caban ⁝ [glyph]

CHICHÉN ITZÁ

It was dark when we arrived last night. We've treated ourselves to the Villa Arqueológica, owned by the Club Méditerranée. It's delightful—none of the yuppie lubriciousness one associates with Club Med—simply a patio of quiet rooms with rounded contours. The architects have built without disturbing the trees that were here: huge guanacastes and palms rise through gaps in the building, a pleasant echo of the ruins.

9 Etznab ⁝ [glyph]

Day of sacrifice. We are in the ruins by half past six, hoping to see sunrise from the top of the Castillo. But the city and surrounding bush stretch away beneath a pewter lid that seems to cover the entire peninsula.

Chichén Itzá is familiar from every travel brochure: the four-sided Castillo; the round Caracol, or Observatory; an immense ballcourt; the Temple of the Warriors; and finally the Sacred Cenote, or Well of Sacrifice, a giant sinkhole that attracts archaeologists, treasure hunters, and assorted cranks in numbers rivaling the Maya pilgrims who visited the site for centuries and perhaps still do.

The name means "Mouth of the Well of the Itzá," and Itzá itself means "Water Wizards." Yucatán has no surface rivers, but the limestone plateau is riddled with underground streams and caverns, some of great size. A *cenote* (from Maya *dzonot*) is formed when the roof of a cave collapses and breaks through to the surface. Such places are revered by the Yucatec Maya, who are always anxious about rainfall. Cenotes are doors to the watery underworld inhabited by Chacs (rain gods), Balams (jaguar spirits, who take many roles), and other entities.

We climb down the Castillo, cross the plaza, and walk along the *sacbe*, the ceremonial road to the cenote. At this hour Indian vendors of soft drinks and handicrafts are just arriving, crouching to release the weight of their huge loads from the forehead tumpline—a gesture identical to that of the lords of time in Classic inscriptions, as they set down the katuns and baktuns at the stages on their journeys through eternity.

The great natural well is almost perfectly round, two hundred feet in diameter, with vertical limestone sides, draped in vines and roots, falling seventy feet to the water's surface. On this sunless day, the water is a sickly pastel green. Soon the guides will arrive with their wide-eyed gringos and tales of how virgins were regularly hurled in to appease the gods. The scene conjured up here hundreds of times a day has immense appeal to restaurateurs throughout Yucatán. Everywhere you eat there's a lurid mural of a heavily made-up, tightly bound, and suspiciously light-skinned Maya virgin being flung into the cenote by burly priests. There isn't a shred of truth in it. Early sources such as Diego de Landa mention that *men* were occasionally sacrificed; and in modern rituals to the water gods only males take part. Several dredgings of the well have retrieved some fifty skeletons of all ages and both sexes—a number that could easily have fallen in by accident. The specialist who examined the bones remarked dryly, "All of the individuals ... may have been virgins, but the osteological evidence does not permit a determination of this nice point."[12]

The archaeology and "history" of Postclassic Yucatán has recently become a case of paradigms lost. Sandwiched between the laconic history of the Classic period and the accounts of Maya civilization set down by Spanish friars lie several centuries of invasion and discord comparable to the first five hundred years of post-Roman Europe. A shadow play of light and darkness is cast on this period by the cryptic books of Chilam Balam and other Maya documents.

Until the 1930s there was a seductive hypothesis of Old and New Maya empires corresponding to the Classic and Postclassic periods. According to this, survivors of the Maya collapse migrated north to the Yucatán Peninsula and there founded cities such as Uxmal and Chichén Itzá. Even when it became clear that the Maya had never created anything resembling an empire, it was still assumed that Yucatán's cities were later than those of the Petén, and that a last Maya florescence took place under Toltec tutelage at Chichén Itzá. Here, plain for anyone to see, are two distinct styles of monumental architecture. One is typically Maya; the other—for example, the Castillo pyramid, the Temple of the Warriors, and the ballcourt—shows strong influence from highland Mexico. It seemed logical that the Maya part of Chichén had been built first; then a warlike group of Toltecs, led by a king bearing the ubiquitous name of Quetzalcóatl, had invaded Yucatán and made Chichén the capital of a brief and bloodthirsty Mexican state.

Almost every aspect of this neat reconstruction is now being challenged. First, it appears that Yucatec cities such as Uxmal are *not* later than those of the Petén Classic. Second, there's circumstantial evidence that the "Maya" and "Toltec" parts of Chichén Itzá were built at the same time. Last, and most disquieting, is that a void of several centuries now seems to exist between the ruins themselves and their "history" recorded in colonial sources. Even the Thompson correlation has been rattled: some Yucatán specialists argue that a shortened chronology, putting the end of the Classic in the thirteenth century instead of the tenth, would best close the gap. Unfortunately, such a revision is hard to reconcile with radiocarbon dates from wooden lintels and much of the astronomical data in Classic inscriptions. As for the books of Chilam Balam, they are as esoteric as the Bible, the Vedas, or the prophecies of Nostradamus: you can find what you want in them, and everybody does.[13]

Clemency Coggins has recently proposed that Chichén Itzá was built specifically to celebrate and symbolize the end of Baktun 9 and a Mexican Calendar Round in the years 830–31. According to her ideas, a Mexican or Mexicanized Maya group moved into Yucatán shortly beforehand and built the Caracol observatory to determine the exact date of astronomical events such as the nocturnal zenith of the Pleiades, when New Fire would be drilled on the chest of a stone "Chac-Mool."

A.D. 830 must have been a year of acute anxiety for both

halves of the Mesoamerican hourglass. The Mexicans feared the end of the world whenever their fifty-two-year cycle returned to its starting position; and the Maya, who normally took a much longer view, were dreading the approach of the new baktun because the inauspicious number ten, a death lord with a fleshless jaw, would take up office and preside for the next four hundred years. Indeed, his malevolent influence was already being felt as the Classic order began to fall apart. Coggins believes a vast building program was undertaken at Chichén Itzá not only to forestall a cosmic cataclysm at this liminal time but to inaugurate a new calendrical and political order: the birth of an age in which the Mexican calendar system would eclipse and subsume the Long Count.

Certainly there's an extroversion to the Toltec buildings that is trying to make some momentous public statement. The symmetrical Castillo, with its four staircases, resembles the hieroglyph for completion of an era; the total number of its steps is 365; and when the rising equinoctial sun strikes the balustrades, feathered serpents carved there can be seen to wriggle from heaven to earth. The ballcourt, more than five hundred feet long and two hundred wide, the largest in Mesoamerica, seems to have been built for an epic struggle between elemental forces. And at the top of the so-called Temple of the Warriors (a building I've always disliked) a reclining Chac-Mool waits with sinister patience, empty dish held on chest for sacrifice.

This enigmatic sculpture inspired Henry Moore's *Reclining Figure*, though it has none of the "freak potato" softness of a Moore. The Chac-Mool unsettles you with its odd, stiff pose and chill mien of endless expectation. You feel what Alexander Kinglake felt when he saw the Sphinx. "The stone idol," Kinglake wrote, "bears awful semblance of Deity—unchangefulness in the midst of change—the same seeming will, and intent for ever, and ever inexorable."[14] The Chac-Mool gazes westward, the direction of darkness, death, and the color black. He is flanked by feathered-serpent pillars that once formed the temple door. His eyes meet yours as you reach the top of the stairs—almond eyes, cut in stone, that on a second glance look through you and on, into the hereafter. The cold hard stare of a cat: what have you got to offer; what have I got to lose? But the Chac-Mool isn't worried; he knows he has everything to gain and nothing to lose. All he has to do is wait. And sometimes, after aeons of waiting, fate sends an offering his way. Not long ago a well-known archaeologist was unwary enough to climb the Chac-Mool's pyramid when the sky had turned black with an impending storm; he was killed by lightning on the spot.

10 Cauac

In the volumes of Stephens and Catherwood, who made the first thorough explorations of Yucatán in the 1840s, there is one of Catherwood's magnificent engravings, entitled *The Mask of Izamal*. With his eye for the dramatic he showed it by moonlight, a huge lugubrious face with open mouth, hawk nose, and bulbous, staring eyes, framed by vines and bromeliads.

The mask has since disappeared, but I have always wanted to visit Izamal—an easy detour on our way to Mérida. We are now in the northwestern part of Yucatán, the most arid, but also the most populous, and so flat that Izamal's one surviving pyramid is visible for miles.

The land here is divided into vast rectangular fields separated by dry stone walls; bedrock shows through the thin soil like skin through a beggar's rags. The sky also hangs in patches, blue peeping through gray as the norther of the past week begins to go to holes. The crop is henequen, the native agave turned into rope and money by the hacendados of the nineteenth and twentieth centuries. Monoculture is a fearful thing: bristly clusters in rank and file make the land a molted scrubbing brush from road to sky.

When Diego de Landa was writing his *Relation of the Things of Yucatán* (c. 1566), mainly to atone for having destroyed so many of them, he mentioned the beauty and wealth of Yucatán's architecture, singling out Izamal and Tiho (Mérida) as two of the finest ancient cities. At Izamal he tells of the great pyramid "of astonishing height and beauty . . . and on top a beautiful chapel of finely worked stone."[15] This temple was dedicated to Itzamná, supreme creator and embodiment of the universe. Landa and his fellow Franciscans pulled it down to build a church and monastery with a precinct larger than that of St. Peter's in Rome. But the old god made a comeback through his wife, Ixchel, patroness of weaving, childbirth, and healing arts. Like Tonantzin-Guadalupe, she appeared to some recently "converted" Indians and was recognized as a manifestation of the Virgin. The events did not pass unnoted in the books of Chilam Balam:

> Destroyed was the town of Emal the Great,
> And Izamal,
> Where there descended . . .
> The Queen,
> The Virgin,
> The Holy Person.[16]

The colonnades and facade have recently been given a fresh coat of ocher with white trim, and in the dark coolness of the church, in a small chamber at the back, we see the Virgin attended by burning candles on waxy flagstones. We also see a portrait of Landa himself, the single man most hated and praised by Mayanists—hated for his destruction and cruelty, praised for his *Relación*, which proved a key document in understanding the Maya calendar and script. He was a small, brittle man, dark hair balding on top, a prominent Roman nose, a weak chin. His cheeks sagged from his nose in two heavy folds, and his eyes were downcast in an attitude of disdainful piety: holier than thou. He was a fanatic who could burn Maya books and Maya nobles with equal zeal. Back rooms of the Franciscan convents in Mérida and Izamal became torture chambers where Indians suspected of even the smallest lapse into idolatry were jailed and tormented with all the righteous terror of the Inquisition.

Landa's purges were considered excessive even by the standards of his day. Eventually he was recalled to Spain and tried. As part of his defense he wrote down whatever he could remember of the civilization he had striven to obliterate. He was neither an agile thinker nor a careful ethnographer. His work is hasty and superficial, and his knowledge of Maya culture was greatly inferior to that of Avendaño, who later visited Tayasal and learned to read and write in Maya hieroglyphics. But Avendaño's book is lost and only infuriating Landa remains:

> These people ... used certain characters or letters with which they wrote in their books about their ancient things and sciences.... We found a great number of books in these letters of theirs, and because they contained nothing but superstition and the devil's falsehoods, we burned the lot, which upset [the Indians] most grievously and caused them great pain.[17]

One day, with his usual arrogance, Landa decided to "learn" the Maya writing system. "What is the Maya letter for *A?*" he asked an informant (presumably a scribe or shaman-priest none too anxious to divulge his knowledge). Landa, assuming that all writing worked the same way, made him give a Maya sign for each letter of the Spanish alphabet, and the poor man put down whatever glyph came closest to the sounds uttered by the Spaniard. Beside *B,* he put the glyph for *be,* the Maya word for "road"; and so on. Landa suspected he wasn't getting the whole story, but didn't really care. "They also wrote in parts [syllables], in one way or another," he added breezily, "which I note here merely to give a complete account."

Until about 1950, scholars regarded Landa's alphabet as virtually useless. It was clear from the inventory of Maya glyphs—close to one thousand—that the writing couldn't possibly have been alphabetic. Even a syllabic system wouldn't have needed many more than one hundred signs. The orthodox view held that Maya writing was ideographic and logographic: glyphs stood for individual ideas and words, modified by affixes and rebuses.

In 1952 Yuri Knorosov, an obscure Russian researcher, announced he had made a breakthrough by applying computer analysis and "Marxist-Leninist principles" to Landa's information. He claimed far too much for himself and was wittily excoriated by Sir Eric Thompson, but David Kelley and a few other freethinkers sensed that Knorosov was onto something. They have since shown that Maya writing, like Egyptian, is a mixed system. A Maya scribe could choose to write ideographically, phonetically, or both (as we do when writing a check in figures as well as words). On public texts—stelae and temple tablets—important data such as a ruler's name were often reiterated in different ways. For example, at Palenque the name of Pacal (Shield) is shown by the ideograph for "shield" and by a syllabic sequence reading *pa-ca-l[a]*. The same phonetic method was used nine hundred years later by the man commanded to write something, *anything*, by irascible Landa. He put down *ma-in-ka-ti*—"I don't want to."

11 Ahau

We spent last night in Mérida and drove today to Uxmal, the loveliest of all Yucatán's ancient cities. The road took us south to the little town of Muna and over the gentle foothills of the Puuc "range," rolling country that would hardly be called hills if it weren't for the perfect flatness of most of the peninsula. The Puuc region gives its name to the local Maya architecture, an expansive style that emphasizes the horizontal dimension and achieves perfect balance between form and ornament. The norther has dispersed, and the day is hot—one of those clear blue skies marbled with white so typical of Yucatán.

UXMAL

The 140-foot Pyramid of the Magician dominates the site, but its dominion is gentle, softened by the round, smooth surface of the building. It is oval—identical in plan to a Yucatec Maya house of the eighth century or the twentieth.

From the summit you can see the whole city. Directly below, at the "back," is the so-called Nunnery quadrangle, one of the masterpieces of Maya design. You enter the courtyard by a large corbeled arch. It's a tranquil space, enclosed and calmed by the smooth ashlars of the palace walls. All ornamentation is confined to the upper half of the buildings, above a cornice. The rooms are cool, smelling slightly of bats, and very dark beneath the cheese-colored facades in the midday light. At Puuc sites the corbeled vault reached its greatest refinement. The architects widened and curved it until, one feels, they were on the point of discovering the true arch. Their technique here was most ingenious. Uxmal's buildings are made of masses of lime concrete covered by a thin veneer of finely cut blocks. The vault stones are boot shaped and tenoned deeply into the concrete, so that each is a miniature cantilever that directs the thrust to its neighbor.

Although in detail the Puuc style, with its baroque feathered serpents, tapir-snouted Chac masks, and geometric entablatures, is wholly foreign, the way it handles proportion and perspective is reminiscent of Classical Greece. The side of the Nunnery directly opposite the entrance is raised above the others on an imposing platform, approached by a flight of steps flanked by columned halls. And the House of the Turtles, just beyond the ballcourt, has the unity and simplicity of the Doric order.

One building at Uxmal has been called the finest ever erected in ancient America (some admirers drop the "ancient"). This is the Palace of the Governors, standing by itself at the south end of the city on an enormous artificial platform. For once the Spaniards guessed rightly with their name—the Governors' Palace must have been the residence of a ruler of Uxmal, perhaps King Chac, whose name appears in a few scanty inscriptions. It is a single, perfectly symmetrical structure, 320 feet wide, broken into three wings by cuneiform archways that spring just above ground level, uniting the plain and ornamented halves of the facade. The sculpture is almost entirely geometric, a lavish but restrained montage of stepfrets and arabesques emanating from a central human figure surrounded by quetzal plumes. The vaulting is bold—the central chamber is almost seventy feet long, fifteen feet wide, and twenty-five feet high at the apex. This building, like others at Uxmal and those of Palenque, reveals a Maya architecture that was fully mature, confident in its structural techniques, self-confident in its deft use of ornament. There is none of the sinister magnificence of Chichén, or the grandiosity of Tikal.

We have a late lunch at the Los Almendros restaurant in Ticul, a short drive from Uxmal. Ticul is a thriving town of ten thousand, about half Ladino, half Indian, bustling with Maya men in cowboy hats and women in embroidered huipiles carrying jars and baskets on their heads. The restaurant has become well known for offering *comida yucateca para los dzules*— Yucatec cooking for foreigners. They do a wonderful *sopa de lima*—bits of toasted tortilla with chicken breast and chiles in a broth flavored with lime juice. After this Janice orders turkey in black sauce; I have turkey in white sauce. The source of the turkeys is no mystery: a patio next to the outdoor kitchen is full of *guajolotes*, puffing, hissing, and gobbling with futile arrogance while former members of their group are bubbling on the stove.

"Say, you from the States?" comes an elderly voice from the next table. The speaker has checked shorts and a Tyrolean hat complete with feather. His wife favors a polyester dress— the sort Lenny Bruce once described as "the kind you can see through and you don't wanna."

"Say, what are you guys eating there? Is it okay?"

"It's wonderful. Try the turkey in white sauce."

"Or black."

"We'll have what they're having," they tell the waiter. Five minutes later there's a frantic gobbling followed by a gringo scream:

"Oh, my gosh! Did you see that? Did you see them wring the poor turkey's neck?"

"At least you know it's fresh, dear."

*   *   *

Evening. Back at Uxmal for the sound and light show. The
search for a good *son et lumière* is a running feature for Janice
and me. I don't like them, she still thinks she'll find a good one
somewhere. The one she saw at Karnak (and I didn't) was good,
apparently. The one we both saw at Giza was bad. Charlton
Heston was the Sphinx.

8:00 P.M. The upper terrace of the Nunnery quadrangle is full of
green plastic chairs. Steel lids have been removed from lighting
channels cut into the courtyard's ancient floor. Appallingly
loud music thunders from loudspeakers in the corners. I've
heard this music before—electro-Maya, popular in Mérida
nightclubs.

> FIRST VOICE: Princess Zac Nicté, White Flower of Mayab,
> the Maya realm, light of the Moon, tender dove, limpid
> water, daughter of the Evening Star, the hour of your des-
> tiny is coming! You know this and you wait, Princess Zac
> Nicté, you who have given your heart to Prince Ulil of
> Uxmal.

> SECOND VOICE: Prince Canek of Chichén Itzá, do you not
> want to touch the Morning Star? Do you not wish to pluck
> for yourself the White Flower of Mayab? What will you say,
> prince of the Itzá, when you discover she is promised to
> another?

> THIRD VOICE: At the wedding feast for Princess Zac Nicté
> and Prince Ulil the guests have waited three days for the
> lord of Chichén Itzá but he has not arrived!

> FIRST VOICE: He has come! At the appointed hour, here in
> Uxmal, with sixty warriors! He has climbed to the altar
> where the priests are singing and the nuptial incense
> burns! He is dressed for war, with the heraldic arms of the
> Itzá upon his chest!

> SECOND VOICE: Prince Canek sweeps Zac Nicté in his
> arms! He steals the sweet dove who must be his by order of
> the black gods of the Sacrificial Well!

FIRST VOICE: Oh, the vengeance that will befall Chichén Itzá! Weapons are being prepared once more in Mayab, and the standards of war are being raised. Uxmal and Mayapán have joined against Chichén Itzá.

And so on. Peace shatters; there is drought. Famine stalks the land, all because the evil prince of Chichén must have the woman of his desire. What a travesty of the books of Chilam Balam, what a feast of anachronisms. The lights are better. Green, blue, yellow, and red play on the pyramids and palaces; and individual motifs in the sculpture of the Nunnery facades are picked out with color. But wait, the text sounds oddly familiar. Indeed it's nothing but an abridged version of one of the jewels of Yucatec Ladino literature, *Land of the Pheasant and the Deer*, written by Antonio Mediz Bolio in the 1920s. "I ... have made a stylization of the Maya spirit," the author claimed. "The themes are taken from tradition, from the traces of the ancient books, from the very soul of the Indians. . . ."[18]

The Chac masks are illuminated now in green. The corn has died. The people of Uxmal are dying of thirst, virgins are being offered to the rain god, and the chorus chants *Chac! Chac! Chac!* with all the ham fervor of a children's play. Soon the chant changes to another word: *Maní, Maní, Maní! We must go to Maní, where there is water.* Here we're on firmer ground. The lordly family of Xiu, which collaborated with the Spaniards and claimed, perhaps falsely, to have built Uxmal, did migrate to the small town of Maní where their descendants still live. (One of them received Queen Elizabeth when she visited Yucatán some years ago.)

But Maní has another history of the sort that doesn't get into sound and light shows. There was death and sacrifice there all right—directed by Diego de Landa. In 1562, outraged by reports of religious backsliding among the Xiu, he conducted an auto da fé, hanging and burning Maya lords, even digging up and scattering the bones of Christians he suspected of apostasy. And when his deeds provoked an outcry, he went so far as to have letters forged and sent to the king of Spain. These, purporting to come from Indian batabs, overflowed with affection for Landa and praise for his purge. They were written in Maya with attached translations—all in the same hand, including the signatures. They may have fooled Philip II, but they didn't fool the Indians.[19] Lord Xiu, a man so loyal to his Spanish allies that he had been baptized with the name of Yucatán's conquistador, himself wrote to the king:

Sacred Catholic Majesty:

After we learned the good, in knowing God our Lord as the only true god, leaving our blindness and idolatries, and your majesty as temporal lord . . . there came upon us a persecution of the worst that can be imagined; and it was in the year '62, on the part of the Franciscan religious, who had taken us to teach the doctrine, instead of which they began to torment us, hanging us by the hands and whipping us cruelly, hanging weights of stone on our feet, torturing many of us on a windlass, giving the torture of the water, from which many died or were maimed. . . .

Not content with this, the religious and thy royal Justice, held at Maní a solemn *auto* of inquisition, where they seized many statues, disinterred many dead and burned them there in public; made slaves of many to serve the Spaniards for from eight to ten years. . . . The one and the other gave us great wonder and fear, because we did not know what it all was, having been recently baptized and not informed; and when we returned to our people . . . [the friars] seized us, put us in prison and chains, like slaves, in the monastery at Mérida, where many of us died; and they told us we would be burned. . . .

The religious of San Francisco of this province have written certain letters to your majesty and to the general of the [Franciscan] order, in praise of fray Diego de Landa and his other companions. . . . May your majesty understand that they are not ours, we who are chiefs of this land. . . . May fray Diego de

Landa and his companions suffer the penance for the evils they have done to us, and may our descendants to the fourth generation be recompensed [for] the great persecution that came on us.

May God guard your majesty. . . . From Yucatán, the 12 of April, 1567.

[signed] Don Francisco de Montejo Xiu

12 Imix

XAMAN HA

Christmas Eve. Back here for the holidays.

The hotel is a tasteful imitation of the colonial style, with limestone columns and Moorish ogees. Musicians are playing guitars in the lobby when we arrive; several employees have gathered to listen, speaking quietly among themselves in Maya.

"I'm sorry, sir," the desk clerk says. "We can't let you have the seafront room you wanted. They've all been taken by a large party of VIPs."

"VIPs?"

"Yes. I'm not really supposed to tell anyone, but"— he swells and leans across the desk confidentially—"the *ex-presidente* of the United States!"

"Which *ex-presidente?* Not Nixon?"

"Yimmy Carter and his family."

"They're here now?"

"Not yet, but we expect them at any moment."

"Damn," says Janice to me. "We booked first. Why should Jimmy Carter get our room? I didn't think they liked him much in Mexico—not after he made jokes about Montezuma's revenge."

There's no hot water. Not a disaster in this climate, but one doesn't expect cold showers at the rates charged here. When I complain I'm told to run the tap for twenty minutes. When that doesn't work I'm told that the tank is in the process of being heated. *"Mañana, seguro, habrá agua caliente."*

13 Ik

Christmas Day, Day of Wind; and there's certainly a lot of hot air about the hot water. Now they tell me the system is broken and they expect some vital parts to arrive "at any moment" from Mérida.

"What about Yimmy Carter? Don't you think he'd like some hot water, too?"

"He hasn't come yet. Please be patient, señor."

Waiting for Carter, it seems, is like waiting for Godot.

We can't use the swimming pool, either. It's in the process of being filled. I wouldn't believe that Carter or any other VIP was within a hundred miles of this place were it not for the "spooks"—burly men in three-piece suits bulging with hardware, perched around the pool, the bar, the restaurant, all with dark glasses, walkie-talkies, and bottles of Coca-Cola. Every so often one of them takes out his walkie-talkie and whispers into it furtively, affectionately, like a priest telling a dirty joke to an old friend.

Evening. The *ex-presidente* has arrived! Suddenly there's hot water and the swimming pool is full.

We have a turkey dinner at a small restaurant on the plaza, followed by dancing and drinking. Margaritas can have a strange and sudden effect on Janice. At eleven-forty she's fine; at eleven forty-five her legs turn to rubber and we stagger back to the hotel in a drunken embrace.

At the top of the stairs she twists away from my grasp and lunges in the direction of the Carters' rooms. A Secret Service man is standing, arms folded, back to the wall, at the end of the passage.

"I've got something I want to say! Let's go down there and hassle that guy!"

1 Akbal

Darkness. A bad day; hangovers. A fragile afternoon on the beach.

3 Chicchan

CANCÚN

Janice caught her flight back to Toronto from here. I ordered coffee and sat in the observation lounge, watching her plane take off. Not such a sad farewell as last time. My own journey is also near its end: a few days at a conference in Mérida, and then to the middle of Quintana Roo, where I hope to visit the militant descendants of the Caste War Maya—if they'll let me. The Santa Cruz have a well-earned reputation for hostility, but I want to see X-Cacal Guardia, where the Speaking Cross itself is said to reside.

Chapter 18

4 Cimi :

Traveling on a Death day again.

MÉRIDA

Back at the Posada Toledo, now filled with guests attending the conference on Latin American Indian literature. Supper at Mérida's Los Almendros—similar to the parent restaurant at Ticul, but there are no live turkeys here.

5 Manik |

Quite a mix of people at the conference: linguists, writers, native speakers of Quechua and Maya, and anything ideologically from Marxist academics to fundamentalist missionaries.

This morning's most interesting paper was given by Domingo Dzul Poot of the Academy of the Maya Language, a distinguished, dapper man with thick iron gray hair and a neat moustache. He began by welcoming everyone in Maya, something that was conspicuously *not* done at the official opening last night. He recounted a legend about the sculptured feet at

356

the ruins of Chacmultún, of how three greedy brothers had tried to uncover a treasure of jade guarded by a seven-headed monster. A local sorcerer heard of their intentions and magically buried the brothers in the ancient building, but he left their feet sticking out because "a person's feet are controlled by his head and are not themselves to blame for wickedness." Dzul Poot told it with masterly poise and wit, in both languages. I spoke to him afterward and learned that he has published books of Maya legends, and is one of the collaborators on a definitive new dictionary of Yucatec Maya.

There are several others like him—educated people who are ethnically Indian and proud of it, something not easily achieved in Latin America. Most of them are not academics; they are simply Maya to whom the Maya heritage is important, not as an intellectual curiosity but as a worldview they are eager to sustain. I must visit this academy.

In the afternoon we're given a bus tour of the city. I've seen the historic sites before, but the chinoiserie mansion of an ex-madam who married a wealthy politician is a new delight. A large man with gangling limbs and thick horn-rimmed spectacles sits next to me. His eyes bulge like boiled onions; his elbow dislodges mine from the armrest; his knee pushes mine toward the wall.

"Wilbur Trench," he says, extending a hand like a baseball mitt. "What brings you here?" I say I've come mainly for interest, and because I've been invited to read from my book on Peru. Trench is with the Summer Institute of Linguistics (alias Wycliffe Bible Translators) and works in highland Guatemala. He continues to spread, with each jolt of the bus, like a collapsing blancmange. He seems completely unaware of this encroachment—a reflection, I suppose, of the missionary's essential solipsism, the inability to sense limits and avoid intrusion.

"Ah'm just finishing a translation of the Scriptures into Quiché."

"Do you find much similarity with Yucatec?"

"What's that? I never heard of that before."

"Are you sure? Yucatec Maya. They speak it here—it's related to Quiché."

"Is that right?" The boiled onions focus on the scene outside the window.

Mérida's origins are mysterious. The early Spaniards, among them Landa, settled here in a ruined city called Tiho—a name still current among Maya speakers. It must have been something like Uxmal, only bigger, but not a trace remains except a slight rise where the Mérida barracks stand on the footing of a major pyramid. So complete is the obliteration of Tiho that archaeologists tend to forget it in their reconstructions of Yucatán's past. Yet the very name suggests that it was once the most important of all Yucatán's Classic cities, at least in the western half of the peninsula. Tiho means "The Fifth Place," or "At the Five," and the Chilam Balam books often give it the resounding title Ichcaanziho—"Tiho Born of Heaven." Five is the number of the center or zenith in the system of world directions: the position of hegemony. Though it must have been abandoned centuries before the Spanish conquest, Tiho's rank had not been forgotten.

The Maya regard a ruined city the way we regard a parked car. Its desolation is temporary; it has an owner or owners; it is as capable of life in the future as in the past. When a Maya peasant looks at the sculptures of Uxmal or Chichén, he doesn't see lifeless art: he sees the ancient rulers and inhabitants turned to stone; and their petrifaction is by no means irreversible.

Because of Tiho's traditions of hegemony, the Xiu encouraged their European allies to resettle it. To the Spaniards it was simply a convenient location—a ready-made quarry that reminded them of Roman remains at home. "[We] occupied a city here, and called it Mérida, because of the strangeness and grandeur of the buildings,"[1] Landa wrote, mentioning a pyramid "so large and beautiful that . . . I don't think it will ever be used up."[2] He also describes "a round, rather tall building"—presumably something like the observatory at Chichén—and three other pyramids with vaulted temples still standing on their summits. His most detailed description is of a quadrangle very similar to Uxmal's Nunnery, but even grander, which the Franciscans promptly pulled down: "We . . . have made from its own stones a proper monastery . . . and a fine church which we call the Mother of God. There was so much stone . . . that we gave a lot to the Spaniards for their houses."[3]

In the Chilam Balam books one senses the anger and awe of the Maya at seeing their ancient city destroyed and then replaced by a new, strange architecture that nevertheless exercised a familiar form of religious autocracy. The cathedral replaced the great pyramid as the focus of mystery and power:

> 13 Etz'nab was the day when the land was
>   established . . .
> when they measured off by paces the cathedral,
> the dark house of instruction . . .
> In the middle of Tihoo . . .
> the fiery house,
> the mountainous house,
> the dark house,
> for the benefit of God the Father,
> God the Son and God the Holy Spirit.[4]

The books of Chilam Balam were living documents of the Yucatec Maya—part bible, part community charter, part almanac, part chronicle—added to and revised as the years passed and divine patterns were recognized in human events. Long passages are almost certainly transcriptions or digests of codices burned by Landa and his minions. Some parts may have come down from the Classic period; others were written as recently as the nineteenth century. The books are chronological but not diachronic, obsessed with time, yet timeless. Maya time was a circle, a spiral, wheels within wheels affording glimpses of recurring symmetry: the "ancient future" of the katun cycles, the flux of peoples and dynasties, the populating and abandonment of stone cities that had a life of their own, whether occupied by human beings or wild beasts. The Maya "contained" the Spanish invasion by internalizing it, by claiming they had foreseen it in detail, by wresting it from European triumphalism and embedding it in Maya time. In this way the books are both fatalistic and subversive. Chilam Balam, which means "Jaguar Prophet" or "Spokesman of God," refers both to a religious office and to an individual said to have uttered this prophecy while in trance:

> Know all of you that the time has come. . . . the rulers as well as the people shall suffer. . . . When these times arrive in these provinces of Mayapán and Ziyancaan and in this peninsula which will be called Yucatán, you will leave as dying deer. . . . Vultures will enter the houses in your villages because of the great numbers of dead Mayas and dead animals. . . . The Petén [general word for "the land"] will be sold, and all the people will be moved. At the end of the Nicté [Flower or War] Katun you will be seen bowing your heads to the archbishop . . . you will have to follow the True God called Christ. . . . heaven and earth will thunder, for then, sorrowfully, our rulers' time will end and that which was written on the monuments will be fulfilled.[5]

The Mayas' attitude to the "True God" was ambivalent. Like the Incas and many other peoples colonized by Europe, they recognized ethical value in his teachings. But they were outraged by the horrors and hypocrisy that accompanied his gospel:

> [Katun] 11 Ahau is the beginning of the count,
> because this was the katun when the foreigners
>   arrived. . . .
> Then Christianity also began. . . .
> The katun is established at Ichcaanzihoo [Mérida]. . . .
> Then with the true God, the true *Dios*,
> came the beginning of our misery.
> It was the beginning of tribute . . .
> the beginning of strife by trampling on people,
> the beginning of robbery with violence,
> the beginning of forced debts,

the beginning of debts enforced by false testimony,
the beginning of individual strife,
a beginning of vexation. . . .
This was the origin of service to the Spaniards and
    priests. . . .
It was by Antichrist on earth. . . .[6]

6 Lamat

Day of Venus; New Year's Eve. The session today was on Quechua, the Inca language of Peru, which I know a bit. In the evening I go out with the *quechuistas:* Don Gabriél, a folklorist from Cusco; Silvia, a specialist in Andean music; and a few others. We end up at a nightclub called Pancho Villa's, a corny gringo place. But we find a corner to drink the new year in, singing *waynos*—the bawdy, beautiful songs of the Andes— and listening to Don Gabriél's Quechua insults: "Your sister is like an old green bus that everyone climbs on. Your arse is cold as a river stone."

7 Muluc

New Year's Day. Edmonson has written, "The Maya thought it very clever of the Spanish to have their own year. They learned it rapidly and found it child's play."[7] The Yucatec Maya were greatly intrigued by the European system and they ransacked it with an intellectual glee that puts the Europeans, interested only in gold and souls, to shame.

The week appealed for several reasons: it divided the moon's cycle into four parts; it went fifty-two times into the year, thus resonating with the fifty-two-year Calendar Round; and its seven daynames acted as a new kind of Year-Bearer cycle, because if one year begins on a Sunday, the next will begin on a Monday, and so on. Leap years presented a problem, but since they fell quadrennially they were always in step with one of the Maya Year-Bearers and could be handled by a separate count. But what interested the Maya more than anything were the remnants of pre-Christian astrology and science—the knowledge of the Arabs and the Classical world—that traveled in the baggage of the "Christian" system. The days of the week, clearly ruled by ancient gods, must have seemed strangely familiar. And then there was the zodiac, which the Maya associated with the plagues brought from Europe by the Spaniards: "The curse of Sagittarius, which has the body of a horse and the head of a man, begins with ... smallpox."[8] Before long the Maya were writing splendidly eclectic almanacs that included the new influences beside the old:

January: This month has thirty-one days, the moon thirty. . . . On the eleventh day the sun enters the sign called Aquarius. . . . Men born on the days ruled by this sign are small, always sad, very fond of women, and noted for using great quantities of small chiles with their meals. . . .

January 1st: 10 Oc. The burner begins his fire. [The burners presided over a cycle of sacred fire; each ruled for sixty-five days, a quarter tzolkin.] A good day. The Circumcision. Octave of Saint Stephen.

January 2nd: 11 Chuen. A good day.

January 3rd: 12 Eb. A good day.

January 4th: 13 Ben. A good day.

January 5th: 1 Ix. A bad day. . . .

January 12th: 8 Imix. A bad day. The month Yax begins. . . .

January 17th: 13 Cimi. A good day. Giants are born. . . .

January 29th: 12 Etz'nab. A bad day. Roads used by iguanas are closed.[9]

8 Oc ⦂ 🔲

The Academy of the Maya Language, founded in 1936 by the Yucatec scholar Alfredo Barrera Vásquez, occupies a modest office in a commercial district of Mérida. Cluttered steel desks, old typewriters, stacks of manuscripts and files. Domingo Dzul Poot isn't here, but I'm greeted by Ermilo Yah Pech and Juan Bastarrachea Manzano. Traffic rattles the dusty windowpanes. At times it's difficult to hear what they are saying.

Ermilo Yah Pech is a teacher at a preparatory school in Mérida. He is a slight, small man with the fine features and serious manner of a shy bird. I ask him if he is able to teach at all in Maya.

"I try. In the areas the government calls *zonas indígenas* the first two years of primary school are in Maya. But the problems are many. Parents want what they think is best for their children. They come to me and say, 'What are you teaching Maya for? We already know Maya. We want our kids to learn Spanish so they can progress.' We can't keep our people in a ghetto. So the challenge is to create a new appreciation of Maya as a literary and cultural heritage, to carry the work begun here by our founder not just to scholars but to the Maya themselves."

"We are seeing cultural disintegration," says Bastarrachea, a larger, louder man. "Marijuana. Alcohol. And Coca-Cola, the black venom of the gringos! In the old days we Maya used drugs—alcohol, hallucinogens, tobacco, many things—but in a ritual way, with religious constraints. Now these new things come in and dissolve the social ties that keep us together."

There's a stridency in him that reminds me of Alfredo at Sna Htz'ibahom in San Cristóbal. He is the only one without a Maya surname, as he points out himself.

"One of our projects is to compile a list of Maya proper names. We have several hundred already." He hands me a heavy loose-leaf binder. "The names all mean something; they're usually ancestral totems. Mr. Yah Pech here—his names mean that his totems are the zapote tree, *yah*, and the tick, *pech*. Unfortunately, because of discrimination, people used to change their names. My mother's family was once called Haas—*mamey*, a fruit much like an apple. But at some point they translated it into Spanish as Manzano."

The loss of the name rankles him—history resented.

Among the academy's achievements is the 1980 publication of the *Diccionario Cordemex*, comprising all known lexicons of Yucatec Maya from the sixteenth century to the nineteenth. *"Nuestra biblia"* says Yah Pech, thumping the volume affectionately: "Our Bible." Somehow they got sponsorship from the henequen marketing board (conscience money no doubt)—hence the dictionary's name; the office, too, has been loaned to them by Cordemex. Now they are working on a compendium of modern Maya to be used in teaching and promoting literacy in the native language.

"We also work with other Maya groups. We are studying the *Popol Vuh*, trying to forge cultural links between all members of the Maya heritage, not only in Mexico."

"What about political links—do you ever think there will be a Maya nationalism that could cut across the frontiers created by colonialism and the criollo republics?"

The two look at each other and speak rapidly in their own language:

"The time for that is not yet."

They change the subject (or do they?) to the Caste War.

"Another thing we're doing is studying the letters written by Maya leaders to the Ladinos during the war. We are making transcriptions which we hope to publish."

It is usually the winners who write history, but in these letters is the Maya view, the voice of a people wronged and ignored for centuries, finally stirred to rebel:

If we are killing you now, you first showed us the way. If the homes and the haciendas of the Whites are burning, it is because previously you burned the town of Tepich, and all the ranches on which there were poor Indians. . . .
    I inform you of the reason why we are fighting:

because those Commanders and your Governor gave the order for them to kill us . . . old and young, and the youths they seized violently in order to shove them into their houses, which they burned . . . I inform you that the cause of the present war is because we have seen the slaughter of those who are of our race.[10]

The letters might have been written by the Maya of modern Guatemala. The atrocities they list are sickeningly familiar: robberies, rapes, burnings, desecrations of churches. And, as in Guatemala, and so many other places throughout the history of Christendom, the oppressors tried to use the piety of the Maya as a way of taming them. Ladino priests were sent to the Indian leaders with the familiar devices of "thou shalt not kill" and "blessed are the meek." The Maya were no longer taken in: "There is only one thing I have to say to you and to the venerable virtuous curates," wrote the eloquent Francisco Caamal in 1848:

Why didn't they appear or rise to support us when the Whites were killing us? Why didn't they do anything when that priest Herrera . . . put his horse's saddle on a poor Indian, and mounted on him, began to whip him, gashing his belly with his spurs? Why didn't they have compassion when this happened? And now they remember, now they know that there is a true God? When they were killing us, didn't you know that there was a true God? . . . You never believed in his name, but rather even in the dark of the night you were killing us on the gibbet.[11]

One great misfortune of the Caste War is that in western Yucatán it brought the end of the ancient intellectual tradition and broke the continuity that might otherwise have existed between the books of Chilam Balam and the reflexive approach of modern educated Maya. In a few years of conflict, Yucatán's population fell from about half a million to little more than two hundred thousand. The counts of the katuns and the tzolkin died with those who kept them. The machinery of the calendar finally stalled. Today, the Yucatec Mayas' rituals and offerings, though they invoke ancient gods, are tied to saints' days and European almanacs.

Evening. A perfectly golden sky, flocks of blackbirds dilating and shattering like shoals of fish. I sit in the plaza, have my shoes shined, and watch the afterglow of sunset spill down through the great trees. Opposite is the tall, plain facade of the cathedral, "the fiery house, the mountainous house, the dark house" of God the Father, Son, and Holy Ghost. In 1848 the Maya came very close to capturing this city and this temple built from the ivory stones of Tiho.

A few days after Manuel Ay fell to the firing squad at Valladolid in July 1847, the town of Tepich was sacked by both sides. Troops and events moved quickly over the flat surface of Yucatán. On August 6, the Yucatán parliament stripped Indians of citizenship and deposed all native batabs. The whites fled westward to Mérida, where almost every able-bodied man was hastily conscripted. The rumor spread that Cecilio Chi would take Mérida on August 15, slaughter every Ladino, and crown himself king. The Ladinos panicked: they lynched prominent Mayas, including loyal ones, and burned outlying villages that couldn't be "defended." The war raged across the woods, trails, and cornfields. There was no real front: towns changed hands, pockets of resistance held out, guerrilla forces attacked and faded into the bush.

Early in 1848, moderate Ladinos, led by Miguel Bar-bachano, began negotiating with Jacinto Pat. Peace talks were held, but an armistice dissolved almost as soon as it was agreed. In March, Valladolid fell to the Maya.

The whites were by this time desperately short of weapons and supplies. All Indian rebellions in the Americas, before and since, ultimately failed because the whites had supply lines to the outside world and the Indians did not. During the first year of the Caste War this situation was reversed. The Maya were trading booty for guns with British gunrunners in Belize; the Ladinos were cut off by a United States blockade of Mexican ports. Mérida sent envoys to Washington to try to change this, but when the American press heard of Jacinto Pat they assumed, from his name, that the Maya leader had Irish blood and championed his cause.[12]

In April there were further negotiations between Barbachano and Pat. The terms agreed on by the two leaders would have set up a dual government of Yucatán, with Barbachano as perpetual head of the Ladinos, and Pat the "Gran Cacique" of all Indians. Indians were to have free access to public lands, an end to tribute and debt peonage, and the right to bear arms. The agreement was a good one, but neither leader could sell it to his followers. The Ladinos saw Barbachano's lifetime governorship as an end to "democracy." The Maya, ever anarchical, had no wish for a Gran Cacique. The deal particularly stank in the nostrils of Cecilio Chi, who wrecked it forthwith by taking Maní.

The Maya successes continued. On May 26, Pat's forces took Ticul; on the twenty-eighth, Chi took Izamal. Refugees poured into Mérida; others poured out—a flotilla of Ladino boat people abandoning the peninsula from the western ports. Terrified garrisons waited behind the walls of Mérida and Campeche for the final assault.

But it never came. A satisfactory explanation—satisfactory, that is, to Western ideas of strategy—has never been found. The only explanation from the Maya side was told decades later by Leandro Poot, son of a Caste War commander:

When my father's people took Acanceh they passed a time in feasting, preparing for the taking of Tiho. The day was warm and sultry. All at once the sh'mataneheeles [winged ants, harbingers of the first rain] appeared in great clouds to the north, to the south, to the east, and to the west, all over the world. When my father's people saw this they said to themselves and to their brothers, "Ehen! The time has come for us to make our planting, for if we do not we shall have no Grace of God [corn] to fill the bellies of our children."

... Each [said] to his Batab, "Shickanic"—I am going—and in spite of the supplications and threats of the chiefs, each man rolled up his blanket ... and started for home and his cornfield.

... Thus it can be clearly seen that Fate, and not white soldiers, kept my father's people from taking Tiho and working their will upon it.[13]

Historians have been unconvinced by this, but it seems to me quite credible. As much as the Maya were the people of time, they were the people of corn. The name of the Ixil means exactly that; the *Popol Vuh* declares that mankind is made of corn. The annual planting wasn't merely an economic imperative; it was a sacred duty. The time had come: the ordinary peasants could see no reason why they shouldn't go and plant, and come back later to finish off the dzul. If they didn't, they and their families would starve; the Chacs and Balams would be enraged. They had no knowledge of the international connections the dzul would revive during the respite; of how arms and supplies—even gringo mercenaries—would pour into Yucatán from the outside world. All that was outside their experience; and the batabs, who did understand such things, couldn't convince them otherwise. Chi and Pat held on to a few troops, but the best they could do was make an orderly withdrawal, town by town, to the east.

Barbachano sought political union with Mexico, with Cuba, with the United States—with any white power that might help him regain Yucatán for "civilization." Then the Mexican-American War ended; and in August 1848 Yucatán and Mexico were reunited. Shipments of rifles and food arrived from Havana and New Orleans. The Maya regrouped after the planting season, even routing some American soldiers of fortune attracted to Yucatán by promises of land and secret dreams of carving out a second Texas: "It was easy to kill the strange white men," Leandro Poot recalled, "for they were big and fought in a line.... Their bodies were pink and red in the sunlight and from their throats came a strange war cry, Hu Hu! [Hurrah!] ... I do not think any escaped."[14] They were the first gringo filibusters, the first William Walkers and Oliver Norths, and the Maya beat them. But the white tide nevertheless continued to flow eastward. In December the Ladinos retook Valladolid, and then Tihosuco, home of Jacinto Pat.

Eighteen forty-nine was a bad year for the Maya. Cecilio Chi was murdered by a mestizo he had trusted; Jacinto Pat was killed by one of his lieutenants in a dispute over whether to sue for peace. The Indians decided to retreat into the heavily forested eastern region of the Yucatán Peninsula, now called Quintana Roo.

At desperate moments in the life of an individual, the supernatural may intrude upon intolerable reality. Voices are heard, visions are seen; instructions are received from God. Whether we call it a nervous breakdown, a psychosis, or a religious conversion depends largely on the outcome. It may end in madness or in suicide; it may summon unsuspected strengths and lead to a new and better life. The same is true of nations. When threatened by genocide or foreign domination there may arise a "crisis cult," a belief in divine aid.

In fifteenth-century France a young woman named Joan of Arc heard heavenly voices that told her to put on armor and lead her people against the English. In the last century, as the tribes of North America were falling to smallpox and repeating rifles, a cult called the Ghost Dance arose on the Great Plains. Followers believed that if certain rituals were performed the world of the white man could be made to slough off like a dead skin: railways, wagon trains, and plagues would vanish; the dead buffalo and dead Indians would return. About two thousand years ago, as Rome ruled Judaea through a corrupt and brutal puppet king, a Messiah appeared.

In the sixteenth century God had spoken to the Maya through Chilam Balam. In 1850, he spoke again, from a little wooden cross carved on a mahogany tree beside a cenote in the heart of Quintana Roo.

Chapter 19

10 Eb ||

I took a bus and followed the route of the retreating Maya, east to Valladolid, then south to Tihosuco, where Jacinto Pat first plotted liberation. In the plaza there's a statue of him, life-size: a small bronze figure of a small bronze man.

We stopped an hour before continuing to Chan Santa Cruz—Little Holy Cross—where the Speaking Cross appeared in 1850. I had time to see Tihosuco's great church, built in the sixteenth century and ruined during the Caste War. Three-quarters of the facade has fallen away, leaving a gaunt needle of limestone encrusted with remnants of columns, pediments, and empty niches. The walls are twelve feet thick, pierced only by small windows and gun slits: a fortress for king and Christ. The nave is more than two hundred feet long, half of it open to the sky. Grass and wildflowers grow at one end; an altar and a Christmas crèche occupy the other. It's a liminal space: half-ruin, half-shrine; nature and culture in equilibrium.

The priest was chasing a large pig out of the vestry. He was a Spaniard from Barcelona, with a plump boyish face and a blue chin.

"The people here are better than in Spain," he said. "When Mayas get drunk they speak of God; when Spaniards drink they deny Him."

Many of the colonial houses are still as ruined as the church, grass and trees growing on their walls, ornate doorways blocked with stones to make pigpens and poultry yards. One feels that the Indians did not entirely lose. Ladinos never returned; Tihosuco was abandoned to the forest, and when people came back in the 1930s, it was the Maya who claimed this land.

Don Julián Xix Ya, the sexton, was one of them. He lives opposite the church in a great house that must have belonged to a hacendado. Large, cool rooms that once heard the frothy accents of Castile echoed now with children's voices speaking Maya. A fingertip was missing from his right hand—reminder of some hard machete work.

"There was nothing here but bush in those days. We had to cut and clear and burn; we put roofs on old houses like this one, and we started to clean up the church. Eventually we asked for a priest, and the American fathers came in 1952. They got people to contribute labor for restoring the roof. Many of us were glad to help, but there were those who said this was a return to the old days, to the slavery we suffered in the past."

I asked if he knew exactly what had happened to the church.

"The Mayas of Santa Cruz came with explosives in the 1850s. They dug a ditch beneath the front, filled it with gunpowder, and blew down the facade. *¡Sólo por coraje, imagínese!*—Imagine, just from anger, for revenge! People say they took a golden bell. Who knows where it is now? And they took all the saints, like prisoners of war!"

The Caste War also left scars on the map of Yucatán. After the Mexicans conquered the Santa Cruz Maya in 1901, they divided the peninsula in three. The state of Yucatán was allowed to keep only the north; the state of Campeche was formed in the southwest; and the eastern stronghold of the rebel Maya became the federal territory of Quintana Roo, denied statehood until 1974. Chan Santa Cruz had its name changed to Carrillo Puerto (after a martyred politician); Chetumal, near the Belize border, soon eclipsed it.

Quintana Roo had always been a marginal region. There were few Classic settlements of any size. When the Spaniards invaded in the 1520s, brutal campaigns and Old World diseases quickly destroyed the small Indian towns, despite a gallant resistance led by Gonzalo Guerrero, a Spaniard who had joined the Maya after being shipwrecked near Cozumel some years before. Survivors scattered deep into the interior. Once English pirates began raiding along the Caribbean coast in the seventeenth and eighteenth centuries, these Maya remained effectively beyond Spanish control.

When Stephens visited Tulum by boat only five years before the Caste War broke out, he remarked that Quintana Roo "is not traversed by a single road. . . . It is a region entirely unknown; no white man ever enters it." A romantic notion that had gripped him in Guatemala returned: "I conceive it to be not impossible that within this secluded region may exist to this day . . . a living aboriginal city, occupied by relics of the ancient race, who still worship in the temples of their fathers."[1] He was almost right. There was no living city of the kind he imagined, but there were Maya who had had little contact with whites for two hundred years, and who *did* still worship in the ruined temples of their ancestors.

Valladolid and Tihosuco, where the Caste War began, bordered this wild region; and two years later the shattered forces of Pat and Chi found sanctuary here after their failure to reconquer all of Yucatán.

It is dark when I arrive in Carrillo Puerto, the former Chan Santa Cruz. By night, the streetlights and bright shops seem to belong to a modern city, wholly absorbed into the Mexican nation. And when I walk across the plaza, beneath royal palms and a flagpole flying the eagle and serpent of Mexico, past benches full of lovers and old men, crotons in neat flowerbeds, smooth concrete underfoot, it's hard to believe that anything remains from the past.

I ask a cabdriver to take me to the best hotel, and he's honest enough to say that I don't need him—it's just on the far corner, the Hotel Chan Santa Cruz: acceptable but not extravagant. My room is a little damp, but clean. Clouds of gnats dance around the outside lamps; crickets and frogs applaud the night.

11 Ben

The place that seemed so large and modern by electric light resolves itself into a small, sleepy town beneath a hard sun and cobalt sky. A minute or two from the plaza you're among typical Maya houses, apsidal or rectangular; roofs of thatch or corrugated iron; fruit trees, turkeys, pigs, and chickens behind dry stone walls.

In a small dell on the western end of town where the streets lose their paving and ridges of limestone break through the earth like ancient bones there is a little cave with glaucous water at the bottom. This is where, in 1850, a cross carved on a mahogany tree spoke to the defeated Maya:

> On the fifteenth
> Of the count
> Of October . . .
> I began to speak
> With my children here in the world. . . .
> I reside
> In the village . . .
> Of Jaguar House. . . .
> There have arrived,
> The day
> And the hour
> For me to show you
> A sign . . .[2]
> Because it has come,
> The time
> For the uprising of Yucatán
> Over the Whites
> For once and for all![3]

The Speaking Cross prophesied victory and issued tactical instructions. It told the Maya that they were the chosen race, the true Christians, the children of God. Like Old Testament Jehovah, it blamed their woes on spiritual impurity and promised triumph to true believers. Although final victory never came, the Cross did help the Indians to resist for fifty years; and even now its followers still believe that the prophecies will one day be fulfilled.

A few yards away, above the cenote, stands a tall stone shrine with an arched roof made of lime concrete laid over wooden poles. It is open at the front and you can see a blue cross painted on the back wall. It looks abandoned. Wild figs are sprouting from the arch, tentacle roots clasping the old masonry. To reach it you have to walk through someone's banana grove. An old woman comes over to see what I'm doing.

"Does anyone ever come here?" I ask her.

"Oh, yes. Often. The *antiguos* and one or two tourists like yourself."

She explains that by *antiguos*, "ancient ones," she means the Maya of outlying villages, those who maintain the cult of the Cross more than eighty years after their city fell to the Mexican federal army. They repudiated the peace made later between their leaders and the revolutionary government of Mexico; and, calling themselves *los separados*, the "Separate Ones," took themselves off into the woods and founded new villages where they guard their rites and remain latently hostile.

The outline of events is this:

1849: The Maya forces retreat to Quintana Roo and mingle with local Maya.

1850: The Speaking Cross appears at the cenote and issues instructions for renewing the war against the whites.

1850–58: Maya fortunes ebb and flow, but the Indians manage to survive attacks on their stronghold.

1858: The Maya win a decisive victory by taking the fortress of Bacalar (near modern Chetumal). At Chan Santa Cruz they begin building a ceremonial capital, complete with a church, schools, palaces, and barracks. They become effectively independent from the rest of Mexico.

1863–1893: The Indian state is given de facto recognition by the British at Belize. The Maya suffer from epidemics and internal disputes.

1893: Mexico and Britain negotiate a border treaty; supply of arms to the Indians is cut off.

1901: The Mexican federal army, under General Ignacio Bravo, takes Chan Santa Cruz.

1901–15: Brutal Mexican occupation; continuing guerrilla raids from Maya scattered in the forest.

1915: The Mexicans pull out and return Quintana Roo to the Maya.

1917–20: Influenza and smallpox epidemics.

1920–29: Chicle boom. General May, the Indian leader, negotiates peace with Mexico.

1929: The more militant Indians repudiate May's "sellout" and reestablish the cult of the Cross at X-Cacal Guardia.

"When do they come?"

"On certain days throughout the year, and especially on May third, the day of the Holy Cross."

So the Cross is not forgotten in its birthplace. The cult, superficially a Christian heresy, stemmed also from a long tradition of Maya belief. For centuries, possibly millennia, crosses had been associated with water, ancestors, and cosmic order. "Son, have you seen the green water-holes in the rock?" asks a riddle in The Chilam Balam of Chumayel: "There are two of them; a cross is raised between them. They are a man's eyes."[4] And in another early text it is written, "The lord of Maní, who was called Mochan Xiu . . . had that sign of the cross and others made of cut stone and placed in the courtyards of the temples where it could be seen by all, and he said that it was the green tree of the world."[5]

Nor was a speaking god anything new. Early Spaniards reported seeing one at Cozumel; Tayasal had a speaking oracle until the conquest of 1697 (only 150 years before the Caste War); and just a century ago, when the Guatemalan Mams were forced to plant coffee instead of maize, ears of corn uttered warnings of hunger and misery.[6]

Invaders and foreign visitors to Chan Santa Cruz scoffed at the ventriloquism and sound chambers that allowed the Cross to speak, but recent study of the surviving cult reveals a more sophisticated approach. The Indians knew perfectly well it was a human voice: a human voice inspired by God—like the prophetic utterances of Chilam Balam.[7] Crosses and sound chambers were the medium, not the message.

I walk back to the plaza, wondering how to get below the skin of this place, to uncover what is really here. A modern municipal palace stands on the site of Chikin Ik, the "West Wind," palace of the latter-day priest-kings who led the Maya after the coming of the Cross. It has a few neo-Maya motifs and a mural showing the usual icons of Mexico: Father Hidalgo ringing his liberty bell in 1810; Benito Juárez clasping his book of laws. Opposite, on the east side of the plaza, half hidden from here by palms and almond trees, is the craggy bulk of a church. It is massive and graceless, similar to Tihosuco's fortress-church but not so big: a stubby, unfinished bell tower, a few young trees sprouting along the parapet. But this is not a colonial structure. It was built by the Maya after their victory at Bacalar in 1858. The war had turned very ugly by that time. Barbachano had begun selling Maya prisoners into slavery on the sugar plantations of Cuba; the Maya countered by making their prisoners build a ceremonial capital worthy of their new city-state. This church was in reality a Maya temple, and, like those of Tikal a thousand years before, the tutelar spirit of the jaguar presided over it. The building was called Balam Na, "Jaguar House," a name also applied to the town.

The Balam Na is cool and dark inside, smelling of damp mortar, whitewash, and incense. Its nave is more than a hundred feet long, and almost forty wide. It has a high, barrel-vaulted ceiling supported on stone arches rising from slender columns engaged with the walls. The heaviness of the exterior, with its huge buttresses to take the thrust of the vault, is rewarded here by a feeling of spaciousness and austere taste. After Mexican troops occupied the town in 1901, the building became a prison, a boxing ring, and later a cinema; but in the 1950s, American Maryknoll priests reconsecrated it to the

Holy Cross, in the hope of winning the Maya back to Rome. The stubby tower, however, has never been completed; and the separado Maya believe it will remain so until they regain their freedom and their city.

Voices come from the vestry; a few minutes later three gringos emerge and walk toward the door.

"No, I'm sorry, I can't help you," an Irish voice is saying. "I'm here for the pastoral care of this parish. This isn't a flophouse, you know!"

"Sanctuary, Father. Where's your Christian charity?"

"You fellas be off now, and don't come bothering me or the sisters again."

The two supplicants shuffle out—fossil hippies, tangled blond hair, wavy beards, fair complexions: not so different from Mexican images of Christ. The third figure, the Irishman, is a short man in his late forties with graying hair, a ruddy face, and sapphire eyes.

"And what can I be doing for you? I don't suppose you'll be after wanting free bed and breakfast yourself?"

I suddenly feel very conscious of my sandals, jeans, and none-too-crisp shirt. I introduce myself and explain my interest in the church.

"Are you the priest here?"

"That I am. Ray Comiskey. Sorry I got you wrong. You see we get these boms—no other word for 'em—trying to bom free lodging. Americans mostly, don't want to work, just travelin', beggin' off the poor Indians and the clergy. Give 'em an inch and they take a moile." He smiles and looks me up and down. "Now I see you're what you say you are. But I can't tell you moch about the building. It's colonial I tink."

Father Ray is with the Legion of Christ, a Catholic missionary organization, based in the States, that has taken over from the Maryknolls.

"You see, we're trying to win the confidence of these Maya Indians. They're Catholics really, but they've been so long without priests they've got it all confused. They've got the three crosses of Calvary mixed up with the Holy Trinity and Lord knows what else. They don't trost the Mexicans, so the

Legion always sends Irish or American fathers down here. I speak the lingo meself—I say mass in Maya—made me own translation of the liturgy, based on Bishop Landa's.

"I've got to go now to visit an old lady who's sick. Come back after mass tonight and we'll have a little chat."

I have a good lunch at the 24-Hours restaurant on the main road that runs between Cancún and Chetumal: turkey in *mole poblano*, a spicy bitter chocolate sauce, served with a pile of steaming tortillas, and extra chiles on the side.

State elections are coming. On a wall across the street is a slogan neatly painted in the green, red, and white colors of the Institutional Revolutionary Party, which has ruled Mexico for more than fifty years. I SHALL RESPECT THE TRADITIONS AND KNOWLEDGE OF THE MAYAS, says the *candidato*, whose victory is of course a foregone thing.

On the way back to my hotel I see another sign, crudely painted on a board beside a house: YOUR GOD IS DEAD, TRY MINE.

Evening. In the plaza the steel lamp standards with their flying-saucer tops haven't yet dispersed a navy blue sky bleeding in the west. Palms, almond trees, and jackfruits, silhouetted by the glow, are alive with long-tailed blackbirds defending their roosts with quizzical, ascending whistles. Several Maya and Mexican women leave the Balam Na, followed by two nuns. Father Ray comes out, incense wafting from his clothes. "There you are. Come on over to the *casa cural* and we'll have a cop of coffee."

The house he occupies is a rambling, run-down building that badly needs some paint and new sheets of iron on the roof. I follow him to the kitchen at the back: a table covered in oilcloth, a stereo system, and some bookshelves.

"I've been thinking about who could help you with local history. I don't know as much about it as I should. There's an old fellow owns a hardware store, Don Fernando's his name. He could tell you a ting or two. Speaks Maya, though he's not a Maya himself. People here have all sorts of stories about the war—that's what they call it—the War, as if there hadn't been any others since."

I ask if he's read Nelson Reed's *The Caste War of Yucatán.*

"I've got it. It's here someplace, but the only one I ever read was that *Lost World of Quintana Roo*—by a French fella who hiked down the coast. That's a good read. Personally I find history rather boring." He pours me instant coffee and gets a diet Coke from the fridge for himself.

"Can't take coffee, unfortunately. Or sugar. A bit of a medical problem. Only ting I can find to drink around here is this diet stoff."

I have with me the remains of my Christmas scotch: "I was going to offer you a belated New Year's drink . . . but maybe it's not good for you?"

"Whiskey we can drink! Let's have a little drop!"

"I saw a sign today: 'Your God is dead, try mine.' Do you get much competition from Evangelicals?"

"Very moch. They're a royal pain in the neck. And you wouldn't mind it so much if it was real evangelizing. Bot it's always *against*—against the Catholic church, against the images, against the Blessed Virgin, against the pope. Bot I'll say one thing for 'em, they're very good at getting people to give op the drink."

"Have another?"

"Your health!" He lifts his glass and studies it for a moment. Then: "The only consolation is that there's so many different kinds of them. Pentecostals, Baptists, Assemblies of God—I've lost count. Only a handful of members in each. As long as they keep sayin' everyone can read the Bible his own way they'll always have that problem. Always will. If they ever united it'd be a serious matter. Bot then if they did that they'd be Catholics, wouldn't they?" He laughs heartily.

I ask how he sees the separado Maya—as schismatics, as heretics?

"Lord no! We don't throw words like that around anymore. They tink they're Catholics. *Iglesia Mazehual* they call themselves, which means sometin' like 'the ordinary man's church,' 'the Maya church.' Its past is totally Catholic. People say they've got a lot of pagan beliefs and all, bot I don't think so.

The only thing from their past is the *Yumtzil*—the Lords of the Forest—but half of them have saints' names anyway.

"You ought to see the church there at X-Cacal Guardia, their main village. Its like a great big Indian house, all whitewashed, with a big thatch roof, almost as big inside as my church here. They invited me to say a mass there once—they've got their own so-called priests but they like having a real one come in once in a while. Anyway, I go, and they're all there with their rusty old guns and the whole business. I could tell they were very wary—could feel their eyes on me, watching. They're very cagey. They have this *ting* about guarding something."

Father Ray chuckles and shakes his head.

"You know what I tink?" he continues. "I tink it all began when some old priest was dyin', and he gave 'em the church plate and the images or whatever, and he told them to guard it all. And they've kept on guarding and guarding and they haven't the faintest idea what it is! One of the sisters was op there too, and she took a peek in a wooden box they keep. It was empty! There was nothin' but dost inside. And they don't know it's empty because they never look!"

12 Ix ·‖ 🔲

It was almost midnight when Father Ray and I killed the bottle. It seems he doesn't know much about the past of the Mazehuales, as the Santa Cruz Maya call themselves, and I don't think he really wants to. By seeing them simply as Catholics who have lost their way on certain points of dogma, he can diminish the gap between their beliefs and his.

The guard system is not at all what he imagines. The rebels and refugees who fled to Quintana Roo in 1849 were from many parts of the peninsula. After the deaths of Chi and Pat, they shared no allegiance to a single batab or town; their kinship networks were in shreds; they were far from ancestral lands. If they were to keep their freedom they had to create a political structure, a new nation. Two models were available: the religious sanction of a tutelar god; and the practical organization they had learned in the Yucatán militia. They successfully united these things and transformed them. The high priest of the Cross, the supreme interpreter of God's will, became the *Nohoch Tata*, "Great Father," a Maya pope and king. His right-hand man was the General of the Plaza. Below him were captains, lieutenants, and sergeants. The Mazehual soldiers were organized in companies of about 150 men each. Though they lived near their cornfields most of the time, they assembled in large barrack buildings around the plaza of Santa Cruz for periods of *guardia* duty by rotation. There they drilled, made weapons, and prayed for hours in the Balam Na, listening to the uncanny orations of the Cross. In this way the Maya forged a city-state, similar in outline to those of the pre-Columbian past, but equipped with the military expertise of the mid-nineteenth century.

Two young British officers were among the first foreigners to see the Balam Na and the strange theocracy the Maya had created. In March 1861, Lieutenants Plumridge and Twigge were sent by the superintendent of Belize to Santa Cruz with a chilly note for the Nohoch Tata, Venancio Puc. There had been trouble along the border between Belize and the Indian state. The English and Maya shared a mutual interest in guns and hatred of Mexico, but certain Ladino refugees had tried to interrupt the gunrunning, causing retaliatory raids. Puc told the young officers that matters were out of his hands: they would have to speak to God. At midnight, in complete darkness, the two lieutenants were led to the altar of the Jaguar House, already full of worshiping Maya.

> At that moment the soft music and singing that till then had pervaded the building ceased and was followed by a deafening and prolonged sound similar to thunder when heard at a distance. This too ceased, and in the midst of the silence that followed was heard a . . . voice which seemed to originate in the midst of the air. . . .[8]

God raged about the superintendent's "very insulting letter," and suggested that if the Englishmen wanted to leave Santa Cruz unscathed they had better arrange for the shipment of one thousand barrels of gunpowder at a decent price. On the next day, the Nohoch Tata threw a drunken party at which the Englishmen were "subjected to the most degrading familiarities."[9] Other members of the Maya hierarchy did not approve: within a year or two Puc was overthrown; and his successors cultivated better relations with Her Majesty.

Afternoon. Don Fernando has skin like ink-stained parchment: large blots on his cheeks, smaller spots across his forehead; faint lines of faded script. He sits on a bench just inside the heavy double doors of his windowless shop, out of the sun that his complexion can no longer endure. Pale blue eyes, sharp with business acumen, watch you as you walk in. His stock is a relic from the days when an Indian or an outlaw could make a small fortune tapping the chewing-gum trees of Quintana Roo: machetes, leather scabbards, galvanized buckets, lanterns, drums of kerosene.

He is proud of that pale skin and those blue eyes. His father was from Spain, and he grew up on Cozumel, moving here not long after the last of the Indian generals, Francisco May, made peace with the Mexican government. Those were the days when chicle gum was high. The Maya got soft with easy money. Their leaders, especially May, became rich. Windup gramophones could be heard playing the tunes of the jazz age in the bush.

"There were only four hundred people in town then—Chinese, Lebanese, Indians, Yucatecans, Spaniards. In those days the peso was worth something. Not the rubbish it is now!"

Another man, even older and much darker than Don Fernando, comes in and sits down on the bench.

"Here's the man you should be talking to!" says Don Fernando, in a patronizing tone. "Allow me to present Don Simón Poot Cimé, *de la pura raza*, Maya right through to the marrow of his bones! Isn't that right, Don Simón? In those days one hundred pesos could buy a cow and her calf!"

"*Sí*," the old Maya says dreamily. "You could get a good cow for fifty."

Poot Cimé is walnut faced, willowy, and very old. Like several Santa Cruz Maya, he has a little African blood—from runaway Belizean blacks who joined the Indians. At regular intervals he gives involuntary grunts, as if fighting for air.

"More than eighty years old!" says Don Fernando. "He was born not long after General Bravo took this town in 1902."

"1901," Poot Cimé corrects. (Trust a Maya to get the date right.) "It was 1901 when Bravo took Noh Cah Santa Cruz."

"You mean Chan Santa Cruz?"

No, they both agree, it wasn't called that once it became the Maya capital. It was known as Noh Cah, "Great City," or Santa Cruz Balam Na after the temple of the Cross.

"And he should know—his mother was a half sister of General May!"

Poot Cimé confirms this with a nod and a grunt. His uncle, the old general whose name means "epoch" or "cycle," had a long life. Born in 1889 or thereabouts, May rose to power after the Mexican withdrawal (during the Revolution) in 1915. He was a short, stocky man, with busy eyes. He usually wore a collarless shirt, cotton trousers, leather sandals, and a heavy Colt .45 stuck in a cartridge belt.[10] A plaque near the Balam Na commemorates his death in 1969, forty years after the Mexicans returned and stripped him of his power.

13 Men ⦂⦀ 🔲

Rain today. I did a little more poking about in town. Beside the Balam Na is a long colonnade, once the front of a religious school where Mazehual youngsters learned the way of the Cross. On the wall nearest the church hangs a bizarre crucifix, a wooden cross of heavy timbers with a Christ that appears at first to be a carving, but when you look closely you see it's simply a piece of strangler fig that has grown in the shape of the murdered god. There are other relics: some stone blocks of

Classic date with eroded glyphs on them, and rusty fragments of a steam engine—bits of boiler and cylinders like the dismembered carcass of a lobster. The stones were found when the new municipal offices were built. Perhaps the West Wind palace had been built on the site of an ancient ruin. Or were the blocks brought from somewhere else and incorporated into it? The steam engine is easier to trace.

The beginning of the twentieth century stalked the free Maya with as much malignancy as any baleful katun or baktun. In 1893 Britain and Mexico signed a treaty that cut off the supply of weapons. In 1898 the Mexican government anchored an armored barge on the Hondo River, which forms the Belizean border, just to make sure. In the same year, Mexican garrisons reoccupied the ruins of Tihosuco and other towns in the no-man's-land to the north and west of the Maya state. The Indians were encircled.

In 1900, General Ignacio Bravo began his slow advance on Santa Cruz. The Mazehuales found their muskets and cannon little use against machine guns and breech-loading artillery. It was their misfortune that they had defied the white world during a half century of unprecedented material progress. Western technology had begun to run away with itself, and it had left the little peoples of the earth behind. The Mazehuales, the Zulus, the Sioux, the Mahdists—all those who had challenged the West and succeeded for a while—were eventually outgunned.

But it wasn't only technology that took the Mazehuales by surprise. The plagues that had been the true conquerors of America returned, cutting down the Indians even more rapidly than General Bravo's guns. When the Mexicans finally reached the holy city in May 1901, they found it deserted. The survivors had scattered into the forest; trees were already growing on the walls of the Balam Na.

Bravo built a narrow-gauge railway from Santa Cruz to the Caribbean coast to be his supply line and an outlet for chicle, which was just becoming fashionable in the land of the gringos. The Maya were down but not out: they constantly sabotaged Bravo's railway, and after the Mexicans withdrew in 1915 they finished it off in a Luddite orgy. These fragments beside the Balam Na are some of the remains.

The Mazehuales never really reoccupied their capital. General Bravo had stabled convict labor in the Balam Na—political prisoners, murderers, sex offenders—men and women all shut in together like cattle every night. The Cross would not return to a temple defiled by killing, rape, and human filth. The Maya believed that "bad winds," left by the Mexicans, haunted the city. And in a sense they were right: smallpox broke out again, reducing them to a mere four thousand—less than a tenth of their numbers in 1850.

In the 1920s the survivors regrouped in three ministates, surrounding the old capital like disarticulated petals of a flower. The most powerful group—led by General May—settled to the south and built a new shrine center called Chan Cah Veracruz, "Little Town of the True Cross." A second group was based in the northeast at Chunpom; and a third to the northwest at X-Cacal Guardia. These three little towns still endure, each the religious and political hub of a dozen villages.

The Separate Ones of X-Cacal Guardia emerged as the most militant of the three. In 1929 they sent a raiding party to Chan Cah Veracruz and took the Speaking Cross away from an effete General May.[11] At about the same time the Tulum crosses also moved to X-Cacal. Nowadays all three groups regard X-Cacal as the senior partner in matters spiritual.

1 Cib .

Father Ray invited me to attend a private mass this evening at San Andrés, a small village subordinate to Chan Cah Veracruz.

"I find the Chan Cah lot easiest to deal with. They're more open, a little bit more modern. This mass they want me to do—it's a *quinceaños*, a sort of coming-out party for a girl on her fifteenth birthday. It's entirely a Spanish custom—a few years ago they would never have been interested, but now they've picked op some city ways, and so they want it."

* * *

He turns up at my hotel, late afternoon, in his truck—a Jeep pickup with chrome wheels, balloon tires, and a lurid red-and-orange paint job—the sort of vehicle "bush" can buy in Orange Walk.

"She's not a bad rig. You need a good one. I'm always giving lifts, acting as an ambulance driver—you can't refuse."

We drive south down the highway that leads eventually to Bacalar, Chetumal, and the frontier of Belize. Yellow butterflies, warming themselves on the hot tarmac, lift at our approach and blow like confetti around the truck.

"I hate to see the little bodies crushed on the windscreen, bot there's nothin' you can do about it. The Maya believe butterflies are souls of the dead, you know. You can't convince them otherwise."

SAN ANDRÉS

The sun is about to set as we enter the straggling village, turning the women's dresses pink and the leaves of the mango trees to greenish gold. A smell of fires, tortillas, rotting vegetation in a ditch.

The thatched church has pole walls, rounded at the ends. Inside you can see the care that went into its construction: unusually massive posts support the tie beams and rafters; the palm thatch is very neat. Tiger stripes of orange light enter through the walls and fall on the white clay floor. The altar, known as the *Gloria*, has six wooden crosses dressed in richly embroidered huipiles. It is a rustic platform raised on forked poles and covered by a sort of arch, made of saplings and a clean white cloth, representing the celestial vault. On one side is a wooden table and some gourds used for serving a sacramental drink of honey and corn.

"Ah, good, a table!" Father Ray exclaims, setting the gourds on the floor. "We're locky to find one. Can't say mass without it. Sometimes I have to use a folding Coca-Cola table I carry in the trock."

The table stands unsteadily on the clay floor.

"We'll fix this the Maya way." He picks a pebble loose and jams it under a leg. Then he takes his vestments and paraphernalia from a small brown suitcase.

People begin to arrive: older women and little girls in huipiles; adolescent friends of the *quinceañera* in their best party dresses. The young men have tight shirts and longish hair. There are babies at breasts; dogs wander in and out; someone chases away a pig. I can hear people gossiping outside, a radio playing ranchero music in the distance. Eventually there are fifty or sixty in the small church.

Father Ray confesses the girl in a corner; then says a brief mass. His Maya sounds a lot like Dublin. The congregation are diffident, unsure of the responses; but they do better with hymns.

Outside I'm approached by the girl's father. He's seen my camera; would I be kind enough to take some pictures of the family? Later, when I have prints made to send back, I notice how tiny the people are—I didn't stoop enough, and photographed them all from above.

2 Caban

How to approach X-Cacal Guardia, where the Cross still lives, and where I plan to end my journey? I pondered the question over breakfast. X-Cacal is not the sort of place one just turns up. Uninvited visitors are likely to be met by guards brandishing antique but serviceable rifles. I decide to visit one of X-Cacal's subsidiary villages first; there it might be possible to gain an introduction.

Tusik is a half-hour bus ride and an hour's walk down a dirt road through the bush. I pass an occasional milpa, the ripe corn standing tall with squash and bean vines spiraling up its stems. I hear a rhythmical squeaking that at first sounds like an insect. It gets closer. Turning round, I see a man not far behind. The squeaking comes from a long machete in its scabbard, grazing the red earth as he walks.

"*Buenas tardes*," he calls. "Where are you going?"

"To Tusik."

"Do you know anyone there?" His Spanish is good and he seems amiable. I have the name of the local schoolmaster, a certain Maestro Chan Chin.

"Chan Chin's away," my companion says, "because it's holiday time." I change the subject. How is the farming this year; is there enough good land to go around?

"There's enough land but there's no high jungle anymore. We used to get the best crops in virgin clearings, but it's all gone."

"What about game?"

"There's a lot of wild pigs. And the *tepezcuintles* are fat because it's harvest time."

We come to a little shrine at the side of the road—a cross inside a thatched shelter. These crosses guard the paths leading out of all Mazehual villages. They correspond to the four directions and are associated with the Lords of the Forest, the Chacs, and the *Pauahtun*—stone giants who stand at the corners of the Maya world. Farmers light a candle on their way out of town to put themselves right with these and other field guardians. But my companion is anxious to conceal any such beliefs:

"See that cross?" he volunteers. "Someone is buried there."

"An accident?"

"Yes, an accident."

"A car accident?"

"Exactly, a car accident."

He marches off after giving me a biker handshake, thumbs locked. Where on earth did he learn that? From hippies at Tulum, or is it something that came with runaway blacks from Belize?

Fifty years ago, anthropologist Alfonso Villa Rojas lived here and later wrote the only substantial ethnography of the Mazehual Maya. In his day Tusik had no clearly defined streets—just houses and yards at random among the trees with a church and plaza in the middle. Now it looks like any small Yucatec town. The plaza has been squared off and the houses arranged more or less in blocks. I buy a cold Coke from a corner store that also sells Alka-Seltzer, chocolates, cheap dresses, and *Playboy* T-shirts. A pile of railway ties, stacked for shipment in the plaza, shows where the last of the high jungle has gone. There's a tall concrete water tank, installed recently by the Mexican government, and a microwave tower, sited here (I suspect) to give government officials an excuse to drop in and keep an eye on things.

In the middle of the plaza stands the church, like the one I saw last night but bigger. The doors are padlocked. An old bronze bell, perhaps a war trophy, hangs between two posts.

A man with rum on his breath and a shotgun in his hand comes up.

"¿De dónde eres tú, jefe? (Where are you from, boss?)" The familiar form is intentionally insulting, and the "boss" sarcastic.

"Canada."

"What are you doing here, boss?"

I explain I'm looking for the subdelegado—the village chief.

"Canada . . ." He ponders the name, as if trying to remember whether it is numbered among the Mayas' enemies. "Is Canada further than Mexico?"

He's relieved to hear that it is. His face relaxes and the shotgun is lowered. "The subdelegate's house is down that street, where those pigs are. Ask for Don Jacinto Aké Itzá."

It's a fine house with whitewashed masonry walls to waist height and vertical poles above. A man in his early thirties invites me in and pulls out a low stool for me to sit on—the only chair in the place. He and his wife are reclining drowsily in cotton hammocks. When my eyes adapt to the gloom I notice the shiny concrete floor, a glass-fronted cabinet, a large radio against the far wall, a new bicycle on its stand. Everything is clean and neat. I wait quietly, assuming someone has gone to fetch the subdelegate. I am expecting an older man. After a long, uncomfortable pause the young man reveals he is Jacinto Aké Itzá and asks what I want.

I tell him I'm interested in Maya history, and that an anthropologist I spoke to before leaving Canada suggested that people in Tusik might be willing to talk about it. Aké Itzá leans forward in his hammock, bare feet touching the floor. He's naked from the waist up, his bronze chest hairless as a baby's;

he listens with gaze averted, judging my words with the hauteur of a Maya lord from the murals of Bonampak.

"Yes, I remember Pablo, the *antropólogo*. He was here in '83. Last year we had another visitor. His name was Jaime—he was from Canada like yourself."

"From where in Canada? Do you remember which city?"

"From the same city—Canada." I realize Aké Itzá is thinking in terms of the Maya political model: the city-state. Patterns persist in this part of the world: Mexico, Guatemala, and Belize are all named for their principal cities; he assumes Canada is the same.

I am curious not only about the war but also *The Chilam Balam of Tusik*, a document last seen here in the early 1970s.[12] Apparently its owner or guardian was killed a few years ago, and the book's whereabouts since then are unknown. It is possible that the Mazehuales have others. In the 1960s an American journalist, who later wrote a sensational account for *Argosy* magazine, was told that a hieroglyphic codex still existed. The information came from no less an authority than Juan Bautista Vega, Nohoch Tata of Chunpom.[13] The journalist was told he could see the codex only if he returned with cases of guns for the Maya cause, a condition he wasn't able to meet.

"*Yo no sabe, señor,*" Aké Itzá says, in broken Spanish, to my questions. "Perhaps my father can help you. But he speaks only Maya." He sends his wife to fetch the old man from another house in the same compound. The father comes in, white haired and suspicious. There's a long conversation with his son. It turns out that he "doesn't know"—or doesn't want to tell. Fair enough.

As I rise to leave, Aké Itzá gives a tersely eloquent dismissal: "Pablo spoke Maya. Jaime spoke Maya. You don't speak Maya."

3 Etz'nab ⦂ 🖃 *Day of sacrifice.*

I was planning to leave today—a simple matter of catching a bus to Cancún and a plane to Toronto. After yesterday's reception at Tusik, there seemed little chance of accomplishing anything at X-Cacal Guardia. I was having breakfast, as usual at the 24-Hours, when Father Ray's Jeep pulled up.

"Look, I've been tinking. I've been after getting in touch with them there at X-Cacal, to invite them to a kind of ecumenical meeting we've got planned. They might not like it if I just turned op meself, no warning like, so I'm sending Don Rómulo, our catechist, along with the invitation and a few gifts. He speaks Maya perfectly. Thought you might like to go too—it would give you a look at the place. I've got some brass bells you can take. They lov little bells—anytime they're praying they ring them. And pick op a couple of rosaries from the sisters. Nice ones with crosses on. They like those."

Father Ray sat down and ordered a cup of tea.

"It's an amazing ting, that big white church, and the barrack huts beside it—an amazing ting. You can't get the Indians to come to holy communion, you can't get them to come to mass, but they'll go there to X-Cacal and spend a whole week! A whole week doing their guardia. And they don't even know what it is they're supposed to be guarding!"

Don Rómulo is an elderly man with hooded eyes and a soft grandfatherly voice. His hands are large and gentle, as if used to holding fragile objects. You can tell by the way he drives: never a sudden turn on the wheel or a rough gear change, never an ungainly movement.

"We'll go the long way round through Yaxley, where you can still see some high jungle. Padre Raimundo said you were English."

"Born and bred."

"Excellent! That'll make things much easier. They like the

English, they consider you allies. Have you got any pictures of the queen?"

"I'm afraid not."

"They remember Queen Victoria. They've even got English flags—hidden away because the Mexicans don't approve."

Except for Plumridge and Twigge, Englishmen were always well received at Santa Cruz Balam Na, and Mazehual leaders were equally welcome at Government House in Belize. In 1887 the Santa Cruz Maya formally asked to join the British Empire.[14] The request was turned down because of its international complications, but the Mazehuales never lost their affection for the queen and her flag of three crosses (a symbol that might have been chosen to win their hearts). I wonder how things would have turned out if Britain *had* annexed the Maya state. Would the Indians have been allowed to keep their lands and leaders, like the Fijians who voluntarily joined the empire in 1874? Or would they have been treated the same as other Maya in British Honduras—driven from their homes by logging companies and plantations? The Icaiché, who claimed northwestern Belize as their own, certainly had no love for Queen Victoria.

"I hope they don't remember how we abandoned them in the end."

"They still hope the old alliance can be revived. About four years ago, when the Colony got independence, they heard that a senior British official would be visiting for the celebrations. An old fellow from X-Cacal went down to the border and said he wanted to talk to the queen's representative. When they asked him why, he admitted he was hoping to get guns to fight the Mexicans." Don Rómulo shakes with laughter. He's a Yucatecan, and Yucatecans also like to dream of fighting Mexicans.

The *monte alto*, or "high jungle," is in bloom: sprays of small white flowers like daisies, the crimson candles of epiphytes, purple and mauve morning glories cascading down and flowing across the rutted track. Old *chicozapote* trees, scarred like warriors by the chevron cuts of chicle gatherers; smells of skunk and wild allspice. Here and there piles of railway ties wait for shipment.

X-CACAL GUARDIA

At dusk we come to X-Cacal. At the boundary of the town is the usual shelter with crosses and offerings inside. I expected a rustic place: the Separate Ones are in a way the Maya Amish, keeping alive an old order fastened in the nineteenth century. But X-Cacal has not rejected everything the twentieth can offer: it has a basketball court, water tower, and electric light. Many of the houses on the plaza are substantial masonry constructions, identical to those of mestizos and *mayeros* (citified Maya) elsewhere.

Don Rómulo explains that there are really two parts to the town: this, the secular center; and a ceremonial precinct with the barracks, the meeting hall, and the church. We turn down a muddy street lined with traditional pole-and-thatch houses. Don Rómulo stops here and asks a boy for someone called Don Marcelino. "I'm not sure exactly what his position is," he adds, turning to me, "but I think he's a lieutenant."

A middle-aged man comes out of the nearest house. Don Rómulo gets out to meet him, telling me to stay in the truck. I hear them speaking in Maya. They approach the truck; Don Marcelino glances suspiciously at the cab. He's tall for a Maya, about fifty, with a full hawk nose and a shaggy haircut frosting in front and at the temples. He wears the collarless cotton shirt and white knee britches of the Caste War period, and in his left ear is a small silver earring. I hear the words *Inglés* and *Gran Bretaña*. The lieutenant's face brightens and he peers in through the window, saying, "*¡Muy bien! ¡Muy bien!*" He gets in the back and we continue toward the ceremonial precinct. After two or three hundred yards, the road passes between some large and rather dilapidated huts—these are the barracks, one for each of the tributary companies, grouped around the border of a plaza. At the far side is a great church, the largest modern Maya building I've seen, about eighty feet long and forty wide, with rounded ends. Its walls are of whitewashed masonry with blue trim around the doors; the thatch is thick and even. Don Rómulo points out the corral, opposite the west end. Here "bullfights" are held and sacred ceiba trees are "planted." As in Chiapas, the "bull" is a man in costume, part rodeo clown, part sacrificial beast: the conqueror's game both burlesqued and incorporated into Maya rituals of fertility. Behind the church is the Popol Na, or "Council Hall," almost as large but built of poles.

We follow Don Marcelino to the church's main entrance, in the curved west end. Two men with rifles are standing on either side of large green doors painted with blue crosses. We are told to remove our shoes; we enter and sit on some chairs along the north wall. There are no windows, and the sun has already set. A single light bulb, burning far up in the thatch above strings of cutout paper flags, throws a mosaic of shadows on the tiled floor. The walls have a white dado with blue above, perhaps representing earth and sky. Showing through the paint are earlier motifs: crosses, squares, ladders, and a tree of life. Some women and children enter quietly and sit down cross-legged just inside the door.

After a few minutes a man of about forty arrives. He has a thick moustache and the easy confidence of one accustomed to leading. His six-foot frame and dark face suggest some African blood. With him is a tiny, wizened man who peers at us from a knit, disapproving brow. There are introductions and more biker handshakes. The tall man is Isidro Ek, Nohoch Tata, Great Father of the Holy Cross, supreme religious authority of the Mazehual Maya. His companion, Juan Ek, is custodian of the Tulum crosses and second in command. (Ek—"Star"—is a common Maya surname. Apparently they are no relation to each other; and none, I presume, to Ignacio Ek, the old Icaiché I met all those years ago at Kohunlich.)

"*Buenas tardes, Padre,*" Juan Ek says, taking me for a priest, despite my jeans. I hear *Inglés* again; his brow unfurls.

"I've introduced you as a subject of the queen, friend and emissary of Father Raymond," Don Rómulo says.

An emissary of the padre? I hear Don Rómulo say in Spanish "*Somos todos católicos, pues*" ("We are all Catholics anyway"), as part of his pitch for the "ecumenical meeting." Except in my case, that much is true—the Mazehuales consider themselves Catholics, the truest Catholics of all. It's a strange encounter, both groups subscribing to the same title, even worshiping occasionally in each other's churches. But for one the center of the world is Rome; for the other it is here, this temple, these forests, this Jaguar House standing between the nine levels of the underworld and thirteen tiers of heaven, at the crossroads of the four directions, in a metaphysical space big enough for Balams, Chacs, and "God Three Persons"—the triune godhead of the Speaking Cross.

The Nohoch Tata takes me aside to a table covered in buckets and gourds for the sacred drink. Above this, hanging from a main crossbeam, are two large wooden drums. "*Maya pax*," he says. I recall that the hieroglyph of the month Pax resembles just such a drum with curlicues of sound emanating from its skin. Ek asks Don Rómulo to interpret.

"He wants to know if they can play *Maya pax*—Maya music—at the meeting, and whether Padre Raimundo could help them by providing a violin. I said he would have to ask the padre himself." (Thank heaven for that—I've heard Father Ray's opinion of Maya music: "They get stinkin' dronk and play any old ting they like.")

Don Rómulo passes me a plastic bag containing the rosaries and bells: "Now is a good time to hand over the gifts."

The rosaries are examined closely, the small carved crosses noted and admired. Then come the brass bells, bought in Ireland by Father Ray but probably made in Hong Kong. The Maya scrutinize them under the light bulb and test their sound with the absorption of concert musicians. Smiles and nods of approval.

"We must pray now," Don Rómulo adds. "Take these candles and give them to the Angel—that soldier on guard beside the Gloria."

The Gloria sanctuary, which occupies all of the eastern apse, is set apart from the rest of the church by a low crenellated stone wall with painted crosses. An arched doorway in the middle leads to an offering table and an altar roofed with branches and cloth like the one I saw at San Andrés. But here there is a third structure I haven't seen before: an inner sanctum, a masonry vault screened by a white curtain beautifully embroidered with a cross and floral border. Whatever is behind this curtain is for the eyes of the Nohoch Tata alone. It is said to conceal *La Santísima*, the holy of holies, the Speaking Cross itself.

We approach the "Angel," a diminutive guardsman sitting at a table. A rifle leans against the wall behind him. He rises, receives the candles, and tells us to follow him into the Gloria. The gifts are brought and reverently placed on the offering table. Thirteen candles are set out and lit. A smell of beeswax and soot. The electric bulb at the far end of the church goes out. We kneel at the altar, the flames throwing feathered shadows on the embroidery that hides the Cross. I hear the others praying quietly in Maya, a language so much older than my own.

If I could understand that language, perhaps the Cross would express to me, as it has recently to other Anglo-Saxons, the hope that the British and Americans will help its people to be free. In the early 1970s, a spokesman of the Cross suggested to linguist Alan Burns that the Americans should forget about the South Vietnamese and come instead to the aid of the Maya. Then, in the rhetorical voice of his god, the old man spoke of the Caste War, the Cuban Revolution, President Nixon, and finally the struggle between the Maya and the Mexicans: a struggle as old as Tikal and Teotihuacán.

> The Mexicans have entered Noh Cah Santa Cruz
>   Balam Na.
> They have taken everything.
> Everything has been grabbed by them,
> everything has been eaten . . . .
>
> Those that are called English
> and those that are called Americans, red-red men.
> They will put up the tower on my temple.
> That is the only truth.
>
> I've made it true until the sun ends.
> There you will get . . . the things you need,
> there with those who are called English,
> with those who are called Americans, red-red men.
> They are my servants. . . .
>
> *I am . . . the Cross,*
> *I am . . . Noh Cah Santa Cruz Balam Na.*[15]

The irony is heartbreaking. If the Mazehuales knew the real nature of American and British involvement in Meso-america—the support, whether tacit or active, of dictators, racists, and Westernized plutocracies—they would despair. But the enemy they know is Mexico. And they remember the English queen who was once their ally; and the friendly Americans who dig in the ancient cities and know how to read what is written there. In those words of the Speaking Cross, spoken only a decade ago, the unfinished tower of the Jaguar House becomes the symbol of unfinished history.

Epilogue

If I have learned anything on this journey, it is that the history of the Maya is no more finished than the history of the English. One could say that the Maya are shattered: by the white men's countries drawn between and around them, by their own many languages, by the creeping replacement of Maya with Spanish (or English in Belize), by the loss of the calendar in some places and its retention in others, by the many faiths they have kept and acquired. The Maya may be shattered, but they have always been so. Disunity may be a weakness but it is also their strength. The Spaniards conquered the Maya again and again but never broke them. Even in Guatemala, where the war of conquest has been renewed, Maya culture survives.

Here in the Jaguar House of X-Cacal Guardia it comes to me how much of this journey has been spent in churches and shrines. I have knelt at more Maya altars than at any others in my adult life. I am not myself a believer but I recognize the power of belief. The Maya are intensely religious; in their shrines and churches, as in their ancient temples, one finds the articulation of their culture. But they are not rigid. Many times in the past they have shown their ability to take a foreign religion, intended to destroy their beliefs, and turn it instead into a new expression of Maya identity. In Guatemala they absorbed Catholicism into the worship of Earth, Sky, and the ancestors; here they created the Speaking Cross. The latest assaults—whether from fundamentalism or materialism—will, if history is any guide, be deflected and transformed in similar ways. The Maya are a subtle, ancient people who have overcome many things. They know this themselves. "What is a man on the road?" asks a riddle; and the answer is "Time."[1]

The modern Maya are traveling many roads: the hard road of armed resistance, the silent road of refuge; the seductive road of accommodation. For a people conscious of time, all roads are perhaps expedients, temporary fortunes in a journey as short as a single day, as long as the eternity so elegantly measured by the Maya calendar. On my own journey I have not found what I feared: that the Maya face extinction—much more than the rest of us do. If there is to be a twenty-first century, the Maya will be part of it. And if, on the winter solstice of 2012, human beings witness the beginning of Baktun 13, some of them will be members of the civilization that invented that count. And thirteen is a very good number for the Maya.

Glossary

AGUARDIENTE. Cane alcohol.

ALAUTUN. Period of LONG COUNT Maya calendar, equivalent to 160,000 BAKTUNS, or about 63,000,000 years. (The term was coined for convenience by students of ancient Maya thought; the original name is unknown.)

ANTIGUOS. Ancients. In central Quintana Roo this term refers to those who still keep the cult of the "Speaking Cross."

AUTO DA FE. "Act of faith." Purge of heretics, apostates, or idolaters, often by burning at the stake.

BAKTUN. Period of LONG COUNT Maya calendar, equivalent to 144,000 days, or slightly less than four centuries.

BALCHE. Ceremonial drink of fermented bark and honey, used especially by the Lacandón Maya.

BATAB. Native Maya aristocrat and/or community leader in colonial Yucatán.

BOLONTIKU. Nine Gods. The lords of the underworld and of the night in ancient Maya religion. Their diurnal counterparts were the *Oxlahuntiku*, or Thirteen Gods of Heaven. Both may be considered multiple aspects of greater deities.

CACIQUE. Originally a Carib word for "native chief." A political boss.

CALENDAR ROUND. Endlessly repeating 52-year cycle of the MESO-AMERICAN calendar, formed by the combination of the 365-day solar year and the 260-day TZOLKIN.

CAMIONETA. Guatemalan word for bus; elsewhere it usually means a light van or truck.

CAMPESINO. Peasant or country-dweller. The term may become politically or racially loaded when it is substituted for INDIO or INDÍGENA.

CANTINA. Bar or tavern.

CARAJO. Spanish expletive, literally meaning "penis."

CASA CURAL. House of Catholic priest.

CEIBA. Silk-cotton or kapok tree native to Central American lowlands. Regarded as sacred by Maya.

CENOTE. Sinkhole common in the limestone flatlands of the Yucatán Peninsula. From Maya *dzonot*.

CHACHALACA. Raucous jungle fowl, about the size of a chicken.

CHICLE. Tree sap from which chewing gum is made.

CHICOZAPOTE. Sapodilla. Tree from which CHICLE gum is extracted.

CHILAM BALAM, BOOKS OF. Name applied to about a dozen texts, written in Maya using the Roman alphabet, from colonial Yucatán. Some of the historical and mythological content is common to all, and was presumably salvaged from earlier hieroglyphic codices destroyed by the Spaniards. The various books are named for the towns in which they were kept; some include additions and revisions from the 16th century until the early 19th.

CHUCHKAHAU. "Mother-father." Title of lineage head among the modern Quichés of Guatemala. Such a person is usually also a DAY-KEEPER.

CHUH. Belted tunic resembling a poncho with the sides sewn together, worn by the Tzotzil Maya of highland Chiapas.

COFRADE. Member of a COFRADÍA.

COFRADÍA. Religious brotherhood, dedicated to a particular saint or saints, common among the Maya of highland Guatemala. Cofradías combine Catholic elements with ancient Maya patterns of worship and social structure.

CONTRA. The counterrevolutionary, anti-Sandinista forces of Nicaragua and Miami.

CORREGIDOR. Magistrate and/or administrator in colonial and 19th-century Spanish America.

CORTE. In Guatemala, a long, wraparound skirt worn by Maya women.

COSTUMBRE. Custom. Specifically, traditional religious practices of the highland Maya.

COSTUMBRISTA. Practitioner (especially an expert) of COSTUMBRES.

CREOLE. In Belize, general term for Afro-Caribbean Belizeans and the variety of English they speak. Not to be confused with Spanish CRIOLLO.

CRIOLLO. Person of Spanish descent born in the New World. Such people have generally formed the ruling class of Latin America since independence.

DAYKEEPER. English term for present-day Maya shamans and diviners who keep the MESOAMERICAN calendar.

DUEÑO DEL MONTE. Lord of the Forest. The god or gods believed to inhabit and protect the wilderness. Spanish translation of Maya YUMTZIL.

DZUL. Yucatec Maya term for foreigner or outsider, whether of a different race or other Maya group. Often applied nowadays to whites and MESTIZOS, though it is also a common Maya surname.

EJIDO. Landholding community. Refers both to pre-Columbian structures such as the *calpulli* and to peasant communes formed since the Mexican Revolution.

ENTRADA. Colonial Spanish term for an invasion or military expedition into unconquered territory.

EVANGÉLICO. Christian Evangelical or fundamentalist, especially a missionary.

EXISTENCIALISTA. Existentialist, or GRINGO living bohemian life in Mexico.

FINCA. Guatemalan term for hacienda, plantation, or country estate.

FOCO. Focus. Term used by the Castro and Guevara school of guerrilla warfare for a base in remote country intended to be the catalyst and core of revolution.

GRINGO. Any North European or North American, especially a citizen of the United States. Not always pejorative.

GUAJOLOTE. Domestic turkey of Mexico (from which all other domestic turkeys are ultimately derived).

GUANACASTE. Conocaste. Large tropical American timber tree.

GUARDIA. Guard. In central Quintana Roo, specifically the system of guard duty practiced by followers of the "Speaking Cross."

GUERRILLERO. Guerrilla fighter.

HUIPIL. Blouse or shift worn by Maya woman, often richly woven or embroidered.

INDÍGENA. Indigenous person. Polite term for native Indians throughout Latin America.

INDIGENISMO. Indianism or indigenism. Sincere but often naïve intellectual movement intended to support Indians, their culture, and their contribution to the national culture of countries such as Mexico, Guatemala, and Peru.

INDIO. Indian. The word has been used pejoratively for so long in Latin America that INDÍGENA is now generally preferred.

INTENDENTE. Superintendent or administrator. In Guatemala, these officials are generally LADINO appointees of the state, with power over the Indians' own representatives.

KAIBILES. Usually translated as "Tigers"—the name of the crack counterinsurgency troops of the Guatemalan army. The Maya word actually implies a "double" or something of double strength.

KATUN. Period of LONG COUNT Maya calendar, equivalent to 7,200 days, or slightly less than 20 solar years.

KIN. Yucatec Maya word meaning day, sun, and/or time.

LADINO. Latin. Term used, especially in Guatemala, to refer to any-one who is not ethnically an Indian. Whites, MESTIZOS, and even Indians who have assimilated to Hispanic culture are all consid-ered *Ladino*.

LIMOSNA. Alms, charity.

LONG COUNT. Sometimes called Initial Series. Calendar used by Maya during the Classic period (circa A.D. 250–900). It differs from all other MESOAMERICAN calendars in being counted from a datum point in the past without repetition. Because it is a count of days (KIN) it achieved remarkable precision, but the exact correlation with our calendar is still a matter of dispute.

MACAL. Wild elephant-ear taro.

MAM. Grandfather. The name of the "Year-Bearer," or TZOLKIN day on which the solar year begins. Also the name of a Maya people and language of western Guatemala.

MARIMBA. Large xylophone, very popular in Guatemala.

MAX. Maya word for tobacco. Also a Maya form of the name Tomás.

MAY. Maya word for calendrical era, especially the SHORT COUNT cycle of thirteen KATUNS.

MAYERO. Modern Yucatec term for a Maya, especially one who is urban or educated yet retains an Indian identity.

MAZEHUAL. Word of Toltec origin meaning commoner. Used by the Maya of central Quintana Roo to refer to themselves. (In north-ern Yucatán *mazehual* tends to be pejorative.)

MECAPAL. Forehead tumpline for carrying heavy loads.

MESOAMERICA. Contiguous area of Mexico and Central America where high civilizations arose. Includes central and southern Mexico, the Yucatán Peninsula, all of Guatemala and Belize, and western parts of Honduras and El Salvador.

MESTIZAJE. Mixing of Indian and Spaniard. Often used to advocate the blending of indigenous and Hispanic cultures to create a new society—a spurious aim while political and economic power remain in the hands of only the Hispanic sector.

MESTIZO. Person of mixed Indian and Spanish blood. Like most "racial" terms in Latin America, it is more of a cultural definition than a genetic one. Mestizos are usually part of the Hispanic or Ladino cultural sector.

MILPA. Cornfield or garden plot, usually cut from the bush in shifting slash-and-burn agriculture.

MONTE. Scrub, bush, or jungle.

MUY BIEN. Spanish for "Very good" or "That's fine."

NAHUATL. Language spoken by the Aztecs. Best-known member of the Nahua group, to which Toltec also belonged. Not to be confused with NAWAL.

NAWAL. Guardian spirit acquired by person at birth. The *nawal* (or *nahual*) is usually an animal "double," capable of magical deeds.

NOCHE TRISTE. The "Sad Night," probably July 10, 1520, when the Aztecs routed the Spaniards and drove them from the city of Mexico.

NOHOCH TATA. "Great Father." Title of the supreme religious leaders of the MAZEHUAL Maya of Quintana Roo.

NORTE. Norther. Cold wind that brings wet and cloudy winter weather.

OCOTE. Pitch pine. Used for torches and offering fires.

PANAMERICANA. Pan American Highway.

PAX. Yucatec Maya word for upright drum with leather membrane. The name of the "month" Pax, whose glyph shows a drum.

POK-TA-POK. Yucatec Maya name for the ritual ball game played in stone courts throughout ancient MESOAMERICA.

POLO DE DESARROLLO. "Development pole." Euphemistic term for clusters of fortified villages created by the Guatemalan army as a counterinsurgency tactic.

POX. Home-distilled alcohol made by the Maya of Chiapas.

QUECHUISTA. Expert in Quechua (or Runasimi), the Inca language of Peru.

QUETZAL. Spectacular tropical bird of Central America. Its long emerald tail feathers were highly prized in ancient times. Also, the currency of Guatemala, at par with the U.S. dollar until recent years.

QUETZALCÓATL. "Feathered Serpent" or "Precious Twin." God and hero of MESOAMERICA, around whom there is a vast cycle of myth and legend. Many kings were named after him, and he himself had many other names.

RANCHERO. Ranch-style song, cooking, etc.

RANCHITO. Shack or hovel, whether in the country or an urban slum.

RANCHO. Ranch or homestead of any size.

REDUCCIÓN. Reduction. Strategic settlement, usually fortified and staffed by priests, into which Indians were herded for indoctrination and control during the colonial period.

RELIGIOSIDAD POPULAR. Popular piety, folk Catholicism.

SACBE. "White road." Ceremonial causeway leading to temple precinct or running between one ancient city and another, especially in Yucatán.

SEPARADOS. "Separate Ones." The strictest adherents of the "Speaking Cross" in Quintana Roo.

SHORT COUNT. Maya calendrical cycle of thirteen KATUNS, or about 256 solar years, used especially in Postclassic Yucatán. Because the KATUNS are named only by their last TZOLKIN day, the cycle (also called a MAY) repeats endlessly without reference to the larger BAKTUN cycle of the LONG COUNT.

SUBVERSIVO. Subversive. Pejorative term, used by the Central American Right, for left-winger or revolutionary.

TAMAL. Maize dumpling with meat and chile in the middle, steamed inside a banana leaf or corn husk.

TAXISTA. Taxi driver.

TEPEZCUINTLE. Paca or spotted cavy. Large rodent hunted for its flesh; known in Belize CREOLE as *gibnut*.

TRAJE. Suit or clothes, especially the distinctive dress of highland Maya communities.

TUN. Maya for stone, and for the 360-day "year" in the LONG and SHORT COUNT calendars. Twenty tuns form one KATUN.

TZOLKIN. "Count of days." Endlessly repeating 260-day ritual cycle formed by the combination of 20 daynames and the numbers one to thirteen. The count, still kept by many highland Maya, acts as almanac, horoscope, and religious calendar.

TZUT. Headcloth or scarf worn by highland Maya.

UINAL. Sequence of 20 named days forming both the Mesoamerican 20-day "month" and the basis of the TZOLKIN. Although the order of the days never changes, the first day of the solar year, known as the Year-Bearer, shifts by 5 names each year because there are 18¼ *uinals* in the 365-day solar year.

XTABAY. Supernatural seductress who appears to men alone in the forest and leads them astray.

YANQUI. Yankee. Pejorative term for any citizen of the United States.

YAXCHE. Yucatec Maya for the CEIBA tree, which is also symbolically a tree of life at the center of any conceptual space.

YUMTZIL. Yucatec Maya for the lord or lords of the forest, supernatural beings who "own" the bush and its game, and must be placated when hunting or making MILPA.

ZAHORÍN. Old Moorish word for diviner or seer, applied in Guatemala to Maya shamans.

ZÓCALO. The central square of any Mexican town or city. (Literally the socle, or plinth, of a statue.)

ZONA INDÍGENA. "Indigenous zone." Parts of Mexico with dense Indian populations, sometimes designated for special programs in education and administration.

ZOPILOTE. Vulture, turkey buzzard.

Notes

PROLOGUE

1. Reed 1964:201–05.
2. López de Cogolludo 1971:500.
3. Coe 1966:131.

CHAPTER 1

1. León-Portilla 1973:93.
. 2. Morley and Brainerd 1983:524.
3. Throughout this book I follow the 584,283 correlation constant. See Morley and Brainerd 1983:598–603.
4. León-Portilla 1973:24.

CHAPTER 2

1. López de Cogolludo 1971:215;216.
2. Chamberlain 1948:235.
3. Pendergast 1985a:101.
4. Jones 1977:167; Dobson 1973:222.
5. Gann 1925:67–68.

CHAPTER 3

1. Roys 1967:126.
2. Handy 1984:249.
3. Mondragón 1983:33–34.
4. Falla 1984:116–17.
5. Black 1984:132.

6. Handy 1984:271.
7. Pendergast 1967:194–98.
8. Pendergast 1967:5.
9. Pendergast 1967:115.
10. Pendergast 1967:175.
11. Stephens 1841, vol. 1:249.
12. Huxley 1984:65.
13. Handy 1984:51.
14. Handy 1984:50.
15. Pendergast 1967:167–68.
16. Quoted in Handy 1984:167.
17. Black 1984:22.
18. Handy 1984:161–62.
19. Pendergast 1967:81.
20. Edmonson 1982.
21. *Four Quartets*, "Burnt Norton" 1943.
22. Roys 1967:136; Morley and Brainerd 1983:159; Coe 1966:129.
23. Roys 1967:82–83.
24. León-Portilla 1980:95; Scholes and Roys 1968:271–72.
25. Gómara 1964:360.
26. López de Cogolludo 1971:230.
27. López de Cogolludo 1971:229.
28. López de Cogolludo 1971:231.
29. López de Cogolludo 1971:324.
30. Thompson 1977:28.
31. Quoted in Bricker 1981:23.
32. Roys 1967:184; Thompson 1966:166–67.
33. Craine and Reindorp 1979:174.
34. Pendergast 1967:161.

CHAPTER 4

1. Rough estimate based on Caufield 1986:38. Guatemala is expected to lose one-third of its remaining rain forest between 1981 and 2000. If we estimate 10,000 square miles of rain forest in 1981, then annual loss is about 175 square miles.
2. Caufield 1986:112.
3. Barry, Wood, and Preusch 1983:25.
4. Caufield 1986:108–09; Barry, Wood, and Preusch 1983:25.
5. Navarrete 1982a:158–59.
6. My calculations are based on data in Hammond 1982:292. See also Morley and Brainerd 1983:566.

7. Schele and Miller 1986:321. See also Morley and Brainerd 1983:548;559.
8. Thompson 1966:14.
9. Brotherston 1986.
10. Coe 1966:99.
11. Thompson 1950:155.
12. Morley and Brainerd 1983:107ff; 277–93.
13. Coggins cited in Morley and Brainerd 1983:118–19.
14. In Morley and Brainerd 1983:543.
15. Hammond 1982:110.

CHAPTER 5

1. Recinos 1980:109–11.
2. Statistics supplied by Immigration Public Affairs, Ottawa.
3. Black 1984:99.
4. *Noticias de Guatemala* February 4, 1980, quoted in Handy 1984:247.
5. Painter 1987:xvii;4.
6. Quoted in McClintock 1985:258–59.

CHAPTER 6

1. Handy 1984:63.
2. Handy 1984:63;57.
3. Handy 1984:69.
4. Handy 1984:71.
5. Huxley 1984:39.
6. Woodward 1985:180.
7. Schlesinger and Kinzer 1983:67;75.
8. Handy 1984:97.
9. Handy 1984:93.
10. Handy 1984:106.
11. Schlesinger and Kinzer 1983:43.
12. Handy 1984:115.
13. Handy 1984:139; Schlesinger and Kinzer 1983:101.
14. Handy 1984:128.
15. Schlesinger and Kinzer 1983:55.
16. Handy 1984:129.
17. Handy 1984:142.
18. Schlesinger and Kinzer 1983:182.
19. Schlesinger and Kinzer 1983:185.

20. Schlesinger and Kinzer 1983:184.
21. Black 1984:12; Schlesinger and Kinzer 1983:184.
22. *El Imparcial* July 28, 1954, quoted in Schlesinger and Kinzer 1983:200.
23. Schlesinger and Kinzer 1983:234; Barry, Wood and Preusch 1983:120.
24. Handy 1984:79.
25. Crosby 1973:38.
26. Recinos, Goetz, and Chonay 1953:116.
27. Roys 1967:83.
28. Ashmore 1980:23.
29. Huxley 1984:26.
30. Stephens 1841, vol. 2:124.
31. Hammond 1982:207.

CHAPTER 7

1. *The Concise Oxford Dictionary*, 6th ed., 1976:725.
2. Sexton 1985:375.
3. *Prensa Libre* (Guatemala) November 29, 1985.
4. *New York Times* November 9, 1977. For more details, see Barry, Wood, and Preusch 1983:29.
5. Hammond 1982:276–77.
6. Recinos 1980:155.
7. Recinos 1980:164.
8. Asturias de Barrios 1985:92–93.
9. Recinos 1980:105.
10. Handy 1984:249.
11. Anonymous 1982:151;169.
12. *Title of the House Ixquin Nehaib* (Quiché document, c. 1550); León-Portilla 1980:96–100.
13. Handy 1984:98.
14. *Toronto Star* November 3, 1985.
15. Sexton 1985:410.
16. Quoted in Sexton 1985:378.
17. Black 1984:22.

CHAPTER 8

1. Fuentes 1985:12.
2. Fox 1978:187.

3. Carmack 1981:43–48.
4. Carmack 1981:134–6; Fox 1978:3–4.
5. Recinos 1980:81.
6. Recinos, Goetz, and Chonay 1953:115–17; Recinos 1980:95–96.
7. Carmack 1981:114.
8. Recinos 1980:102–03.
9. Recinos 1980:103.
10. Recinos 1980:107.
11. Quoted in Mondragón 1983:12–22.
12. Schlesinger and Kinzer 1983:221.
13. Schlesinger and Kinzer 1983:219;221.
14. Sexton 1985:12–13.
15. Handy 1984:189.
16. Quoted in McClintock 1985:134.
17. *New York Times* July 28, 1985.
18. Mendelson 1965:94.
19. *Survival International News* no. 9, 1985.
20. Sexton 1981:110.
21. Mendelson 1965:131–32; 139.
22. Mendelson 1965:jacket.

CHAPTER 9

1. *Guatemala: Masacres Cometidas por el Ejército, 1981–85.* Map published by Guatemalan Church in Exile.
2. Martínez Peláez 1971:594.
3. Martínez Peláez 1971:596;603.
4. Martínez Peláez 1971:594ff.
5. Martínez Peláez 1971:609–10.
6. Martínez Peláez 1971:612.
7. For a more recent but equally flawed attack on Maya ethnicity, see Hawkins 1984.
8. Tedlock 1985:71.
9. Tedlock 1985:27.
10. Tedlock 1985:71.
11. Tedlock 1985:72–73.
12. Brotherston in the *Times Literary Supplement* April 18, 1986:408.
13. Tedlock 1985:167.
14. Tedlock 1985:170.
15. Carmack 1981:181;352.

16. Craine and Reindorp 1979:74, n. 43.
17. Carmack 1981:361.

CHAPTER 10

1. *Wall Street Journal* October 30, 1985:1.
2. Black 1984:154–55.
3. Tedlock 1985:18.
4. K'ucumatz, the Quiché version of Quetzalcóatl, was also the name of Quicab's father, who reigned c. 1400–1425.
5. Stephens 1841, vol. 2:184.
6. Carmack 1981:186.
7. Tedlock 1985:365; see also Perera and Bruce 1982.
8. Tedlock 1985:14.
9. Tedlock 1985:57;322;360.
10. Tedlock 1985:13.
11. Tedlock 1982:176.
12. Thompson 1950:128.
13. Thompson 1950:66.
14. Tedlock 1985:221–22.

CHAPTER 11

1. Recinos 1980:27–29.
2. Recinos 1980:129.
3. Tedlock 1982:111.
4. Bricker 1981:77–84.
5. Tedlock 1982:21–22.
6. *Guatemala: Masacres Cometidas por el Ejército 1981–85.* Map published by Guatemalan Church in Exile.
7. Sexton 1985:424.
8. Fuentes y Guzmán quoted in Lovell 1985:61–62.
9. Fuentes y Guzmán quoted in Lovell 1985:62.
10. Jonas, McCaughan, and Sutherland 1984:160–61.
11. Sexton 1985:393.
12. Stephens 1841, vol. 2:229.
13. Stephens 1841, vol. 2:231–32.
14. Stephens 1841, vol. 1:232; vol. 2:125; vol. 2:250.
15. Stephens 1841, vol. 2:230.
16. Quoted in Lovell 1985:17.
17. Oakes 1951a:24.

18. McClintock 1985:257.
19. Sexton 1985:419.

CHAPTER 12

1. Morley and Brainerd 1983:432–33.
2. Stephens 1841, vol. 2:195–96.
3. *Polémica* (San José, Costa Rica) nos. 10–11, 1983:87.
4. Robert Burkitt, quoted in Lovell 1986a:29.
5. Payeras 1983:72–76.
6. McClintock 1985:137.
7. *Polémica* no. 3, 1982:40; Colby and Colby 1981:36.
8. *Polémica* no. 3, 1982:40.
9. *Guatemala: A Nation of Prisoners,* Americas Watch report, January 1984:90.
10. Sexton 1985:423.
11. Nairn 1983:17.
12. Colby and Colby 1981:38–39.
13. León-Portilla 1973:49.
14. León-Portilla 1973:85–86.
15. Brotherston 1979:250–251; cf. León-Portilla 1973:88–89.

CHAPTER 13

1. Lovell 1985:65–66.
2. Carmack 1981:159.
3. Menchú 1984:169–70.
4. Martínez Peláez 1982:54–55.
5. Menchú 1985:196.
6. Menchú 1984:13.
7. Menchú 1984:38;40.
8. Reviewed in *American Anthropologist* 1985, vol. 87:992.
9. Martínez Peláez 1982:52.
10. Maslow 1986:215.

CHAPTER 14

1. Rus 1983:138.
2. Llorente 1984:172.
3. Tedlock 1985:353.
4. Tedlock 1985:157.

5. Morris 1984:5.
6. They have opted to use the letter *j* to represent the Maya aspirate. For consistency, and to avoid confusing English readers, I've changed it to *h*.
7. Gossen 1974:3.
8. Sna Htz'ibahom receives help and support from Cultural Survival Inc., coordinated by Robert M. Laughlin, the Smithsonian Institution, Washington, D.C.
9. Paz 1988:176.
10. Rus 1983:154.
11. Gossen 1974:42.
12. See Bricker 1973:111, where "God's jaguar" is said to have defended him against the Jews.
13. Lawrence 1961:241.
14. Bricker 1981:140–41.

CHAPTER 15

1. Lafaye 1976.
2. Schele and Miller 1986:48.
3. Morley and Brainerd 1983:127.
4. Also known to Mayanists as Bolon Tzacab and the Manikin Scepter.
5. Schele and Miller 1986:60. I have changed their Gregorian dates by two days to conform to the 584,283 correlation used throughout this book.
6. Schele and Miller 1986:274.
7. Greene 1939:187.

CHAPTER 16

1. Perera and Bruce 1982:4.
2. Perera and Bruce 1982:5.
3. Miller 1986:32.
4. Greene 1980a:3.
5. Huxley 1984:28–29.
6. Huxley 1984:73.
7. Morley and Brainerd 1983:416.
8. Miller 1986:151.
9. Perera 1986b:6.
10. Perera and Bruce 1982:2.
11. Perera 1986b:1.

12. Perera 1986b:7;12.
13. Perera 1986b:12.

CHAPTER 17

1. Díaz 1963:23.
2. Morley and Brainerd 1983:571.
3. For the Viking analogy, see Miller 1985.
4. Quoted in Stephens 1963, vol. 2:278.
5. Stephens 1963, vol. 2:264.
6. Stephens 1963, vol. 2:273.
7. Bartolomé and Barabas 1981:49.
8. Schele and Miller 1986:320–21.
9. Reed 1964:24.
10. Edmonson 1982:43.
11. Edmonson 1982:xix.
12. Hooton quoted in Coe 1966:127.
13. For example: Edmonson 1982, 1986; Chase 1985; Lincoln 1985; Kelley 1983.
14. Kinglake 1982:174–75.
15. Landa 1982:107–08.
16. Edmonson 1986:145–46.
17. Landa 1982:104–05.
18. Mediz Bolio 1983:12–13.
19. Landa 1978:114–17.

CHAPTER 18

1. Landa 1982:109.
2. Landa 1982:111.
3. Landa 1982:112.
4. Roys 1967:125–26 (minor changes).
5. Craine and Reindorp 1979:65–68.
6. Roys 1967:77–79 (some changes in format).
7. Edmonson 1986:12.
8. Craine and Reindorp 1979:57.
9. Craine and Reindorp 1979:19–23.
10. Quoted in Bricker 1981:97–98.
11. Quoted in Bricker 1981:94.
12. Reed 1964:86–87. In this very brief sketch of the war I have relied heavily on Reed's superb account.

13. Reed 1964:99; also in Bricker 1981:102.
14. Reed 1964:112.

CHAPTER 19

1. Stephens 1963, vol. 2:280.
2. Bricker 1981:156.
3. Bricker 1981:104.
4. Roys 1967:127; cf. Edmonson 1986:197.
5. *Relación de Mérida* quoted in Pearce 1984:19.
6. Reed 1964:134.
7. Burns 1977.
8. Quoted in Villa Rojas 1945:22; and Reed 1964:182.
9. Quoted in Jones 1974:674.
10. Villa Rojas 1978:126.
11. Bartolomé and Barabas 1981:49.
12. See Villa Rojas 1945:73. The document he saw was an 1875 copy of a text dated 1628.
13. Machlin and Marx 1971:19.
14. Reed 1964:224.
15. Burns 1983:85;87 (some changes in spelling and presentation).

EPILOGUE

1. Edmonson 1986:50.

Bibliography

Acker, Alison
 1986　*Children of the Volcano*
　　　　Toronto: Between the Lines Press
Adams, Richard E. W., ed.
 1977　*The Origins of Maya Civilization*
　　　　Albuquerque: University of New Mexico Press
Anonymous
 1982　"Baile de la Conquista"
　　　　Tradiciones de Guatemala, nos. 17–18
Ashmore, Wendy
 1980　"The Classic Maya Settlement at Quiriguá"
　　　　Expedition 23 (1):20–27
Asturias, Miguel Angel
 1970　*The Mulatta and Mr. Fly*
　　　　(Gregory Rabassa, trans.)
　　　　Harmondsworth: Penguin Books (1st ed., in Spanish, 1963)
 1983　*El Señor Presidente*
　　　　San José, Costa Rica: Editorial Universitaria Centroamericana (4th ed.)
Asturias de Barrios, Linda
 1985　*Comalapa: Native Dress and its Significance*
　　　　Guatemala: Ixchel Museum Publications
Aveni, Anthony F.
 1980　*Skywatchers of Ancient Mexico*
　　　　Austin: University of Texas Press
Aveni, Anthony F., and Gordon Brotherston, eds.
 1983　*Calendars in Mesoamerica and Peru: Native American Computations of Time*

419

Oxford: British Archaeological Reports (BAR International Series 174)

Barrera Vásquez, Alfredo
1984   *Códice de Calkiní, Cantares de Dzitbalché*
        Campeche: CORACEC

Barry, Tom, Beth Wood, and Deb Preusch
1983   *Dollars and Dictators*
        London: Zed Press

Bartolomé, Miguel Alberto, and Alicia Mabel Barabas
1981   *La Resistencia Maya*
        México DF: Instituto Nacional de Antropología e Historia

Becker, Marshall Joseph
1979   "Priests, Peasants, and Ceremonial Centers: The Intellectual History of a Model"
        in Hammond and Willey, eds. 1979:3–20

Benson, Elizabeth P., ed.
1981   *Mesoamerican Sites and Worldviews*
        Washington: Dumbarton Oaks, Harvard University

Becquelin, Pierre
1969   *Archéologie de la Région de Nébaj (Guatémala)*
        Paris: Institut d'Ethnologie

Bierhorst, John, trans.
1985   *Cantares Mexicanos: Songs of the Aztecs*
        Stanford: Stanford University Press

Black, George
1984   *Garrison Guatemala*
        New York: Monthly Review Press

Bricker, Victoria R.
1973   *Ritual Humor in Highland Chiapas*
        Austin: University of Texas Press
1981   *The Indian Christ, the Indian King*
        Austin: University of Texas Press
1986   *A Grammar of Mayan Hieroglyphs*
        New Orleans: Tulane University, Publication 56

Brintnall, Douglas E.
1979   *Revolt Against the Dead: The Modernization of a Mayan Community in the Highlands of Guatemala*
        New York: Gordon and Breach

Brotherston, Gordon
1979   "Continuity in Maya Writing: New Readings of Two Pas-

sages in the Book of Chilam Balam of Chumayel"
in Hammond and Willey, eds. 1979:241–258

1986 "The Zodiac, the Ritual Year, and Astronomical Time in Mesoamerica"
Paper presented at the Second Oxford International Conference on Archaeoastronomy, Mérida, Yucatán, January 13–17

Browman, David L., ed.
1978 *Cultural Continuity in Mesoamerica*
The Hague, Paris: Mouton Publishers

Bruce, Robert D.
1974 *El Libro de Chan K'in*
México DF: Instituto Nacional de Antropología e Historia

Bruce, Robert D., Carlos Robles, and Enriqueta Ramos
1971 *Los Lacandones, 2: Cosmovisión Maya*
México DF: Instituto Nacional de Antropología e Historia

Brunhouse, Robert L.
1975 *Pursuit of the Ancient Maya: Some Archaeologists of Yesterday*
Albuquerque: University of New Mexico Press

Bunzel, Ruth
1959 *Chichicastenango: A Guatemalan Village*
Seattle: University of Washington Press (2nd printing)

Burkitt, Robert
1924 "A Journey in Northern Guatemala"
The Museum Journal, June 1924:115–45
Philadelphia: University of Pennsylvania
1930 "Explorations in the Highlands of Western Guatemala"
The Museum Journal, vol. 21, no. 1:41–72

Burns, Allan F.
1977 "The Caste War in the 1970's: Present-Day Accounts from Village Quintana Roo"
in Jones, ed. 1977:259–73
1983 *An Epoch of Miracles: Oral Literature of the Yucatec Maya*
Austin: University of Texas Press

Carmack, Robert M.
1973 *Quichean Civilization*
Berkeley: University of California Press

1981 *The Quiché Mayas of Utatlán*
Norman: University of Oklahoma Press

Caufield, Catherine
1986 *In the Rainforest*
London: Pan Books

Chamberlain, Robert S.
1948 *The Conquest and Colonization of Yucatán, 1517–1550*
Washington: Carnegie Institution (Publication 582)

Chamix, Pedro
1982 "La Importancia Revolucionaria de Conocer los Movimientos Indígenas"
Polémica, no. 3:47–57

Chase, Arlen F.
1985 "Time Depth or Vacuum: The 11. 3. 0. 0. 0 Correlation and the Lowland Maya Postclassic"
in Sabloff and Andrews, eds. 1985:99–140

Chase, Arlen, and Prudence M. Rice, eds.
1985 *The Lowland Maya Postclassic*
Austin: University of Texas Press

Coe, Michael D.
1966 *The Maya*
London: Thames and Hudson
1967 *Tikal*
Philadelphia: The University Museum
1978 *Lords of the Underworld: Masterpieces of Classic Maya Ceramics*
Princeton: Princeton University Press

Coggins, Clemency
1979 "A New Order and the Role of the Calendar: Some Characteristics of the Middle Classic Period at Tikal"
in Hammond and Willey, eds. 1979:38–50
1986 "A New Sun at Chichén Itzá"
Paper presented at the Second Oxford International Conference on Archaeoastronomy, Mérida, Yucatán, January 13–17

Colby, Benjamin N., and Lore M. Colby
1981 *The Daykeeper: The Life and Discourse of an Ixil Diviner*
Cambridge, Mass: Harvard University Press

Colby, Benjamin N., and Pierre L. van den Berghe
1969 *Ixil Country: A Plural Society in Highland Guatemala*
Berkeley: University of California Press

Collier, George A.
   1975   *Fields of the Tzotzil, the Ecological Bases of Tradition in
           Highland Chiapas*
           Austin: University of Texas Press
Collier, Jane Fishburne
   1973   *Law and Social Change in Zinacantán*
           Stanford: Stanford University Press
Conrad, Geoffrey W., and Arthur A. Demarest
   1984   *Religion and Empire: The Dynamics of Aztec and Inca
           Expansionism*
           London and New York: Cambridge University Press
Cowgill, George L.
   1979   "Teotihuacan, Internal Militaristic Competition, and the
           Fall of the Classic Maya"
           in Hammond and Willey, eds. 1979:51–62
Craine, Eugene R., and Reginald C. Reindorp, trans. and eds.
   1979   *The Codex Pérez and the Book of Chilam Balam of Maní*
           Norman: University of Oklahoma Press
Crosby, Alfred W.
   1973   *The Columbian Exchange*
           Westport Conn.: Greenwood Press
   1986   *Ecological Imperialism*
           New York: Cambridge University Press
Culbert, T. Patrick, ed.
   1973   *The Classic Maya Collapse*
           Albuquerque: University of New Mexico Press
De Vos, Jan
   1980   *La Paz de Dios y del Rey*
           San Cristóbal de Las Casas, Chiapas:
           Colección Ceiba
   1985   *La Batalla del Sumidero*
           México DF: Editorial Katún
Díaz, Bernal
   1963   *The Conquest of New Spain*
   [c. 1575]   (J. M. Cohen, trans.)
           Harmondsworth: Penguin Books
Dobson, Narda
   1973   *A History of Belize*
           London: Longman Caribbean
Dzul Poot, Domingo
   1985   *Cuentos Mayas*
           Mérida, Yucatán: Maldonado Editores

Edmonson, Munro S., trans.

1982 *The Ancient Future of the Itzá: The Book of Chilam Balam of Tizimín*
Austin: University of Texas Press

1986 *Heaven Born Mérida and Its Destiny: The Book of Chilam Balam of Chumayel*
Austin: University of Texas Press

Ekholm, Susanna M.

1979 "The Lagartero Figurines"
in Hammond and Willey, eds. 1979:172–186

Fagen, Richard R., and Olga Pellicer, eds.

1983 *The Future of Central America: Policy Choices for the U.S. and Mexico*
Stanford: Stanford University Press

Falla, Ricardo

1984 "We Charge Genocide"
in Jonas, McCaughan, and Sutherland, eds. 1984:112–19

Farriss, Nancy M.

1984 *Maya Society Under Colonial Rule: The Collective Enterprise of Survival*
Princeton: Princeton University Press

Folan, William J., Ellen R. Kintz, and Laraine A. Fletcher

1983 *Cobá, A Classic Maya Metropolis*
New York and London: Academic Press

Fox, John

1978 *Quiché Conquest*
Albuquerque: University of New Mexico Press

Fuentes, Carlos

1985 *Latin America at War with the Past*
Toronto: CBC Enterprises

Gage, Thomas

1928 *The English-American*
[1648] London: Routledge

Gallenkamp, Charles

1985 *Maya: The Riddle and Rediscovery of a Lost Civilization*
New York: Viking

Gallenkamp, Charles, and Regina Elise Johnson, eds.

1985 *Maya: Treasures of an Ancient Civilization*
Albuquerque: The Albuquerque Museum

Gann, Thomas

1925 *Mystery Cities: Exploration and Adventure in Lubaantun*
London: Duckworth

1926   *Ancient Cities and Modern Tribes*
        London: Duckworth
Gates, William
    1978   *An Outline Dictionary of Maya Glyphs*
            New York: Dover Publications
Gerhard, Peter
    1979   *The Southeast Frontier of New Spain*
            Princeton: Princeton University Press
Goldman, Francisco
    1986   "Guatemalan Death Masque: pomp and terror in a dark
            country"
            Harper's, January:56–63
Gómara, Francisco López de
    1964   *Cortés: The Life of the Conqueror by His Secretary*
            (Lesley Byrd Simpson, trans. and ed.)
            Berkeley: University of California Press
Gossen, Gary H.
    1974   *Chamulas in the World of the Sun*
            Cambridge, Mass.: Harvard University Press
Graham, Elizabeth, Grant D. Jones, and Robert R. Kautz
    1985   "Archaeology and Ethnohistory on a Spanish Colonial
            Frontier: The Macal-Tipu Project in Western Belize"
            in Chase and Rice, eds. 1985:206–14
Graham, Ian, ed.
    1975   *Corpus of Maya Hieroglyphic Inscriptions*, vol. 1: "Intro-
            duction"
            Harvard University: Peabody Museum of Archaeology
            and Ethnology
    1979   *Corpus of Maya Hieroglyphic Inscriptions*, vol. 3, pt 2:
            "Yaxchilan"
            Harvard University: Peabody Museum of Archaeology
            and Ethnology
    1982   *Corpus of Maya Hieroglyphic Inscriptions*, vol. 3, pt 3:
            "Yaxchilan"
            Harvard University: Peabody Museum of Archaeology
            and Ethnology
Greene, Graham
    1939   *The Lawless Roads*
            London: Longmans, Green, and Co.
Greene Robertson, Merle
    1980a   "The Giles G. Healey 1946 Bonampak Photographs"
            in Greene, ed. 1980:3–44

Greene Robertson, Merle, ed.
  1974 *Primera Mesa Redonda de Palenque, Parts 1 and 2*
        Pebble Beach, Calif.: The Robert Louis Stevenson
        School
  1980b *Third Palenque Round Table, 1978 Part 2*
        Austin: University of Texas Press
  1983 *The Sculpture of Palenque*, vol. 1
        Princeton: Princeton University Press
Greene, Merle, and J. Eric S. Thompson
  1967 *Ancient Maya Relief Sculpture*
        New York: Museum of Primitive Art
Gregory, James R.
  1984 *The Mopan: Culture and Ethnicity in a Changing Beli-
        zean Community*
        Columbia: University of Missouri Press
Hammond, Norman
  1974 ed. *Mesoamerican Archaeology: New Approaches*
        London: Duckworth
  1982 *Ancient Maya Civilization*
        Cambridge: Cambridge University Press
Hammond, Norman, and Gordon R. Willey, eds.
  1979 *Maya Archaeology and Ethnohistory*
        Austin: University of Texas Press
Handy, Jim
  1984 *Gift of the Devil: A History of Guatemala*
        Toronto: Between the Lines Press
Harris, A., and M. Sartor, eds.
  1984 *Gertrude Blom Bearing Witness*
        Wilmington: North Carolina University Press
Harrison, Peter D.
  1979 "The Lobil Postclassic Phase in the Southern Interior of
        the Yucatán Peninsula"
        in Hammond and Willey, eds. 1979:189–207
Harrison, Peter D., and B. L. Turner II, eds.
  1978 *Pre-Hispanic Maya Agriculture*
        Albuquerque: University of New Mexico Press
Haviland, John Beard
  1977 *Gossip, Reputation, and Knowledge in Zinacantán*
        Chicago: University of Chicago Press
Hawkins, John
  1984 *Inverse Images*
        Albuquerque: University of New Mexico Press

Henderson, John S.
1981   *The World of the Ancient Maya*
        Ithaca: Cornell University Press
Heyden, Doris
1975   "An Interpretation of the Cave Underneath the Pyramid of
        the Sun in Teotihuacan, Mexico"
        American Antiquity 40:131–47
Humphreys, R. A.
1961   *The Diplomatic History of British Honduras 1638–1901*
        London and New York: Oxford University Press
Hunter, C. Bruce
1974   *A Guide to Ancient Maya Ruins*
        Norman: University of Oklahoma Press
Huxley, Aldous
1984   *Beyond the Mexique Bay*
        London: Triad/Paladin (1st ed. 1934)
Jonas, Susanne, Ed McCaughan, and Elizabeth Sutherland, eds.
1984   *Guatemala: Tyranny on Trial*
        San Francisco: Synthesis Publications
Jones, Grant D.
1974   "Revolution and Continuity in a Santa Cruz Maya So-
        ciety"
        American Ethnologist, vol. 1, no. 4:659–84
1977   ed. *Anthropology and History in Yucatán*
        Austin: University of Texas Press
1984   "Maya-Spanish Relations in Sixteenth-Century Belize"
        Belcast Journal of Belizean Affairs, vol. 1, no. 1:28–40
Jones, Grant D., Robert R. Kautz, and Elizabeth Graham
1986   "Tipu: A Maya Town on the Spanish Colonial Frontier"
        Archaeology, Jan–Feb:38–47
Kaufman, Wallace, ed.
1984   *The Voice of the Maya*
        Carrboro, N.C.: Signal Books
Kelley, David H.
1962   "Glyphic Evidence for a Dynastic Sequence at Quiriguá,
        Guatemala"
        American Antiquity, vol. 27, no. 3:323–35
1974   "Eurasian Evidence and the Mayan Calendar Correlation
        Problem"
        in Hammond, ed. 1974:135–43
1976   *Deciphering the Maya Script*
        Austin: University of Texas Press

1983   "The Maya Calendar Correlation Problem"
        in Leventhal and Kolata, eds. 1983:157–208

Kinglake, A. W.
1982   *Eothen*
        London: Century

La Farge, Oliver
1947   *Santa Eulalia: The Religion of a Cuchumatán Indian Town*
        Chicago: University of Chicago Press

La Farge, Oliver, and Douglas Byers
1931   *The Year Bearer's People*
        New Orleans: Tulane University Press

Lafaye, Jacques
1976   *Quetzalcóatl and Guadalupe: The Formation of Mexican National Consciousness 1531–1813*
        Chicago: University of Chicago Press

LaFeber, Walter
1983   *Inevitable Revolutions: The United States in Central America*
        New York: W. W. Norton

Landa, Diego de
1978   *Yucatán Before and After the Conquest*
        (William Gates, trans. and ed.)
        New York: Dover Publications (reprint of 1937 edition)
1982   *Relación de las Cosas de Yucatán*
[1566]   México DF: Editorial Porrúa

Las Casas, Bartolomé de
1984   *Brevísima Relación de la Destrucción de las Indias*
[1552]   México DF: Editorial Fontamara

Laughlin, Robert
1975   *The Great Tzotzil Dictionary of San Lorenzo Zinacantán*
        Washington: Smithsonian (Contributions to Anthropology #19)

Lawrence, D. H.
1961   *The Plumed Serpent*
        Harmondsworth: Penguin Books (1st ed. 1926)

León-Portilla, Miguel
1962   *The Broken Spears*
        London: Constable
1973   *Time and Reality in the Thought of the Maya*
        Boston: Beacon Press (Spanish ed. 1968, UNAM)

1980 *El Reverso de la Conquista*
México DF: Editorial Joaquín Mortiz (7th ed.)

Leventhal, Richard M., and Alan L. Kolata
1983 *Civilization in the Ancient Americas*
Cambridge, Mass.: University of New Mexico Press and Peabody Museum, Harvard

Lincoln, Charles E.
1985 "The Chronology of Chichén Itzá: A Review of the Literature"
in Sabloff and Andrews, eds. 1985:141–96

Llorente, J. A.
1984 "Vida de Fray Bartolomé de Las Casas, Obispo de Chiapa, en América"
in Las Casas 1984:123–200

López de Cogolludo, Diego
1971 *Los Tres Siglos de la Dominación Española en Yucatán, o sea Historia de Esta Provincia*
[1688] Graz, Austria: Academische Druck (reprint)

Loten, H. Stanley
1985 "Lamanai Postclassic"
in Chase and Rice, eds. 1985:85–90

Lothrop, S. K.
1924 *Tulum: An Archaeological Study of the East Coast of Yucatán*
Washington D.C.: CIW Publication 335

Lounsbury, Floyd G.
1980 "Some Problems in the Interpretation of the Mythological Portion of the Hieroglyphic Text of the Temple of the Cross at Palenque"
in Greene, ed. 1980:99–115

Lovell, W. George
1985 *Conquest and Survival in Colonial Guatemala*
Montreal: McGill-Queen's University Press
1986 "Rethinking Conquest: The Colonial Experience in Latin America"
Journal of Historical Geography, vol. 12, no. 3:310–17
1988 "Surviving Conquest: The Maya of Guatemala in Historical Perspective"
Latin American Research Review, vol. 23, no. 2:25–57

430   BIBLIOGRAPHY

Lowe, John W. G.
1985   *The Dynamics of Apocalypse: A Systems Simulation of the Classic Maya Collapse*
Albuquerque: University of New Mexico Press

Luján Muñoz, Jorge, ed.
1982   *Historia y Antropología de Guatemala*
Guatemala: Universided de San Carlos

Luna, Leonel
1982   "El Racismo y la Revolución Guatemalteca"
Polémica, no. 3:47–55

Mace, Carroll Edward
1970   *Two Spanish-Quiché Dance-Dramas of Rabinal*
New Orleans: Tulane University

Machlin, Milt, & Bob Marx
1971   "First Visit to Three Forbidden Cities"
Argosy 372 (May):18–29

MacLeod, Murdo, and Robert Wasserstrom, eds.
1983   *Spaniards and Indians in Southeastern Mesoamerica*
Lincoln: University of Nebraska Press

Marcus, Joyce
1976   *Emblem and State in the Classic Maya Lowlands*
Washington: Dumbarton Oaks, Harvard University

Martínez Peláez, Severo
1971   *La Patria del Criollo*
San José, Costa Rica: Editorial Universitaria Centroamericana
1982   "Los Pueblos Indígenas y el Proceso Revolucionario"
Polémica, no. 3:47–56

Maslow, Jonathan Evan
1986   *Bird of Life, Bird of Death*
New York: Simon and Schuster

Mathews, Peter
1980   "Notes on the Dynastic Sequence of Bonampak, Part 1."
in Greene, ed. 1980:60–73
1984   ed. *Corpus of Maya Hieroglyphic Inscriptions*, vol. 6, pt. 1: "Toniná"
Cambridge, Mass.: Peabody Museum, Harvard University Press

Mathews, Peter, and Linda Schele
1974   "Lords of Palenque—The Glyphic Evidence"
in Greene, ed. 1974, *Pt. 1*:63–75

McClintock, Michael
  1985 *The American Connection: State Terror and Popular Resistance in Guatemala*
        London: Zed Books
Means, Philip Ainsworth
  1917 "History of the Spanish Conquest of Yucatan and of the Itzas"
        Cambridge, Mass.: Papers of the Peabody Museum of American Archaeology and Ethnology, vol. 7
Mediz Bolio, Antonio
  1983 *La Tierra del Faisán y del Venado*
        Mérida, Yucatán: Ediciones Dante
Mendelson, E. Michael
  1965 *Los Escándalos de Maximón*
        Guatemala: Ministerio de Educación
Menchú, Rigoberta
  1984 *I, Rigoberta Menchú*
        (Elizabeth Burgos, ed., Ann Wright, trans.)
        London: Verso
  1985 *Me Llamo Rigoberta Menchú y Así Me Nació la Conciencia*
        (Elizabeth Burgos, ed.)
        México DF: Siglo XXI
Miller, Arthur G.
  1979 "Religious Syncretism in Colonial Yucatán: The Archaeological and Ethnohistorical Evidence from Tancah, Quintana Roo"
        in Hammond and Willey, eds. 1979:223–240
  1985 "From the Maya Margins: Images of Postclassic Power Politics"
        in Sabloff and Andrews, eds. 1985:199–222
Miller, Mary Ellen
  1986 *The Murals of Bonampak*
        Princeton: Princeton University Press
Mondragón, Rafael
  1983 *De Indios y Cristianos en Guatemala*
        México DF: Copec
Montejo, Victor Dionicio
  1984 *El Kanil, Man of Lightning*
        (Wallace Kaufman, trans.)
        Carrboro, N.C.: Signal Books

Morley, Sylvanus G., and George W. Brainerd; rev. by Robert J. Sharer
    1983   *The Ancient Maya*
           Stanford: Stanford University Press
Morris, Walter
    1984   *A Millennium of Weaving in Chiapas*
           San Cristóbal de Las Casas, México: Walter Morris
    1987   *Living Maya*
           New York: Harry N. Abrams
Nairn, Allan
    1983   "The Guns of Guatemala: the merciless mission of Ríos
           Montt's army"
           The New Republic 188. 14:17–21
Nairn, Allan, and Jean-Marie Simon
    1986   "Bureaucracy of Death"
           The New Republic, 194. 26:13–17
Nash, Manning
    1967   *Machine Age Maya*
           Chicago: University of Chicago Press
Navarrete, Carlos
    1982a "Otra Vez Modesto Méndez, Ambrosio Tut, y el Mod-
           erno Descubrimiento de Tikal"
           in Luján, ed. 1982:155–70
    1982b *San Pascualito Rey y el Culto a la Muerte en Chiapas*
           México DF: Universidad Nacional Autónoma de México
Oakes, Maud
    1951a *The Two Crosses of Todos Santos: Survivals of Mayan
           Religious Rituals*
           New York: Pantheon Books
    1951b *Beyond the Windy Place: Life in the Guatemalan High-
           lands*
           New York: Farrar, Straus and Young
Painter, James
    1987   *Guatemala: False Hope, False Freedom*
           London: Catholic Institute for International Relations
Payeras, Mario
    1983   *Days of the Jungle*
           New York: Monthly Review Press
Paz, Octavio
    1988   "The Telltale Mirror" in *Lives on the Line*
           (Doris Meyer, ed.)
           Berkeley: University of California Press

Pearce, Kenneth
    1984   *The View from the Top of the Temple*
            Albuquerque: University of New Mexico Press
Peissel, Michel
    1963   *The Lost World of Quintana Roo*
            New York: E. P. Dutton and Co.
Pendergast, David M.
    1967   ed. *Palenque: The Walker–Caddy Expedition to the
            Ancient Maya City, 1839–1840*
            Norman: University of Oklahoma Press
    1985a   "Lamanai, Belize: An Updated View"
            in Chase and Rice, eds. 1985:91–103
    1985b   "Stability Through Change: Lamanai, Belize, from the
            Ninth to the Seventeenth Century"
            in Sabloff and Andrews, eds. 1985:223–49
Perera, Victor
    1986a   *Rites: A Guatemalan Boyhood*
            New York: Harcourt Brace Jovanovich
    1986b   "Chan K'in: The Last Days of a Maya Storyteller"
            (manuscript)
Perera, Victor, and Robert D. Bruce
    1982   *The Last Lords of Palenque: the Lacandón Mayas of the
            Mexican Rain Forest*
            Boston and Toronto: Little, Brown and Co.
Pozas, Ricardo
    1962   *Juan the Chamula*
            Berkeley: University of California Press (4th printing
            1971)
Price, Christine, and Gertrude Duby Blom
    1972   *A Portrait of the Lacandón Indians*
            New York: Charles Scribner's Sons
Proskouriakoff, Tatiana
    1960   "Historical Implications of a Pattern of Dates at Piedras
            Negras"
            American Antiquity 25:454–75
    1963   *An Album of Maya Architecture*
            Norman: University of Oklahoma Press (new ed.)
Puleston, D. E.
    1979   "An Epistemological Pathology and the Collapse, or Why
            the Maya Kept the Short Count"
            in Hammond and Willey, eds. 1979:63–71

1983 *The Settlement Survey of Tikal*
University Museum, University of Pennsylvania Tikal Report 13

Quirarte, Jacinto
1979 "The Representation of Underworld Processions in Maya Vase Painting: An Iconographic Study"
in Hammond and Willey, eds. 1979:116–148

Recinos, Adrián, trans.
1980 *Memorial de Sololá, Anales de los Cakchiqueles*
Guatemala: Editorial Piedra Santa

Recinos, Adrián, Delia Goetz, and Dionisio José Chonay, trans.
1953 *The Annals of the Cakchiquels*
Norman: University of Oklahoma Press

Redfield, Robert
1941 *The Folk Culture of Yucatán*
Chicago: University of Chicago Press

Reed, Nelson
1964 *The Caste War of Yucatán*
Stanford, Calif.: Stanford University Press

Robicsek, Francis
1978 *The Smoking Gods*
Norman: University of Oklahoma Press
1981 *The Maya Book of the Dead*
Charlottesville: University of Virginia Art Museum

Roys, Ralph L.
1967 *The Book of Chilam Balam of Chumayel*
Norman: University of Oklahoma Press
1972 *The Indian Background of Colonial Yucatán*
Norman: University of Oklahoma Press (new ed.; orig. 1943)

Rus, Jan
1983 "Whose Caste War? Indians, Ladinos, and the Chiapas 'Caste War' of 1869"
in MacLeod and Wasserstrom, eds. 1983:127–168

Rus, Jan, and Robert Wasserstrom
1980 "Civil-Religious Hierarchies in Central Chiapas: A Critical Perspective"
American Ethnologist, vol. 7 no. 3:466–78

Rushdie, Salman
1987 *The Jaguar Smile*
New York: Viking

Sabloff, Jeremy A., and E. Wyllys Andrews V, eds.
    1985   *Late Lowland Maya Civilization: Classic to Postclassic*
           Albuquerque: University of New Mexico Press
Sánchez, George I.
    1961   *Arithmetic in Maya*
           Austin, Tex.: George Sánchez
Schele, Linda
    1982   *Maya Glyphs: The Verbs*
           Austin: University of Texas Press
Schele, Linda, and Mary Ellen Miller
    1986   *The Blood of Kings*
           New York: George Braziller, Inc.
Schlesinger, Stephen, and Stephen Kinzer
    1983   *Bitter Fruit: The Untold Story of the American Coup in
           Guatemala*
           New York: Doubleday/Anchor Press
Scholes, France V., and Ralph L. Roys
    1968   *The Maya-Chontal Indians of Acalán-Tixchel*
           Norman: University of Oklahoma Press (new ed.)
Sexton, James D., trans. and ed.
    1981   *Son of Tecún Umán, A Maya Indian Tells His Life Story*
           Tucson: University of Arizona Press
    1985   *Campesino, The Diary of a Guatemalan Indian*
           Tucson: University of Arizona Press
Shane, D. R.
    1985   *Hoofprints on the Forest: Cattle Ranching and the
           Destruction of Latin America's Tropical Forests*
           London: Institute for the Study of Human Issues
Sharer, Robert J.
    1980   "The Quiriguá Project, 1974–1979"
           Expedition 23(1):5–10
    1985   "Terminal Events in the Southeastern Lowlands: A View
           from Quiriguá"
           in Chase and Rice, eds. 1985:245–53
Stephens, John L.
    1841   *Incidents of Travel in Central America, Chiapas, and
           Yucatán*, vols. 1 and 2
           London: John Murray
    1963   *Incidents of Travel in Yucatán*, vols. 1 and 2
           New York: Dover (reprint of 1843 ed.)
Stuart, George E., and Gene S. Stuart

1985 *The Mysterious Maya*
Washington, D.C.: National Geographic Society (3d printing)

Tedlock, Barbara
1982 *Time and the Highland Maya*
Albuquerque: University of New Mexico Press

Tedlock, Dennis, trans.
1985 *Popol Vuh*
New York: Simon and Schuster

Thompson, J. Eric
1930 *Ethnology of the Mayas of Southern and Central British Honduras*
Chicago: Field Museum of Natural History (Anthropological Series, vol. 17, no. 2)
1950 *Maya Hieroglyphic Writing*
Washington, D.C.: Carnegie Institution (Publication 589)
1962 *A Catalog of Maya Hieroglyphs*
Norman: University of Oklahoma Press
1963 *Maya Archaeologist*
Norman: University of Oklahoma Press
1966 *The Rise and Fall of Maya Civilization*
Norman: University of Oklahoma Press (2d ed.)
1977 "A Proposal for Constituting a Maya Subgroup, Cultural and Linguistic, in the Petén and Adjacent Regions"
in Jones, ed. 1977:3–42

Todorov, Tzvetan
1984 *The Conquest of America*
New York: Harper and Row

Tozzer, Alfred M.
1907 *A Comparative Study of the Mayas and the Lacandones*
New York: Macmillan (AMS reprint, New York, 1978)

Trik, H. W., and M. E. Kampen
1983 *The Graffiti of Tikal*
Philadelphia: University Museum, University of Pennsylvania (Tikal Report 31)

Turner, B. L.
1974 "Prehistoric Intensive Agriculture in the Maya Lowlands"
Science, vol. 185:118–24

Turner, B. L., and Peter D. Harrison
1983 *Pulltrouser Swamp*
Austin: University of Texas Press

Varner, John G., and Jeannette Johnson Varner
  1983   *Dogs of the Conquest*
         Norman: University of Oklahoma Press
Villa Rojas, Alfonso
  1945   *The Maya of East Central Quintana Roo*
         Washington, D.C.: Carnegie Institution (Publication 559)
  1978   *Los Elegidos de Dios: Etnografía de los Mayas de Quin-*
         tana Roo
         México DF: Instituto Nacional Indígena (Serie de Antro-
         pología Social, Collección INI no. 56)
Vogt, Evon Z.
  1969   *Zinacantán*
         Cambridge, Mass.: Harvard University Press
Wachtel, Nathan
  1977   *The Vision of the Vanquished*
         Hassocks, Sussex: The Harvester Press (1st ed., in French,
         1971)
Warren, Kay B.
  1978   *The Symbolism of Subordination: Indian Identity in a*
         Guatemalan Town
         Austin: University of Texas Press
Wasserstrom, Robert
  1978   "A Caste War That Never Was: the Tzeltal Conspiracy of
         1848"
         Peasant Studies, vol. 7, no. 2:73–85
  1983   *Class and Society in Central Chiapas*
         Berkeley: University of California Press
Wilk, Richard R.
  1985   "History and Mayan Ethnicity in Belize"
         Belcast Journal of Belizean Affairs, vol. 2, no. 1:12–16
Willey, Gordon R.
  1977   "The Rise of Maya Civilization: A Summary View"
         in Adams, ed. 1977:383–423
Woodward, Ralph Lee, Jr.
  1985   *Central America: A Nation Divided*
         Oxford and New York: Oxford University Press
Wright, Ronald
  1985   "The Lamanai Enigma"
         Equinox no. 24:28–43
Young, Colville
  1980   *Creole Proverbs of Belize*
         Belize City: Angelus Press

Index

Academy of the Maya Language, 363–364

Acul, 237–242

agriculture, 11, 27, 54, 133, 137, 150, 238, 367–368, 388

Agua Azul, 293

Ahau (Lord), 28, 34, 35, 76–77, 148

Ah Cacau, King, 95, 96, 115, 298

Ahpo-Hel, Lady, 300

Aké Itzá, Don Jacinto, 389–390

alautun, 91

Alfredo (Mexican), 280–283

alienation, 55–56, 117, 195–196

Alta Verapaz, 256

Alvarado, Gonzalo de, 219

Alvarado, Pedro de, 64, 87, 104, 151–155, 168–169, 173, 176

K'umarcaah and, 202–203, 204, 219

American Wycliffe Bible Translators (Summer Institute of Linguistics), 308, 357–358

Americas Watch, 229

Ancient Maya, The (Morley), 28, 33

Anglican Church, 26–27

Annals of the Cakchiquels, 104, 138, 151–152, 166

Antigua, 104–105, 108, 165, 172–173

Arabs, 29, 362

Arana Osorio, Colonel, 74, 127, 160, 235, 240

Arbenz, Jacobo, 125, 132–136, 161, 170, 180, 221

Arcadio, Don, 243–250

arches, in Palenque, 297

architecture, 163

  in Belize City, 26

  in Belmopan, 36

in Chichén Itzá, 340, 342, 343–344

in Palenque, 294–295, 297–301

Puuc-style, 347–349

in San Cristóbal de las Casas, 268–269

in Tulum, 335

see also churches; houses; palaces; pyramids; stelae

Arenas Barrera, Luis, 236

Arévalo, Juan José, 125, 130–132, 134, 160

Argosy, 390

arithmetic, 29, 91, 95

Armando (guide), 231–232, 243

army, Guatemalan, 64–67, 85, 116, 121, 150, 160, 162, 174, 175, 220–221, 223, 226

  in Acul, 238–242

  age of, 41

  Arbenz and, 135–136

  Arévalo and, 131–132

  in Flores, 71–72, 74

  Indian identity eroded by, 195–196

  Ladinoization of, 125, 126

  in Nebaj, 228, 230, 235–236, 237

  Spanish embassy protest and, 109–110

  in Uspantán, 253–254

art, 96, 99, 166

  see also paintings; sculpture

astronomy, 28–29, 90–91, 95, 296

Asturias, Miguel Angel, 146, 147, 175

Atitlán, Lake, 174–176, 181

Avendaño, Andrés de, 82, 346

Ay, Manuel, 339, 366

Aztecs, 11, 37, 54, 97, 283

  calendar of, 106, 107

Aztecs, (*Cont.*)
 conquest of, 12, 78, 79, 82, 137, 165, 265
 diseases and, 138
 gods of, 201, 273
 Quichés and, 167–168
 Spaniards compared with, 273

Babylonians, 29
Baer, Philip, 308
baktuns, 29, 33, 34, 76, 91, 342, 343, 400
Balam Na (Jaguar House), 376–378, 381–385
ballcourt, in Chichén Itzá, 340, 342
Ballplayer, the, 146
Baluartes, 330–331
Barbachano, Miguel, 366–368, 376
bargaining, 98–99
Barrera Vásquez, Alfredo, 363
Barrios, Justo Rufino, 125–126, 178, 217
Bastarrachea Manzano, Juan, 363
batabs, 339, 352, 366, 368
Bautista Vega, Juan, 390
Baymen, 24
Beleheb Tz'i, 197, 202–203
Belehé Qat, King, 170
Belize (formerly British Honduras), 6, 15, 17–57, 81
 El Salvador compared with, 14
 ethnic distribution in, 27
 frontiersmen and fugitives in, 49
 Guatemala and, 21, 47, 49, 61–62, 157
 Maya cities abandoned in, 9
 names in, 21, 27, 30
 origin of name, 24
 refugees in, 13–14, 21–22
 see also specific cities
"Belize Breeze" ("bush"), 22
Belize City, 7, 22–31, 33, 69
Belmopan, 32–38
Benque Viejo, 49, 50, 56
Berlin, Heinrich, 89
Beyond the Mexique Bay (Huxley), 70
bilingualism, 255, 279, 281, 339, 363
Bird of Life, Bird of Death (Maslow), 112
Blatherwycke, Myron, 107–109, 227, 230
Bliss, Baron, 27
Bliss Institute, 27–30
Blom, Frans, 302
Blom, Trudi, 302, 320, 321
blue, Maya, 52
Bobbie (English woman), 50–51, 52
Bolivia, 37, 129, 134
Bonampak, 303, 304, 307, 310–316

Bravo, Ignacio, 375, 383, 384, 385
Brazil, 129
British Honduras, 24, 49, 62, 392
 see also Belize
Brol, Enrique, 236, 237
Brotherston, Gordon, 249–250
Bruce, Robert, 301, 307, 309, 318, 320, 323, 324
"bullfights," 393–394
Burkitt, Robert, 235
Burns, Alan, 396
bus travel:
 in Belize, 19–23, 31–32
 in Guatemala, 63–68, 71, 85, 259–260
 in Mexico, 263, 330
butterflies, 50–52

Caamal, Francisco, 365
Caddy, John, 68–70, 75, 83
Cakchiquel Maya, 104, 148, 151–153, 165–170, 174–176, 206
 language of, 206, 212
calendar, Maya, 5, 12, 28–30, 33–35, 90–91, 93, 94, 151, 197–199, 214–215, 271–272, 361–362
 baktuns and, 29, 33, 34, 76, 91, 342, 343, 400
 Short Count and, 76, 96, 107, 338
 at Xunantunich, 52, 53
 see also daykeepers; Long Count; *tzolkin*; Year-Bearers
Calendar of Mundo, 179
Calendar Round, 106–107, 272, 299, 342, 361
Cambridge University's Museum of Archaeology and Ethnology, 139, 142–144
Campeche, 77, 81, 267–268, 329–331
Campeche, state of, 371
camping, in Palenque, 295–296
Canada, Guatemalan refugees in, 108–109
canals, 54
Cancún, 274, 333–334, 355
Can Ek, King, 62, 79–83
Canek, Prince, 350
cannibalism, 67
Cantel, 126
Canul, Marcus, 7
capitalism, 128–129, 133, 255
Caracol observatory, 340, 342
Caracol, stelae, 28–30, 38
Cárdenas, Lázaro, 281
Carlos (Guatemalan), 119–21, 245
Carpentier, Alejo, 187
Carpio Nicolle, Jorge, 159–161, 290

Carrera, Rafael, 70–71, 125, 126, 217, 221
Carrillo Puerto (formerly Chan Santa Cruz; Noh Cah Santa Cruz), 370–371
cars, 111–112, 124, 164
Carter, Jimmy, 132, 353, 354
Caste War, 6, 15, 21, 48, 287, 336, 337, 339, 355, 364–372, 379
Caste War of Yucatán, The (Reed), 379
Castillo, in Chichén Itzá, 340, 342, 343
Castillo Armas, Carlos, 134–136, 160, 170–171
Caterina (Tzeltal Maya), 276
Catherwood, Frederick, 69, 139, 156, 200, 234, 344
Catholic Action, 178–180, 191, 221, 226, 244, 287
Catholic Church:
  conversion to, 79–82, 178, 265, 293, 338, 345
  in Guatemala, 68, 79–82, 173, 178, 202, 245
  heresy vs. sanctity and, 293
  in Mexico, 266–268, 282, 287, 293, 351–353, 376–380, 394–395
  see also priests
cattle, 86, 134
Cauac Sky, King, 140, 141, 142, 144
Cayo District, 39–46
ceiba (world-tree), 12, 46, 79, 259, 270, 293, 393–394
cenotes, 340–341
center-periphery dichotomy, 145–146
Central American federation, 62, 70, 217, 273
Central Intelligence Agency (CIA), 27, 63, 74, 129, 132, 134–135, 171, 282
Cerezo, Vinicio, 159–161, 248, 290
Chaa Creek, 40–41, 46, 47
Chaan Muan, 315, 316
Chac (god), 79
Chac, King, 348
Chac-Mool, 342, 343–344
Chajul, 251
Champotón, 330
Chamula Center, 282, 285–289
Chamulas, 264, 278–281, 283, 285–289
  monkey dance of, 271–272
Chamula township, 280–283
Chan Bahlum, King, 299–300
Chan Bor, 311
Chan Cah Veracruz, 385
Chancalá, 318, 325
Chan Chin, 388
Chan K'in, 309, 310, 317, 319

Chan K'in, Old, 302, 309–310, 320, 322–324
Chan Santa Cruz, see Carrillo Puerto
Chetumal, 45, 371, 374
Chi, Cecilio, 339, 366–369, 380
Chiapas, 6, 15, 217, 258, 261–325
  Guatemala and, 264, 273
  land ownership in, 280–281, 306
  see also specific towns and cities
Chicbal, Basilio, 175–176
Chichén Itzá, 77, 334, 335, 338, 340–344
  Maya vs. Toltec styles in, 342
Chichicastenango, 108, 181–196, 212
  Santa Cruz del Quiché compared with, 195, 196
Chichupac, 220
Chilam Balam, books of, 75–78, 83, 96, 138–139, 186, 249–250, 339, 341, 342, 345, 358–361, 365, 375, 390
Chimaltenango, 175
Chinese, 115
chingar, 269
Chinic, Apolinario, 193
Chitam, King, 96, 99–100
Chixoy, 234, 256
Chol language, 297
Chol Maya, 295
Chontal Maya, 79, 333–334
Christian Democrats, Guatemalan, 159–160, 248
Christianity, 35, 44, 45
  Maya acceptance of, 12, 61, 79–81, 83, 286, 360
  Maya religion compared with, 201–202
  see also Catholic Church; fundamentalists; missionaries; priests; Protestants
chuchkahau (mother-fathers), 185
Chunpom, 385
churches, 26–27, 75, 147
  in Carrillo Puerto, 376–378, 381–382, 383
  in Chamula Center, 288–289
  in Chichicastenango, 185, 191–192
  fundamentalist, 67–68
  in Izamal, 345
  in San Andrés, 386
  in Santiago Atitlán, 177, 178
  in Tihosuco, 370, 371
  in X-Cacal Guardia, 380, 391, 393–397, 399
  Zincantán, 284
Churchill, Sir Winston, 132
Ciudad Vieja, 104

Classic period, 12, 13, 52, 94, 177, 233, 297, 336, 338, 341
  collapse of, 9, 34, 53–54, 86, 141, 300, 334, 341, 342, 343
  late, 9, 53, 75, 97
  paintings of, 311–315
  political structure in, 89–90
class structure:
  cars and, 111–112
  in Guatemala, 120, 125
  in Mexico, 273, 281
  upper, 13, 54, 82–83, 95–96, 125, 273
clothes:
  in Guatemala, 64, 98, 105, 107, 127, 147, 174, 176, 177, 182, 184, 192, 223, 224, 229
  in Mexico, 264, 275, 277, 284, 285, 332–333
Cobá, 91, 334, 336–339
Coca-Cola, 127
  ritual use of, 288–289
Coe, Michael, 12
coffee, 113, 126, 129, 375
cofradías (brotherhoods), 178–180, 191–194, 243
Coggins, Clemency, 96, 342–343
collecting, 114–115
colonialism, internal, 118
Columbus, Christopher, 6, 264
Comalapa, 152–153, 170
COMAR (Mexican commission for refugees), 331
Comiskey, Ray, 377–380, 385–387, 391, 394, 395
communism, 275
  in Guatemala, 66–67, 121, 131, 132, 134, 136, 171, 237
Congress, U.S., 121, 132
Conquest Dance, 153–154
Copán, 13, 53, 100, 140, 141, 142, 177, 207
Córdoba, Hernández de, 330
corn, 238, 367–368, 375
Corozal Town, 7, 9, 19
Cortés, Hernán, 78–80, 82, 106, 168, 330
Costa Rica, 70, 171
costumbristas, 203, 205–212, 246, 268
Council of the Indies, 265
Cozumel, 258, 331, 333–334, 375
Creoles, in Belize, 21, 27, 32, 37, 47–48, 98
criollos, 118, 125, 128, 129, 217, 330, 337
crosses, 12, 190, 225–226, 277, 285, 383, 388

  dressed in women's clothes, 48
  see also Speaking Cross, cult of
Crushton, 277
Cuauhtémoc, 78–79
CUC, see Peasant Unity Committee
Cuchumatanes, 222, 227–228, 229
cultural diversity, national unity vs., 117–118, 120
Curl Nose, King, 96
currency, Guatemalan, 112–113
Curuchich, Andrés, 148, 151, 152
Cuyamel Fruit, 130

dancing, 27, 271–272, 284–285
David (journalist friend), 163–169, 174–175, 189, 192–193, 210–212, 224, 226, 227–233, 239, 244, 248
  arrival of, 155–158
  chicken eating of, 257–258
  in K'umarcaah, 198, 199, 203–206, 210–11
  lateness of, 107, 109, 119, 124
  luck of, 156–157, 198
daykeepers, 156, 202, 205, 208–211, 215, 225, 246–249
  in Nebaj, 246
death squads in Guatemala, 66, 74, 109, 127, 132, 161, 171–172, 174, 230, 231
Declaration of Iximché, 169–170, 174
Decree Law 1995, Guatemalan, 159
Decree Law 1996, Guatemalan, 159
democracy, in Guatemala, 63, 66, 74, 113, 121, 130–131, 136
Díaz, Bernal, 330
Díaz, Porfirio, 129, 332
Diccioinario Cordemex, 364
Diego, Juan, 293
disease, 10, 137–139, 168, 374, 375, 384, 385
dogs, 256–257, 277–279
Dogs of War (film), 24
dollar, U.S., 112–113
Dresden Codex, 90–91
drugs, 22–23, 363
Dulles, Allen, 132–133, 134
Dulles, John Foster, 132–133, 134
dzul (foreigners), 49, 78, 339, 368
Dzul Poot, Domingo, 356–357, 363

Eamonn (Irishman), 25–26
earthquakes, 64, 264
  in Guatemala, 104–105, 148, 165, 172, 252
ecology, 54, 85–86, 97, 321, 324
economy, economics, 128–129

capitalism, 128–129, 133, 255
  Guatemalan, 112–113, 117, 121, 129,
    132, 133, 171, 255
  Maya, 54, 96
Edmonson, Munro, 338, 361
education, 55, 217, 252, 255, 286, 363
  see also literacy
EGP, see Guerrilla Army of the Poor
Egypt, ancient, Mesoamerican civiliza-
    tion compared with, 93–94
8 Monkey, 198–199, 214, 215, 216, 272
Eisenhower, Dwight D., 134
Eisenhower administration, 132–135
ejidos (collective homestead lands), 281,
    306
Ek, Ignacio, 5–7, 15, 394
Ek, Isidro, 394–395
Ek, Juan, 394
Ekholm, Susanna, 269–272, 277–279,
    283–284, 289, 291
El Chupadero, 274
El Cruce, 71, 85
elections:
  in Guatemala, 66, 74, 119, 130, 132,
    159–161, 197, 258, 290
  in Honduras, 107
electricity, 177, 240
Eliot, T. S., 76
Elizabeth (student), 277–278
Elizabeth, Queen of England, 351
El Progreso, 126
El Salvador, 116, 117, 121, 163
  Belize compared with, 14
  refugees from, 13, 14
English language, 279, 282–283
Escuintla, 259
Esquipulas, 135
Estrada Cabrera, Manuel, 130, 147, 197,
    217
evangelicals, see fundamentalists

Falklands War, 21
Fascism, 129, 161, 241
Fernando, Don (hardware store owner),
    378, 382–383
Finca Panama, 149–150
Fleming, Lucy, 40–41, 65, 105
Fleming, Mick, 40–42, 52, 105
Flores, 62, 71–85, 103
food:
  Guatemalan, 122, 182, 238
  Mexican, 122, 333
  see also agriculture; restaurants
Francis of Assisi, Saint, 293
Frank (American psychologist), 329–330
Fuensalida, Padre, 80–81

Fuentes, Carlos, 163
fundamentalists:
  in Guatemala, 67–68, 173
  in Mexico, 282, 286–287, 316, 379

G2 (military intelligence unit), 196
Gabriél, Don (folklorist), 361
Gann, Thomas, 50, 53, 314, 336
García, Lucas, 231, 240, 241
García Márquez, Gabriel, 257
Garifuna Settlement Day, 27
gasoline, 227–229, 237, 333
genocide, 117, 118, 129, 162, 254–255
George (fisherman), 41–46
God K, 300
gods of Mesoamerica, 199, 201–202
  see also specific gods
Goodman, Thomas, 34
Gospel Outreach, 68
Government House (Belize), 26, 392
Graham, Elizabeth, 44
Great Britain, British, 10, 37, 214—215,
    384, 397
  in Belize, 6, 21, 49, 50—51, 56, 366
    374
  in British Honduras, 24, 26–27, 49, 62
  in Santa Cruz and, 6–7, 374, 375, 392
Great Tzotzil Dictionary of San Lorenzo
  Zinacantán, The (Laughlin), 272
Greeks, ancient, 29, 91
Greene, Graham, 301, 314
Gregory XIII, Pope, 214
Grenada, 134, 135
Guadalupe Virgin, pilgrimage in honor
  of, 292–293
Guatemala, 6, 12, 47, 49, 61–260
  army in, see army, Guatemalan
  Belize and, 21, 47, 49, 61–62, 157
  Carrera revolution in, 70–71
  Catholic Church in, 68, 79–82, 173,
    178, 202, 245
  center-periphery dichotomy in, 145–
    146
  Chiapas and, 264, 273
  civil patrols in, 222–223, 224
  civil wars in, 13, 14–15, 30, 63–64,
    66–67, 68, 70–71, 120–121, 217,
    220–221, 226, 239, 252–254
  culture of, 116–117, 146–147, 183–
    184, 252–253, 399
  customs in, 62, 260
  death squads in, 66, 74, 109, 127, 132,
    161, 171–172, 174, 230, 231
  democracy in, 63, 66, 74, 113, 121,
    130–131, 136
  displaced persons in, 63, 64–65, 121

Guatemala, (*Cont.*)
economy of, 112–113, 117, 121, 129, 132, 133, 171, 255
elections in, 66, 74, 119, 130, 132, 159–161, 197, 258, 290
fundamentalists in, 67–68, 173
guerrillas in, *see* guerrillas, Guatemalan
highland, 101–260
killing of Indians in, 109–110, 126, 152–153, 162, 169–172, 174, 197, 212, 229, 254–255, 399
Ladinoization in, 116–117, 177, 183–184, 195–196, 229
Maya cities abandoned in, 9
Mexico compared with, 218, 291
"model villages" in, 45, 104, 237–242
as nightmare country, 63–64
origin of name, 104
origins of most recent cycle of violence in, 170–172
paper vs. real, 145
population distribution in, 116
Protestant-Right alliance in, 68
refugees from, 13, 14, 63, 108–109, 267–268
torture in, 67, 78, 220, 253–254
U.S. aid to, 72, 74, 121, 160, 171
see also Petén; Quiché; *specific cities*
Guatemala City, 62, 82, 84, 103–126, 136, 146–163, 258
history of, 104–105
national museum in, 115–16
National Palace in, 147, 217
nightlife in, 158
Sixth Avenue in, 105–106, 122
Guerrero, Gonzalo, 372
Guerrilla Army of the Poor (EGP), 226, 236–237
guerrillas, Guatemalan, 41, 64, 65, 74, 84, 85, 107, 149, 196, 221
in Acul, 239
"armies" of, 244
Indians and, 116, 171, 223, 226, 252, 254, 255
subversivos vs., 239
Guevara, Ernesto (Che), 136
guns, 50–51, 82–83, 330, 339, 368, 384

hamburger connection, 86
Hammarskjöld, Dag, 135
Healey, Giles, 311
Hernández Martinez, Maximiliano, 117
Hindus, 29, 201
hippies, 174, 236–237, 377
Hispaniola, 264

Hondo River, 384
Honduras, 14, 27, 70, 78, 79, 107, 121, 130
Operation Success and, 134, 135
horse, cult of, 79, 80
Hotel Chan Santa Cruz, 372
Hotel La Cañada, 303–305
Hotel Ruinas, 293, 303
Hotel Santo Tomás, 181–183
Hotel Zaculeu, 218
House of the Turtles, 348
houses, 48, 320
Maya, 10, 13, 22, 37, 244, 277, 332, 373
squatter, 13, 14
Huehuetenango, 108, 216–218, 239
army base in, 67
Huitzilopochtli, 201, 273
human rights, 132, 181
Hunahpu, 203, 204, 271
Hun Batz (One Spider Monkey), 271
Hun Chuen (One Howler Monkey), 271
Huxley, Aldous, 70, 126, 139, 141–142, 314

I, Rigoberta Menchú (Menchú), 254
Icaiché, 7, 8, 10, 49, 392
Icaiché, Mexico, 5–6
Iglesia Mazehual, 379
Incas, 12, 37, 137, 165, 265, 279, 360
myths and legends of, 48, 205
rebellions of, 83, 129, 216–217
Incidents of Travel in Central America, Chiapas, and Yucatan (Stephens), 69–70
Indian Church, *see* Lamanai
Indians:
genocide vs. cultural integration for, 117–118
Las Casas-Sepúlveda debate on, 265
modern vs. ancient, 37, 87
"reductions" of, 45
second conquest of, 128–129, 255
see also specific groups
industry, 126, 130–31, 132
infant mortality, 116, 171, 177
Inkarí, myth of, 205
intellectuals, Maya, 82, 91, 185–186
International Bank for Reconstruction and Development, 132
International Railways of Central America, 125
Israel, 72, 121, 196
Iturbide, 62
Itzá, 45, 62, 68, 75-83, 96, 307, 330, 334, 338–339

Itzamná (Lizard House, Hunab Ku), 93, 142, 176, 179, 186, 205, 345
Ixcán, 236
Ixchel, 314, 345
Ixchel Museum, 151–152
Ixil Maya, 109–110, 147, 229–238, 240–249, 251–252, 368
Ixil Triangle, 229, 236, 240
Iximché, 104, 165–172, 199, 218
Izabal, 74, 171
Izamal, 77, 344–347, 367
Iztayul, Juan, 211–212

Jade Sky, 141
Jaguar Inn, 87, 92
Jaguar Paw, King, 96, 98
"Jaguar Prophet," 75
James, Saint, 273
Janice (author's wife), 155, 157, 334-337, 340, 349, 350, 353, 354-355
Jenkins' Ear, War of (1739), 27
Jenny (upper-class Guatemalan), 148–151
Jim (American living in Guatemala City), 148–150
John Paul II, Pope, 267
Johnson, Samuel, 279
jokes:
    in Guatemala, 122–123, 125, 147, 174, 231
    Mexican, 292
Jones, Christopher, 99
Juárez, Benito, 7, 285, 376
Judaism, 202
Julian calendar, 29, 214–215

Kaibiles (Tigers), 66–67, 220, 231
Kaibil Balam (Double Jaguar), 219
Kaminalhuyú, 163
Kanjobal Maya, 235
Kan Xul, King, 300
Kashlan, Mikel, 287
katuns (Maya "decade"), 28, 29, 34, 53, 338, 365
    upheavals and, 76–77, 81–82, 83
Kayum One, 318–321
Kayum senior, 318–319
Kayum Two, 318, 320–323
Kekchí Maya, 126, 150, 235
Kelley, David, 95, 347
kidnappings, in Guatemala, 109–110, 237, 253–254
K'in García, 301–302, 319
Kinglake, Alexander, 343
Kinich Ahau, Sun-Eyed Lord, 5, 6
Knorosov, Yuri, 346–347

Koh I, 323
Koh II, 323
Koh III, 323
K'ucumatz, King, 167, 200
K'umarcaah (Utatlán), 168, 173, 188, 197–211, 218
    tunnel in, 203–211

labor, 129, 131, 132, 151, 159, 337, 339, 385
Lacandón, 301–304, 306–311, 316, 319–324
    northern vs. southern, 307, 308, 321
Lacanhá, 307, 308
Ladinoization:
    in Guatemala, 116–117, 177, 183–184, 195–196, 229
    mestizaje vs., 273
Ladinos, 21, 37
    in Guatemala, 37, 49, 70, 72, 99, 116–118, 122, 125, 126, 127, 129, 146–147, 171, 172, 177, 178, 182–184, 195–196, 197, 200, 213, 217, 225, 229, 233, 235–237, 242, 244, 252–256, 259
    in Mexico, 6, 263–264, 285–288, 337, 339, 366–367, 381
Lagartero, 270–272
Lamanai (Indian Church), 7–11, 13, 45, 49
    squatters in, 13–14
La Mano Blanca, 161, 171–172
Landa, Diego de, 283, 341, 344–347, 351–353, 358–359, 378
Land of the Phousant and the Deer (Mediz Bolio), 351
land ownership, 70, 85–86, 121, 126, 130, 131, 133, 150
    in Chiapas, 280–281, 306
    ejidos, 281, 306
    in highland Guatemala, 223–224, 226, 233, 235–236, 241–242, 253
    in Yucatán, 337
land reform, 86, 132–134, 170, 281
language, 167, 279
    bilingualism and, 255, 279, 281, 339, 363
    English, 279, 282–283
    Nahuatl, 173
    Quechua, 279, 361
    Spanish, 63, 184, 185, 279, 280, 363
languages, Maya, 12, 13, 14, 55, 75, 82, 116, 183–184, 390
    Cakchiquel, 206, 212
    Chol, 297
    Ixil, 246–247
    pronunciation of, 49, 52, 110

languages, Maya (*Cont.*)
  Quiché, 182–183, 185, 192, 197, 199, 206, 212, 246–247
  Tzeltal, 280, 282
  Tzotzil, 280, 282
  Yucatec, 78, 198–199, 246–247, 357–358
La Quema del Diablo (Burning of the Devil), 258
Las Casas, Bartolomé de, 126, 264–266
Las Margaritas, 274
Last Lords of Palenque, The (Perera and Bruce), 301, 318, 319–320, 324
late Preclassic period, 9
Latin America:
  capital penetration in, 128
  paper vs. real country in, 145
Laugerud, Kjell, 236
Laughlin, Robert, 272
Lawrence, D. H., 12, 277
legends and myths, Maya, 6, 48, 50, 55, 57, 78, 151, 310, 356–357
  K'umarcaah and, 202, 204–205
Len (concrete businessman), 303–308, 310–312, 316–319, 321, 324, 325
León-Portilla, Miguel, 248–249
Liberals, 49, 70, 71, 125–126, 221
life expectancy, 116
Lima, Byron Disrael, 196
literacy, 185–186, 196, 220–221
Lodge, Henry Cabot, 135
Long Count, 29–30, 33–34, 76, 96, 100, 106, 300, 336, 343
Looting, 114–115
Lucas García, Romeo, 236
Lynd, Norman, 149

McNatt, Logan, 36–37
mahogany, 321, 322, 324
Mali, 291–292
Malintzin, 154
Mam Maya, 67, 151, 217–222, 251, 375
Maní, 351–353, 367
Marcelino, Don, 393–394
Marcus, Joyce, 89–90
marimba, 183, 204
Marines, U.S., 107
markets, 24, 98–99, 285
Martínez Peláez, Severo, 183–184, 252–253, 255–256
Maryan (Chamula Maya), 280–282
Mask of Izamal, The (Catherwood), 344
masks, 38, 56, 153–154
Maslow, Jonathan Evan, 112
Massacre, The, 117
Mathews, Peter, 298, 311

Maudslay, Alfred, 139, 143
Mauricio (INAH epigrapher), 311
Maximón, 179–180
May, Francisco, 382, 383, 385
Maya:
  ancestors of, 11
  city-states of, 11–12, 49, 89
  collapse of, 9, 34, 53–54, 86
  conservatism of, 83
  cooperatives and community organizations of, 171–172, 236
  development of civilization of, 11
  disunity of, 11–12, 49, 165, 217, 279, 322, 337–338, 380–381, 399
  eclecticism of, 12, 191, 207, 208, 275, 361–362, 399
  as Greeks of New World, 11–12
  Guatemalan civil war and, 14–15
  independent states of, 6–7
  Old vs. New empires of, 341–342
  peacefulness of, 94–95
  as people of time, 28–30, 91, 94, 95, 249, 359–360; see also calendar, Maya
  rich, 213–214, 254, 285, 339, 382
  sense of loss and, 13, 14–15
  survival of, 12, 183, 249, 399–400
  unfinished history of, 397, 399
  see also specific topics
Mayapán, 77
mayors, 197, 207–208
Mazehual Maya, 379–397
Mediz Bolio, Antonio, 351
Mejía Victores, 68
Melchor de Mencos, 62–64
Menchú, Vicente, 252–254
Menchú Tum, Rigoberta, 252–254
Méndez, Modesto, 87–88
Méndez Montenegro, Julio César, 160
Mérida, 332, 344, 347, 356–366
Mesoamerica, 11–12
  see also specific countries and cities
mestizaje, 273
Mestizo, 127
mestizos, 87, 125, 337
Mexica, see Aztecs
Mexican-American War, 339, 368
Mexican Empire, 62, 273
Mexican Orthodox church, 287–289
Mexican Revolution (1910), 5, 273, 281, 287
Mexico, 118, 163, 260–397
  Belize and, 49, 62
  Catholic Church in, 266–268, 282, 287, 293, 351–353, 376–380, 394–395

constitution of, 281
culture of, 273
fundamentalists in, 282, 286–287, 316, 379
Guatemala compared with, 218, 291
Guatemalan refugees in, 267–268, 274–275, 331
Ladinos in, 6, 263–264, 285–288, 337, 339, 366–367, 381
land reform in, 281
Spanish conquest of, 12, 78, 79, 82, 137, 165, 168, 265
see also Chiapas; Yucatán Peninsula; *specific cities*
Mexico City, 78
Miller, Mary, 316
missionaries, 68, 307, 308
in Lamanai, 9, 10
Mochan Xiu, 375
Moctezuma, 263
Momostenango, 198, 212, 213, 214, 216, 217, 271
Monique (French linguist), 291–293, 296, 303
Moore, Henry, 343
Mopan Hotel, 25
Morley, Sylvanus G., 28
Mormons, 268–272
Morris, Walter, 275–276
Mosquito Coast, 27
Motagua Valley, 137, 140, 145
Mundo, *see* Tiox Mundo
murals, in Bonampak, 311–315
music, 79, 191–192, 284, 395
calypso, 22
marimba, 183, 204
ranchero, 19
reggae, 31, 63
Muslims, 202, 291
myths, *see* legends and myths, Maya

Na Bolom (Jaguar House), 302
Nahá, 302, 308, 309, 318–325
Nahá Lacandon, 201
Nahua, 11
Nahualá, 213
Nahuatl language, 173, 269, 292
National Indigenous Institute (INI), 280
National Liberation Movement (MLN), 160–161, 241
national unity, cultural diversity vs., 117–118, 120
Nebaj, 228–238, 243–251
Negroman, 41, 43
Netzahualcóyotl, library of, 283

New World Archaeological Foundation (NWAF), 268–272, 277
New York Times, 134
Nicaragua, 27, 70, 130, 134, 163
Nixon, Richard M., 136, 170
Noh Cah Santa Cruz, *see* Carillo Puerto
Northern Development Belt, 235–236, 238
numbers, Maya fascination with, 77–78, 93, 336
Nunnery quadrangle, 348, 350

Oakes, Maud, 225
observatories, 90–91, 340, 342, 358
octopi, 329–330
oil and minerals, discovery of, 235–236
Olmecs, 11, 29
Operation Success, 134–135
oracles, speaking, 375–376
see also Speaking Cross, cult of
Orange Walk, 7, 9, 20–22
Orbita, Padre, 80–81, 191
Orellana, Enrique, 105
Organization of American States, 135
Organization of the People in Arms (ORPA), 149–150, 175
Oxchuc, 282
Oxib Queh, 197, 202–203

Pacal (Shield), King, 298, 299, 300
Pacheco, Alonso, 45
paintings, 52, 148, 151, 152, 302, 318
in Bonampak, 311–315
Palace of the Governor, 348, 349
palaces:
in Bonampak, 311–313
in Carrillo Puerto, 376
in Palenque, 295, 297, 300, 301
Palacios, Isaías, 235
Palenque, 12, 13, 201, 290–305, 307, 335, 347
architecture in, 294–295, 297–301
artistic legacy of, 301
collapse of, 53, 100
dynastic history of, 298–300
Tikal compared with, 294, 297
tombs in, 94, 295, 298
Walker-Caddy journey to, 68–70
women of, 298
Palenque Triad, 298–300
"Palestinianizing" the Maya, 196
Panajachel, 108, 174, 181
Panama, 171
Pantí, Mr. (Xunantunich warden), 52–53, 55–56
Pascual Abah, 189–191, 203

Pascual Rey, San, (San Pascualito Muerte), 287–289
Pat, Jacinto, 339, 366–370, 380
Patria del Criollo, La (Martínez), 183–184
Patt, Urbano, 50
Patzicía, 174
Patzún, 174
Paz, Octavio, 283
peasants, 54, 117
  in Guatemala, 70, 74, 116, 120, 133, 196, 220–221, 223, 240–241
Peasant Unity Committee (CUC), 169, 172, 253
Pendergast, David, 9, 10
Pensión Bonifaz, 214
Pensión Las Tres Hermanas (The Three Sisters), 230–232, 236–237
Perera, Victor, 301, 318, 320, 322, 324
Peru, 37, 118, 128, 129, 133, 138, 205
pesticides, 150, 253, 259
Petén, 15, 31, 45, 49, 59–100, 145, 171, 230, 256, 342
  Walker-Caddy journey in, 68–71
  see also Flores; Tayasal; Tikal
Petén Itzá Lake, 72, 77, 81, 82, 85
Philippe (Frenchman), 291, 296, 299, 303
Piedras Negras, 95, 100
Pizarro, Francisco, 138
Playboy, 316
Plumed Serpent, The (Lawrence), 289
Plumridge, Lieutenant, 381–382, 392
Pocomchí Maya, 126
Poland, 68, 267
police:
  in Belize, 20, 23
  in Guatemala, 73, 84, 108, 110, 124–125, 147, 159, 230
  in Mexico, 289, 331
political prisoners, in Guatemala, 73–74, 75
political structure, 89–90, 163, 196–197, 286, 337–338, 381
polos de desarrollo (poles of development), 120
Poot, Leandro, 367–368
Poot Cimé, Don Simón, 382–383
Popol Vuh, 156, 167, 185–189, 197, 199, 201, 204, 210, 212, 234, 271, 300, 364, 368
Popol Vuh Museum, 153–154
Posada Belén, 105, 114–115, 147, 258
Posada Toledo, 332, 356
Postclassic period, 44, 75, 78, 188, 233, 336, 338, 341
pottery, 38, 52, 233–234, 270–272

priests, 79, 171, 172, 178–180, 287, 376–378
  murders of, 68, 221
prophecy, 75–76, 81, 83, 151–152, 339, 373–374
Proskouriakoff, Tatiana, 95
Protestants, 67–68, 202, 221, 244–246
  Anglican Church, 26–27
  see also fundamentalists
Proxmire, William, 272
Puc, Venancio, 381–382
Putun Maya, 333–334, 335
Puuc region, 347
Puuc-style architecture, 347–349
Pyramid of the Magician, 347–348
pyramids, 5, 270
  in Chichén Itzá, 342
  Egyptian, 93–94
  in Iximché, 166
  in Izamal, 345
  in K'umarcaah, 199–201
  in Lagartero, 271
  in Lamanai, 9, 10–11
  in Nebaj, 233, 234
  in Teotihuacán, 204
  in Tiho, 358–359
  in Tikal, 86, 88–90, 92–100, 115
  as tombs, 94, 96, 115
  in Tulum, 335, 336
  in Xunantunich, 47, 52, 55, 56–57
  in Zaculeu, 218, 221

Quechua, 279, 361
quetzal, 112–113, 257
Quetzalcóatl, 190, 200, 289
Quetzalcóatl, Toltec King, 342
Quetzaltenango, 154–155, 168, 211, 213–216
Quicab, King, 167, 204
Quiché, 108, 109, 151, 181–217, 227–256
Quiché Maya, 98–99, 109–110, 126, 151, 165, 167–168, 170, 173, 182, 229, 240, 252–254
  Conquest Dance of, 153
  creation myth and history of, 186–189
  language of, 182–183, 185, 192, 197, 199, 206, 212, 246–247
  rebellions of, 216–217
quinceaños, 385–387
Quintana Roo, 5–7, 15, 77, 91, 267–268, 335, 355, 369, 371–397
  see also specific towns
Quiriguá, 91, 95, 100, 124, 127, 137–144, 205
  Great Plaza of, 139–141

Rabbit, Lady, 315
Rafael ("guide"), 297
railroads, 384–385
ranchitos, 306
Ray (student), 277–278
Reagan administration, 121
Recinos, Adrián, 212
Reclining Figure (Moore), 343
"reductions" of Indians, 45
Reed, Nelson, 379
refugees, Guatemalan, 63
    in Belize, 13, 14
    in Canada, 108–109
    in Mexico, 267–268, 274–275, 331
Relation of the Things of Yucatán
    (Landa), 344–346
religion:
    Christian, *see* Catholic Church;
        Christianity; fundamentalists; missionaries; priests; Protestants
    Maya, 12, 44, 75, 79–81, 93, 97, 178–
        180, 199–211, 286, 399–400; *see*
        also cofradías; costumbristas;
        Speaking Cross, cult of; *specific gods*
    see also churches
religiosidad popular, 268
Requirement, 219
restaurants, 122, 158, 257–258, 330–
    331, 335, 349, 356, 378
Ricardo (Mexican), 274–275
Ríos Montt, Efraín, 68, 150, 173, 175,
    221, 231, 240, 244
Rise and Fall of Maya Civilization, The
    (Thompson) 88
roads, 81, 124–125, 237–238, 283, 305–
    306
    in Belize, 22–23, 31
    repair of, 124–125
Robertson, Merle Greene, 298
Roger (Englishman), 50–51
Rokché, Eulogio, 197–200, 202–206,
    208, 211
Romans, ancient, 29, 167
Romerillo, 277
Romero, Oscar, 266
Rómulo, Don (catechist), 391–396
Roosevelt, Franklin D., 131
Rose, Saint, 286
Royal Ontario Museum, 8
Ruíz, Samuel, 266–268
Ruz, Alberto, 94, 295

Sacapulas, 227–228
sacrifices:
    human, 78, 81, 93, 97, 201, 300, 341
    pottery in, 271

St. John's Cathedral, 26–27
saints, 286, 287, 371
    care of, 178, 179–180, 191–194
San Andrés, 386–387
San Cristóbal de las Casas, 263–280,
    290, 302
Sandoval, Mario, 160–161
San Francisco, 67
San Ignacio, 39–40, 46–47
San Lorenzo church, 284
Santa Cruz (Holy Cross), 6–7, 21–22, 49,
    355
    see also Speaking Cross, cult of
Santa Cruz del Quiché, 194–197, 199,
    200
Santiago, 201
Santiago Atitlán, 175–180
Santo Mundo, *see* Tiox Mundo
Santo Tomás, church of, 185, 191–192
Schele, Linda, 298
sculpture, 141–143, 163, 343–344, 348–
    349
selva lacandona, 306
Señor Presidente, El (Asturias), 146, 147
Sepúlveda, Juan Ginés de, 265
"serial massacre," 174
shaman-priests, 179–180, 182, 185, 202,
    288–289
Shaw, Mr., 30
Short Count, 76, 96, 107, 338
Six Death, 300
skeletons, decrease in size of, 54
Sky Xul, King, 142
slaves 21 27 129 169 170 252
Sna Holobil (The Weavers' House), 276
Sna Htz'ibahom, 280, 282
snakes, 304, 325
Soc, Felipa, 216
Social Democrats, Guatemalan, 160
Sololá, 175, 181–183
Somoza, Anastasio, 134
son et lumière shows, 350–351
Spain, Spaniards, 12, 37, 45, 48, 70, 75–
    76, 78–79, 201, 229, 264–266, 335,
    359–360, 370
    Aztecs compared with, 273
    Aztecs conquered by, 12, 78, 79, 82,
        137, 165, 265
    in Belize, 9–10, 62
    cultural diversity in, 117–118
    Lacandón and, 301, 307–308
    paternalism of, 128
    in Quintana Roo, 371–372
    in Tayasal, 79–83
    in Uspantán, 251–252
    in Zaculeu, 218–219

Spanish language, 63, 184, 185, 279, 280, 363
Speaking Cross, cult of, 6–7, 22, 48, 336, 355, 369, 370–371, 373–376, 380–385, 387–397, 399
squatters, 13–14, 109
State Department, U.S., 86, 134, 231
stelae, 94, 100, 115, 301
　in Bliss Institute, 28–30
　in Cobá, 336
　at Quiriguá, 139–42, 144
　at Tikal, 91, 95–96, 99
　at Xunantunich, 52–53
Stephens, John Lloyd, 68–69, 139, 156, 200, 234, 335, 336, 344, 372
stereotypes, 37
stone, whistling, 48–49
Stormy Sky, King, 96
Succotz, 47–50, 55
Summer Institute of Linguistics (American Wycliffe Bible Translators), 308, 357–358
Survival International, 175

Tactic, 251, 256–258
taxis, 32, 47–48, 85, 157, 291–292, 332
Tayasal, 75, 79–83, 307, 346, 375
technology, 83, 137, 384
Tecpan Guatemala, 165, 169
Tecún, María, 207
Tecún Umán, 152–155, 159, 168, 202, 203, 205, 207, 211, 213
Tedlock, Barbara, 202, 214–215
Tedlock, Dennis, 156, 186, 202, 204, 205, 212, 214, 215
Temple of Inscriptions, 295, 298, 299
Temple of the Warriors, 340, 342, 343–344
Tenejapa, 282
Teotihuacán, 96, 163, 166, 189, 204
Tepich, 366
textiles, 126, 151, 243, 274, 275–276
Tezcatlipoca, 201–202
theater, 280, 281
Thomas, Mr., 42–43, 46
Thompson, Sir Eric, 34, 52, 88, 91, 94, 95, 198, 207, 214, 342, 347
Ticayehuatl, José, 292
Ticul, 349, 367
Tiho, 358–359, 366, 367–368
Tihosuco, 370–371, 372
Tikal, 13, 41, 53, 62, 85–100, 115, 163, 166, 234
　discovery of, 87–88
　dynastic history of, 95–96
　as national symbol, 87

Palenque compared with, 294, 297
Quiriguá compared with, 139–140, 141
Time and the Highland Maya (Tedlock), 214–215
Tiox Mundo (Santo Mundo), 178–179, 185, 205, 206, 208
Tipú, Belize, 41–45
Todorov, Tzvetan, 137, 138
Todos Santos Cuchumatán, 67, 222–226
Tohil, temple of, 199, 200–201, 211
Toltecs, 11, 97, 167, 188, 200, 201, 334, 342, 343
tombs, 234
　looting of, 115
　in Palenque, 94, 295, 298
　pyramid, 94, 96, 115
Toniná, 100, 300
Tonantzin, temple of, 293
T'o'ohil, 201
Topsey, Harriot, 36, 38
torture, 67, 78, 220, 253–254, 345
Totonicapán, 216–217
tourism, Indians affected by, 177
trade, 140, 334
Trench, Wilbur, 357–358
Tula, 188–189
Tula, Seven Caves of, 204
Tulum, 314, 334–336, 372, 385
tun, 191–192
Tupaq Amaru II, 129, 216
turkeys, 283, 349
Tusik, 387–391
Tut, Ambrosio, 87–88
Tuxtla, 288
"twenty-candle" ceremony, 248–250
Twigge, Lieutenant, 381–382, 392
Two Crosses of Todos Santos, The (Oakes), 225
Tzeltal Maya, 275–277
　language of, 280, 282
Tzeltal Revolt, 286
tzolkin, 30, 34–35, 76, 90, 93, 179, 204, 207, 211, 214–215, 248, 365
Tzotzil Maya, 275–277, 286
　language of, 280, 282
Tzul, Atanasio, 216
Tzutuhil Maya, 165, 175

Uaxactun, 53
Ubico, Jorge, 130, 132, 159, 170, 217
Uck, Candelario, 44–46
Ulil, Prince, 350
Union of the National Center (UCN), 159–161
unions, 127

United Fruit Company (UFCo), 125, 129–130, 132–135, 137, 218
United Nations, 275
United Nations Security Council, 135
United States, 116, 163, 339, 368, 396, 397
   Caste War and, 366–367, 368
   DMZ recommended by, 275
   Guatemala aided by, 72, 74, 121, 160, 171
Uquín, Jorge, 193–194
Uspantán, 251–256
Uspanteca, 229, 251–252
Usumacinta River, 317–318
Utatlán, *see* K'umarcaah
utopias, 126, 264–265
Uxmal, 342, 347–351, 358

Valencia, Raúl, 37, 38
Valladolid, 337–339, 366, 370, 372
Vatican, 68, 267
Venezuela, 264–265
Venus, 90–91
Verapaz (True Peace), 126, 265
Victoria, Queen of England, 7, 49, 392
Villa Arqueológica, 340
Villa Rojas, Alfonso, 388
Vinak, Max, 211–212
Volcan Agua, 164
von Däniken, Erich, 298
voting rights, 170

waiters, 182–183, 330–331
Walker, Patrick, 68–71, 83
Wallace (buccaneer), 24
Wall Street Journal, 196
weaving, *see* textiles
When the Mountains Tremble (film), 254
Wilson, Gahan, 316
women, in Mayan art, 313–314

Wright, Ronald (author), academic background of, 7–8, 294
writing system, hieroglyphic, 13, 35, 82, 94, 95, 185, 346–347

Xaman Ha, 333, 353–355
Xbalanqué, 203, 204, 271
X-Cacal Guardia, 336, 355, 375, 380, 385, 387, 391–397, 399
Xibalbá, 205
Xicotencatl, Doña Luisa, 173
Ximénez, Francisco, 185
Xiu, 334, 338, 351, 358
Xiu, Don Francisco de Montejo, 352–353
Xix Ya, Don Julián, 371
Xtabay, 43, 50
Xunantunich, 47–57
Xu'tan, 324

Yah Pech, Ermilo, 363–364
Yaxchilán, 100, 303, 304, 307, 311, 315, 317, 318
Yax Kin, King, 96
Year-Bearers, 106, 207–208, 247–248, 338, 361–362
Young Chan K'in, 309, 319–322
Yucatán Peninsula, 45, 49, 89, 274, 327–397
   Caste War in, *see* Caste War
   Maya cities abandoned in, 9
   Spanish invasion of, 77
   see also specific cities and towns

Zac Kuk, Lady, 298
Zac Nicté, Princess, 350
Zaculeu, 218–222
zero, use of, 29
Zinacantán, 282, 284–285, 286
zoomorphs, 142–143
Zoque Indians, 288